THE CANBERRA
GARDENER

TENTH EDITION

Published by
THE HORTICULTURAL SOCIETY OF CANBERRA INC.
2010

Cover: *Correa* 'Canberra Bells' which has been selected as the plant to mark Canberra's centenary in 2013. It is a small rounded shrub growing to about 1 m high and thrives in light shade to full sun. It is expected to be available through garden centres in autumn 2012. (*Photo supplied by Bywong Nursery.*)

First edition 1948
Second edition 1951
Third edition 1959
Fourth edition 1966
Fifth edition 1969
Reprinted 1972
Sixth edition 1972
© 1976
Reprinted 1976
Seventh edition 1982
Eighth edition 1991
Ninth edition 2004
Tenth edition 2010

National Library of Australia card number and
ISBN 978-0-646-54061-0

Printed in Australia by Goanna Print
Designed by Design One, Canberra

Disclaimer

Preface

The Horticultural Society of Canberra Inc. is very pleased to bring you a new edition of The Canberra Gardener, especially as we fast approach Canberra's centenary. Our Society has worked to develop gardening in the Canberra area for over 80 of those years.

Over the past decade it has become clear that Canberra's gardeners must use less water than was usual in the past. This new edition reflects the lessons we have learned. Most importantly, we know now that we can cope with a lot less water provided we use it carefully and get all the other elements for plant health correct.

The plant suggestions reflect this adaptation to more economical water use, and are also greatly influenced by the many new cultivars and plant species which have proven their worth here. Some other plants have not coped too well and are no longer included.

Many people have been involved in the preparation of this edition. Principal thanks must go to the other members of the Editorial Committee, Merylyn Condon and Chris Ryan. They have contributed substantially to the text, in some cases without any acknowledgment in the body of the book. Each has given unstintingly of their expertise and time. The meetings of the Editorial Committee have been helped no end by their ability to work together so happily.

The authors and reviewers, including those shown at the start of each chapter, were:

Bronwyn Beechey, Keith Brew, Cedric Bryant, Adam Burgess, Ivan and Joy Colaric, Merylyn Condon, Graeme Davis, Tony Davis, Lyn Edwards, Peter Ellerman, Ruth Kerruish, John Le Mesurier, Marie Lenon, Jane Lindsay, Neil Mitchell, Susan Orgill, Lynne Phelan, Christine and David Ross, Glenn Sheldrick, Phillip Unger, Brian Usback, John Woodfield, Brian Wray, and Jane Wright.

We were helped also by staff of the Bureau of Meteorology, members of the African Violet and Gesneriad section of our Horticultural Society, and by members of the Cacti and Succulent Society of the ACT Inc. We are very grateful also to the many readers of the ninth edition who offered their thoughts on plants and techniques.

Many of the people named as authors of particular chapters helped also by providing advice on particular aspects of other chapters. For some chapters no author is shown; the Editorial Committee as a team prepared these.

The photos came from many sources and were taken by Bronwyn Beechey, Cedric Bryant, Ian Collier, Keith Colls, Merylyn Condon, Rik Condon, Suzanne Cooper, Chris Francis, Sheila Hodgson, Sherry McArdle-English, Barry di Salvia, Lyn Edwards, Geoff Ludowyk, Josephine Nef, Denae Starkovski, Paul Tyerman, Phillip Unger and Victoria Willard. Most of the drawings in Chapter 28 are by Adrienne Walkington. We are grateful also for assistance from Bywong Native Plant Nursery, Yates (Dow Agrosciences), and the NSW Department of Industry and Investment.

We hope you will gain as much pleasure in reading this volume as was gained in its production; and that like many of us you will discover new pleasures and treasures for your Canberra garden.

John Le Mesurier
Convenor, Editorial Committee

Contents

PART A: Introduction

Chapter 1 tells you what is special about Canberra's climate and soils.

Chapter 2 discusses things to think about before starting on the physical work of building a new garden; and then suggests ways in which you can make the most of the Canberra regional environment to create a garden taking advantage of all that our climate and location can offer.

CHAPTER 1:
The Canberra environment

In any Australian bookstore you can find a whole range of gardening books, including some excellent general guides for Australian gardeners. So why bother to produce another guide, one especially for Canberra, Queanbeyan and Yass gardeners?

The answer is that the Canberra area is a little different when it comes to gardens because we have extremes of weather. Our weather and our soils, the two things most important to plants, differ from those of the other major cities of Australia where the bulk of the population lives. And, of course, it is for that larger population that those books are written.

Our winters in particular are different, and this presents us with some special opportunities in terms of the seasonal displays our gardens can provide.

In writing *The Canberra Gardener* our aim has been to concentrate on the opportunities our gardens present, and on plants and gardening practices that work well here. The plants suggested all make worthy additions to your garden — plants that are marginal in our conditions, or which will grow well here but give only a minimal contribution to the garden, have generally been ignored.

Canberra's weather

Two aspects of our weather are particularly important to the Canberra gardener. The first point to notice is that we get frosts — among the other capital cities only Hobart usually gets frosts, but not many. Second, our rainfall is low, undependable and at the wrong time of year. The table on the next page summarises our weather, month by month.

Our maximum temperatures, humidity, evaporation and winds are not very special by Australian standards. We get occasional days of high winds, but these are exceptional, and for most of the year our winds are gentle and from the northwest.

The combination of our weather and soils means that for plants growing naturally there are three main growth periods — one period before and one after winter, the length of which depend on the amount of rain and the dates of the first and last frost, and then a third period during the summer in which there are spurts of growth as it rains. In the home garden we can provide an environment to extend growth over a longer period.

Some aspects of Canberra's weather

The Canberra rainfall, which has averaged about 615 mm at the airport, would appear from the table on the next page to be fairly regularly distributed over the year. The averages shown tend to overstate what you might expect in any month, especially in warmer months. This is because the averages are distorted by the occasional years in which we get a lot of rain. The data from the Bureau of Meteorology suggests that in the course of 100 Januarys in Canberra we could have ten years with less than 8 mm of rain and another ten with more than 117 mm, compared with an average of 59.2 mm.

Rainfall statistics have been recorded for quite a bit longer in Queanbeyan and Yass. Yass has had an average annual rainfall of 647 mm over the past 111 years and Queanbeyan was a little drier with an average of 592 mm over the 139 years 1870 to 2009. The number of frosts in these two centres is likely the same as Canberra. Temperatures are much the same in the three centres.

There is nothing we can do about the amount of rain we get but in the past Canberrans have been easily able to supplement the rainfall with reticulated water. That ease has now gone and we must learn how to use our water more efficiently and to use that water to grow plants which best suit our conditions. Selection of plants, preparation of the soil, mulching and watering practices are critical to success and are the major themes of this book.

The occurrence of frost largely governs what can be grown in Canberra, and also governs the time when certain plantings can be made. The main growing season extends from October to March, in effect starting after the last frost of winter and ending with the first frost of the next winter.

The table shows the average number of frosts at the Canberra Airport, but this can be a poor guide to what will actually happen in your garden. Frosts can be influenced by many things. Your garden may be on an eastern or a western slope or in a hollow, or might be wind-prone. In a mature garden trees and shrubs will create a special microclimate. It can be very useful to compile your own record of frosts to give you a better idea of what you can expect from year to year.

Selected climate figures for Canberra, 1939 to 2009

| | Temperature (degrees C) | | | Rainfall | |
	Average Maximum	Average Minimum	No. of frosts	Median (mm)	Average (mm)
January	28.0	13.2	0	48.8	59.2
February	27.1	13.1	0	51.4	55.4
March	24.5	10.7	0	31.1	50.2
April	20.0	6.7	4	32.5	46.4
May	15.6	3.2	13	37.9	44.1
June	12.2	1.0	18	31.8	40.7
July	11.3	-0.1	21	36.4	41.2
August	13.0	1.0	18	45.6	46.0
September	16.2	3.2	12	52.8	52.2
October	19.4	6.1	5	54.4	62.1
November	22.7	8.8	1	59.9	63.9
December	26.1	11.4	0	44.0	53.8
Annual	19.7	6.5	93	616.6	615.0

Source: Data published by the Bureau of Meteorology for Canberra Airport.

Acer campestre 'Aureo-variegata' showing its autumn colours

Unseasonal frosts can occur in late spring, so you need to be very careful about early spring planting of frost-tender crops like tomatoes, beans and rock melons and many of the more tender annual flowers.

Autumn is ushered in towards the end of March with a light frost or two. Towards the end of April, severe frosts commence and kill what is left of summer crops like tomatoes, beans, the various cucurbits, and most of the summer annuals. Plant growth during this period is reduced markedly; during winter the growth of even the hardiest garden plants is practically at a standstill. Nevertheless, there are some plants which come into their own in winter.

Frosts are essential for many of the plants that do very well here. Many of the spring bulbs, spring blossoms and fruit trees depend on below zero temperatures to form and induce their flowers. The other great advantage we gain from our winters is that the marked seasonal change is just what is needed to bring out the colours in the best deciduous trees and shrubs, and that autumn beauty is something that distinguishes Canberra from many other parts of Australia.

Canberra's soils

Canberra's poor rainfall can be made worse by the nature of our soils, which tend to repel moisture and inhibit infiltration.

Much of Canberra's urban area is characterised by undulating terrain with soft (and easily weathered) shales and siltstone and more resistant volcanics (for example Black Mountain). It is also interesting to note (and sometimes hard to believe!) that Canberra was once submerged under the ocean and our landscape has undergone significant changes over the past millions of years.

Major soil types of the Canberra region range from Rudosols or skeletal, acidic, rocky soils near the crests of hills, through to Kurosols and Chromosols on hillslopes with a distinct boundary between the lightly textured loams of the topsoil and heavy, densely packed clays of the subsoil, down to Sodosols with heavy subsoils which disperse and set hard upon disturbance and Alluvial soils along drainage lines. As a general rule, as you move down the slope; soil increases in depth, decreases in rock content and increases in soil fertility and pH.

The major limitations of Canberra's soils are: topsoil depth, poor soil structure, soil acidity and inherent low fertility particularly of nitrogen, phosphorus, sulphur and calcium. While our native and established plants are well adapted to these conditions, intensive horticulture requires an approach to gardening which ultimately increases organic matter, nutrient supply and groundcover.

Improving soil health, learning how to cope with our low and unreliable rainfall, and selecting plants that thrive in Canberra's weather are the keys to a successful Canberra garden.

CHAPTER 2:
Designing your garden

Christine Ross, David Ross and Merylyn Condon

If you are not a gardener, then how do you decide what sort of a garden you want? It may be that you've been inspired by gardens you have visited, by reading books and magazines or watching television garden shows and listening to local radio programs. Even if all these are still not exactly what you would like and even if the plants are totally unsuitable for Canberra, there may still be ideas that you can adapt in planning your own garden.

If a garden is well-designed, aesthetically pleasing and enhances your home, then it will add to the value of your property. That alone is a good reason to aim for such a garden, but as well, you can make the garden work for you. It can, in some cases, become an extension of the house. Hopefully, this chapter will give you a few tips on how to do that and the points you should consider when creating a new garden.

Whether you design your own garden, or

Welcome to my garden

engage a professional designer or landscaper, it must meet your needs. Using a professional landscaper is by far the easiest way, but it is an expensive option. Even so, there are still decisions to be made, and you will need to settle on a design that suits your lifestyle. You will have to choose paving and other construction materials as well as plant material, though a professional landscaper can advise on all these aspects.

If you intend to engage a landscaper you should think first about what you want in your garden. It could be an expensive exercise to have someone prepare a garden design which is totally unsuitable. Think about how much time you can devote to maintenance, for this will help determine the design, and the ratio and nature of plantings to any paving or other surfaces within the landscape. If you have little time or inclination to spend time in the garden, it makes sense that your garden should be planted with fewer plants and that those plants should be both tough and hardy, though still worth a place in any good garden.

A few things to think about

While you may like the new design trends, there are as many ways to design a garden as there are plants to choose from, so your garden can be a very individual thing. With the vast range of plants available, it is easy to inject your own personality into your garden, and at the same time make the garden an extension to your home. So look around and take note of gardens. If a plant grabs your attention, ask about it. Observe how other people use their space and think about how you can apply any favourite ideas to your space.

In recent years, water restrictions have become a reality, and sadly, many of the gardens designed to take this into account display a sameness in the use of architectural 'easy care' plants. In time, even easy care gardens will need some maintenance. In many cases, plants deteriorate soon after planting simply because they are promoted as 'low water usage' and house owners have taken that to mean 'no water usage'. Most shrubs and trees need some moisture during the first year, which can be tapered off over time. Other plants such as flaxes and grasses, while looking 'tough' can be accustomed to receiving more water in their native environment than they will ever receive in Canberra and can therefore deteriorate very quickly in this climate.

You will need to settle on how much of your area can be devoted to a garden and you will need to establish where all your underground services lie. Location of stormwater and sewerage drains, and any underground gas and electricity lines should be checked before the garden is begun and before anything is planted. Consider whether you have room for trees, Nowadays, houses are larger and blocks are significantly smaller than they once were. It is therefore important to decide up front whether there is any possibility of achieving what you want in the space you have available. Even in a small space, with a little careful planning, you can still translate some of those ideas into the area you have available.

Plans

Having assembled your ideas, it's time to make some notes and sketches. Look at your block, its aspect and views including borrowed landscape, levels, drainage, soil type, the prevailing winds, fences, sun and shade. Measure the boundaries of your property, the driveway, house, garage and distances from buildings to boundary. Do some copies. On one of these copies, prepare a site analysis marking in all the water pipes, stormwater drains, power, gas, phone and any other underground services. It is also useful to include external fixtures such as air conditioning units, taps etc. Include any existing trees, even those outside your boundaries, for they may be close enough to throw shade and therefore will affect what you grow.

Prunus serrula is a lovely tree at any time but the bark makes it a standout for winter.

You will need to establish your directions by marking North on your site analysis. This will help you to know what areas of the garden will be shady and where the garden will be warmer. Mark where the prevailing winds come from, and if the soil has areas that are damp, rocky or frosty, mark these as well.

Indicate on your sketch where people tend to walk, for this will be the most useful way to direct your paths.

Next make some lists of all those things that your garden should contain (not just plants). Your list might include a clothesline, a compost heap, a dog kennel, somewhere to store the bins, tools and gardening products, tanks. Next you will need to list all those items you would like to include in your garden, whether it's a swimming pool, outdoor entertainment area, swings, cubby house or other playground equipment, a sandpit, a dog run, chook pen, pond, pergola or a lawn, greywater system or all of the above or something altogether different. One important thought is access – if you want to be able to bring a vehicle or truck into the yard at any time in the future to deliver mulch, bricks etc, you will need to plan for this contingency.

The available space will to some degree determine how much garden you can have, but even if the space around your house or unit is limited, it is still possible to enjoy an attractive garden on a smaller scale. If you enjoy gardening, you should expect to do a few hours of maintenance each week, with a little weeding, watering and trimming periodically. Do you want a productive garden? Do you want to be able to enjoy your garden alone or with friends, having an entertainment area with barbeque or pizza oven with a shaded area for summer gatherings? The list could go on *ad infinitum*, but it's wise to get all your thoughts on paper.

You might also think about the types of gardens you have seen and those you like. Some are very formal, with clipped hedges, lots of flower beds surrounding a small lawn, or no lawn, with treed areas and winding paths, or perhaps one that is totally unstructured and perhaps a little 'wild'. We all have our own preferences and a few are covered in more detail in the following paragraphs.

Timing

While you can have a design for the entire site, funds may not be available to do everything at once, but no matter. If you keep the site mulched and tidy, you can identify your priorities and work to achieve those before proceeding to less vital inclusions.

Soil preparation is best done before any planting or structures are put into the garden. Access for garden machinery can be problematic as time goes on, although 1 m wide machines are available for access to smaller sites. It is best to get the site ripped before any other work takes place. Adding gypsum to a clay soil will help soil structure, and covering your soil with a mixture of animal manure and fine mulch will help control weeds and in time, improve your soil ready for planting. Not everything has to be done at once, and the garden may be developed as funds or time allow. Some gardens can still enjoy rhododendrons and other moisture lovers, but new gardens do not have the luxury of shade from existing plants. This type of plant is best left for gardens which can provide shade and moisture, or left to plant after that shade is available. In a larger garden, particularly if you choose to grow tender plants, it is best to identify some larger plants which will create a canopy and therefore shelter your tender plants. Grow the canopy first and then the tender plants. Most sites have a little shelter, though a new home in a new suburb can present a few problems in establishing the garden especially if your block is one of many in an estate that has few trees. In such a situation, a shelter such as four stakes with shade cloth or hessian attached might be enough to give your tree or trees protection from the prevailing winds until they are actively growing. Planting guidance is given in chapter 25.

In thinking about what you are going to plant, be aware that some plants may use more water and will take more time to look after than others. Vegetables and fruit trees will require regular tending and watering, so it's best to decide up front whether this is the way you want to go. Fruit trees will require care: codling moth, fruit fly and many other insects are out there waiting to infest your fruit. You will need to do something to protect your fruit, whether you cover it in some way or use sprays. You may still opt for a productive garden rather than an ornamental one, and many families enjoy growing their own.

Think about how you are going to water your garden. It is possible to do this and still fall within the daily allocation of water per household, but you need to be a smart gardener and take advice wherever you can about using water in the most thoughtful way (see Chapter 6). Enthusiastic new gardeners often plant too many of each vegetable, when it's better to plant them sequentially to avoid a glut when everything matures at one. Planting in much smaller spaces than traditionally advised has proven to be quite successful. For specific guidance on vegetable gardening in small spaces, an excellent book 'One Magic Square, Grow Your Own Food On One Square Metre', by Lolo Houbein, Hyde Park Press,

Raised garden beds can be made in all shapes and forms.

Adelaide, 2008 has proven to be useful to gardeners.

The site: What can you do?

By now you've decided on the placement of all those vital features discussed above. Now it's time to think about the remainder of your garden and decide what you can do with it. A few options are discussed below.

A productive garden

Whether you have plenty of land or just a small area for gardening, you can enjoy a productive garden. On a large block, you should aim for a sunny site with good drainage. Raised beds are good, or you can edge your beds with timber or bricks. There are interlocking edges available in either timber or concrete block. Aim for four to six beds so that crops can be rotated annually.

If you are limited to a small area, then you will need to think more carefully about how you can successfully grow a range of plants, but it is certainly possible. You can grow vegetables (or other plants) in vertical planters, and many fruit trees respond well to being espaliered.

A fruiting grape can provide shade in summer when it's needed as well as give you fruit. You may only have a narrow passage along the side of your home between you and the next door neighbour but as long as that passage receives a fair percentage of sun during the day, vegetables will grow there.

Vegetables growing beautifully in raised modular beds.

There may be another area on the block where vegetables will receive the sun they need. You can affix tubs and planters to either your fence or the wall of your house and fill them with good quality planting compost. After you plant, you will need to be diligent with watering, as containers dry out much more quickly than garden beds. There is also the option to use large 'waterwell' pots. Most vegetables and herbs will need sun, while others such as spinach and beet will tolerate part shade. It is simply a matter of knowing what to grow where.

There are also squat tanks primarily made for balconies and porches which make good-sized planter boxes. These are manufactured by water tank firms, and as well there is the Table Garden®, an innovative metal trough on castors made locally. Both are good ideas for small spaces and they are useful for people who have difficulty bending down.

Fruit trees such as apples, quinces, figs and citrus make excellent espaliered plants, pruned to grow vertically against a wall or fence and, if trained carefully, climbing plants such as kiwi fruit and grapes can provide summer shade in addition to their prime purpose of fruit-bearing. There are columnar fruiting trees such as the Ballerina series of apples and crabapples or 'Pinkabelle', a dwarf 'Pink Lady' apple; also many fruit trees are now grafted onto dwarf rootstocks which results in a smaller overall plant.

The ornamental garden

Living in Canberra presents some special opportunities to enjoy four distinct seasons. This makes it easy to design and plant a garden which will look good all year round. In the following paragraphs you will find suggestions for all four seasons – remember that some plants will be more drought tolerant than others which may require a little more care to get them started. All are cold tolerant plants.

Spring is an exciting time in the Canberra garden. *Garrya elliptica* displays intriguing green tassel flowers (catkins) in late winter and early spring. You can enjoy the blooms of *Camellia japonica* and *Camellia reticulata* or some of the wattles. In protected gardens, you might see rhododendrons and azaleas, with deciduous azaleas in a vibrant range of colours which will then turn on a great show of autumn foliage colour. Pieris is a superb shrub with flower racemes of white or pink, followed by brilliant red foliage. Perfume is especially noticeable in spring if you grow *Osmanthus fragrans, Daphne*

Flowering Cherry.

odora or *Viburnum carlesii* and you will find there are many more perfumed plants well worth growing. Brown boronia, though not long lived, has perfume that can fill a whole garden.

Create your own Floriade with spring bulbs such as daffodils, bluebells, freesias, snowdrops, Lily of the Valley and many more. Most spring bulbs are drought tolerant and will flower easily with a little care. Once the foliage has died down, the bulbs prefer to stay dry through summer, deep down in the soil. Even in a tiny garden, a tub or large pot filled with spring bulbs can be a welcome feature. The beautiful flowers of the bearded iris belie their tough drought tolerance and put on a great spectacle in October. Pansies, poppies and annual bulbs like anemones and ranunculi will also turn on wonderful displays, and even in times of water shortage, a planter of spring flowering annuals can be enjoyed providing you add compost to the soil mix and cover with mulch for moisture retention.

Flowering trees, such as prunus (cherries, plums, peaches, apricots and almonds), the flowering pears, crab apples, magnolias and dogwoods will be at their best in spring. The foliage on some of these trees is an added bonus, and the Japanese maples are outstanding with a range of beautiful foliage colours and shapes. Wisteria, lilacs and Dutch irises mark the end of the spring flush as they flower in early October while in November you can enjoy the full flush of roses. Try to choose fragrant varieties.

Summer is the season for many flowering perennials, daylilies, bulbous lilies, more brilliant annuals, lavender, some native shrubs and, where it's shady, the hydrangeas. Vegetables and berries are in full production by summer.

Autumn is a beautiful season in Canberra. Many roses will be flowering again and autumn-flowering bulbs will be appearing. Fruit, tomatoes and vegetables will be ready to pick, dahlias are at their riotous best and the first of the sasanqua camellias will be flowering. Chrysanthemums come into flower at the end of autumn. Autumn colour is all around Canberra. Look for trees and shrubs which, apart from producing flowers or their fresh new leaves in spring, will provide a second show for autumn — for example, the dogwoods, Japanese maples and the flowering cherries. Some shrubs, like the Spindle Bush (*Euonymus alatus*) are worth growing simply for the vibrant autumn colour.

Winter in a cold climate has the potential to be drab and miserable, but with careful planting you can avoid this. Even the bare branches of some deciduous trees can be striking so look for those that have interesting bark, patterned, peeling, coloured, there are many different ways the bark can be interesting. Always read the label for such a characteristic may only appear on the mature tree. There are a number of plants which have especially attractive or interesting bark, though take care, for many are suited to higher rainfall areas than ours. Some maples have interesting trunks and the snake bark maples are great, while *Prunus serrula*, the Tibetan cherry, makes a wonderful feature with its dark red varnish-like trunk.

Through the use of dwarf conifers, you can have colour in your garden in winter, but many of these will change colour through the seasons and provide additional interest. The fruit of lemons and other citrus varieties brighten the garden as the cold weather approaches, and the brilliant orange fruit of the persimmon stands out like a beacon. Flowers are a bit harder to come by in the depths of winter, but there are some which are well worth growing, such as Wintersweet and the Witch Hazel family, the latter producing their perfumed yellow flowers on the coldest days of winter, as well as the sasanqua camellias, hellebores, perennial wallflowers, and towards the end of the season, *Iris stylosa* (syn. *I. unguicularis*).

Even a small spot can be both attractive and productive.

A Rock Garden

The rock garden has evolved over time to be a home for Mediterranean plants, smaller Australian plants or cacti and succulents, to name a few. It is a place where rocks and boulders can be used in such a way as to reflect the natural habitat of many different types of plants. By visiting local garden centres throughout the year, you can choose plants in flower so that you can have a few flowers all year round. You can also have year-round interest in a rock garden by including plants with attractive foliage. Silvers, blues and greys are colours commonly found in sun-tolerant and hardy plants.

The ideal site will face east with some shade from the west. This may come from deciduous shrubs and trees or a fence or wall. Not all gardens have the ideal site and dense shade and west-facing gardens are difficult. A sloping site can be useful, but it is possible to make an attractive and effective rock garden in most positions. If your garden must, of necessity, be in a less favourable position, then take care in your choice of plants and choose plants which will thrive in such a location.

Any perennial weeds such as couch must be removed before planting, and of all the tasks involved in building a rock garden, this will be the most important. Timing is important with perennial weeds, and best results will be obtained if spraying is carried out during active growth. Spray the desired area with herbicide and leave for at least two weeks (remember spray drift can kill indiscriminately, so be careful to protect any valued shrubs). It may be necessary to respray before planting to ensure that you have killed all the weeds. This will become evident after the first week or so, when the weeds start to yellow.

Rock gardens on a sloping site look best with the rocks arranged in tiers down the slope, tilting the rocks back slightly so rainwater will wash back towards the plants. The best rocks will be those which will look as if they belong to the site, and they should be well-embedded to look natural, preferably two-thirds below ground level. Try to choose the rocks yourself and include plenty of large ones, limited only by your capacity to lift them. The aim is to make the rocks look as if they have been there forever, so give some thought to this when you arrange them.

Even on a flat site, beds can be built up using rocks, gravel, scalpings and soil, and they will become a haven for plants which need perfect drainage. Paths should slope slightly to avoid puddling in wet weather. While you may be inclined to put rocks all round the garden bed, try to avoid this, for even though soil may spill onto a path or the lawn after rain, once your carefully chosen ground-hugging plants have assumed their role in the landscape, the task of holding the soil will be achieved much more naturally.

A Vertical Garden

Your home may have a large footprint, leaving very little space for a garden. Don't despair, for your garden may be created vertically as a wall garden. If you envisage a brick wall fully covered with plant material, then it's wise to call in professionals for advice as you will need appropriate plants, a means of affixing each plant to the wall and a suitable irrigation system. Hydroponic systems could meet the need very well. If you intend to use a common wall between your property and a neighbour's, you will need to consider whether there will be any potential moisture

A water garden.

seepage problems, and if so, work to avoid them. Do some research and you might be pleasantly surprised, for these gardens are becoming more popular all over the world, and they meet a need where space is at a premium.

A Water Garden

You may have always liked the idea of a tranquil water garden. If you do have room for a real water feature, then give its placement careful thought, for it should look natural and if it is an informal pool, then ideally, it should be at the lowest point in the garden, as a depression which one might expect, would normally fill with water in the event of heavy rain. The butyl rubber liner needs to be laid on sand to avoid wear and tear and should be firmly anchored all around with boulders or rocks. Water pumps, fountains and solar power to drive these are all options, but will need some degree of expertise to install. Water irises and other border plants will eventually soften the edge and make the whole scene appear more natural. If there is no room for a pond or other in-ground water feature, then you might consider acquiring a large glazed bowl. Get one as large as is

Mandevilla laxa, growing against a sheltered west wall.

practical for the space you have, adding a few water plants, one or two goldfish (to control mosquitoes) and a pump to suit the size of the bowl. If you live near a busy street, the sound of moving water will mask the noise of traffic and if placed thoughtfully, you can still enjoy the tranquillity of water in the landscape.

Plants: A few suggestions to help the choice

Look for plants that have seasonal interest, whether it is flowering times, foliage colour, interesting bark (some plants combine a few different features). Some plants flower in winter and have an important role to play in keeping a Canberra garden interesting with flowers, bark, changing foliage colours or texture – all of these are ways to keep your garden interesting all year round.

Include some bird-attracting shrubs and a source of water, even if just a bowl, for visiting birds.

Whether your choice is for Australian plants or other plants, drought and frost tolerance are vital considerations. Not all Australian plants are suited to Canberra's conditions so choose carefully. In this book a considerable number of Australian plants are included in the general lists of shrubs, trees etc. The Society for Growing Australian Plants is another good source of advice on local species, and it's best to choose these or buy good hardy stock from local growers. Grafted native plants

Fothergilla gardenii, a small shrub for a sunny spot, showing its autumn colours.

are worthwhile, and the extra outlay will enable you to enjoy a plant that you might not otherwise have been able to grow.

Annual flowers, while great for quick and easy colour, use considerable amounts of water, but you won't need many to achieve a cheery effect if you fill a few planters and place them thoughtfully.

Lawns, though known as water-guzzlers, remain the cheapest ground cover to establish for children to play on. The difficulty is that in times of water restrictions, watering of lawns with potable water is restricted. Even if allowed, the cost of doing so would be prohibitive. Drought tolerant turf such as 'Santa Ana' and 'Grand Prix' couch is now available as well as 'Sir Walter' buffalo, all of which fade to yellow in winter, but they will soon revive in spring. Think also about the size of your lawn, for you may be able to design your garden as a small green space surrounded by shrubs and trees. You may choose a lawn alternative and you will find some listed in Chapter 3.

Roses, though tough and hardy, do require regular pruning and deadheading, and possibly sprays for disease or pests. Look for disease-resistant varieties (see Chapter 16 for guidance).

Trees and shrubs are important choices for your garden for they are long-lived, so it is important to choose wisely. Your plants can serve you well if you make the right choice. There are some potential pitfalls, and to help you through, here are a few words of advice based on the experience of local gardeners.

» Be sure your garden can accommodate the trees you choose without causing problems to foundations, driveways, paths, pipes and neighbours' amenities. Choosing the wrong plant can be a costly exercise. When picking a tree, consider the size of your block in relation to the ultimate height and spread of the tree, its suitability for the area (frost hardy, drought tolerant, etc). You need to know its usual shape (upright, spreading, pyramidal, rounded) and whether it is deciduous or evergreen. Other interesting qualities can be considered, such as the flowers, the colour or texture of the bark, its fruit, foliage and autumn leaf colour. Remember that the siting of this tree may affect a neighbour's home in years to come.

» Some plants have invasive roots so do your research before planting. Check with your local nurseryman if you don't have all the facts. Tree roots can lift pavers and drive strips while others are efficient seekers of moisture and nutrient so may end up in sewers and drains. Take care in choosing conifers, for you need to know their ultimate size. Many gardeners have planted 'dwarf' conifers in the expectation that they would not exceed a few metres in height, only to find that on reaching maturity, the 'dwarf' is now taking up a third of the front garden and shading the house in winter.

» Drought is tough on some conifers, but others delight in the conditions and there are a few native conifers available, though their ultimate size is more suited to large blocks and farms. Once again, make sure you know your plant before you make your selection.

» Deciduous trees and shrubs facilitate passive solar heating of your house in winter and cooling in summer. The degree to which this will happen depends on the density of the crown of the plant. Evergreen trees and shrubs can provide much needed structure and interest in your garden in winter. If not well-sited, they can hinder the heating of your house in winter but, if properly placed, they can assist in reducing the house temperature in summer.

» If you don't have room for a tree, but do need shade, think about climbers. An evergreen climber such as *Trachelospermum jasminoides* is slow growing but, in time, will be a most attractive plant with perfumed white flowers and shiny leaves. *Mandevilla laxa* (Chilean Jasmine), though slightly frost tender when young, can become a most attractive plant if mulched around the roots in the first year or two. It is partly deciduous with perfumed white flowers in summer and long green beans.

» Grapes, either ornamental or fruiting, can be grown on trellises or pergolas, and Boston Ivy is one to enjoy for its vibrant red autumn colour. Ornamental grapes have spectacular autumn colour, but you might prefer to grow fruiting grapes. If you want speed of coverage, then the white flowered potato creeper will give you that, though its vigour can present a few problems if you ever decide you don't want to grow it, for then removing it can result in suckering of the remaining roots. These are hurdles which can be dealt with if you are aware of a plant's characteristics.

» Wisteria is a beautiful long-lived plant. A mature vine in full flower can be a sight to behold. You need to know that with age it will develop a tree-like trunk and if it is grown near a brick wall, it has the potential to lift the wall and crack it. This does not mean you should not plant wisteria, you just need know its habit and plant accordingly.

» When choosing shrubs, check their features and what conditions they like. Shrubs make a valuable windbreak or privacy screen, while small native shrubs and miniature conifers are excellent plants for year round accents in your garden.

As a potential garden designer, we've included these ideas and comments to help you and to make your job easier. Don't be put off by the possible worries we have talked about. They are discussed simply as scraps of knowledge to accumulate before you make your choices, for if you know a plant's characteristics, then you can make the most of its best points and plant it in the right place!

PART B: The water conscious gardener

Here we look at effective ways of working with Canberra's water and soil environment.

» The challenges and answers for one of the first questions in any new garden — lawns, paving or other alternatives.

» Ways of improving your soil's quality and water retention, making mulch, and compost and how to use them.

» Finally, Chapter 6 discusses how best to water.

In Parts C and D we talk about plants that do well in Canberra. You may be surprised at how wide the choice is.

CHAPTER 3:
The water aware garden

Merylyn Condon

Canberra is a dry area and though drought has been a concern for farmers since first settlement here, now the lack of water is a genuine concern for city and country dwellers alike. Water shortages are here to stay and water restrictions have become the norm.

Gardens and green spaces are vital in preserving our planet in soaking up some of that surplus carbon dioxide but in order to provide those wider benefits and indeed, to enjoy the benefits of a garden, we must ensure that we use every drop of available water to best advantage, whether rainwater or recycled. That's not all we can do, for we can to work to make the soil better able to hold and retain moisture. We can most definitely enjoy good gardens with less water, though we will need to revise our ways and garden smarter.

With all this effort, you might ask why bother at all. It's hard work, time-consuming and sometimes costly to maintain a garden and to keep plants growing when watering times are restricted and water costs are rising. Trees all around Canberra are dying or dead and many thousands of street trees have already been removed. Sometimes this is just life cycle, but very often it is because of insufficient water for the particular trees chosen. Because current water restrictions do not allow for the watering of lawns and most lawns are deteriorating or worse, some people have chosen to remove their lawns and replace them with paving, with artificial turf or with mulched shrubberies. Some people have

A homemade solution to water storage using recycled olive drums

decided that it's all too much, and abandoned the idea of a garden altogether.

The overall effect of the loss of so many plants combined with more paving and hard, reflective surfaces will cause our environment, whether immediate or as a whole, to become warmer in summer and when that happens, being creatures of comfort, we will simply turn on our air conditioners and fans to cool off. So, it's just one big circle, and unless we do something to help ourselves, it will only worsen.

Our water shortages are directly linked to our impact on the environment. Plants have a natural cooling mechanism through transpiration, where water is taken in by the plant's roots and released through the leaves. This causes a cooling effect not only for the plant, but also for the surrounding air. If we only use our gardens to help to reduce summer temperatures indoors by a few degrees, and to raise the temperatures in winter by planning for the winter sun to shine into our homes, we will be doing ourselves a favour and ultimately the environment. A lush garden with abundant plantings will serve to provide cooling effects in summer and reduce the need for air conditioners. In winter, with careful selection and placement of deciduous trees and shrubs around the house, we can enjoy the effects of winter sunshine and it will help warm a home naturally. Shading the ground around one's home with plants and mulch can also help keep summer temperatures down while that same mulch will insulate the soil and help to reduce the effects of frost damage to plants in winter.

So why not plant and nurture a new tree or shrub where possible? Too many have already been lost in these extraordinarily dry times. If you have a street tree out on the nature strip include it in your watering regime, and avoid another casualty.

While saving the planet is by far the best reason for having a garden, there are other more selfish reasons. Gardening can be a very healthy activity, but even if one only sees a garden purely from a monetary perspective, a well-designed and maintained garden will significantly increase the value of a home.

On that basis, here are a few ways to drought-proof a garden, starting with a new garden. Some readers will have allocated funds for landscaping, and that's good, but be sure the garden plan meets all your expectations.

Lawns and lawn substitutes

If you have just bought or built a new home, you will be very aware of the need to keep the dust, mud and dirt outside so that it is

Succulents use very little water, but make sure you choose plants which will handle Canberra's winters

not being trampled into the house. Invariably lawns come to mind because they are still the cheapest form of ground cover available, but with water restrictions, lawns need much more thought.

Many of Canberra's large lawns are disappearing; others are looking yellowed or bald, while many have been reduced in size. As intermittent water restrictions severley limit watering of lawns with potable water, some householders have, in order to keep the front garden looking good, opted to remove their lawns and replace them with paving or some other hard surface. Some have simply mulched the area, then incorporated a collection of drought tolerant plants. A number of people have opted for imitation lawns.

A more recent trend has resulted in smaller house blocks and larger homes with garden designers making more use of the backyard for relaxation and entertainment, creating outdoor rooms as an extension of the house. This presents quite a quandary: lawn or paving?

Late afternoon shadows fall across a Canberra lawn planted with one of the newer couch cultivars 'Santa Ana'.

Lawns: the advantages:

» Lawns provide a great cooling effect as they shade the soil and provide natural evaporative cooling.

» They are soft underfoot and perfect for kids to play on

» They are still the quickest way to anchor soil around a new house

» A lawn is permeable and will absorb rainwater

Some disadvantages of lawns:

» Lawns need to be mown, weeded and fertilised.

» They can be ruined by pets

» Lawns may be difficult to establish or grow in shady places or under trees

» They may not take heavy foot traffic

Pavers: the advantages

» Provide a functional outdoor surface for dining, sitting and relaxing

» Good for paths and terraces

» Can be laid so that rainwater flows into nearby garden beds

» If correctly laid, virtually no maintenance is required

» Permeable paving will allow for moisture flow-through to the soil below.

Some disadvantages of pavers

» Generally more expensive to buy and install than turf

» Clay or stone pavers absorb the sun and reflect heat on a hot day

» Require 'softening' with surrounding plants

» Need to be laid properly on sand or concrete

» A tough surface for children's play, sometimes good, sometimes bad

Pavers can be softened with border plantings or by using a stone border or mulch. It does not have to be a choice between pavers or grass, but by blending a small surface of lawn with the hard surface of paving or using permeable paved surfaces, you will allow water to drain through, you can create a useful and interesting outdoor space and thus have the best of both options.

A lawn is still the best surface for children's play. It will keep a garden cooler in summer time, and nowadays turf can be obtained ready to lay once the initial soil preparation has been done. Much work has been done in the field of drought tolerant grasses, eg Sir Walter buffalo and drought tolerant South African hybrid couches, and though these will yellow in a Canberra winter, they are still probably our best option for a lawn. There are also some native grasses now available in seed form although these do not have the appearance of a traditional lawn. Recently, a new Australian native turf Zoysia 'Nara' has been introduced; this is said to be cold-tolerant, though is not yet well known in Canberra.

Lawn alternatives:

Hardy ground covers and drought-tolerant plantings can be lower maintenance than some types of turf. Most require regular watering and mowing, at least in the growing months. Thyme and chamomile lawns, native violets (*Viola hederacea*), baby tears (*Soleirolia soleirolii*) or kidney weed (*Dichondra repens*) are often mentioned as substitutes for lawn though none of these has the exact characteristics of a traditional lawn. Some of these alternatives attract bees, probably not the best option if small children are going to be using the area for play.

Artificial grass can look wonderful, but it still requires maintenance.

In recent years, artificial grass has become popular. Many have welcomed the opportunity to have a soft green space where children can play safely, which needs very little maintenance other than an occasional run with a leaf blower. Price is usually related to quality, but probably corresponds with laying a good quality carpet. There is a variety of green hues for buyers to choose from, some even having a sprinkling of fine yellow. The material is rubber-backed with perforations for drainage, and a deep layer of compacted road base is placed underneath.

A selection of hardy plants, phygelius, santolina, arctotis and blue ceratostigma, providing interest all year long.

The lawn must be edged with cement. While some artificial grasses need to be anchored, the heavier forms do not dislodge on windy days because of their weight.

Caution: Some studies in other countries, especially the USA, have suggested that the use of artificial turf may pose a health risk, due largely to concerns about it being derived from recycled tyres with possible high lead levels and the potential to contain carcinogenic materials. The Horticultural Society of Canberra Inc. has no expertise in this area. If you plan to use artificial turf you might like to seek further information.

Growing the right plant in the right position

One automatically associates Australian plants with drought tolerance, but remember that Australia is a diverse land with many different climatic variations and soils, so it's wise to do some research before you decide what to plant or where to put it. Many plants are bulk-marketed and distributed Australia-wide by growers and some of these plants will simply not grow in Canberra's heavy clay soils, given also our cold winters and hot dry summers. Grafted plants facilitate the growing of many which might once have been quite difficult, particularly West Australian plants which are used to sandy soils and therefore prefer good drainage. One example is the *Pimelea physodes*, (the Qualup Bell) from Western Australia, which as a grafted plant thrives here. In WA it is popular as a cut flower and forms the basis of a thriving industry. Though comparatively new to Canberra, it is growing in popularity, with its large pink and green bellflowers lasting well over two months. The genus eremophila (Emu Bush) also contains many tough plants suited to dry conditions. Some are grafted and others are cutting-grown, but all are worthy of a place because of their extreme drought tolerance.

Species of brachyscome (syn. brachycome), an Australian daisy, are worth growing, and there is an annual species as well as many perennial species. The species is a better choice for toughness than are some of the newer cultivars which are not so frost tolerant.

For a guide on Australian plants, you can do no better than to regularly explore the National Botanic Gardens and try to match the conditions provided there for any plants you admire. Bywong Native Plants is a local wholesale nursery which grows and introduces plants which are well-suited to our conditions, and these are available in many of our garden centres, while Stocks' Native Nursery in Harden propagates hundreds of local species as tubestock. Starting with small plants is by far the best way of growing Australian plants. Another good way of ensuring you choose 'plant survivors' is to go to a Native Plant Sale at the Australian National Botanic Gardens. There are also a number of private propagators living in Canberra who sell locally-grown plants, and the best source of information on such growers is the Society for Growing Australia Plants.

Pride of Madeira flowers in spring and is a most striking plant.

There are many Australian plants which will serve you well, but there are also countless exotics which suit our tough conditions. Grey and silver plants are generally found growing in deserts, on arid plains, mountain tops, seashores and coastal cliffs. These are areas of extreme exposure and these plants tolerate conditions such as intense sunlight, driving winds, periods of drought and in some cases, extreme heat or extreme cold. Not only are they drought-tolerant, but they are beautiful in their own right. Below is a list, not exhaustive, of some proven survivors. There are many such plants.

» *Achillea clypeolata*,

» Acacia (but not all species),

» Agave (succulent),

» Allium (ornamental) species,

» *Arctotis hybrida*,

» Artemesia species,

Callistemom '*Endeavour*', guaranteed to attract Wattle Birds.

- » Brachyscome syn. brachycome species
- » Callistemon species,
- » *Chamelaucium uncinatum*,
- » *Cerastium tomentosum* (a silvery ground cover with tiny white flowers commonly called Snow in Summer),
- » Chrysocephalum species,
- » *Convulvulus mauritanicum* (a creeping plant with mauve flowers), tough and hardy. More recently other forms have been introduced with deeper blue, purple or white flowers.
- » Correa species
- » Darwinia species,
- » *Dianella tasmanica*,
- » Echeverias (succulent),
- » *Echium candicans* (Pride of Madeira),

- » Eryngium species,
- » *Euphorbia myrsinites*,
- » *Festuca glauca* (Blue Grass),
- » Grevillea species,
- » *Hakea species*,
- » *Helichrysum italicum* (the Curry bush),
- » *Lagerstroemia indica*, a proven small tree for drought,
- » Lavendula,
- » *Melaleuca species*,
- » *Murrubium vulgare* 'Scallop Shell',
- » *Nerium oleander* is a proven survivor available in miniature forms through to large shrubs
- » Rosemary, various forms and cultivars,
- » Sage and many of the salvia family,
- » *Santolina chamaecyparissus* (Lavender Cotton), a plant that tolerates extreme dryness and will grow in dry gardens
- » Sedum (succulent)
- » *Teucrium fruticosa* is a silver-leafed shrub with blue-mauve flowers which makes a tough hardy hedge as it responds very well to trimming
- » Thymes make great ground covers.

CHAPTER 4:
Improving the soil

Susan Orgill

This chapter and the next cover three aspects of caring for the soil around your home. We begin with core approaches to improving the quality of the soil, then ways of mulching so as to keep the soil in good condition and reduce water demand; and finally compost, a special form of mulch.

Soil quality

Getting the structure of your soil right is one of the best ways of ensuring that your plants receive the nutrients and the moisture they need. Even a highly nutritious soil will not support plants unless there is moisture to dissolve the nutrients and allow plants to utilise them. Our aim is to describe how you can improve and maintain the quality of your soil and so make it better able to support your plants; and then the best ways of adding moisture to the soil. You don't have to improve the whole garden all at once, but improve it as and when you can and reap the rewards.

Most gardeners realise the importance of soil in providing water, nutrients, oxygen and anchorage for their garden plants. However some are not aware that these four basic functions can be likened to a performer juggling four balls — drop one and the whole act is spoilt!

Basically, the strategy is to encourage your plants to develop a large and deep root system; and you do this by making the soil in which they are growing as hospitable

as you can for the development of such a root system. A large, deep, root system for your plants means that the plants can take advantage of the nutrients and the moisture held in a greater volume of soil and so their ability to withstand drought and all the other stresses of the garden is enhanced.

The autumn berries of *Callicarpa bodnieri*. Callicarpas like a moist, well drained soil.

Roots can develop only where there is moisture so if watering is shallow or topsoil thin, only a poor root system can develop. However, roots also need air and few plants can develop in a continually wet soil, such as you might get where drainage is impeded. Water is also needed to stimulate our beneficial soil microbes which convert nutrients into plant available forms. Nearly all nutrients required by plants must first pass through a soil organism (such as bacteria, fungi or protozoa) before they are plant available. Soil organisms are just like us in that they need water, food, shelter and plenty of oxygen to work!

Gardening in Canberra is made a bit more difficult by the combination of our fairly low and unreliable rainfall with the poor nature of our soils. Our rainfall was discussed in Chapter 1. Our soils present a number of problems:

» Generally, they are not highly fertile, so you need ways of making them more so and then maintaining this increased fertility. Mulch and compost are a great help and you can use supplemental fertilisers. Vegetables and annuals in particular will appreciate this.

» If your topsoil is high in clay, then it is likely you are gardening on former subsoil (and all the topsoil has been removed!). Clay subsoils are not renowned for being high in plant nutrients but they are great at storing moisture if they are well structured. In these cases in particular you will do better if you can improve the fertility of the clay soil.

» Often soils that are low in organic matter will not absorb moisture unless through steady rain for an extended period. These soils are known as 'hydrophobic soils'. Increasing the level of soil organic matter with compost and manures is helpful, and then a layer of mulch will help avoid a recurrence of the problem.

» If your topsoil is high in clay and poorly structured, then the soil moisture can be held so tightly that most plants may struggle to get what they need. Focusing on improving soil structure and using a clay-breaking technique is the answer.

» If your topsoil is compacted then infiltration and aeration may be impeded. Aggregating the clay particles by applying organic material and/or gypsum and well-timed cultivation will help a great deal.

Working soils too often or too soon after rain can break down soil structure. The result may be a hard, compacted or crusted soil in which oxygen levels are low and water tends to run off rather than infiltrate.

There is an excellent book by Kevin Handreck "Gardening Down-under: better soils and potting mixes for better gardens", CSIRO Publications, East Melbourne, 1993 which describes clearly in very practical terms the subjects of this chapter.

Improving poorly structured clay soils

The relative proportions of the various sized particles in the soil (sand being the coarsest and clay the finest), together with the humus and organic content, determine the soil texture, ie whether it is a loam, clay or sandy loam. Our soils contain quite a bit of clay, although the surface soils may also have a lot of weathered gravel particles.

At this point it is important to highlight the difference between soil texture and soil structure. Soil texture is the amount and proportions of clay, silt and sand particles. Soil structure is the way that these particles are arranged. We can change and manage soil structure but not so easily soil texture (for example, without importing large amounts of sand).

A loam soil contains relatively even proportions of clay, silt and sand; an ideal topsoil in most cases. Sand is good for drainage although has minimal nutrient content. Clay is comprised of very fine; microscopic plates stacked one on top of the other. These structures absorb water (and

With time the soil of this well mulched new bed will support a garden to be proud of.

swell) and are also very effective at storing nutrients (as they are negatively charged). Clays are very important; however, if the soil is low in organic matter (the 'biological glue' of soil) when they get wet and swell they can collapse and set hard, impeding infiltration, drainage and aeration. Also, the clay content effects the amount of plant-available water. That is, more water is required than in for example sands. If there is not enough water, then the moisture can be held so tightly in the soil that plants cannot use it even though the soil may appear moist. That said, it is very important not to over water or saturate clay soils. This is why soil structure is so important

An ideal garden soil would include a mix of gritty particles and organic material. A soil like this will more easily absorb water, the excess more easily drains away, and it would not hold onto the water with the same strength as clay does.

So the first strategy in improving your soil is to work at aggregating those tiny clay particles into larger particles. The two most common ways of tackling this are to use gypsum (or some other clay breaker) and to improve the organic content of the soil with composts and mulch. Mulch and compost are the subjects of the next chapter.

Gypsum (calcium sulphate) is a powder which you spread at the rate of 0.5–1 kg a square metre and then dig into the surface soil. Apart from causing the clay particles to aggregate, it reduces the sodium content of the clay and adds sulphur, and this further improves the soil. Adding gypsum or some other proprietary soil conditioner is a very important first step. If your soil is very acidic, then you can increase aggregation at the same time as increasing the pH by applying and incorporating lime (calcium carbonate).

Remember also that the clay is often below a layer of differing texture. In this case, the gypsum etc is unlikely to penetrate far enough to affect the clay, so apply it only if the clay is near the surface.

New maple leaves in spring.

A good method of adding organic matter is to use compost, either worked into the soil or added to the surface as a mulch. Alternatively, fresh plant material such as the remains of vegetables after harvest, weeds (not in seed) and annual bedding plants can be turned into the soil. 'Green manure crops' can be grown specifically for this purpose and include various legumes such as peas which are usually incorporated into the soil at flowering.

It is difficult to change the texture of a clay soil by adding sand — around 50 per cent would need to be thoroughly mixed into the soil. However, when establishing lawns or playing fields, a thick layer of sand is often used to assist drainage and root penetration. If this is done, remember this sandier soil will require more frequent watering and fertilising.

The second basic problem to be tackled is compaction of the soil. Continual foot traffic across a lawn and, in a new garden, the machinery used by builders can result in a compacted soil. The simplest way of reducing compaction is to loosen the soil with a fork. There is no need to turn the soil over; you simply need to break it up a bit. The result is that water and other nutrients and conditioners will soak in much more easily and plant roots will find it easier to develop.

If you are noticing water pearling on the surface around your annual vegetables or citrus plants, another way to increase infiltration is to apply something high in carbohydrates such as molasses or sugar (ordinary sugar you put in your cup of tea is fine!). This stimulates the soil microbes to break up the waxy lattices that cover some clay structures and inhibit water absorption.

CHAPTER 5:
Mulch and compost

Cedric Bryant and Merylyn Condon

Mulch is a term used to cover a wide range of materials placed on the surface of the soil. One of the best ways of keeping the garden in tiptop condition is to mulch all garden beds and regularly top it up. Organic mulches, apart from adding additional nutrients to plants, encourage a whole host of creatures that live in a good soil.

Mulch has many advantages:

» It reduces weed growth and any weeds that do appear will easily pull out.

» It keeps the soil around your shrubs moist and cool, reducing evaporation.

» A good layer of mulch protects the soil from the extremes of weather. Heavy rain, rather than running off or washing away good topsoil will sink into the soils and penetrate to the root zone.

» In the heat of summer it prevents crusting of the surface which will in due course prevent water soaking in.

» When rain does come, a layer of mulch will prevent the soil splashing up onto leaves of plants. This can be a major cause of fungal problems.

» Newly planted trees and shrubs, which have been mulched, will make better progress during the establishment period than those which have to put up with weeds and the periodic drying out of the topsoil.

It is important to keep in mind there is considerable loss of moisture from the soil of a mature garden through the movement of water through plant roots and eventually out the leaves.

Are you selecting a mulch for the benefit of the plants or because it looks good? There is a distinct difference. Although, any mulch is better than no mulch.

There is a wide selection of mulch material available commercially of which not all is ideal for the benefit of the plants. Pinebark, pine needles, shredded plant material such as lucerne, pea and sugar cane straw material; newspapers and cardboard, carpet, and pebbles can all be used as mulch. There are arguments for and against most of them. For example, carpet keeps down weeds but looks most unattractive. It could be used for a path in a vegetable garden. Some fresh mulch material will draw nitrogen from the soil and can temporarily rob the plants you are hoping to help. It may be necessary to provide supplementary feeding. Some non-organic

Chrysocephalum apiculatum (syn. *Helichrysum apiculatum*) Yellow Buttons thriving in a wood chip mulch.

mulches can be used to good effect, but need to be quite deep since most absorb extreme heat in mid-summer. These may consist of river stones of varying sizes or scoria and crushed bricks. For alpines and cacti inorganic mulch such as fine pebbles is preferable as they need to be kept dry at the crown.

Lucerne mulch is excellent for roses and for most other plants and is specifically recommended by Swane's Roses of Sydney. Lucerne, as it breaks down, releases the vital major nutrients of nitrogen, phosphorus and potassium in the right combination to stimulate and promote growth. Lucerne may be obtained in cube form, shredded or in bale form from the farm. Cubes or shredded are the easiest to handle but can be rather expensive if you have a large area. Baled lucerne is available from farm produce stores and at times can be purchased direct from growers straight from the paddock. Second or third cut bales are best if available, as first cut bales often contain more weed seed than later cuts. Bales need to be opened out and spread evenly over areas. Watch as you spread as on occasions some pests may also arrive in the form of earwigs, field mice

or cockroaches. This warning also applies to any other form of mulch in unopened bales. Inhaling the dust from bales of mulch can be a health problem. For safety, wear a mask so you don't inhale the dust.

Consider the following before buying mulch:

» Mulch should be for the benefit of the plants, not for appearance.

» Mulch should be a combination of coarse and fine material.

» Mulch should be dense enough to prevent weed growth, ideally 50–75 mm deep. Keep it away from stems/trunks of plants to prevent collar rot.

» Mulch should allow good water penetration after rain or hand watering. (Some mulch material can be impervious to water.)

» Mulch should break down over time to improve soil. This is the result of decomposition and worm activity. Periodically mulch will need topping up.

» The mulch must be economically viable, especially for large gardens.

» For small courtyard/townhouse gardens and vegetable gardens lucerne hay is specially recommended. However, it is not economically viable for the large garden.

Organic mulches are best as over time they will break down and improve your soil. However, you need to understand the properties of whatever you might choose to use. Some have little nutrient value, others release the right amount required for maintaining plants in top condition, and some take nitrogen from the soil as

A kniphofia thriving in mulch. Note the use of wood blocks and stones to form two swales.

they decompose. An ideal organic mulch available in Canberra is from trimmings and prunings taken to landscape suppliers. This is checked for environmental weeds such as privet, cotoneaster and pyracantha. It is then shredded and stockpiled for several months to compost before being offered for sale. This complies with all of the above attributes for the ideal mulch.

If lawn clippings are used it is best to spread on a path to dry out before using, or mix them sparingly with coarser and dry materials. If used alone, green grass clippings will form a solid mass which water cannot penetrate, so it is best to put them into the compost heap. Pulverised cow manure will also form an impermeable crust, which will prevent water getting through to your plants so it must be mixed with other materials or frequently stirred.

Applying mulch to the garden:

For the greatest benefit apply a mulch of organic material in early spring and before plants put on too much new growth.

It is important to cultivate and water your garden before spreading mulch, and at the same time remove any weeds. Keep the soil in good condition by lightly and regularly cultivating through the mulch, keeping the water content constant. Light cultivation helps decomposing mulch to fully mix with the soil. This improves and maintains the soil condition, and allows moisture to penetrate readily to the root area. Mulch should be maintained throughout the growing season. Some types of mulch will decompose very quickly in the warmer months and may require topping up to maintain the benefit.

Weeds should be removed from mulched areas, before they go to seed. They are easily removed while the mulch is damp.

It used to be common to use black plastic under the mulch to further inhibit weed growth. This is an absolute no as the soil can become waterlogged in periods of heavy rain. The plastic restricts natural evaporation of soil moisture and prevents fertiliser from reaching the root zone. There is also a tendency for plants to create a shallow root system directly below the black plastic.

Compost

Composting is a method for speeding up what occurs naturally in bushland and forests, where leaves and other dead matter rot down and are returned to the soil. Even if you already choose to bury your kitchen scraps in the garden, by starting a compost heap you will have more control over the process. You will then be able to treat your plants to nutrient rich compost and stand back and watch them grow. By incorporating your household and garden waste material into a compost heap, you will reduce the amount you put out for collection each week and importantly, much of your household waste can be returned to your soil in a form available for plant growth.

Depending upon how much time and energy you have, you can have useable compost in anywhere from approximately three weeks to a year or more. The less time the compost takes to make, the more effort you will have to expend, and you will probably need to learn a little more about compost heaps.

Essentially, most composting methods require the assembly of components in a heap or in a container, often in layers. The process can be sped up by using a rotary tumbler or by manually turning over the heap. Composting in a tumbler will be quite different to an open heap, and you may have to check for excess moisture and add a quantity of shredded material at your discretion to soak up any excess moisture.

The compost heap

The primary consideration in having a successful compost heap is the ratio between carbon and nitrogen components. A compost heap will usually work best where there is about 30 times as much carbon as nitrogenous products (see the table which follows). There are also a number of other considerations such as temperature, moisture, oxygen and particle size.

Carbon products:	Nitrogen products
Sawdust (very high)	Lawn clippings
Straw	Weeds
Dead leaves	Animal manures
Paper	Blood and bone Human hair Urine Food scraps

While there are very few hard and fast rules about the composition of a compost heap, too much of any one ingredient will slow the rotting process and so will excess moisture. During prolonged wet weather, it is a good idea to cover the heap with a tarpaulin so that the rotting process can continue. Small pieces of organic matter will decompose far quicker than large ones and you can speed up the process by putting prunings and eucalyptus leaves (or any other larger sized materials) through a shredder before adding them to the heap.

A classic compost heap, but note the pipe in the centre for air and moisture and the removable slats at the front.

The traditional compost heap is closest to nature but the slowest way to compost. You might like to position the heap where it will be unobtrusive, perhaps in the back corner of your yard, or behind the garage. The optimum site will have good air distribution and warmth. You can simply make a mound of the materials you are adding, or you may prefer to use old wooden pallets to enclose the heap at the back and on two sides. You can add anything which has been alive, including newspaper. Avoid using meat scraps in an open heap as they will attract rodents. Dry materials such as straw and autumn leaves should be moistened and as mentioned previously, the heap will decompose more effectively if the components are all similarly-sized.

Sometimes anaerobic (oxygen absent) conditions will develop after continuing rain and the compost heap will become wet and smelly, but even then, nature will take its course and worms will work their way up into the heap, completing the composting process by feeding on the decaying vegetable matter.

The compost will be mature when you can no longer recognise the individual components.

It should smell earthy and be quite dark in colour. In a compost heap, you will find that the material at the base of the heap will be more mature than what has been added most recently, so if you need some compost desperately, you could carefully scratch out a quantity from the bottom of the heap.

The size of the heap will be your choice and when you think it is big enough, that is when it will be time to start all over again with a second heap.

Making compost quickly

To do this, you will need the correct ratio between carbon and nitrogen components and it is best not to work on any more than 1 cubic metre of materials. In Canberra, it is best done during late spring or summer, preferably in a warm situation with plenty of air distribution.

Ensure that all materials are fine, so shred any that are too big and mix all ingredients before making the heap. Moisten any dry materials and once you have built the heap, you may still have to add moisture to create perfect conditions for rapid decomposition.

Leave the heap for about 3–4 days. During this time, the heap should begin to generate heat. Every 3 days turn the heap by shovelling it to another area nearby. Repeat until 14 days later, then you can reduce the turning process to once weekly. After three weeks, the compost should be beginning to break down, and the longer you leave it, the finer it will become.

Other methods of composting

If you don't have space or energy to keep turning the materials, you might try layering the ingredients thinly, assembling them in either a heap or in one of the containers suggested below.

There are many containers suitable for composting, either commercially available or you can recycle an old bin or make one. Some of these are ideal for smaller spaces. Here are a few:

» Wire mesh bins, either fashioned into a cylinder or attached to four star pickets in the shape of a square;

» Bins made of polycarbonate or toughened plastic;

» Wooden bins with slatted sides to allow aeration;

» Three purpose-built adjoining brick bays (or concrete block, railway sleepers or recycled timber) will allow you to use compost from one while the others contain matter at varying stages of decomposition;

» Rotating bins commercially available (at least two are needed);

» Black plastic garbage bags;

» Plastic rubbish bins converted by removing the bases

Some tips on composting

A smaller heap which can be turned quickly and regularly will give a quicker result.

The smaller the individual size of components in a compost heap the faster the heap will decompose.

You can assist the process where there are lots of leaves in the heap by adding extra phosphorus (chook manure, blood and bone etc).

Use a shredder if possible to chop prunings and tough leaves to a smaller size.

If vegetable peelings form a significant component of the heap, every so often you should sprinkle a handful of sawdust and lime mixture (1:1 by volume) and/or soil. Keep a container full nearby for convenience so that it is there when you need it. The sawdust will soak up excess moisture and provide carbon to balance the nitrogen content of the scraps.

Keep the heap moist, especially in summer, so as to keep the rotting process moving — dryness is not a problem if you are using a tumbler or plastic container and you may have to add sawdust or wood mulch to absorb excess moisture.

For good aeration, which will provide the organisms with oxygen, use a compost corkscrew, or roll up chicken wire into tubes and place these vertically into the heap, or fork over the compost heap as often as you can.

Be vigilant with weeds. Try to remove them from your garden before they develop seeds, for while the heat of a compost heap will kill some of the weed seeds, it may not kill them all. It is better to adopt good cultural practices and thus save yourself the headache of spreading weed seed around the garden in the compost.

Avoid placing couch or any other perennial rhizomatous weeds in your compost heap. These should be put into a black plastic garbage bag and the bag left in a hot place for two or three weeks to 'cook'.

If high nitrogen organic matter is not readily available, commercially available urea can be used at the rate of 50 g per bucket of leaves.

CHAPTER 6: Watering

Cedric Bryant

Designing a watering system is a complex task, one that changes as you develop your garden and as new technologies become available. Rather than say very much about this aspect of watering, in this chapter we concentrate on some of the principles behind efficient watering.

Some simple techniques

Wetting agents and water crystals have become popular in recent years. Essentially they are detergents or surfactants, which lower the surface tension of the water, and allow it to move down between the particles. An ordinary kitchen detergent will do this also but will not have a lasting effect and may, in addition, be bad for your plants. Wetting agents need to be reapplied every year or so.

If your garden is on a slope, either of these problems will be exacerbated. You can help water to sink in by slowing the rate at which it runs off, by the use of swales, such as barriers or gravel channels across the line of the land. Using logs, or small retaining walls,

you can break up the fall into more gentle segments and thus allow time for water to soak in. Alternatively, a ditch filled with gravel running across the slope will do the same thing. Refer to the sketch on this page. In a home garden, swales can be subtle variations in the slope and could even comprise a lawn area. Swales are particularly useful for the retention of water for trees and deep rooted shrubs. In the sketch the dotted area suggests the way the water might sink into the soil.

Water spikes can be a practical and inexpensive solution for some gardens, probably best in smaller gardens. Attaching an upended soft drink bottle to the spike, either with the end of the bottle removed for easy application of water, or if you prefer to leave the bottle intact, the plant will receive a slower flow of moisture from the upended bottle. Black agricultural pipe can be used either as a bracelet around a treasured shrub or tree at the drip line, using a joiner and inserting vertical pipe into the bracelet through which you can add water at ground level. Another inexpensive option is to dig a hole beside each plant and insert a black flower pot, through which you can then apply water periodically. The water will drain through the bottom of the pot to a more acceptable level for the plant, and will be less likely to evaporate beneath the pot.

Water storage crystals are useful for establishing new plants. Shrubs and trees can take several years to fully acclimatise to their new homes and should be carefully nurtured through those first years of establishment and not allowed to dry out. There are many water storage crystals on the market, and when put into the planting hole around the new plant, the plant will extract water from the gel if the soil dries out. As the water in the gel is used up, the gel returns to crystal form, and when you apply water or it rains, the crystals will swell into gel once more. This can go on for about three years or so, making the process a great safeguard for new plantings. But please read the label carefully, as it can be harmful to use too many crystals, the result being their rapid expansion with moisture which can result in the plant being pushed out of the ground. Better to add water gradually to the crystals in a bucket till they have swollen to their full capacity and then spoon the made up gel into planting holes around the plant.

How much water should you apply?

There is no simple answer as it depends very much on what plants are being grown and how well the soil is prepared. In most instances newly planted trees and shrubs will require not necessarily more water but rather more often. Keep in mind no plant can be considered drought tolerant until the roots are well established. This may take up to 6–12 months. Deep, regular watering is the most important thing. Be wary of long watering which may well be running off and into the drains. This equally applies to hand watering. In the Horticulture Society's former rose garden of the Xeriscape garden at Weston the roses were kept in tiptop condition with minimal watering. Drip irrigation and effective mulching has been the secret. Not really a secret, just common sense.

Do not put off watering because the forecast is for rain. The only rain one can count on is that which has already fallen, and even then you need to be sure it has been a significant fall. Look under a mature tree next time even a minimal amount of rain has fallen. You may be surprised to find that none at all has reached the ground. A follow-up watering after a shower can be especially useful.

Light waterings are worse than useless as they encourage root development close to the surface. As soon as the plant has to cope on its own for a few days it will show signs of water stress. Concentrate on developing a deep root system. If water restrictions are limited to hand watering on alternate days, divide the garden into sections and develop a watering plan. Don't try to do it all together, but concentrate on particular sections on set days.

Watch for signs of water stress in your plants and get to understand the needs of the different varieties. Plants can also wilt from overwatering. Many plants naturally allow their leaves to wilt on a hot day to reduce water loss. Hydrangeas for example will droop badly on a hot summer afternoon but they quickly recover in the evening. Other plants may not be quite so gardener-friendly. Applying too much water can damage plants and so can unreliable watering. For example, intermittent periods of drought and moisture will cause blossom end rot in tomatoes because it has the effect of reducing the availability of a chemical important to the plant. The development of flowers and fruit in particular will be much helped by a dependable water supply.

If possible group plants according to their water needs. Vegetables and fruit trees, if

Rhododendron leaves showing symptoms typical of leaf burn, the result of too much exposure to sun.

they are to be at their most productive (better than you can buy at the supermarket) need regular watering too. Plant these in their own areas, away from plants that will compete for their moisture. For example, if fruit trees are planted in lawns the thirsty nature of grass can reduce a fruit crop by up to 40%. Look at the listing of plants in the chapter on annuals and perennials and group plants according to their preferences and needs for moisture and shade.

The proper watering of camellias, rhododendrons, azaleas and daphne is important. Leaf burn, first appearing on the tips of leaves on plants can be caused by direct sunlight or water stress.

Soil should be kept moist but not to the extent that water logging results. These plants come from areas with heavy summer rainfall, so regular watering through Canberra's dry summer is essential.

Many people group Australian plants together in the belief that they all require little water. There are many which, when well established, can cope with little supplementary watering but study the needs of the individual plants before making a decision.

Plants need water at different times of the year, and also need different watering techniques at various stages of growth. For example, daffodils prefer dry conditions in summer, with increasing water as they start to show signs of growth. Mature trees, needing quite large quantities of water, should have an extensive and deep root system and can cope fairly well relying on natural rainfall. In times of extended drought concentrate on watering the established features of your garden, the plants which would be expensive to replace with mature specimens. Let the annuals, perennials and lawn take the stress. They will be much cheaper to replace.

The most efficient method of watering

Drip irrigation is the most efficient way of watering as losses to evaporation are minimised with the drip pipe placed under the mulch. This is preferable to spray irrigation that has been popular in the past. This resulted in the mulch absorbing most of the water only to evaporate during hot days. In addition on windy days the water would often blow everywhere except on the plant. Spraying has it's place in a fernery, but in an exposed garden bed is useless.

With drip irrigation there is no wasteful runoff. It also has the advantages of keeping the foliage dry and of not causing splashing of soil fungi up onto the leaves. Both wet leaves and soil splashes tend to encourage fungal problems for some plants. A drip system installed below the mulch will ensure that the water goes directly to the plants.

Most drip systems deliver 2 litres an hour through emitters spaced approximately every 30 cm along the line. Always buy 'pressure compensating' drip line, which delivers equally to every outlet. For the best advice discuss your needs with a reputable specialist irrigation company. DripEze is one of the better brands manufactured by the well-known Australian company Toro. Drip pipe is generally available in 50 m or 200 m rolls.

The following can be a guide to the amount of water a drip irrigation system uses. Based on using the standard 13 mm drip line, a 50 m roll of DripEze has 166 emitters each delivering 2 litres/hour or 332 litres/hour. An average garden would use a minimum of 5 x 50m rolls: = 1660 litres/hour. If drippers are left on for two hours each week (in high summer) this becomes 3320 litres/hour. Most of the year one hour once a week is sufficient to maintain the water levels to plants. Once the temperatures exceed 25–30°C this would possibly need, depending on the plants, to be increased to two hours once a week. A simple way of monitoring the water output is to place a two litre ice cream container under the drip line. As the drip line delivers 2 litres an hour the container should be full in that time.

If you are hand-watering, use an attachment that delivers a gentle flow of water. Plants don't like being hit by a jet of water any more

than you do. A watering wand can deliver a good quantity of water, where you want it and without hurting the plant or damaging the soil surface. Don't water in the heat of the day. Morning watering is best for some plants as damp foliage overnight may lead to fungal or mildew problems. For most plants it is best to water in the evening so that plant can absorb the moisture before facing the rigours of a summer day. Remember to water plants growing under eaves and smaller plants under trees, especially in winter when they tend to be forgotten. In winter it is probably best to water in the middle of the day. Plants growing near brick walls have to compete with the walls as bricks act as a wick to draw moisture out of the ground and also reflect heat. Don't waste water on paths, roads etc. Eliminate weeds, as they will compete with those plants you want to get the water·

Grey water

Grey water may be used on the garden but be wary of the salts and detergents it contains. These can damage your plants if they become too concentrated in the soil. If you do utilise this water source make sure you do not apply it to any one plant too often, as it will build up toxicity. Be careful it doesn't flow into drains as it will pollute the rivers; and keep it well away from your ponds. Be careful also not to leave grey water sitting in the crown of a plant as this can cause rot.

Choose washing detergents thoughtfully. There are many low-sodium products on the market, and some people have developed simple ways of cleaning their clothes which exclude the use of wash powders completely, so do your investigations and choose a product which suits you. If the garden is desperate for water, you may need to use grey water, but try to save your purest water for edible plants. Grey water should be dispersed to various parts of the garden, trying not to apply grey water to the same area too regularly. Alternatively, mix rinse-water with detergent-water to dilute the effect. If you use grey water on a specific area, make sure than next time you water that area, you use clean water.

Water tanks

Rainwater tanks are growing in popularity as a way of saving water that would otherwise flow into the stormwater system. At current prices for water it is not yet clear that they offer a financial advantage. You will maximise the savings that might be available if you make sure that you actually use the water collected, rather than saving it for a period of drought.

Perhaps the main attraction of your own tank will be that it allows you to water at times or in ways that are not permitted under a rationing system.

Arrange the overflow outlet of the tank so that the overflow water can flow either to the street or be applied to your garden. Only divert overflow water to the garden when you can be sure that it will all soak into your soil and not run into your neighbour's property.

Check with the Water Conservation division of ACTEW Corporation for current restrictions, which can change depending on flows into the storage dams. ACTEW also conduct from time to time free WaterWise Garden Workshops covering all aspects of ground preparation, planting, fertilizing and drip irrigation. See their web site at www.actew.gov.au or call the water conservation office during normal business hours on 6248 3131.

PART C: The ornamental garden

Ornamentals, grown for their flowers, shape, autumn or winter colour, bark and perfume are the backbone of nearly every garden.

In Part C we begin with annuals and perennials, and then we look at the many different types of plants, from Australia and other places, which grow well in our climate: tiny ground covers, bulbs, roses, lots of other shrubs to trees. We even tell you how to care for cut flowers.

CHAPTER 7:
Annuals and perennials

Merylyn Condon

Annuals, ie plants that are grown from seed then mature, flower, set seed and die within one year, have always been valued for quick growth, colour and the ability to provide variety in the garden. Nowadays, limited water supply is a significant concern, and annuals are less favoured for mass plantings.

Biennials (such as foxgloves and wallflowers) take two years to complete their growth cycle, and like annuals, can still have a role to play in the garden, though it is not as great as when water was more plentiful.

Perennials are longer-lived plants and can be divided into two categories, soft-wooded (or evergreen perennials) and herbaceous perennials. Soft-wooded perennials, such as dianthus, do not develop woody tissue like trees and shrubs, and remain green throughout the year. Herbaceous perennials, such as penstemon, have persistent roots, and the foliage of the plant will die down or deteriorate in winter, and regrow in spring. Some perennials such as the variegated forms of euphorbia can be grown purely for their foliage colour.

Annuals

Annuals provide colour quickly, and for new homeowners in the early stages of developing their garden, can be very useful plants. Carpeting annuals can be used as edging and many annuals are used to great effect in baskets, window boxes and large tubs, or to spill over walls and rockeries. With a wide range of colours and growth habits,

they can be used to enhance shrubberies, to vitalise gardens when other plants are not at their peak. Low growing annuals amid tall perennials or around flowering shrubs can provide fill, foliage and colour contrasts, or alternatively, tall flower spikes such as salvia and foxgloves among lower-growing annuals can be very effective.

It is still possible to grow annuals, but regrettably many require more water than is reasonable in the Canberra garden today. They have a new and different role in providing potted colour or highlights when planted in groups, pots, troughs or swathes. You may note that, for this reason, the list of annuals and perennials is more selective than has appeared in some earlier editions of *The Canberra Gardener*.

Perennials

Perennials will live for many years, particularly if divided and cut back after flowering to rejuvenate each clump. They are useful plants and there will be something for every site in your garden: for shady or sunny areas, for hot dry spots, or for boggy areas. They are an interesting and valuable plant form and can be reproduced easily and economically.

Perennials were once planted in borders but, nowadays, architectural styles vary immensely as do the supporting garden designs. Many house blocks are much smaller now, and perennials have gained a valued place in the garden for foliage shape and colour and for their variety of flower colours and forms. Some garden owners prefer their gardens to be informal and relaxed; others aim for definition and formality to enhance the character. There are perennials to fill all these roles. Hedges wax and wane with fashion, and often the border and definition achieved by a hedge can easily be created by substituting perennials.

For anyone wishing to reflect a heritage style home with sympathetic plantings, the range of perennials is good and many old varieties continue to be available simply because they are proven performers. That said, there are many new cultivars so that there is something for everyone's taste. Some plants, such as hellebores and epimediums, will naturalise to form ground cover beneath established trees, others are suited to pot culture (for example, heuchera and *Geranium traversii*) and many will perform best in rockeries or raised beds, for example verbena.

Salvia guaranitica 'Black and Blue'.

Feeding Your Flowers

Like any other plant, annuals and perennials do best if the soil is well prepared before planting. Annuals in particular are fast growers and need frequent applications of fertiliser and organic matter.

Some plants prefer a neutral pH (carnation, stock, sweet pea, Sweet William) so where the soil tends to be acidic, liming is helpful. To check your soil, either buy a pH testing kit or ask your local garden centre to test some samples of your soil for pH (during the week, when they are less busy). A few samples are helpful as soil can vary in different parts of the garden. Most annuals do well with generous proportions of composted animal manures, but you can overdo it, encouraging leaf growth at the expense of flowers. Some

plants such as nasturtium, clarkia, lupins and Livingstone daisy prefer less rather than more manure in their soils, so the best practice is to grow these in soil that has been manured for a previous planting.

Organic fertilisers include animal manures, animal and vegetable by-products. Animal manures supply useful amounts of nutrients to the soil when applied in large quantities and they also benefit soil structure. There are some concerns however, as fresh animal manure such as sheep manure (and sometimes cow manure) may be a source of unwanted pasture weeds. Horse manure can introduce oats. Fresh poultry manure can burn foliage and is harmful to acid-loving plants as it is highly alkaline. Commercially available animal manures are generally safe to use, but more expensive. Animal manures supply more nitrogen than phosphorus or potassium, so while growth may appear good, too much green growth will affect the plant's ability to produce flowers. However, the benefits of using animal manure far outweigh any problems and most of those problems listed above can be overcome by composting the manure before use. Some useful by-products for gardening are blood and bone, dried blood and bone dust, bone meal and fish emulsion. Most plants respond well to an annual addition of composted animal manure but, from the time they form buds, applications of a liquid fertiliser such as Phostrogen® will help to promote flowering.

Plant wastes are also an important source of organic matter. Garden compost is a convenient and inexpensive way of converting waste plant material and, if properly prepared, the heat generated during decomposition of its components will kill most weed seeds within. To avoid nitrogen tie-up problems, compost should not be used on your garden until it has aged to a stage where its individual components are no longer recognisable.

Planting

Canberra's climate is perfect for growing many alpine and rock plants. For most plants, the best site will face east with some shade from the west, though there are exceptions and some plants have very specific needs. Generally, protection provided by deciduous shrubs and trees or a fence or wall is sufficient. Not all gardens have the ideal site, but so long as you do your best to meet the plants' requirements through providing, in most cases, good drainage by raising the bed slightly, it is possible to make an attractive and effective garden for most of the plants recommended.

A clump of herbaceous peonies can really make a spring border.

Many new homeowners will have minimal space for a garden. It is still possible to have a few baskets, pots or tubs, or you can even make durable timber tubs which can be fixed to a wall or fence with brackets. Whatever you choose to grow, just remember that using containers means that you control the nutrient and moisture supply and you need to be aware of the effects of heat and cold on the plants you choose. Make a point of watering and renewing fertiliser (or use controlled release granules), according to the specific needs of your plants. So long as you have chosen plants that are suitable for your location, it should be easy to be satisfied with your gardening efforts. If you are unsure of what to grow, ask your garden centre horticulturist for advice.

You can develop year-round colour in your garden simply by visiting local garden centres throughout the year and buying plants when they are in flower. If you are not familiar with the plant, check with the horticulturist on duty as to whether a plant will be suitable for your garden. After building up a basic collection, you may want to add some of the more rare and unusual plants, and for these you may have to go to specialist nurseries or buy plants by mail order. Careful searching through local garden centres will often be just as rewarding.

In a new garden choose plants which won't mind being exposed to the elements until such time as the garden becomes more protected with the growth of shrubs and trees. Then you will be able to increase the range of more sensitive plants, if you want to do that.

Ensure that there are no perennial weeds such as couch in your new beds. With newly bought topsoil wait a while in case weeds germinate. This is vital where you are growing plants which will spread across the soil and become clumps. Better to completely remove such weeds before you put in your plants, for this will save you many headaches during the growing season. Spray the mulch with glyphosate (Zero®, Roundup®) and leave for at least two weeks. Spray drift can kill indiscriminately, so be careful to avoid valued shrubs by keeping the spray very low to the ground. It may be necessary to respray before planting to ensure that you have killed all the weeds. This will become evident after the first week or so, when the weeds start to yellow. In existing gardens, perennial weeds can be selectively removed by using a small paintbrush dipped in glyphosate solution. Alternatively, wearing a fine kitchen glove, and over that a cotton glove; you can dip your gloved hand into the solution and run your fingers along the weed you wish to kill. This is particularly useful in dealing with couch which has grown through clumps of perennial plants.

Helleborus niger (Photo Ian Collier).

Division of perennials

Herbaceous and soft-wooded perennials are commonly divided to produce new plants and to rejuvenate the plant itself. This is generally when the plant has flowered and passed its peak, at the same time cutting back and tidying up the foliage. If the plant has overgrown the space allocated, the clump can be divided as well. Division is best done in either late autumn or as growth slows.

To divide a plant, firstly give it a light prune. Using a garden fork, loosen the soil around the plant and lift it from the ground, being careful not to damage the root system too much. Wash the clump to remove any soil. In some cases, the clump may be pulled apart by hand, and with plants such as chrysanthemums, the clump can be cut into pieces, discarding the older centre, and retaining the younger, more vigorous outer growth. Do not allow the roots to dry out. Most agapanthus clumps (apart from some of the more delicate herbaceous types) will tolerate division with a mattock or spade.

Some plants (eg *Ranunculus ficaria*, dicentra sp).will have been dormant during winter and can be divided in early spring when fresh new shoots appear above ground, just before the new growth takes off.

Perennials from cuttings

Many perennials may be increased by taking soft-tip cuttings (eg. cranesbill geraniums, penstemon and verbena). Cuttings can be taken at any time during the plant's active growing season.

Remove healthy and actively growing tips from the plant 7 cm to 10 cm long. Use clean sharp secateurs to cut the shoot beneath a node, remove the leaves at the bottom end of the cutting and if the remaining top leaves are large, trim them in half to reduce transpiration. Make sure the cuttings do not wilt while being collected. (They can be kept fresh in a sealed plastic bag with a little water for at least a few hours). Dip the newly cut end of the stem (just below a node) into hormone powder.

Fill a pot with a mixture of clean sharp sand and organic matter (or compost) which has been well watered. Make a hole for each cutting, using a dibbler stick or a pencil. A number of cuttings can be placed into the same pot until it resembles a small forest. Water well and place a plastic bag over the pot and seal to simulate humid conditions. Most softwood cuttings treated this way will strike in two to five weeks.

Pests and diseases

Apart from snails and slugs, annuals and perennials are generally trouble-free and require minimal effort to remain so. There is no real need to use chemical sprays on annuals and perennials, unless your plants are so infested and you place such value on them that you consider you must use some form of control. For most plants, it's better to be wise in your choice of cultivars by seeking out disease-resistant plants and to avoid the need for chemicals.

An exception would seem to be hellebores, which in recent years have become the target of aphids during winter and early spring. These cluster beneath the leaves and even in the centre of flowers, reducing the vigour of an otherwise perfect plant for Canberra's climate. A thorough spray with Confidor® will solve the problem. Check regularly for signs of an outbreak as numbers quickly build up beneath the leaves.

Gardeners can be thankful for the introduction of Confidor®, a low toxicity insecticide for the control of aphids, thrips, lace bug and mealybug, which is also said to pose a minimal risk to most beneficial insects. There is also a new generation of organic pesticides which reflect those recipes used by organic gardeners for many a year.

Observing your plants and watching for signs of any pests or disease can ensure that your plants stay healthy. Removing problem insects or diseased plants and diseased parts of plants as you notice them will often be the best solution to a problem. Pesticides can be indiscriminate and you can do more harm than good by killing helpful insects along with the pests. If one particular cultivar continually gives problems, then you should try something new and avoid buying the troublesome one in future years.

❶ Sun + dry ❷ Sun + moisture ❸ Dry + shade ❹ Shade + moisture ❺ Waterside + bog

Recommended plants:

Plants in the following list have been labelled according to their sun and moisture requirements. The symbols used are:

Plants for sunny, dry positions.	❶
Sun and moisture lovers. (Plants in this section require sun, moisture and good drainage. They are not bog plants.)	❷
Plants for dry shade.	❸
Shade and moisture lovers.	❹
Waterside and bog plants.	❺

The list is not exhaustive, but all are tried and proven performers for Canberra. Some of the plants included are grown for their attractive foliage as much as for their flowers, and are a valued feature for prolonged interest. Some plants are more vigorous than others, a feature which many gardeners welcome and others may frown upon. A small number of plants have the potential to become garden 'thugs', but are nevertheless still valued by busy gardeners, so a warning is included.

❸ **Acanthus mollis** (Bear's breeches). Perennial. Forms dense clumps. Flowers are tall white spikes with soft mauve bracts to 1.5 m and leaves spiny. Propagate by seed, division or root cutting in spring or autumn. This plant is undergoing renewed popularity because of its striking foliage and interesting architectural habit, but it can be snail heaven. It has an extremely persistent root system so make sure you really want to grow this plant for, once planted, it will become a permanent addition to your garden.

❶ **Achillea clypeolata** Perennial, 40 cm. Some achilleas are inclined to be invasive, but this will remain a neat clump. Take care when choosing an achillea, for those with a rhizomatous root system can become a nuisance. A. clypeolata has distinctive silvery fern-like foliage and clear yellow flowers, which can be dried for floral arrangements. Remove spent flower stalks after flowering and remove any woody stems. Propagation is by division of the clump in early spring or autumn.

❶ **Agapanthus**. Perennial, 1 m. These are renowned for their ability to survive in tough conditions. That said, they do need a little regular water to thrive. There are many cultivars including miniatures, variegated types and herbaceous perennials which die back during winter. Remove spent flower stems and dead leaves at the end of winter. Propagate from seed in spring or autumn or division in late winter to early spring.

❷ **Ageratum houstonianum** (Floss flower). Annual. Dwarf varieties up to 25 cm and tall up to 60 cm high. Flowers are borne in large clusters of blue, mauve, pink and white. Useful for borders and mass planting. Will tolerate partial shade. Grow them from seed in spring for planting out in December. 30–100 cm.

❷ **Ajuga reptans**. A perennial which spreads by surface runners with indefinite spread. Dark blue flower spikes up to 15 cm high. A. 'Jungle Beauty' is a larger form than the species, spreading more rapidly, with flower spikes to approximately 20 cm and dark leaves tinged with purple. A. 'Catlin's Giant' is

❶ Sun + dry ❷ Sun + moisture ❸ Dry + shade ❹ Shade + moisture ❺ Waterside + bog

also a larger form worth growing with its dark foliage. *A. reptans* 'Black Mary' has similar dimensions to the species, but with dark leaves. Ajuga plants enjoy light shade or sun, but can become mildewed if grown in deep shade.

❹ ***Alchemilla mollis***. A perennial with wavy silver-edged leaves which hold dew or raindrops to give a sparkling effect. Forms a clump and grows to a height of 40 cm. Masses of small greenish-yellow flowers in late spring–summer. *A. alpina* is a smaller plant 20–30 cm, with a silver border on the leaves. Divide in autumn.

❶ ***Anchusa capensis*** (Cape Forget-me-not). A biennial growing to 30–40 cm. Small bright blue flowers throughout summer and autumn. It likes an open sunny position and rich sandy loam. Usually grown as an annual.

❷ ***Androsace lanuginosa*** (Rock Jasmine). A perennial with clusters of pink flowers in late spring. Forms a dense mat of silvery foliage no more than 7 cm high. *A. sarmentosa* is similar but has brighter pink flowers. Propagate from seed, cuttings in autumn or self-rooted layers.

❹ ***Anemone nemorosa***. Perennial. Delicate creamy white spring flowers and usually under 10 cm high with fine creeping rhizomes. Prefers a moist shaded position. 'Robinsoniana' is lavender-blue, 'Vestal' is late blooming and white flowered. Dormant in winter. Propagate by division in early winter.

❹ *Anemone x hybrida* (Japanese windflower). A perennial which can grow to 1.5 m clumps, producing flowers in early autumn. While there are around 30 cultivars, most nurseries do not list

Kangaroo Paws come in a range of other colours.

cultivar names, but sell plants in flower. The most commonly sold has pure white flowers and prominent stamens ('Honorine Jobert') while another pale pink unnamed hybrid is equally popular. These may take a little time to reach clump size, but once established they will be extremely hardy and can be a welcome addition to the autumn garden. Windflowers have tough rhizomatous roots which can inhibit the growth of other plants in the same area, so they are best grown in isolation. Cut back after flowering and propagate by division.

❶ **Anigozanthos** (Kangaroo Paw). A perennial Australian plant which prefers well-drained sandy or gravely soil and a hot, sunny position. Snails are attracted to the leaves, so take precautions! Though it is drought and fairly frost resistant, extra water during dry conditions will prolong the flowering period. *A. flavidus* is the hardiest of the kangaroo paws with leaves 1–1.5 m long and growing into a clump 1 m across. It has flowers in green, yellow or soft red in spring and summer. The 'Bush Gem' series, bred for

❶ Sun + dry ❷ Sun + moisture ❸ Dry + shade ❹ Shade + moisture ❺ Waterside + bog

A clump of aquilegias are a delight.

resistance to Inkspot disease (a fungus which blackens the foliage), is offered in a colour range through yellow, gold, orange, red, burgundy to green. You can divide large clumps in autumn.

❶ **Antirrhinum majus** (Snapdragon). A short-lived perennial usually grown as an annual. Needs a moderately rich well drained soil but can become tall and leggy if over-manured. Nip out tops of young plants to encourage branching. Tall (65 cm), dwarf (25 cm) and semi-dwarf (45 cm) varieties are available in white, yellow, red and mixed colours. A good cut flower. Rust used to be a serious disease of snapdragons but most new varieties are rust-resistant. Always choose recommended rust-resistant varieties.

❷ **Aquilegia** (Columbine, Granny's bonnet). Perennial. Most aquilegias are between 30 and 45 cm high, with the exception of A. flabellata which is smaller at approximately 20 cm. All flower in late spring–early summer and can be cut back after flowering. Divide in autumn or obtain seeds of named varieties from seed companies.

A. 'Nora Barlow' has double flowers with green and pink petals 45 cm; 'Double White' has small double white flowers on a plant to 45 cm tall; 'Tower Blue' small double pale blue (30 cm); A. alpine single large (45 cm) deep blue; 'Yellow Queen', large (45 cm) single yellow spurred flowers with grey foliage; A. flabellata 'Alba', blue/grey foliage and single white flowers (20 cm).

❶ **Arabis albida**. Perennial. A tough evergreen plant to 30 cm, with grey foliage and a delightful spring display of white flowers. 'Flore Plena' is a double-flowered form. Propagate from seed, cuttings in summer, or division in autumn.

❶ **Arctotis fastuosa** (African daisy). Perennial. 60 cm high with silvery foliage. An interesting range of colours is available from creamy yellow, bright gold through orange to deep pink and claret. Propagate from cuttings or rooted pieces at any time.

❷ **Argyranthemum frutescans** (Marguerite daisy). Perennial. A strong grower that needs to be tip pruned from an early age to encourage bushiness. It eventually becomes a woody plant and should be replaced by easily-struck spring cuttings every few years. Flower colours range from white and yellow to varying shades of pink. The 'Federation daisy'® strain tends to be less tolerant of Canberra's winters and may be short-lived.

❷ **Armeria maritima** (Thrift). Perennial. Grows as a mound 10 cm high with small white or pink 'drumstick' flowers produced in spring and summer. Propagate from seed, division or cuttings in spring or autumn.

❶ Sun + dry   ❷ Sun + moisture   ❸ Dry + shade   ❹ Shade + moisture   ❺ Waterside + bog

❶ **Artemesia** (Wormwood) is a large genus of evergreen and deciduous perennials which has many species from arid and semi-arid environments. They are grown for their silver grey aromatic foliage which can repel insects. Most of the artemesias are particularly frost-hardy and prefer an open sunny situation with light well-drained soil. The flowers are unremarkable. Propagate from cuttings in winter or by division in spring.

A. ludoviciana. Perennial. 'Valerie Finnis' 45 cm has striking silver foliage. *A. schmidtiana* 'Nana' is a rhizomatous plant which grows to 8 cm and forms a delicate mound of finely cut, fragrant silver leaves. Divide in spring or autumn. 'Powys Castle' 60 cm and 'Lambrook' 60 cm, *A. canescens* 15 cm and *A. pedemontana* 10 cm are also recommended. *A. arborescens* is a large spreading plant often available as a potted herb, but remember that it grows to shrub-like dimensions of 1.5 m high x 1.5 m across. If you have the space, it is very hardy.

❷ *Aster novae-angliae.* Annual. Summer annual to about 60 cm. Shallow rooted, it requires regular watering during growing and flowering seasons, rich soil, some top dressing with compost or animal manure and a sunny sheltered position. Flowers can be pink, blue, mauve, maroon or white. Suggested varieties are 'Perfection', 'King', and 'Giant Crego'. The fungal soil-borne disease, fusarium wilt is the most serious disease of asters. Resistant varieties are now available and good drainage and well structured soil will help prevent the problem. Do not plant asters where they were grown the previous year. Plant seeds in spring.

Aster novi-belgii (Perennial aster or Michaelmas daisy). Perennial. Modern perennial asters are mainly hybrids. There are many named varieties. Clustered flower heads of tiny flowers appear in autumn. White, mauve, pink and violet. Some varieties grow to about 90 cm with large flowers, and dwarf types to about 15 cm. Regular division in early spring will help maintain vigour.

❺ *Astilbe x arendsii* hybrids. Perennial. Astilbes need light shade and cool roots, in rich leafy soil that never dries out. Flowering is in early to late summer, and there are a number of hybrids available in a range of colours from white through to scarlet. Propagate by division in winter.

❶ *Aubrieta x cultorum* (Rock cress). Perennial, sprawling plant 15 cm high and 30 cm wide. Shades of white, pink through to deep violet. Some doubles and some variegated. Though the flowers are small the plant will cover itself. The plant is short-lived so take cuttings in summer or divide the rhizomatous root.

❶ *Aurinia saxatilis* syn. *Alyssum saxatile* (Yellow alyssum). Perennial. To 30 cm. Ideal for rockeries, crevices and in dry stone walls. Tiny yellow flowers through spring and summer. After flowering, clip all over with shears. Will self-seed. Division at any time other than when in flower.

❹ *Begonia semperflorens* (Bedding begonia). Perennial. An excellent perennial with glossy foliage for bedding or bordering purposes, but often grown as annuals. 15–30 cm tall, depending on variety. Wide range of foliage colours

❶ Sun + dry **❷** Sun + moisture **❸** Dry + shade **❹** Shade + moisture **❺** Waterside + bog

and flowers ranging from white through pink shades to red. Very frost tender so seedlings should not be planted out before October or November. Frost bitten foliage is best left on the plant through winter months, and new shoots will emerge in early spring when the clump can be tidied up and divided. Can be grown in full sunshine but prefers partial shade. Appreciates a side dressing of general fertiliser in November.

❶ ***Bellis perennis*** (English daisy). Really a perennial, but best treated as an annual. Double flowers of white, pink rose and red. Height about 15 cm, suitable as border plant. Inclined to self seed freely. Prefers sunny position. Sow seed late summer, plant out seedlings in autumn.

❺ **Bergenia** Perennial. Bergenias are an attractive and effective ground cover. B. cordifolia with large rounded fleshy leaves and rose pink tubular flowers on stalks of 30 cm, flowers in late winter–early spring. *B. x schmidtii has* rose pink flattened flowers to 30 cm long and is probably the most vigorous and widely planted bergenia. 'Silberlicht' has pure white to very pale pink flowers with flower stalks up to 45 cm long. Bergenias can develop attractive red tinged foliage in winter. Propagate all bergenias by division in spring after flowering.

❶ ***Brachyscome*** syn. *Brachycome multifida* (Native or Cut Leaf daisy). Perennial. 15–45 cm and clumps to 1 m wide with mauve flowers. Often available in punnets. Blooms in late spring through summer. Hybrids 'Break o' Day', 'Sunburst', 'Outback Sunburst' and

A benchtop display of dahlias in March.

'Amethyst' — white and pink hybrids are often available in punnets but generally are less hardy than the species. They do not cope with frosts. Encourage branching by pinching out shoots. In late winter, cut back to new growth. *B. multifida* can be propagated by using ripe seed, stem cuttings or rooted segments as plants layer easily. Named cultivars should be propagated by stem cuttings or, if the plant layers easily, rooted segments may be used. Division can be done for all in spring or autumn.

❹ ***Brunnera macrophylla***. Perennial. Sprays of intense blue flowers from late winter until late spring. The heart shaped leaves expand through spring to become quite large by summer and a good ground cover. Height 45 cm. Try also *B. macrophylla* 'Betty Bowring' with white flowers. Height 45 cm. Propagate by division in spring or autumn.

❶ ***Calendula officinalis*** (English marigold). Annual. A useful cut flower for winter or spring on stems up to 30 cm in orange and yellow. Require a good soil for best results. May be sown direct or in seed boxes for transplanting to growing position. Liable to self sow if left to form seed heads but self sown plants will be inferior. Sow seeds any time except winter.

❸ **Calibrachoa** An annual or short lived perennial like a miniature petunia, to which it is related. Forms a compact trailing clump. Does very well in hanging baskets in part shade. Water when soil is almost dry.

❷ *Caltha palustris* (Marsh marigold). Perennial. A good plant for full sun and moist heavy soil, it has golden yellow flowers. Propagate by division in spring or immediately after flowering. 45 cm.

❹ *Campanula persicifolia* (Peach-leaved bellflower). Perennial. Height up to 1 m. This comes in shades of deep purple, pale blue and white with a number of double flowering cultivars and two-toned flowers. Does best in moist, well-drained moderately rich soil. While this plant will grow in sunny positions, the flower colour is brightest in shady spots. Some cultivars worthy of growing are 'Chettle Charm' (white edged with blue), 'Pride of Exmouth', double lilac-blue, 'Moerheimii', double white.
Also worth trying are *C. glomerata*, 25 cm–40 cm high, clustered globular bells in violet-blue, also deeper violet, double flowered and white versions; *C. lactiflora*, 1.5 m high, lilac blue, also pink or white; *C. trachelium* (blue), *C. takesimana*, 30 cm – 45 cm, white to pink bells with dark spots on the inside, *C. latifolia* 1 m high (lilac to white), *C. portenschlagiana* (syn. *C. muralis*) 15 cm high and with indefinite spread, profuse violet-blue flowers in late spring and early summer.

Propagate all by division in spring or autumn or from basal cuttings in spring.

❷ *Canna x generalis*. Perennial. Though a tropical plant, cannas may be grown in Canberra and surrounding areas provided the rhizomatous roots are mulched well in winter or lifted in autumn as you would dahlias. They thrive in sun if their roots are kept moist and they do like a heavy feed. Trim back burnt foliage in early spring and divide at the same time. Some cannas are grown specifically for their leaves, with foliage ranging from plain green, through bronze, dark red or variegated. Try 'Tropicanna', a striking foliage plant striped pink and bronze, or 'Bengal Tiger' with gold and green striped foliage. Cannas can be propagated by division almost any time of the year except mid winter. 45 cm to 1.8 m.

❷ **Carex** spp. A perennial grass which grows well in cooler regions, including Canberra. 'Everbright' forms a tussock of long, narrow cream leaves with green margins. *C. albula* 'Frosted Curls' is striking with fine, silvery foliage which curls. It forms a soft tussock of about 30 cm round. Propagated by division of clumps.

❶ *Centaurea cyanus* (Cornflower). Annual. Cornflowers come in shades of pale and deep pink, cerise, crimson, white, purple and blue, 30 cm to 1 m. They like well-drained soil in a sunny position. Sow seed in spring and autumn. *C.* 'Silver Fountain' is an attractive silver leaved form with purple thistle-like flowers and a low scrambling habit, spreading to 1.5 m. The wheat-coloured spent flower heads are a striking extra feature, if only temporary.

❶ Sun + dry ❷ Sun + moisture ❸ Dry + shade ❹ Shade + moisture ❺ Waterside + bog

Everlasting Daisy. There is a photo of a quite different cultivar in Chapter 5.

❶ **Cerastium tomentosum** (Snow in summer). Perennial, 15 cm. A useful ground hugger with silvery foliage and masses of tiny white flowers in spring. Propagated by division and will occasionally self-seed.

❷ **Chrysanthemum**. Perennial. The florist's chrysanthemum is now known as *Dendranthemum morifolium* though it is still often sold under the name chrysanthemum. Heights range from 30 cm to 1.5 m (the taller plants will require staking) and a wide range of colours through white, yellow, red and rusts. Excellent cut flower. After flowering, chrysanthemum clumps send out suckers which develop into short leafy shoots around the plant. These overwinter (protect from snails) and start into active growth in spring. Take suckers, with roots, from the clump, selecting those farthest away from the old plant and plant them out in their permanent position, treating them as though they were annuals. Pinch out the centre of the plant when well established to encourage the development of side shoots. Cuttings may be taken from young shoots also after the spent flower stalks have been trimmed back and the plant is re-shooting.

❷ *C. paludosum*. Annual. Low growing compact bedding or edging chrysanthemum with small yellow-centred white daisy flowers. A hardy plant, it blooms well in either sun or semi-shade and makes a good container plant. Propagate from seed in spring.

❶ **Chrysocephalum apiculatum** syn *Helichrysum apiculatum* (common Everlasting daisy). An Australian perennial, available in many forms

❶ Sun + dry   **❷** Sun + moisture   **❸** Dry + shade   **❹** Shade + moisture   **❺** Waterside + bog

ranging from a prostrate layering variety to a rounded form to 30 cm high by 1 m across. Small golden flower heads are produced from spring to autumn. A hardy species that will grow in most soils and conditions, provided drainage is good. It likes sun and is frost resistant. Prune hard in late winter to encourage new growth.

❷ *Cleome hassleriana* (Spider Flower). Annual. Summer flowering pink and white flowers with long protruding stamens. 1.2 m high and 45 cm wide. Propagate from seed in spring or in early summer.

❶ *Conostylis candicans*. A dwarf grass-like Australian plant with narrow silver sword-shaped leaves to 0.3 m. A striking feature plant which will grow in sun or part shade, and prefers light to medium well-drained soils. Ideal as a rockery or tub plant. Woolly yellow flowers in spring/early summer. Frost hardy.

❹ *Convallaria majalis* (Lily of the valley). Perennial. Sweetly perfumed spring flowering and 20–30 cm high. Propagate from seed or division of rhizomes. The rhizomes should be planted in autumn and if given fertile, humus rich moist soil, they will thrive. The tendency for the root system to mat can deprive other plants of moisture, so take care where you plant. Divide in autumn.

❶ *Convolvulus mauritanicus* (Bindweed). Perennial. A spreading plant with trailing stems approximately 60 cm long with pale blue trumpet flowers. Some newer forms have deeper flower colour and there is a white form. Suited to a large rockery or spilling over a wall. Trim back in winter. It flowers from late spring through to the first frosts and can be

propagated by cutting. Particularly drought-tolerant. Flowers close at night.

❷ *Coreopsis grandiflora* is an excellent plant for drought tolerance, preferring full sun and a fertile well-drained soil. It will tolerate poorer stony soils, and its golden yellow daisies are a pretty sight, growing wild alongside railway lines in outer Sydney. New cultivars are offered with double forms and can be a welcome addition to the garden. *C. verticillata* is a perennial with thin rhizomatous roots and smaller bright yellow daisy flowers from late spring to autumn. *C. verticillata* 'Moonbeam' is a lemon yellow form. Old clumps can be divided in winter or early spring.

❹ *Corydalis flexuosa*. A perennial which forms a small clump around 30 cm tall, with long-spurred tubular clear blue flowers in late spring and early summer. Try also *C. lutea* which has yellow flowers, *C. cashmeriana* with brilliant blue flowers, and *C. ochroleuca* which has cream flowers. Self-seeding may occur in good conditions. Propagate from seed or by division in early spring.

❷ *Cosmos bipinnatus*. Annual. Flowers in summer and autumn, pink red, purple and white. Needs good drainage. 1.5–1.8 m. Wind protection needed because of its height. Sow seed in spring.

❷ **Dahlia** (Bedding varieties). This seedling-grown form of dahlia is used as an annual bedding plant, obtainable in punnets or as 'bloomers' in spring (after the frosts). It requires a sunny sheltered position in well-fertilised, well-drained soil. 30 cm high in a wide range of colours, some with bronze or dark red foliage. Though

❶ Sun + dry   ❷ Sun + moisture   ❸ Dry + shade   ❹ Shade + moisture   ❺ Waterside + bog

Cosmos, an annual where the flowers and foliage are equally attractive.

these seedlings form tubers they are usually treated as annuals. There is however no reason why they cannot be left in the same position for a year or two, after which they will require lifting and dividing to ensure flowering continues the following season. For information about the larger types see the bulbs chapter.

❷ **Delphinium elatum** hybrids. Perennial. A wide range, some with tall spikes to 1.5 m or dwarf types 60 cm to 90 cm, and a wide range of colours. Needs to be watered very well in spring and summer and protected from slugs and snails. Not really suited to Canberra.

D. ajacis (Larkspur). Annual to 90 cm. Sow seeds in permanent position in spring and thin out to desired spacing. Requires a rich well drained soil in a sunny position with shelter from strong winds. Wide range of colours. Good cut flower.

❶ **Derwentia perfoliata** (formerly known as *Parahebe perfoliata*). An Australian perennial growing to 60 cm high and 1 m wide with silver-grey leaves which appear to encircle the stems. White or

pale blue flower spikes appear at the end of each stem in summer. Cut back the old spikes in late winter. Frost hardy and not particularly fussy about location. Propagate by division or cuttings.

❶ **Dianella tasmanica**, the Flax Lily, is an Australian plant with tough strap leaves and deep blue flowers, followed by striking purple berries. Makes a good rockery plant, providing it has some moisture. It is not fussy about soils so long as drainage is fairly good, and it will grow to between 0.5 and 1 m. Frost tolerant and propagated by division.

D. caerulea 'Cassa Blue' is a compact perennial (0.5 m x 0.5 m) with rich blue foliage which can be used for mass planting, as an accent and in low water requirement gardens. It has all the attributes of *D. tasmanica* but is more drought-tolerant. Many cultivars have become available in recent years, some with bi-coloured leaves, and all are useful plants.

❷ **Dianthus**. A large and varied genus of annuals and perennials, including carnations grown for the cut-flower trade, Alpine, Maiden and Modern Pinks, Sweet William and many other cultivated annuals and perennials. Some are useful border plants while some, such as Sweet William and large flowered carnations, can be used further back in the garden. Carnations grow up to 60 cm high with a spread of approximately 30 cm. Stems will need support. Fully double flowers are usually fringed. Large flowered varieties are best if disbudded, ie the leading flower in each cluster is retained and the others pinched off to improve flower quality.

❶ Sun + dry ❷ Sun + moisture ❸ Dry + shade ❹ Shade + moisture ❺ Waterside + bog

D. barbatus (Sweet William) is a hardy biennial which self sows readily, grows to around 45 cm high and 15 cm wide. It has fragrant flowers in late spring and summer which range from white to crimson-purple and often are two-tones. It can be divided.

D. deltoides (Maiden Pink), a dwarf mat-forming evergreen perennial, is ideal for rock gardens. Small flowers with fringed petals in pink, cerise or white, usually with a red centre in spring–early summer to 15 cm high. Trim back after flowering. Easily grown from seed or cutting.

Dianthus (Alpine Pink) is a compact plant forming a mound. Flowers in many colours around 25 to 30 cm above foliage. 'Pike's Pink' is a good cultivar.

Dianthus (Modern Pinks). Try 'Doris', pale pink; 'Valda Wyatt' rose pink; 'Joy' mid pink or *D. allwoodii* which has fringed single pink flowers with a red centre. 35–45 cm.

All dianthus require a well drained sunny position, medium sandy loam; compost or manure is beneficial together with complete fertiliser. Young plants should be pinched back, particularly carnations. After flowering they should be pruned back to the main foliage mass to encourage the next flush of flowers. These are suitable for the cottage garden. Take cuttings in late summer and early autumn. Dianthus may be layered if just a few plants are required. Simply bend down a stem to the soil and secure it against movement with a wire peg.

❷ *Diascia barberae* (Dutchman's breeches). Perennial. Pretty salmon pink flowers bloom from early spring until the first frosts. They make a good underplanting for roses. There are many named forms, mostly in shades of pink and apricot. 'Ruby Field' has salmon pink flowers from summer to autumn, grows from 15 to 30 cm tall and has a spread of 20 cm. Pinch out tips to increase bushiness and cut back old stems after flowering. Divide or take root cuttings in autumn.

❹ *Dicentra formosa* (Bleeding heart). Perennial. Grows to 45 cm high with pink and red flowers in spring and summer. *D. formosa* 'Alba' is a white flowered form. Try also *D. spectabilis*, pink and white flowers on large arching stems 60 – 90 cm tall; *D. spectabilis* 'Alba' has similar dimensions to *D. spectabilis* but with white flowers. Dicentra does well in humus-rich, moist, well-drained soil with some shade but can tolerate dryer conditions. Propagate from seed in autumn or division in late winter.

❹ *Digitalis purpurea* (Foxglove). A short-lived frost-hardy biennial which grows to 1.5 m. *D. purpurea* 'Albiflora', with pure white flowers will come true from seed if isolated from other forms.

❹ *Digitalis x mertonensis* (Strawberry foxglove). Perennial. Summer flowering, to 1 m. Divide after flowering. All foxgloves prefer humus-rich well-drained soil.

❶ *Echinops ritro*. Perennial, 40 cm. A genus which is related to thistles but with striking blue, blue-grey or white globular flower heads, it's more attractive than most thistles. This is an interesting addition to the perennial garden. 'Ritro' is clear dark blue. Propagate by division or seed.

❶ Sun + dry ❷ Sun + moisture ❸ Dry + shade ❹ Shade + moisture ❺ Waterside + bog

The spring flowers of the perennial epimedium, growing in light dry shade. The leaves are attractive too, colouring well in autumn.

❸ **Epimedium grandiflorum**. Perennial. 'Rose Queen' has spidery pink or purple flowers with white spurs held above the foliage on 30 cm stems. Best displayed as a clump rather than as a ground cover. *E. x youngianum* 'Niveum', white flowered, forms an attractive clump 45 cm high. Leaves are tinted bronze in spring. *E. x versicolour* 'Sulphureum' is a carpeting perennial 30 cm high, with leaves tinted red when young. Clusters of sulphur yellow flowers with red spurs in spring. Epimediums have elegant foliage with heart-shaped leaves and sprays of delicate, sometimes spurred flowers. Propagate from ripe seed or by division in autumn.

❶ **Erigeron** (Fleabane, Seaside daisy). Perennial. 60 cm. A family of daisy flowers, preferring full sun and good drainage but will grow in any soil. This plant seeds and re-grows readily. While it may assume weed proportions, many gardeners welcome its presence as a cottage garden plant. Try *E. andersonii*, mauve daisy type flowers with yellow centre.

❷ **Erodium chrysanthum**. Perennial. A member of the geranium family, with silvery green foliage and sulphur yellow flowers through summer. It requires well-drained soil which is not too fertile. Propagated from cuttings in summer or from ripe seed.

❶ **Eryngium** (Sea Holly). Perennial. Good drainage is necessary. *E. giganteum* 'Miss Willmott's Ghost' 1.2 m, *E. tripartitum* 60 cm and *E. alpinum* 60 cm are all striking plants. To appreciate them fully, they should be sited with the afternoon sun behind them. Fresh seed or root cuttings in winter or division in spring.

❷ **Erysimum syn. Cheiranthus** (Wallflower). Both biennials and perennials. A number are winter flowering, but take care in choosing, for whilst wallflowers are renowned for their perfume, some of the new varieties have none. *E.* 'Winter Cheer' is a welcome sight in a winter garden in Canberra with purple/pink flowers. *E.* 'Bowles' Mauve', syn. *E.* 'E.A. Bowles' is a dense mounded bush to 1 m with mauve flowers over a lengthy period. *E.* 'Apricot Twist' is a smaller plant, with pretty apricot/orange flowers. All appreciate a good trim after flowering to retain good shape and dense growth. Propagate by cutting in summer.

❶ **Eschscholzia californica** (Californian Poppy). Perennial with cup-shaped flowers from grey-green feathery foliage. Colour range now extends to bronze, yellow, cream, scarlet, mauve and dark red. Spring flowering but flowers close on cloudy days. 30 cm high. Sow where they are to grow in poor, well-drained soil in spring. This plant self-seeds readily and

1 Sun + dry **2** Sun + moisture **3** Dry + shade **4** Shade + moisture **5** Waterside + bog

has become naturalised in many parts of Australia. Though it is not a weed in the ACT, be aware of its potential as its fine seeds can be carried by insects or water. Seeds will easily germinate in the cracks in paving.

Euphorbia. A wide range of these hardy annuals and perennials do well in Canberra. Euphorbias hybridise easily and do not generally reproduce accurately from seed, but if you do grow seedlings, transplant them shortly after germination as larger seedlings do not transplant easily.

3 *Euphorbia amygdaloides var robbiae*. Perennial. This forms spreading rosettes of dark green leaves. It grows to 60 cm high and wide and has lime green floral bracts. Divide in early spring or autumn.

3 *Euphorbia characias subsp wulfenii*. Perennial. Blue-green leaves and chartreuse flower heads. *E.characias* will self-seed so faded flower heads should be removed to avoid a problem with seedlings.

2 *E. characias* 'Tasmanian Tiger'. A spectacular new plant selected for its uniformly coloured variegated foliage. Leaves are grey-green with clear white margins. Tall pale green stems support cream-white bracts with small green centres.

1 *E. myrsinites* is a sprawling low evergreen plant. It has heads of green flowers with yellow bracts at the tips of stems. It is attractive on the edge of a rockery or down a wall.

2 *E. dulcis* 'Chameleon' has claret foliage and bracts, grows to 40 cm. *E. griffithii* 'Fireglow' has orange red bracts in

Euphorbia myrsinites is a tough ground cover.

summer. Rhizomatous euphorbias such as *E. griffithii* and *E.* 'Chameleon' can be easily divided in early spring when new shoots appear.

2 *E. marginata* (Snow on the Mountain) is a striking annual with variegated leaves and small white flowers surrounded by petal-like bracts. Sow seed in spring. Grows to 60 cm.

1 *Felicia amelloides* (Blue daisy). Perennial, 60 cm high and 120 cm wide. *F. petiolata* is prostrate with spread of 1 m and pale pink daisies. Either will scramble through adjoining plants. Propagate from cuttings in late summer or autumn or from seed in spring.

2 *Foeniculum vulgare* 'Purpureum' (Bronze fennel). A tall, graceful perennial growing to 1.8 m with masses of feathery foliage and clusters of yellow flowers. A striking feature plant. Remove spent flowers to prevent self-seeding and propagate from seed in spring.

1 **Gaillardia hybrids**. Perennial. *G.* 'Norgate's Red' is an interesting rich tan-red. 'Goblin' is a compact plant almost never without flowers. It grows to 20 cm, and 'Norgate's Red' grows to around

❶ Sun + dry **❷** Sun + moisture **❸** Dry + shade **❹** Shade + moisture **❺** Waterside + bog

Euphorbia 'Tasmanian Tiger'.

40 cm and both are suitable for rockeries. 'Mandarin' has low foliage to 25 cm but with strong flower stems to 40 cm, making it better for picking. Gaillardias are extremely hardy and tolerate extreme heat, cold, dryness, strong winds and poor soils. Propagate from seed in spring or early summer, or division in spring.

❷ ***Gaura lindheimeri***. Perennial. Clump forming and long flowering for use in the mixed border. There are several smaller cultivars now available, e.g. 'Siskyou Pink' with rose pink flowers to around 80 cm or 'White Butterfly' with white flowers 80 cm. This plant tends to self seed and can become weedy. Divide in autumn.

❶ **Gazania**. Perennial. Hardy prostrate plants to 30 cm, bearing many brightly coloured daisy-like flowers over spring, summer and autumn. Valuable in a hot sunny position with their colours of cream, gold, pinks, orange and mahogany tones. Best divided every few years to maintain vigour. They can self-seed and may become weedy in some gardens.

❸ **Geranium** (the Cranesbill). The notes that follow are about the true geraniums, not the plants commonly sold as geraniums

which are in fact pelargoniums. Many cranesbills are ideal for dry positions in the garden and many feature attractive foliage.

❸ *Geranium macrorrhizum*. This perennial cranesbill has pink flowers and is ideal for dry conditions. It forms a dense clump. There is a white form 'Album', and 'Czakor' is a deep rose pink. Leaves redden in winter.

❸ *G. phaeum* (Mourning Widow). Perennial. This has maroon, almost black flowers. It is renowned for its ability to grow in deep dry shade. There are several variants worthy of growing; 'Lily Lovell' (rich mauve flowers) and 'Samobor' (typical flowers but large leaves with brown markings). Division or seed. Cultivars by division.

❷ *G. traversii* 'Sea Spray'. Perennial. This hybrid forms a 30 cm mound of grey foliage spreading to around 1 m when established. The flowers vary from pale pink to near white and are almost continual through the growing season. Appreciates a little moisture.

❷ *G. x* 'Phillipe Vapelle' has felty blue-grey foliage and blue-purple flowers with veins over a long period. Sunny position and a little moisture.

❶ *G. sanguineum* (the Bloody Cranesbill), *G. sanguineum album*, *G. malviflorum* (winter-flowering), *G. pratense var. striatum*, *G. pratense* and *G. pratense* 'Johnson's Blue' are all good. *G. sanguineum var. striatum* has large blush pink flowers veined with deeper pink over a long season. Propagate by dividing in autumn or seed in spring.

❶ Sun + dry ❷ Sun + moisture ❸ Dry + shade ❹ Shade + moisture ❺ Waterside + bog

Geranium 'Ann Folkard'.

❷ *Geranium x cantabrigiense*. Perennial. Soft, rosy pink flowers in summer. To 15 cm. Likes morning sun. 'Biokovo' has white flowers with pink veining in summer. Height 30 cm. Morning sun. Propagate by division or cuttings.

❶ ***Gypsophila elegans***. Annual. 30–60 cm. Thrives in a light soil of medium fertility dressed with lime. Sow in position and thin out. Flowers in white and pale shades. Excellent cut flower.

❶ *G. paniculata*. (Baby's breath) is a perennial, growing 50–75 cm. Flowers of white, pink and lavender pink in summer. Good for drying for winter decoration.

❷ ***Hakonechloa macra***, a perennial grass which grows in a graceful clump 30–45 cm and will colour in autumn to orange-bronze. There are variegated forms which will also colour in autumn. Propagate by division.

❷ ***Helianthemum nummularium*** (Sun Rose, Rock Rose). Perennial. This comes in a variety of colours, flowering in spring. Cut back after flowering to encourage compact new growth. Propagate from seed or cutting in autumn.

❷ **Helianthus** (Sunflower). Perennial. Very large flowers in autumn. Needs good garden loam and sunny position. Recommended variety *H. salicifolius*, 1.5 m, bright yellow flowers. Propagate by division. 30–45 cm.

❶ ***Helichrysum bracteatum*** syn *Bracteantha bracteata* (Golden everlasting daisy). Many forms are available, both as annuals or perennials. In most, the flowers are large with shiny papery bracts appearing over a long period in spring and summer. 'Diamond Head' is a compact dwarf perennial to 20 cm high and 60 cm across with papery yellow flowers from late spring through summer. Sow seed of annuals in spring or autumn. 'Dargan Hill Monarch' is a sturdy perennial to 50 cm high and 1 m across with large yellow paper daisies in spring and summer. All make spectacular displays in summer. Look for cultivars in flower. A good cut flower, this plant prefers a sunny position with good drainage and some moisture. Keep the soil damp, though not wet, with deep watering once a week, more often during summer. Allow the foliage to dry completely between watering and if possible, water before the flowers open.

Helichrysum bracteatum (Straw flower). Annual. 60–120 cm. Native to Australia. Wide range of colours.

Sun + dry   Sun + moisture   Dry + shade ❹ Shade + moisture ❺ Waterside + bog

Helleborus x ballardiae, another of the hellebores which do so well in Canberra, flowering in late winter and spring (*Photo Ian Collier*).

❹ **Helleborus**. Perennial. *Helleborus x hybridus* are available in an ever-increasing variety of colours and markings ranging from singles to doubles, solid colours from the darkest red through to spotted flowers and picotee forms. An excellent winter or spring flowering plant. *H. foetidus* is also a welcome sight in winter with interesting foliage and pale green well shaped flowers. Also try *H. corsicus* for green flowers. Some trimming back of the leaves on deciduous varieties is necessary as the buds appear. Divide in autumn or allow to seed where it is being grown. Watch for aphids, which congregate under leaves or inside the flowers. Confidor® or a Pest Oil/ Eco-oil® spray should control the problem. 40–45 cm.

❹ **Heuchera** (Coral Bells). Perennial. *H. sanguinea* is the best known of the heuchera family, and has bright coral to scarlet flowers. Heucheras form clumps of scalloped leaves, which are often tinted bronze, purple or variegated. They produce stems bearing masses of dainty white, crimson, pink or green bell-shaped flowers over a long flowering season. Recommended cultivars are:

H. cylindrica 'Greenfinch' which has leaves of pale green with marked veins and pale delicate flowers, and the plant will occasionally self-seed. 'Rachel' has leaves attractively scalloped and bronze with flowers soft rose-pink. 'White Spires' is a vigorous plant, with dark green scalloped leaves and strong-stemmed white flowers.

❶ Sun + dry   **❷** Sun + moisture   **❸** Dry + shade   **❹** Shade + moisture   **❺** Waterside + bog

H. micrantha var. diversifolia 'Palace Purple', grown for its striking lustrous dark red leaves and panicles of tiny white flowers on dark red stems in summer. It is clump forming with a height and spread of 45 cm. 'Amethyst Queen' has lustrous leaves with a distinctive network of silvery veins and pink flowers on dark red stems.

New cultivars with foliage colour of lime, caramel, coffee, peach can be quite striking as a contrast in the garden. All heucheras can be divided in autumn or spring, using the young outer portions of the crown. Can tolerate heat if roots are moist, but better in light shade. 60 cm high.

❹ *Heucherella tiarelloides*. Perennial. Heucherellas are a hybrid between Heuchera and Tiarella, both members of the Saxifraga family. Plants are clumping, easy to grow and thrive in leafy, rich, moist but well-drained soil. Flowers of 'Bridget Bloom' are soft pastel pink and freely produced on plants 30 cm tall. 'Snow White' has pure white flowers, freely produced and the plant will grow to 30 cm tall. Divide in autumn or spring.

❹ **Hosta**. Perennial. Hostas are easily grown in moist rich soil, and are also good in pots and hanging baskets. There are many forms available; some with miniature leaves, others with leaves 30 cm wide. Heights vary from 5 cm to 80 cm. The flowers are very attractive, either bell or funnel shaped on tall stems. Colours are mainly mauve with a few good purples or whites. The leaves last well in floral arrangements. Snails and slugs love hosta leaves though blue-grey leaved forms are the last on the snail menu. It pays to be vigilant and collecting snails by torchlight can reduce numbers significantly, at the same time using an iron-based repellent spray where possible. Copper strips can act as an efficient barrier. Diggers or Garden Express and garden centres are sources of this, and leadlighting suppliers market adhesive copper tape. Crowns can be divided with a knife and re-planted or potted during dormancy.

❺ *H.* 'Hadspen Blue' 50 cm, 'Halcyon' 50 cm, and 'Krossa Regal' 75 cm have attractive blue foliage and slate mauve flowers. For lime to yellow foliage, try 'Chinese Sunrise' 35 cm, 'Gold Standard' 50 cm or 'Piedmont Gold'. For green leaves, try 'Green Fountain' 60 cm, 'Royal Standard' 45 cm. For variegated leaves, try 'Francee' 60 cm, 'Frances Williams' 60 cm or 'Wide Brim' 60 cm.

❷ *Iberis sempervirens*. (Candytuft). Small evergreen sub-shrub suited to the rockery. Produces masses of pure white flowers in spring through to summer. There is a small form called 'Little Gem'. Propagate from cuttings in summer. To 30 cm.

❶ *I. umbellata*. (Globe Candytuft). Annual. A long lived annual which, with trimming, will flower again the following season. Its flowers are globular and showy, and in hard conditions its foliage will be dense and glossy. 30 cm high and 20 cm wide, in shades of pink, mauve and white. It self seeds but not to nuisance levels.

❷ *Imperata cylindrica* 'Rubra' (Japanese Blood Grass). Perennial, growing 30–40 cm. Japanese Blood Grass has erect, mid

❶ Sun + dry ❷ Sun + moisture ❸ Dry + shade ❹ Shade + moisture ❺ Waterside + bog

Bees love lavenders.

green leaves and in summer the leaf ends turn red, hence its name. By autumn, the whole plant turns to a vibrant red. This is a wonderful plant for contrast, and with good siting, it can make a striking feature. It likes either full sun or dappled shade and humus rich, moist soil. Propagation is usually by division.

❷ *Lathyrus odoratus* (Sweet pea). Annual. Available in climbing or dwarf forms. Dwarf forms can be grown in rockeries or pots. Climbing types are best grown on a fence, trellis or frame facing north or north-west. They need full sun and protection from strong winds. Good soil preparation is important. A soil rich in humus, with plenty of animal manure and good drainage will improve the results. Permanent support is needed from the time the plants are about 15 cm high. Apply dressings of complete fertiliser several times during the growing period and liquid fertiliser when buds appear. Sow seed in early autumn.

There is also a perennial sweet pea, which unfortunately has no scent, *L. latifolius*, perennial or everlasting pea. This grows to about 1.8 m with dense white, pink or rose flowers in spring

or summer. Seed should be planted between mid March and mid April, or divide in early spring.

❶ **Lavender**. While lavenders are technically shrubs, they are included here because they complement perennials. Countless varieties are now available from specialist nurseries, many of them valuable additions to the garden. Always trim lavenders after flowering to prevent plants becoming woody. Propagate from summer cuttings.

The traditional forms of lavender are *Lavandula x allardii* (Mitchum Lavender) 1.5 x 1 m, *L. angustifolia*, the traditional English lavender, *L. dentata* (French Lavender), *L. stoechas* (Spanish Lavender) and *L. latifolia* (Spike Lavender).

'Hidcote' to 60 cm and 'Munstead' (60 cm) are dwarf cultivars available as punneted seedlings for use in low hedges.

Of the newer introductions, try *L. stoechas* 'Marshwood', pale mauve spikes, long flowering 50 x 70 cm, 'Sidonie', fine purple spikes 1 x 1 m, *L. stoechas* 'Kew Red' 50 x 40 cm, magenta flowers from spring through to summer and grey foliage; 'Wine' 60 cm x 50 cm burgundy flowers in spring to autumn, with grey foliage. *L. x intermedia* 'Bogong' has mauve flowers in summer, with grey foliage 80 x 75 cm.

L. stoechas 'Butterfly' 60 x 60 cm has lavender flowers in spring to autumn and grey foliage.

❷ *Leucanthemum x superbum* (Shasta daisy). A popular perennial with several

❶ Sun + dry ❷ Sun + moisture ❸ Dry + shade ❹ Shade + moisture ❺ Waterside + bog

forms that make long lasting cut blooms. The variety 'Esther Read' has a double white flower, the centre of which is a massed pin cushion dome of fine petals. 'Chiffon' has a double row of narrow petals frilled and divided at the ends giving a lacy effect. Propagate by division when not in flower. 60 cm tall and 90 cm wide.

❶ *Limonium sinuatum* (Statice). Annual in blue, white and pastel shades, to 60 cm. Small flowers of the 'everlasting' type which will dry to a papery texture. The flowers are tiny but the calyces surrounding the flowers are long-lasting. Requires a fairly rich soil with the addition of some lime. Suitable as a cut flower and can be dried for winter decoration. Sow seed in late winter–early spring.

L. perezii. A perennial species growing to 60 cm with insignificant white petals and deep mauve-blue calyces which provide a long lasting papery flower. It can be dried for long use in floral decoration. *L. perezii* requires good drainage. It can be propagated by division in spring.

L. platiphyllum syn latifolium. Perennial. Tiny panicles of pale violet flowers in summer. Propagate by seed or division in spring or root cuttings in winter.

❶ *Linaria maroccana* (Toad flax). Annual, growing 20–40 cm. Dainty plant with small flowers resembling miniature snapdragons; useful for decorative work or spring garden displays in borders. Sow seeds in permanent position in either early spring or autumn and thin out. Will grow in most soils. Wide range of colours. Trim after flowering for more flowers. Can self-seed.

❶ *Lobularia maritima* (Sweet Alyssum or Sweet Alice). Annual or perennial forms, spreading, producing masses of tiny, honey-scented flowers from spring to autumn. Full sun, with fertile well-drained soil. Can be direct sown from late spring to autumn.

❶ *Lomandra confertifolia.* A small Australian grass growing to a height of 30 cm and 70 cm across. A frost-resistant light green tufting plant, which is useful in the garden or as a container plant. Should be cut back in late winter to promote lush growth, the feature of this plant. New cultivars are being introduced regularly, with a variety of foliage colours. The blue forms have a shorter life. Propagate by division in early spring or autumn.

❷ **Lupinus** (Russell hybrids). Perennial. 1 m. Require a well-drained moderately fertile, slightly acidic soil. Come in a variety of colours from cream, through to violet and red with bi-colours. As they are hybrids propagate by cutting or division in spring.

❷ *Matthiola incana* (Stock). Annual. Perfumed. Require moist, well-drained neutral soil. Staking may be necessary. Propagate by seed in spring and cull spindly seedlings in favour of sturdier ones. 60 cm.

❹ *Meconopsis betonicifolia* (Himalayan Poppy). Perennial. Part or full shade. Dormant in winter. This plant is reputed to be difficult to grow but so long as it is given good drainage, to the extent of incorporating fine gravel or washed river sand in your soil when planting, you will be rewarded by the most intense

① Sun + dry **②** Sun + moisture **③** Dry + shade **④** Shade + moisture **⑤** Waterside + bog

Miscanthus sinensis 'Aureo-variegata' in the foreground and *Miscanthus sinensis* 'Flamingo' behind.

blue poppy flowers. When the plant produces its first buds, remove them for this will assist in prolonging the life of this beautiful plant. Height 1–1.2 m. Propagate by fresh seed in late summer. *M. cambrica* (Welsh Poppy) grows to 30–45 cm and has lemon-yellow or orange blooms. It will grow in sun and self-seeds.

② *Mimulus aurantiacus*. Though botanically a shrub, this plant is at home with annuals and perennials. It grows to only 50 cm and has pretty apricot flowers over a long period. Take cuttings when flowers diminish in number.

② **Miscanthus**. A family of deciduous perennial grasses which like good drainage. There are a number of cultivars available, but *M. sinensis* 'Variegata' is an exceptional plant for visual impact

most of the year. Growing to 1.2 m high and approximately as wide, it has illuminating cream leaves with green bands from spring through to autumn when the foliage changes to a wheat colour. Feathery flower heads and wheat coloured foliage will remain until you trim it back to ground level in late winter in preparation for new spring growth. Divide after trimming or in early spring before growth commences.

① *Myosotis alpestris* (Forget-me-not). Annual. Hardy plant 15–30 cm that will tolerate light shade. Flowers in blue, white and pink. A useful plant for mixing with bulbs. Prefers a moderately rich soil. Self seeds, often to nuisance level, but if plants are carefully removed before the seed matures, they can be used to advantage both as a weed-suppressant and for spring impact.

❶ Sun + dry   ❷ Sun + moisture   ❸ Dry + shade   ❹ Shade + moisture   ❺ Waterside + bog

❷ **Nemesia** cultivars are often available as potted colour. These grow around 40 cm and flower colours vary through shades of blue and pink, as well as pure white. Nemesia seed can be sown in early spring or small divisions of root taken, but existing plants can self-seed in good conditions.

❶ *Nepeta x faassenii*. (Cat Mint). Perennial. An aromatic grey-foliaged plant with lavender flowers in summer. Grows to 45 cm and is used as an edging, or to complement heritage rose plantings. Clip after flowering to avoid woodiness. Divide during late summer. Will self-seed in ideal conditions.

❷ *Omphalodes cappadocica*. Perennial. A spreading plant with purple blue sprays of flowers in spring. *O. verna* has loose sprays of bright blue flowers with white eyes on 25–30 cm stems above dark green leaves. Good ground cover which can be divided every 2 years.

O. linifolia (Navelwort). Annual. Its common name belies the beauty of this plant, which is a treasure in the spring garden, growing to 40 cm. Fine silver-grey leaves and profuse white forget-me-not flowers. Sprinkle seed in autumn where you want it to grow.

❷ *Pæonia lactiflora* (herbaceous peony). Perennial to 90 cm. Best in rich, deep, well-drained cool soil. Will tolerate part shade. Leave undisturbed for years, but mulch and top-dress heavily. In heavy soils mound the soil around the new plant rather than planting it too deeply. When new shoots appear, sprinkle lime around the mound as a snail deterrent. Flowers

Herbaceous peonies flower in spring.

are large and showy in pink, red, white and purple colours. Single and double varieties, often with striking bronze tinted spring foliage and reddish tints in autumn. They can be propagated by division in winter, but they do resent being disturbed and may take several years to resume flowering.

Pansy see Viola

Papaver. Many types of annual and perennial poppies flourish in Canberra

❷ *Papaver nudicaule* (Iceland poppy). Perennial but best treated as an annual; sow in January and plant out March to early April to establish before cold weather. Sunny sheltered position. Wide range of colours provided by the large number of strains. Remove dead flowers to promote flowering and maintain quality.

❷ *P. orientale* (Oriental poppy). Perennial growing 90–120 cm. Hairy foliage; likes rich soil with plenty of moisture, but well drained. Spectacular large flowers in early summer. Plant dies down during winter. Varieties of orange, red through to pink, single and double, with or without a dark base. Sow seed in spring or early autumn.

❶ Sun + dry ❷ Sun + moisture ❸ Dry + shade ❹ Shade + moisture ❺ Waterside + bog

Oriental poppy.

❶ *P. rhoeas* (Flanders poppy and also the Shirley poppy). Annuals growing 30–36 cm. Sow in autumn for spring. If sown in March, the plants should be grown under shelter during winter. Like a light rich soil. Attractive cut flower in single and double varieties. Wide range of shades from white to deep red and orange.

❶ *P. paeoniflorum* (Peony poppy) syn. *P. somniferum* does well in Canberra. It has large flowers, usually double in white, pink, red or purple, in summer. Sow seed in autumn.

❶ *Patersonia occidentalis*. Native iris, a tussock-forming Australian plant that grows to about 30 cm with purple flowers in spring. It will grow in full sun or filtered shade but needs good drainage.

❶ *Pelargonium fragrans* (Nutmeg geranium). A bushy small shrub to 30 cm which is included with the perennials because of its size. Its grey foliage is aromatic and it has tiny white flowers over a very long period. Propagate from cuttings in spring or autumn. Many other pelargoniums are available at garden centres, some for garden culture and many for sheltered positions. The

Canberra Geranium and Fuchsia Society Inc. (www.geraniumsfuchsias.websyte. com.au) is a good source of information and plants on this genus.

❷ **Penstemon**. Perennial. Sunny well-drained position. Some cultivars worth growing: 'Firebird' red, 'Evelyn' pale pink, 'Hidcote' rose pink, 'White Bedder' white, 'Pennington Gem' deep pink, 'Alice Hindley' blue and white, 'Purple Bedder' claret. 1–1.2 m tall. Species can be grown by seed in spring or autumn, cultivars by division in spring or cuttings in late summer.

❶ *Petunia x hybrida*. There are annuals and perennials available. Spreading annuals are available also, ideal for baskets and tubs. All like well-drained fertile soil in a sunny position, and protection from wind. Pinch back to encourage branching and deadhead regularly. Purchase seedlings in early summer. Seed propagation not recommended.

❷ *Phlox drummondii.* Annual. Grows quickly to 35 cm. In summer and autumn it has small flattish flowers in reds, pinks, purples and creams. Needs fertile, well-drained moist soil and, particularly, moisture while growing. Propagate by seed.

P. paniculata (Perennial phlox). There are many cultivars in colours ranging through violet, red, salmon and white. 1 m high, flowering in summer. Propagate by division .

P. subulata (Alpine phlox) is another perennial. Again there are many colours ranging from white, blue through pinks to dark pink and two toned flowers. Propagate by division or root cutting.

❶ Sun + dry　❷ Sun + moisture　❸ Dry + shade　❹ Shade + moisture　❺ Waterside + bog

❷ ***Phormium tenax*** (New Zealand Flax). Evergreen, 1.5–2.5 m. Stemless plant, consisting of clumps of strap-like leaves. An excellent feature plant but, as a NZ plant it needs extra water to grow well in Canberra. Flower stems grow above leaves, carrying end sprays of orange red flowers, followed by brownish seed pods. There is a wide range of leaf colours and combinations in new named varieties, many of which are smaller than the species, ranging from shades of pink and coral through to bright variegations.

❷ ***Phygelius aequalis***. Perennial, 1–1.5 m. Summer and autumn flowering. 'Yellow Trumpet' and 'Moonraker' are both creamy yellow, although the latter is more compact. *P. x rectus* 'African Queen' has light red flowers. All like fertile, well-drained soil that has some moisture. They have a long flowering period and are showy plants. Propagation is from cuttings in summer, or division of roots when rejuvenating the plant.

❷ ***Physostegia virginiana*** (Obedient Plant). A rhizomatous perennial, which prefers moist, well-drained soil in sun or very light shade. It is easy to grow, but with rhizomatous roots, can become invasive. Magenta spikes in summer, also pale pink or white. Division is the easiest form of propagation, though it can also be grown from seed or cutting.

❶ ***Poa australis***, Blue Tussock grass. Silvery blue clumping grass to 30 cm. Propagation by division in spring and autumn.

❹ ***Polemonium caeruleum*** (Jacob's ladder). Perennial. Mauve flowers with orange-yellow stamens in early summer,

Physostegia virginiana has the common name of Obedient Plant because if you gently change the direction in which the flowers are pointing they will stay that way.

45–60 cm. Must be divided at least two to three-yearly to avoid deterioration. Propagate by division in spring or from seed sown in autumn or spring.

❹ ***Polygonatum odoratum*** (Solomon's seal). Perennial. This graceful plant grows from 60 cm to 1 m. The form, foliage and flowers provide an interesting plant for a shady spot in the garden, and in spring the greenish-white fragrant bells clustered along the stem make a wonderful display. Prefers moist, humus-rich soil but can tolerate dry shade. Division is best in spring.

❶ ***Portulaca grandiflora***. Annual. Sunny well-drained position and only occasional water is required. 15 cm. Propagation by sowing seed in spring. Seedlings should

❶ Sun + dry **❷** Sun + moisture **❸** Dry + shade **❹** Shade + moisture **❺** Waterside + bog

not be planted out until all danger of spring frosts has passed. Once growing, cuttings can be taken from existing plants in summer to increase stock.

Primula. These do well in Canberra and there is a wide choice of annuals and perennials.

❺ *Primula japonica*. Perennial. Flowers in spring and early summer to 60 cm. *P. florindae* flowers in spring to 60 cm. Both can be propagated by seed in spring, early summer or in autumn by division or from root cuttings. A good tub plant.

❹ *P. malacoides* and *P. obconica* are perennials usually grown as annuals. Both flower from winter through to spring and should be planted out in March. *P. obconica* has larger leaves and flowers than *P. malacoides*. There is a good range of colours ranging from white through to claret. Both like fertile, well-drained soil, part shade and ample water. Sow seed in early autumn. 30 cm.

❹ *P. vulgaris* (English primrose). Perennial. Grows to 20 cm and produces a carpet of bright flowers in spring. The true English primrose is yellow with a dark eye, but garden cultivars come in every colour. The English Cowslip (*P. veris*) grows to 25 cm. Both like fertile, well-drained soil, part shade and ample water. Propagated from seed in spring, early summer or autumn, by division or from root cuttings. Remove dead heads and old foliage after blooming.

❹ *Primula x polyanthus*, the Polyanthus group. Frost-hardy perennials which have cheery bright coloured flowers in every

Polyanthus look great in pots on balconies, providing colour through winter and spring.

possible colour and colour combination, often spotted, striped and picotee forms. They can be found every winter as 'potted bloomers' in garden centres and supermarkets. Will grow to 15 cm and may be propagated by sowing seed in autumn or plants divided in autumn.

❹ ***Pulmonaria officinalis***. Perennial. 'Sissinghurst White' has heavily white spotted leaves and white spring flowers, 30 cm tall. *P. saccharata* 'Highdown' and 'Beth's Blue' have striking blue spring flowers, while 'Majeste' is another striking plant with silver foliage and pale pink flowers. Pulmonarias are best grown in cool, moist, humus-rich light soil. Good pot plants. Propagated by cutting or division in autumn.

❶ Sun + dry   ❷ Sun + moisture   ❸ Dry + shade   ❹ Shade + moisture   ❺ Waterside + bog

❹ ***Ranunculus ficaria***. Perennial. Single bright yellow flowers in spring. It only reaches 5 cm in height and has glossy green leaves with silver markings. 'Brazen Hussy' has dark bronzed leaves and shiny, deep gold flowers. Propagated by division in early spring or autumn.

❺ ***Restio tetraphyllus*** (Tassell Cord-rush). A creeping plant to 1 m with soft bright green weeping foliage, which is hardy, frost resistant, and will tolerate poorly drained soil. Ideal for planting near a pond or in a moist site or may be grown in a water-well pot.

❶ **Rhodanthe**, previously known as Helipterum. An Australian family of small perennial and annual paper daisies in pink and white shades valued for cut flower arrangements and garden display.

R. anthemoides. Small perennials growing to 30 cm high and a spread of 60 cm, these have small grey-green leaves and produce masses of papery purple pointed buds opening to white flowers in spring for an extended time. Good edging and container plants. They prefer a compost rich well drained soil with morning sun and some shade from the summer sun. Good cultivars readily available include 'Paper Star' and 'Paper Cascade'. Highly recommended.

R. chlorocephalala and *R. manglesii* are annual paper daisies. Sow seed in spring where they are to grow. The colour range includes pinks with black or yellow centre. Both types grow to 40 cm, are suitable for rockeries, cottage garden displays and for dried flowers. Prefer sun and are frost sensitive.

❺ ***Rodgersia aesculifolia***. Perennial. A rhizomatous clump-forming plant which produces bold, dark green leaves. Star-shaped yellowish-white, pink or red flowers are borne in panicles on reddish green stems in mid to late summer. Reaches a height of 1 m and spread of 75 cm. Propagate by division in spring or from seed in autumn.

Salvia. Another excellent group of annuals and perennials for this climate as they generally need little water and flower freely. Some of the cultivars being offered locally may not always get through our cold winters but cuttings strike easily to make vigorous new plants and if protected during the colder months, may be planted out after the danger of frosts is over. It is a useful process to do this for all perennial salvias, as they can become woody with age, and are easy to propagate. The taller varieties, both annual and perennial will need a protected site or staking to avoid wind damage.

❷ *S. splendens* (Bonfire salvia). Annual, 1–1.2 m. Sunny position, rich soil and regular watering in hot weather. Propagate from seed in spring but do not transplant into garden before late October. Available in tall or dwarf forms.

❶ *S. chamaedryoides* is a perennial growing to 30 cm with silver foliage and clear bright mid-blue flowers. Frost hardy and suited to edging. *S. azurea*, 1 m, has sky blue flowers. Winter dormant, drought and frost tolerant. *S. involucrata* 'Bethellii' (1 m) with bright pink flowers is herbaceous, drought and frost tolerant, and will even flower in shade. *S. superba*

❶ Sun + dry **❷** Sun + moisture **❸** Dry + shade **❹** Shade + moisture **❺** Waterside + bog

Salvias are wonderfully easy care, low-water plants.

'Blue Queen' grows to 40 cm with dark blue spikes. Repeat flowering, winter dormant, drought and cold hardy.

There are many other perennials: *S. patens* 'Cambridge Blue' has flowers of intense bright blue. Though young plants need protection from frost with mulch, they will thrive in well-drained soil in sun or light shade. *S. guaranitica* has rich deep blue flowers and needs adequate moisture while actively growing to 1–1.5 m. *S. guaranitica* 'Black and Blue' is taller and stronger than the species, with large blue and black flowers. Flowering in late summer to autumn, they are propagated by softwood cuttings in mid-summer. Best cut back in late winter.

❶ ***Santolina chamaecyparissus*** (Lavender cotton). Perennial. 45 cm. Aromatic silver foliage and small yellow button flower heads. Can be used as a quick growing hedge, but do not allow it to become woody. Old woody stems should be reduced by about two thirds to encourage new growth after flowering. Propagate from cuttings in late summer. 'Nana' is a smaller growing form to around 30 cm in height and spread. Cuttings of both types can be taken at any time.

❸ **Saxifraga spp**. There are many evergreen perennials in this family. The foliage and flowers of saxifraga are equally attractive. *Saxifraga stolonifera* (syn. *S. sarmentosa*) is an effective ground cover, particularly useful in dry shade. It has interesting silver-veined foliage, with claret coloured undersides and there are varieties offered with dark red foliage if you are prepared to search the mail order catalogues. It grows to approximately 15 cm high and in spring through to early summer bears delicate white flower panicles. As the name implies, the plant is stoloniferous and its plantlets can be transplanted at any time of the year.

❶ Sun + dry **❷** Sun + moisture **❸** Dry + shade **❹** Shade + moisture **❺** Waterside + bog

❶ *Scabiosa atropurpurea* (Pincushion plant). Annual. 60 cm, in various shades of pink and blue. Sow seed in spring.

S. caucasica is a perennial. Various shades of pink, red, purple, blue 60 cm. Open flowers on tall stems flowering freely through summer. Best in light soil and sun with lime added. Divide in spring or autumn or by cuttings in summer.

❷ *Scleranthus biflorus* (Canberra grass). A cushion-like plant with a spread of 40 cm. Tiny green flowers appear in late spring. It should be grown in a sunny, moist position, in a weed free area. Weeds growing through the cushion can detract from its appearance, so try to keep it weed-free. If weeds get the upper hand, it is easiest to dig up the clump, turn it over and remove the weeds from below as their roots will be quite obviously different. You can then replant the clump and water it in. It is frost-tolerant. Because of its moss-like appearance it is a most attractive plant amongst rocks.

❶ *Stachys byzantina* (Lambs ear). Perennial, 30 cm. Silver woolly leaves with mauve pink flowers. A good ground cover or border plant, ideally suited to growing near roses. Look also for *Stachys* 'Big Ears', a recent introduction with compact foliage. *Stachys officinalis* 'Nivea' and 'Rosea' have dense green foliage and a mass of mauve or pink flowers in summer. Propagated by division year round.

❹ *Stypandra glauca* (Nodding blue lily). This is an Australian perennial with a growth pattern of slender grass like arching stems ending in clusters of beautiful deep blue lily like flowers in late spring. Grow it in a well-drained position with light shade. Once established it is drought-tolerant and is also frost-resistant.

❶ *Tagetes* (Marigold). Annual. Excellent summer–autumn flowers for a bright garden display in colours of lemon, yellow and orange. *T. patula* (French marigold) 20–30 cm and *T. erecta* (African marigold) 75 cm are both frost sensitive. Propagate from seed in spring. Seedlings must be planted by late spring or early summer so that flowering is completed before frosts set in. Thrives in full sun.

❸ *Tellima grandiflora*. Perennial. Clump forming, 60 cm high, this plant has heart shaped purple tinted leaves. Its small bell-shaped cream flowers are borne on 60 cm stems. 'Purpurea' has reddish-purple leaves and pink-tinged cream flowers. Propagate by division in spring.

❹ *Thalictrum aquilegifolium*. Perennial. A clump forming perennial which grows to 1 m with pink, lilac or greenish/white flowers in summer. All thalictrums like shade and moisture.

T. delavayi — ferny leaves appear in spring and sprays of single lavender flowers in summer on tall stems. *T. delavayi* 'Hewitt's double is worth looking for, and also *T. delavayi* 'Album', a pretty white form.

T. dipterocarpum 'Lavender Shower' has a loose spray of lavender flowers from mid to late summer. Very fine foliage to 1.2 m.

❶ Sun + dry **❷** Sun + moisture **❸** Dry + shade **❹** Shade + moisture **❺** Waterside + bog

T. speciosissimum (*T. glaucum*) has grey ferny foliage which goes well with its fluffy yellow flowers. Height 1–1.2 m. Propagate from fresh seed in autumn or division in spring.

❹ *Tiarella cordifolia*. Perennial. Related to heuchera, it is a vigorous spreading evergreen with abundant blooms in spring. Tiny terminal creamy white spikes. Leaves are lobed with marbling and spots and some leaves will colour in autumn, 30 cm. *T. wherryi* is slow-growing and forms a clump 20 cm high and wide. In late spring it has soft pink and white flowers and its leaves turn red in autumn. Tiarella can be divided in autumn or spring, using the young outer portions of the crown.

❶ *Tropaeolum majus* (Nasturtium). Annual. Trailing or low growing pot, window box or bedding favourite. Sow seed in position in late spring and thin out. Poor soil and sunny position most suitable but will tolerate partial shade. Flowers should be picked regularly to extend flowering season.

❶ *Tweedia caerulea* (syn. *Oxypetalum caeruleum*). Perennial 30-45cm tolerating full sun or partial shade. Blue-grey leaves and attractive light blue flowers in late spring to early summer. Appreciates a little water, but do not overwater, as this is a drought tolerant plant. Long shapely seed pods may be left to mature on the plant for harvesting when dry. Pods will split, exposing the seeds which can then be stored. Propagate from softwood cuttings or seed sown direct in early spring.

Pansies seem to get better every year.

❹ *Vancouveria hexandra*. Perennial. A graceful creeping woodland plant related to the epimedium. The leaves are reminiscent of maidenhair fern, rounded and often 3-lobed, but with a flowering stem 20–40 cm. Small pendulous flowers in white or yellow, in spring or summer. Divide or grow afresh from seed in spring.

❶ *Verbena x hybrida*. Perennials which provide a wide range of colours from blues through to red and two toned flowers. Can be propagated by division in spring.

❶ *Veronica peduncularis* 'Oxford Blue'. A perennial ground cover with deep blue flowers in late spring to summer. Root mass can inhibit penetration of moisture to other plants. *V. spicata* grows to 60 cm and 1 m wide. A striking plant with purple spikes in summer. Both can be divided in early spring or autumn.

❹ *Viola*. This much loved genus contains annuals and perennials which prefer cool moist positions. There are two Australian violas and they grow well in Canberra being frost tolerant but both die back in winter.

1 Sun + dry **2** Sun + moisture **3** Dry + shade **4** Shade + moisture **5** Waterside + bog

V. betonicifolia is a tufted plant to 20 cm with long slender leaves and purple or lilac flowers on long stems in spring and summer. This species will grow best in a moist sheltered position with shade but is tolerant of other positions in the garden.

V. hederacea (Ivy-leafed violet), a light spreading groundcover, will cover quite large areas in time with its fine runners, and thrive in shady positions. Good for cascading from pots and rockeries. As well as the usual purple and white flowered plant, there is also a pure blue flowered form 'Baby Blue'.

Viola hybrids Annual. These are the plants we once knew as pansies and violas, no longer distinguishable from each other nor confined to autumn tones as they once were. Violas are now marketed in ranges from soft pastels to raucous hues for every colour scheme and whether you prefer showy large flowers with flounced petals or tiny, cheeky flowers reminiscent of the original Johnny Jump-ups or Heartsease, there will be one for everyone's taste. Growing your own from seeds can be difficult, but if you wish to try, then sow seeds in autumn or spring, under glass.

Viola. Perennial. These cultivars are long flowering and very hardy. 'Jackanapes' has brown upper and yellow lower petals, 'Maggie Mott' has bright purple-blue flowers and 'Huntercombe Purple' has purple flowers with cream centres. Perennial violas are propagated by division or cutting in spring. *V. labradorica* has distinctive small dark purple-toned leaves and attractive blue flowers.

Viola odorata (Violet). Perennial. If you like perfumed plants, then you will already grow violets. Enjoy them, but remember that they have the propensity to become invasive as they germinate readily and spread their seeds very efficiently.

V neapolitana (the Parma Violet) is very fragrant and double flowered.

1 *Zinnia elegans*. Annual, 30–90 cm. An excellent summer and autumn plant. Requires rich soil to which lime has been added, open, sunny, well drained position. Wide range of colours and forms ranging from small to giant-flowered types. Plants are easily raised from seed which should not be sown before October. Pinch out the first bud of medium and tall types but this is not necessary with the shorter plants.

CHAPTER 8: Bulbs and bulbous plants

Tony Davis

Many bulbs and so-called bulbous plants flourish in the colder climates of eastern Australia.

They frequently herald the arrival of spring but careful choice of bulbs will ensure that there is colour in the garden for much of the year. Many of these also make excellent cut flowers. However, they have a relatively short flowering period and are best seen as a small part of the general landscape.

For ease of presentation, this chapter includes bulbs and a number of other plants, such as corms, rhizomes, tuberous roots and tuberous rhizomes.

Cultural requirements

With a few exceptions, bulbs require a sunny, well-drained soil containing organic material such as compost, old straw or well rotted manure. Complete fertiliser should be incorporated into the lower layers of the soil where it will be available to the roots without coming into contact with the bulb. Fresh manure or fertilisers with high nitrogen content should be avoided. A light dressing of complete fertiliser can be applied to the surface of the soil about two months before flowering and weak liquid fertiliser, applied as the bulbs show bud development, will also be beneficial.

Wet feet are perhaps the greatest problem for most bulbs so ensure that the beds have adequate drainage. There are exceptions to this rule such as hostas, *Iris kaempferi*, *Iris pseudacorus* and zantedeschia.

Planting times and depth vary considerably from bulb to bulb — see the Table later in the chapter for a guide to the most commonly grown bulbs.

When cutting flowers, ensure that you leave sufficient foliage for the development of next season's bulb. Do not remove the ageing foliage for the sake of tidiness.

Many bulbs are best left in the garden from year to year and only need lifting when they become overcrowded and unproductive. For best results, tulips, hyacinths and gladioli should be lifted and stored each year. Bulbs, together with foliage and the earth around the roots may be lifted when the foliage is yellowing. They can then be put in a dry place until the tops are dead; soil and tops can then be easily removed.

Bulbs with a protective coating, such as gladiolus, tigridia and freesia should be stored in a dry location. Onion bags or old stockings provide a suitable medium to hang for these types of bulbs.

Propagation

Bulbs and bulbous plants may be propagated

» by natural increase such as the new bulbs which develop around narcissus bulbs;

» from bulbils, cormlets and the like which form on various parts of the parent plant;

» by division of rhizomes, tubers, tuberous roots and the like;

» from seed which has been pollinated by bees or other insects (or hand pollinated with a view to breeding a plant superior to the parents).

Some of the natural processes can be hastened by the use of methods such as twin scaling (e.g. narcissus) or scooping and scoring (e.g hyacinth). For more information on these methods you will need to consult specialist texts.

Container plants.

Most bulbs can be grown in pots or other containers and used to brighten an otherwise dull spot in the garden or to bring indoors instead of cut flowers. Hyacinths, daffodils, tulips and bluebells are frequently used for this purpose. Many of the lower growing species can also be used to good effect. For example, muscari (Grape hyacinths) are very effective if grown in a container with a dwarf fruit tree or other small deciduous plants, but generally smaller bulbs look best in small containers. The use of bulbs in containers is limited only by your imagination.

If they are to be left in the garden, the choice of container is not all that important provided you remember that there are some disadvantages with most of them. Plastic pots are cheap and generally provide good drainage but they tend to heat up quickly in the warmer weather thus risking damage to plant roots. Placing the pot inside another larger pot will provide insulation. Clay pots provide better air circulation but require more frequent watering. Whatever you choose, there will be some trade-offs involved.

Growing in containers allows the gardener to provide optimum soil conditions. However, for most bulbs it is essential that the potting mix drains freely.

Plant the bulbs much closer to the surface than you would in the garden (to allow maximum root growth) and resist the temptation to crowd the pot unless you propose to treat the bulbs as annuals. Remember that bulbs frequently have a very strong root system so three or four narcissus bulbs in a 30 cm pot would be adequate. The pots should be left outside except for those short periods when they are used inside for decoration.

Daffodils come in a wide range of shapes, sizes and colours.

Pests and diseases

Bulbs and the like are remarkably free from attack by diseases and pests so don't be put off by the next few paragraphs. Nearly all things that do attack these plants are carried over from season to season in or on the bulb. It is, therefore, important to check bulbs carefully after lifting. Any unhealthy ones should be discarded and the rest stored in a dry, airy place. Prior to planting in well-drained soil they should be checked again and any with signs of deterioration discarded. Take care to avoid damaging them when digging for storage or division or when cultivating as injury will provide a point of entry for disease organisms. See the pests and diseases chapter for more detailed information.

Snails and slugs are probably the most serious pests of these plants and can severely damage new shoots, leaves, flower stems and buds. Eliminate hiding places and use snail baits when the shoots first appear to prevent damage.

Virus diseases may cause light and dark green mottling of the foliage in bulbs such as daffodils and irises while in others such as tulips they cause variegated flowers (colour breaking). It is difficult to control virus diseases because they are spread by propagating from infected plants and by insects, usually aphids. Purchased bulbs are mostly free from virus diseases but if grown near old plantings may eventually become infected. Bulbs from visibly diseased plants should not be used for propagation. In a home garden it is almost impossible to control the insect vectors.

Fungal leaf spots occur commonly on some plants in wet seasons. If you have this problem avoid overhead watering and overcrowding of plants. Clearing away old leaves before new growth starts will do much to reduce this minor problem.

Aphids may infest young growth causing distortion of buds, shoots, foliage and flowers and weaken the entire plant. They can be controlled by spraying or dusting infested plants with an insecticide — dusts work best.

Caterpillars of various moths may feed on leaves and stems, others may attack the floral parts and destroy the developing buds. If there are only a few caterpillars remove them by hand, otherwise spray or dust with an insecticide.

Bulbs not flowering

The most common reason bulbs don't flower is poor growing conditions, particularly heavy shade or strong competition from tree roots. Overcrowding of some bulb species or planting too deeply can also reduce the number and size of flowers. Excessive use of nitrogen fertiliser can cause bulbs to make soft sappy growth to the detriment of next year's flowers. The size of bulbs or corms can also be an important factor. For example, bulb offsets of narcissus and hippeastrum can take a number of years to reach flowering size.

Some species of the following genera are suitable for growing in partial shade.

Agapanthus

Alstroemeria

Anemones (some types)

Bulbinella

Clivia

Chionodoxa

Convallaria

Crinum

Cyclamen

Eranthis

Erythronium

Hosta

Hyacinthoides

Ipheion

Leucojum

Lycoris

Muscari

Ornithogalum

Polygonatum

Sparaxis

Trillium

Zantedeschia

List of species

Acis autumnale syn *Leucojum autumnale* is a dwarf autumn flowering species that produces white flowers tinged with pink, on 10–15 cm stems.

Agapanthus (African or Nile lily). A tough garden plant that does best in full sun or partial shade but will survive in deep shade. Summer flowers of blue or white on stems 50–90 cm. Divide when necessary immediately after flowering; cut back the leaves to half their length and plant the roots shallowly. However, it is best to leave undisturbed for years as they frequently will not flower in the first year after division. Flowers are good for indoor arrangements. The root system is invasive. While they are drought hardy they will grow better with lots of water. Remove spent flower heads to avoid over germination and potential weed problems.

Allium (Onion flowers). A large group of bulbs, becoming more readily available in Australia. By and large they require full sun with a fairly dry dormancy period; partial shade and summer water are tolerated by some species. Foliage can have a strong onion odour when crushed. Generally propagated by division of clump or by seed, planting bulbs in autumn about 8 cm deep and 10 cm apart. These bulbs are never fully dormant and should not be left out of the ground for an extended period. If growing alliums from seed, chill prior to sowing. Most take three to four years to reach flowering size.

A. christophii (syn. *A. albopilosum)* with spikes about 50 cm high and mauve flower heads about 15–20 cm across is an eye-catching species. Flowers are long lasting.

A. neapolitanum, with heads of white flowers on stems of 40 cm should be planted about 10 cm apart. It makes a good cut flower.

A. murrayanum, with pink flowers on short stems, is a useful plant for the border.

A. cernuum is a lovely summer flowering species with a succession of pink to purple flowers on 40 cm stems. While not as showy as some of the larger alliums, its long flowering period makes it a desirable bulb. Plant bulbs about 15 cm apart.

A. giganteum with round balls of lilac flowers on stems of more than a metre is a striking garden species. However, the leaves can be unattractive by flowering time so some thought should be given to the planting location.

Alstroemeria (Peruvian lily). A tuberous-rooted family not as widely grown as the excellent cut flowers would perhaps justify. It looks well in the garden, flowering in late spring and summer, in a range of pinks, reds, yellow and white, usually blotched with brown. Smaller types such as the 'Princess Lilies' grow to around 25 cm; taller types can be up to 1.5 m tall and need some staking and wind protection. Divide in late autumn. Plant rootstocks 10–12 cm deep in rich soil. Seed germinates readily. *A. psittacina* can become a pest in some gardens though its red and green flowers at Christmas are valued by many.

Amaryllis belladonna (Belladonna lily or Naked lady). These require an open sunny position. Flowers are carried on spikes of 50–70 cm in late summer or early autumn in colours of pink, rose-red or white. They are produced before the leaves appear. Divide the clumps while the bulbs are dormant (late spring, early summer) replanting about 25 cm apart with the neck at soil level. *A. belladonna* resents division and may not flower in the first year so do not divide unless seriously overcrowded.

Amaryllis Naked Ladies are one of the easiest and showiest bulbs you can grow.

Anemone. One of the most commonly grown spring flowering bulbs, producing good cut flowers when grown in full sun. Soil rich in humus with the addition of lime prior to planting gives best results. Plant the corms 3–5 cm deep and 20 cm apart. Because these corms are cheap they can be treated as annuals. They are usually hybrids of *A. coronaria* but some of the lesser-grown species are worth a place in the home garden.

> *A. blanda* with daisy-like flowers is usually available in shades of blue with a height of 10 cm or less. It grows nicely in partial shade or full sun. Corms are available commercially and it will self- seed if conditions are to its liking.

Arum lilies see *Zantedeschia,*

Babiana (Baboon flower). Late spring flowers on stems 20–40 cm in red, blue, purple, white and yellow. In Canberra they are marginal but grow best when planted deeply (15–20 cm) and about 10 cm apart. Plant in autumn and leave undisturbed for several years. Propagation is by division of the corms. Grows well in pots in our climate.

Begonia x tuberhybrida. The tuberous begonias we know today have a most spectacular range of colour, form and size of flowers. While being frost tender, with reasonable care and thought they can provide a spectacular display through summer and autumn in our climate.

There are two main types worth growing: the tall, large, double-flowered type with flowers resembling a large camellia or rose, many with ruffled edges; and the multiflora non-stop type which has many smaller single, semi-double or double flowers for several months. Flowering can be prolonged by removing faded flowers regularly.

Tubers of named cultivars and unnamed seedlings of both types are available from specialist growers from winter to early spring or as potted plants in many local garden centres in late spring.

Tubers should be started in small pots or trays in a frost-free area in late September in a coarse free-draining mix and kept damp without waterlogging. Begonias develop roots all round the tuber so potting mix can just cover the tuber to encourage a good root system. Tubers are planted with the hollow side up. As growth increases to 8 cm high repot into 15 cm pots. Do not use a large pot at this stage. Allow only one or two main stems to remain. Excess stems should be carefully removed and grown on as cuttings in sharp sand and peat. They will form small tubers for next season. In early December increase pot size to 20–30 cm and place in growing position in an open area free from harsh sun and wind but where there will be air circulation to prevent mildew and other fungal problems.

Tuberous begonias will grow underneath trees, or hanging in trees, on the south or south–east side of the house, on patios or in a shade house where the only direct sun they receive is early morning sun. Glasshouses can be too hot in summer and likewise if the sun shines directly through, windows can be detrimental.

Smaller non-stop tuberous begonias can be planted into the garden as an attractive border plant in semi-shaded positions. Normally these do not require additional support, particularly if grown close together. Protect them from snails and slugs.

Larger flowering plants will grow taller and require small stakes and ties to support them and stop them being blown over. On larger types remove the smaller side buds of each flower spike and leave the larger centre male bud for an increase in flower size. Face the leaves to the front at all times as this is where most flowers appear and face.

For best results use a good quality free-draining slightly acidic mix. Do not overwater at any time, as this will quickly rot the fine hair-like roots which grow from the tubers. Use a three-month slow release fertiliser high in potash at final potting stage and apply a soluble seaweed or fish emulsion fortnightly until April.

By mid-April reduce watering and return plants to a frost-free area to die down. Stems will fall off as growth stops and then tubers may be removed from the soil and placed in a tray with a little dry potting mix. Place the tray in a plastic bag and store in a frost-free area until next spring when the process can be repeated.

Bluebells see *Hyacinthoides*

Brodiaea syn. Ipheion. Looking rather like a miniature agapanthus but with leaves that generally die away at or before flowering, brodiaeas need to be massed in a group to be seen at their best. The one usually available is 'Queen Fabiola'. Umbels of deep blue flowers are held on 45 cm stems. Easily grown in full sun, preferably in light soil with good drainage. Plant 6 cm deep and 7 cm apart.

Bulbinella floribunda (Cat's Tail). Long lasting, yellow flowers in late winter, early spring. Many flowers on a poker-type stem. A fibrous-rooted plant that can be divided when dormant (November–December). Replant with the crown at soil level being careful not to let the roots dry while out of the ground. Water

Brodiaea californica

well during the growing and flowering period. Tolerates light shade.

Calla lily see *Zantedeschia*

Canna. Summer–autumn flowers on stems up to 2 m high, largely in reds, pinks and yellows and including bicolours. Easily propagated by division of the fleshy rhizomes in late winter. Replant with the rhizome just below soil level. Likes a light soil with a high humus content and should be kept moist in hot weather. Foliage is frost sensitive. There are many hybrids.

Chionodoxa (Glory of the snow). Early spring flowering bulb with spikes up to 15 cm in blue, white and pink. It flowers best if left undisturbed. Propagation is by division of the clumps, planting 5–10 cm deep in clumps in early autumn. *C. luciliae* and *C. gigantea* are suitable for Canberra. Will tolerate light shade.

Clivia (Kaffir lily). Red, orange, yellow or cream flowers in spring on spikes of 40–50 cm. Suitable for pot culture or for a sheltered position in the garden in cold climates. Can be disappointing in the open Canberra garden. Normally propagated by offsets but seeds will flower in two years. Bulbs should be planted in autumn about

50 cm apart with the crown clear of the soil. Divide only when overcrowded.

Colchicum (Autumn crocus, Meadow saffron, Naked boys). Crocus-like flowers to 30 cm mainly in pink, white, lilac and bicolours. The common name varies from place to place. Corms should be planted in clumps 5–8 cm deep in January with 10–15 cm between each. Propagation is by division of the clumps which should be done only when plants show signs of deterioration e.g. fewer flowers and poor foliage. They do best in a sunny sheltered position but will tolerate light shade. Suitable for pot culture. Good value in Canberra.

Convallaria majalis (Lily of the valley). Highly perfumed spring flowers in pink or white. Flower spikes 5–15 cm make an excellent small cut flower. Propagation is by division of the clumps and this should be done in autumn, replanting the crowns 5 cm below the surface and 15 cm apart. They do best in a cool partly shaded position. Do not disturb for 4–5 years. A top dressing of about 2 cm of well-rotted manure each winter will give good results. Suitable for pots. Can become a weed in time if not kept under control.

Crocosmia x crocosmiiflora (Montbretia). Summer flowers in orange and yellow on 60–120 cm wiry stems, resembling small gladioli. They make good cut flowers. Plant corms 10 cm deep and 15 cm apart in early winter. Corms increase rapidly in average garden soil but can be left 3–4 years before lifting and dividing. The species can become a weed but there are a few attractive hybrids worth growing —- 'Citronella', usually only available from specialist bulb suppliers, 'Emily McKenzie', 'Lucifer' and 'Solfatare'.

Crocus. Among the first of the spring flowering corms although there are some excellent autumn flowering species. Available in a wide range of colours with flower stems 15–30 cm. Plant in clumps in February–March, 8–10 cm deep with a similar spacing. Suitable for pots.

Cyclamen. This is a delightful group of tuberous dwarf plants that are particularly attractive under deciduous trees and shrubs. While the flowers in white, pinks and red are beautiful in their own right, cyclamens could also be grown for the excellent foliage shapes and markings. Flowering times vary from autumn through to spring. A key consideration is to ensure that the plants are not overgrown by taller more vigorous plants.

C. coum, a winter flowering species in shades of pink, is readily available and easily grown. However, it does not spread as easily or rapidly as C. hederifolium.

C. hederifolium, in white through to various shades of pink, is easy to grow in shade or partial shade and is now readily available in Australia. This species self-seeds reasonably freely to form a carpet after a while.

C. graecum is a pink autumn flowered species with shiny foliage. A hot, dry summer period is required for this species so it would perhaps be best placed in a dry rock garden. It may not flower in the first season.

C. repandum is a rich pink spring flowering species for partial shade.

All will multiply from self-sown seed or seed can be collected from all species when ripe (usually December). Grown in pots outside they will usually flower in three years.

Daffodil see Narcissus

Dahlia. One of Canberra's best plants for flower production. Summer–autumn flowers in an extensive colour range and in many flower forms. Bushes range in height from 1 m. They thrive in a well-drained, sunny position sheltered from strong winds. Soil should be prepared in early spring about six weeks before planting; dig in liberal quantities of well-rotted compost and give a dressing of lime. Fertiliser should not be necessary until the plant is approaching the budding stage.

Plant tubers in October– November or green plants (taken from tip cuttings) towards the end of November. Plants should be about 75 cm apart.

A Canberra-grown dahlia seedling called 'Darbro Marianne'.

It is important that the taller growing cultivars be staked and tied at regular intervals; bedding types do not require staking. Drive in hardwood stakes at the required spacing before planting. Tubers should be planted 8–10 cm deep with the growth eye of the tuber about 5 cm from the stake. Providing the soil was reasonably moist at planting time, it should not be necessary to water again until the plants have emerged from the

Eranthis, or winter aconite, is one of the lesser known bulbs. It flowers in Canberra's early spring.

A bench top display of Canberra-grown dahlias at Lanyon.

ground. One good watering a week should keep them growing strongly until the budding stage.

Pinch out the centre of the plant just above the third set of leaves to encourage a good framework for the plant. When approaching the flowering stage some disbudding will improve the quality of the flowers. Blooms allowed to develop on the plant should be removed as soon as they are spent, cutting back to the last lateral which has been allowed to remain.

Dahlias are excellent cut flowers if picked and handled correctly. Make sure the flowers have reached full development before picking. Always pick the flowers in the evening and leave in a bucket of water overnight before arranging.

In the early spring dig the clumps that have died down over winter (the tops can be removed after the frosts have dried them off). Gently hose off the soil and divide them for later planting. They are best divided with the aid of secateurs and a knife. Notice that the growth eyes are on the crown and not on the tuber proper. Take care that each tuber has at least one eye and also not to break the neck of the tuber.

Dahlias are relatively free from pests and diseases. They can be susceptible to powdery mildew late in the growing season and are sometimes attacked by aphids.

Dierama (Wand Flower, Fairy Fishing Rods). Summer flowering on 90–180 cm stems in colours of white, pink or maroon. As the flowers open the flower spike arches over and the bell shaped flowers hang in a single row on the lower side.

> *D. pulcherrimum* (a taller species up to 180 cm) makes a graceful garden decoration in colder climates.

Dierama may be propagated by division of clumps or from seed, which takes two to three years to flower. Plant new corms in groups 10 cm deep and 15 cm apart in early winter.

Endymion see *Hyacinthoides*

Eranthis (Winter aconite). Yellow buttercup flowers on 10–15 cm stems in early spring. Plant the tuberous roots in January–February about 8 cm deep and 10 cm apart. Plants should be out of the ground for as short a period as possible. Leave undisturbed for as long as possible as the tubers take a year or more to establish. They will self-seed in good growing conditions.

Erythronium (Dog's tooth violet, Trout lily). Does best in shade or partial shade in soil containing plenty of organic matter. Requires adequate moisture at all times. Plant in groups 8 cm deep and 10 cm apart in autumn.

> *E. hendersonii* in lilac grows to 40 cm and *E. oregonum* with white-cream flowers and mottled leaves are attractive garden plants. 'White Beauty' is thought to be a hybrid of this species.

Propagation of erythroniums is usually by division of the bulbs in autumn but seeds germinate readily and flower in about 4–5 years.

Erythronium citrinum, a dog's tooth violet.

The pineapple lily now comes in a lovely pink form as well as this traditional green and white.

Eucomis (Pineapple lily). Creamy green flowers in summer on 30–45 cm stems. Bulbs are planted in winter with the top of the bulb at about soil level and 30 cm apart in rich soil and full sun. Provide ample water during the growing season.

> *E. bicolour* has green petals edged or suffused with purple.

> *E. comosa* has creamy green flowers with a distinct pink flush with the ovary turning purple as the flower matures.

Eucomis are suitable for pot culture and are good for cut flowers. Propagation is by division of offsets in winter

Freesia refracta (and many hybrids). Small spring flowering bulbs with a strong fragrance. Available in many colours with some hybrids having stems up to 50 cm. They require a warm position with some protection from severe frost. Plant corms 5 cm deep in clumps with 5–8 cm between corms. Divide only when overcrowded. Excellent cut flowers.

Fritillaria. A group that consists of many species with attractive bell-shaped flowers borne in a small cluster at or near the top of the unbranched stem. Unfortunately many of

A well established clump of *Fritillaria meleagris*, the Snake's head fritillaria.

these are not readily available in Australia and of those that are easily obtained not all are easy to grow. Fritillaria do best in well-drained soil and should be left undisturbed for as long as possible.

F. acmopetala grows to 45 cm, has green bells with a brown interior. It prefers a semi-shaded position and is relatively easy to grow.

F. imperialis (Crown imperial) with its tall spires (up to 150 cm) of orange or yellow bells is without doubt the most spectacular member of the family. It is best planted with a layer of coarse sand around the bulb to help prevent rotting. It is also advisable to keep it as dry as possible over the summer dormant period.

F. meleagris (Snake's head) has flower stems up to 30 cm. This species is good for growing in a perennial border, as it needs to be kept moist over summer. The white and reddish-purple chequered petals are attractive and unusual in the bulb world. *F. meleagris* is slow to increase naturally but can be grown readily from fresh seed and can be expected to flower in 2–3 years.

F. pontica is one of the easiest species to grow. Stems of 45 cm carry green-tipped brown bells. This species requires semi-shade for best results.

Galanthus (Snowdrops). These generally flower from early winter. Flowers are white with green tips on the inner petals. Stems are short (10–20 cm). Propagation is by division or by seed (which takes up to five years to flower). Division is best undertaken in late spring or autumn and bulbs should not be held out of the ground for any significant length of time. Plant bulbs 8–10 cm deep in clumps for best results. All the spring flowering species require regular water.

Galanthus flowering in mid-August.

G. caucasicus is a nice winter flowering species with relatively large flowers. *G. elwesii* is similar.

G. nivalis is sometimes hard to find, but worth the effort, as are its named cultivars.

G. reginae-olgae is an autumn flowered species that likes a drier sunny spot in the garden. The flowers appear before the leaves.

Galtonia candicans (Cape hyacinth). A summer flowering bulb with many fragrant white flowers on stems up to 120 cm. Plant in clumps in winter 5–10 cm deep and 20–25 cm apart.

Leave undisturbed until overcrowded. Propagate it by division of bulbs but it can also be grown from seed, taking one to two years to flower. Will tolerate light shade, but likes good drainage. Snails love it.

Gladiolus. Modern gladioli hybrids come in a wide range of colours. Spikes may exceed a metre but the shorter stemmed types are best for most uses and are less susceptible to damage by strong winds. Plant corms 10–12 cm deep and 15–20 cm apart.

Gladioli are best lifted about six weeks after flowering while the leaves are still green, when the small cormlets are still attached to the original corm. Avoid leaving cormlets in the soil as these will invariably grow and become a nuisance. The cormlets can be replanted in spring and will reach flowering size in 2–3 years.

Although the modern hybrids form the basis of the cut flower gladiolus collection, many of the lesser known species are available and are well worth growing. These include *G. byzantium* which has 60 cm magenta flower spikes, *G. colvillii* and *G. nanus* are in a range of colours and *G. tristis* has perfumed cream flower spikes up to 60 cm. *G. natalensis* has orange flowers in winter.

Gladiolus thrip is a serious pest of gladioli and a few other plants, attacking the foliage, flowers and corm which can be damaged during storage. The corms become sticky, hard and scaly and the young root buds may be injured. The pale-coloured varieties don't show the effects as badly. To control the pest, regular sprays of insecticide are required from the time when the shoots are about 20 cm high. The best method of control is to store the dormant bulbs in a cold area; dip them in an insecticide before replanting.

Gloriosa (Climbing lily, Flame lily). A lily with tendrils at the tips of the long tapering leaves which grows to 120 cm or more in very good conditions. Plant in October with the top of the tubers horizontal and 5–8 cm below the soil. Flowers in shades of red, orange and yellow are produced near the ends of the branches in summer. A support frame such as that used for sweet peas is needed. Plants die down soon after flowering and should be kept dry in the dormant period. *G. rothschildiana* is the showiest species with broad crimson flower segments, yellow at the base. *G. superba* is also a good species with long narrow segments of orange and red.

Divide tubers in spring, making sure each piece has an eye to shoot from. Can be grown from seed but this will take three to four years to flower.

Grape hyacinth see Muscari

Hemerocallis (Day lily). Hardy, summer flowering, with flowers in a wide range of colours on stems 60–120 cm. Spikes provide a succession of individual flowers each of which lasts only one day. Divide the clumps every few years in late winter to early spring. Tolerates partial shade. Some are evergreen, others may die back completely in winter.

Hippeastrum. Spring flowering bulb with up to four large flowers on strong 30–60 cm stems. Hybridisation has provided a wide colour range, often striped or mottled. Plant in humus-rich soil in winter with the neck of the bulb above the soil. They will tolerate light shade, make excellent cut flowers and are very good for pot culture. Protect against snails in spring. Divide after they die down.

Hosta (Plantain lily). Grown more for the attractive broad foliage than for the short-lived flowers that appear in spring and summer. They come in a wide range of leaf colours and textures, some variegated. Divide large clumps after the foliage dies down in winter, replanting with the crown of the plant at soil level and 30–50 cm apart. Best grown in semi-shade. They need a rich moist soil for best results. Hostas are particularly susceptible to attack by snails. The grey leafed ones are less susceptible. Copper strips surrounding pots or a heaped circle of coffee grounds will act as a barrier.

Hyacinthoides (Bluebells). Hardy bulbs suited to growing among shrubs or for naturalising in partial shade. They flower in mid to late spring on 30 cm stems mostly in blue, but white and pink forms are also available. Plant bulbs 5–8 cm deep in autumn. They multiply readily to form large clumps. *H. non-scripta* (English bluebell) is smaller than *H. hispanica* (Spanish bluebell) and less commonly grown. Propagation is by division in autumn or any time after flowering.

Hyacinthus (Hyacinth). Popular spring flowering bulb available in a wide range of colours. Highly perfumed flowers on spikes of 20–30 cm. Plant 10–15 cm deep and 15 cm apart in late summer. Bulbs should be lifted each year after the leaves yellow in December. Good for cut flowers and suitable for container culture. Apart from the many hybrids grown for garden display there are a number of species which are excellent specimens but, unfortunately, are very difficult to obtain.

Bulbs seldom last more than two seasons. It is better in Canberra to replace them rather than try to propagate.

Hymenocallis (Spider lily, Ismene). White/cream summer flowers on 50–70 cm stems. Plant in early spring with the neck of the bulb at soil level. For best effect they can be grown in clumps with the bulbs 20 cm apart.

> *H. narcissiflora* is the most popular species grown with a few very fragrant white flowers.
>
> *H x festalis* is a vigorous hybrid with fragrant white flowers. Propagate by dividing the clumps in late autumn. Well suited to pot culture.

Ipheion uniflorum syn Tritelia (Spring star). Small white, blue or mid violet flowers carried on 15 cm stems in spring. Leaves have a pungent smell when bruised. Plant 5 cm deep and a similar distance apart in autumn. Its low growth habit makes it suitable for large rock gardens, borders and containers. Can be left undisturbed for 4–5 years. Tolerates partial shade. Can be invasive.

Iris See the Iris Chapter

Ismene see Hymenocallis

Ixia (African corn lily) Delightful spring flowering corms with small, star-shaped flowers on a wiry, unbranched 30–60 cm stem. Fragrant flowers in a wide range of colours. Slightly frost sensitive. Plant corms in autumn 5–8 cm deep and 8 cm apart in a light well drained soil. A good cut flower and suitable for growing in containers. Propagate by division in autumn.

Kniphofia (Red hot poker, Torch lily). An evergreen plant with a number of species and many hybrids from which to choose. The result is that there are kniphofias available for flowering in all seasons. The traditional colours are red and/or yellow but hybridisation has given a wide range of pastel colours as well as plants from 50 cm to more than 150 cm in height. Propagate before the new growth commences by dividing the clumps every 3 years or so; you can take to the clumps with an axe and it won't do any lasting harm. Plants should be set about 50 cm apart. Because the long strap-like leaves can become unsightly they are best cut back to near ground level before the new season's growth commences. Watch for mealy bugs around the neck of the clump and if necessary spray with horticultural oil.

Kniphofias come in a range of colours from yellows to red.

Lachenalia (Cape cowslip, Soldier boys). Spring flowering bulbs on 20–30 cm stems, available in yellow/red, mauve, purple and pink/red. They prefer a rich well-drained soil in full sun. Propagation is by offsets which should be planted in autumn, 8–10 cm deep and 5–10 cm apart. Replant only when overcrowded, choosing the plumpest bulbs for best floral effect. More suitable for container cultivation. Not easy to grow in the open garden in Canberra.

Lapeirousia laxa (Scarlet freesia). Early summer flowering bulb with small scarlet or white flowers carried on 15–25 cm stems. Plant corms in full sun or semi-shade in autumn 5 cm deep and 2–5 cm apart to achieve a massed effect. Needs protection from heavy frosts. Suitable for growing in pots. Propagation is by seed which reaches flowering size in 2 years. Lapeirousia will self-seed but not so much as to become a major pest.

Leucojum (Snowflakes). Similar to galanthus (Snowdrops) but with coarser, daffodil-like foliage and taller flower spikes ending with a few pendulous flowers. They are gross feeders. Flowers white, tipped green, drooping and bell-shaped. Plant 5–10 cm deep and a similar distance apart in clumps for best effect. Propagation is usually by bulb offsets. Tolerates light shade.

L. aestivum is late winter to early spring flowering on 45–60 cm spikes.

Lilium. A large genus containing many large showy species with sweetly scented, often richly coloured flowers on stems usually over 1 m. Dwarf species on stems of 30–90 cm are also available. Most liliums grow exceptionally well in cool climates. Lilium bulbs have fleshy overlapping scales and should not remain out of the ground for any longer than necessary. Bulbs should be left undisturbed for years but may be lifted and divided when the tops die down. At transplanting the roots should not be damaged or allowed to dry out. April to July is the normal planting period. Liliums do best in a rich, very well-drained soil (drainage is most important).

Liliums do very well in Canberra. This is one of the Asiatic lilies, which flower in November/December. They are an easy-care pot plant.

Most of the choice garden varieties are stem rooting, that is, they produce roots on the flowering stem between the top of the bulb and the soil level. These varieties should be planted 15–20 cm deep. Other cultivars that root from the base of the bulb should be planted 5–10 cm deep. The taller growing varieties should be spaced 45 cm apart while the smaller varieties can be grown closer together.

Liliums prefer a cool root run but flower best in full sun. Surface mulching with compost or well-rotted manure is beneficial. Stakes for the taller varieties should be put in at the same time as you plant the bulbs to ensure the feeding roots are not damaged.

Most varieties flower between November and February. Spent flowers should be removed regularly (unless you want to propagate from seed). They make good cut flowers but take care when handling them as fresh pollen can stain clothes.

Propagate liliums by dividing clumps after they have died down, growing on the bulbils (or bulblets) produced by some species at the leaf axils or by striking the bulb scales (see specialist literature for more details).

Apart from the many hybrids which form the basis of most garden plantings, many of the species from which these are bred are readily available and well worth growing. The catalogues of specialist suppliers contain good descriptions of these together with helpful growing hints.

Lycoris (Spider lily). Autumn flowering bulbs very similar to the Nerines. Clusters of flowers on 30–45 cm stems. Readily available in red (*L. radiata*) and yellow (*L. aurea*) forms but pink (*L. squamigera*) is also available at times. They thrive in partial shade and prefer some protection from severe frosts. Plant bulbs twice their length deep and 10 cm apart in winter. Good cut flowers and suitable for growing in pots. Propagation is by careful division of the bulbs but they dislike disturbance so division should only be carried out when plants are overcrowded.

Montbretia see Crocosmia

Moraea (Peacock iris) Native to Africa and quite easy to grow in any well-drained soil in a sunny position. Two popular species are *M. aristata*, pastel blue with peacock eyes of deep blue-violet; and *M. villosa*, usually blue or pink with iridescent eye markings. Both grow to 30 cm. Plant in autumn. Flowers in spring.

Muscari (Grape hyacinth). Short spikes of fragrant small flowers carried in grape-like clusters. Early spring flowers in blue, white, violet and yellow. Plant bulbs in clumps in autumn, 10 cm deep and 10 cm apart. Tolerates light shade. Suitable for growing in containers. The disadvantage with muscari is that they have lush leaf growth compared to the relatively short flower spikes. Propagation is by division although most will multiply by seed.

M. armeniacum is the most commonly available species and the selection "Blue Spike" with sterile, double, blue flowers is worth seeking out.

M. azureum is a bright blue with shorter leaves.

M. botryoides in pale blue or white forms also has shorter leaves and flowers later than most Muscari.

For something different, *M. macrocarpum* with perfumed bright yellow flowers is worth a position in the garden. This species can be a little difficult to find but is available from time to time.

One of the muscari family.

Narcissus

Spring flowering bulbs with many species and a vast number of hybrids for garden cultivation. They are available in a range of colours with white, yellow or apricot outer petals and cups of white, yellow, red, orange, apricot and pink. Height of the flower stem varies from a few centimetres to more than 60 cm according to the variety and growing conditions. They make excellent pot plants.

Narcissus are hardy and can be grown in a range of situations but prefer a well drained soil rich in organic material. Full sun is important in the growing period but some shade or a mulch in the dormant period is beneficial. They benefit from a complete fertiliser, rich in potash and low in nitrogen. Slow release fertilisers (provided they have low nitrogen content) are excellent as nutrients are available to the plant throughout the growth cycle.

Plant the bulbs in autumn after the worst of the hot weather has passed. Depth of planting depends on the size of the bulb. As a general guide the bulb should be covered by soil twice the length of the bulb (measured from the base to the start of the neck). In practice, this means from about 5 cm for small bulbs to 12–15 cm for large bulbs. Spacing also depends on size but generally 10–20 cm will be required. They look best in clumps.

Propagation is usually by division of bulbs. Seed germinates readily and reaches flowering size in 3 to 8 years depending on the species.

Lift and replant about every four years. Bulbs should not be lifted until the foliage has died

A hoop-petticoat daffodil, easy to grow in Canberra.

down (about early December) — do not cut or tie the foliage for the sake of tidiness as next year's flowers are dependent on healthy foliage throughout this year's growing season. Bulbs should be dried in a cool, airy situation out of the sun and then cleaned of soil and the outer loose dry tunics and shrivelled leaves. The bulbs are then stored in an airy situation.

There has been much progress in the development of new *Narcissus* hybrids and a recommended list would soon be out of date. Well known varieties such as King Alfred, Ansett, Ceylon and Fortune, while still providing colour in many gardens, have been superseded by varieties that provide the same colour but have greater texture, thus giving better value in the harsh weather often experienced in spring.

Apart from the very extensive range of named hybrids of the commonly grown trumpet or cup types available from specialist growers, many of the lesser grown species and hybrids are also available and are worth growing in their own right. These include:

N. bulbocodium (the Hoop-petticoat daffodil) is a dwarf species with small pale primrose to rich gold flowers consisting mainly of the greatly enlarged funnel-shaped cup or trumpet with very insignificant narrow perianth segments. Flowers are borne singly on stems up to 10 cm. Does well in a hot dry summer location.

N. cyclamineus has small blooms consisting of a long narrow trumpet with the petals reflexed back like cyclamen petals. Stems usually 20 cm or less. This species should be kept moist at all times of the year.

A fine clump of *Narcissus cyclamineus*.

N. jonquilla has clusters of 1 to 6 very fragrant flowers.

N. poeticus has a single fragrant flower with white petals and a yellow or green cup edged with red or orange. Usually very late flowering.

N. tazetta and hybrids of tazetta origin have bunches of very sweetly scented flowers, usually with a yellow cup. Many of these flower before the majority of Narcissus and are often incorrectly called jonquils.

N. triandrus is a dwarf species with drooping flowers (one to six per stem). The cup is bowl shaped and the petals usually reflexed. This species must be kept cool and dry over summer.

Nerine. An autumn flowering bulb that is excellent for both cut flowers and garden display. Clusters of red, pink or white flowers on 30–60 cm stems. Propagation is usually by division of the bulbs in the dormant period. This can be either summer or winter, depending on the species. Propagation can also be carried out by twin scaling but this would only be used if large numbers are required.

Nerines flower best when left undisturbed and a bit crowded.

Replant the bulbs about 15 cm apart with the neck of the bulb above ground level and leave undisturbed for as long as possible as nerines will often not flower for a year or two after transplanting; they like to be part of the crowd.

> *N. bowdenii* with soft pink flowers in mid autumn is an easy and rewarding species to grow.

> *N. filifolia* with its grass-like leaves and short, dainty, pink flowers is a gem for its late summer flowers. It has a winter dormancy period.

> *N. sarniensis* (the Guernsey lily) with strong red flowers is another gem worth growing.

There are also a number of good hybrids including 'Fothergillii major' and 'Salmonia'.

Ornithogalum (Star of Bethlehem). Spring flowering bulb with stems of 15–60 cm. Flowers usually white, sometimes combined with green centres or stripes. Plant in autumn 10–15 cm deep and 15 cm apart. Will tolerate light shade. Propagation is by division of the bulbs which can multiply quite rapidly in the more dwarf species.

> *O. thyrsoides* (Chincherinchee), a summer flowering species, is a particularly good cut flower.

> *O. umbellatum* is less desirable as a cut flower because it closes at night. It can also be a pest as it multiplies rapidly.

> *O. reverchonii* is perhaps the most desirable species but is very difficult to find in Australia.

Polygonatum (Solomon's seal). White flowers with green tips carried on arching 60–90 cm stems. The spring flowers hang on the underside of the stems with the leaves on the upper surface. Plant 5–8 cm deep, 25–30 cm apart in autumn or winter. They prefer a cool shady position. The foliage dies down in autumn and care should be taken when tidying up as the fleshy roots are very shallow. Good cut flower.

Ranunculus asiaticus. Spring flowers on 30–45 cm stems in a wide range of colours. Plant in a rich well drained soil in autumn, about 5 cm deep with the claws down and about 15 cm apart. They benefit from regular applications of liquid fertiliser from the time the flower buds first appear. The tuberous roots can be lifted when the foliage dies down in early summer and stored for replanting in autumn. Alternatively, in view of the potential losses in storage and the relatively low cost of the tubers, they can be discarded after flowering and new stock bought the following season. Suitable for cut flowers.

Rhodohypoxis. A delightful little plant producing masses of flowers in summer. Available in white, red and shades of pink with flower stems up to 10 cm tall. Plant the corms in autumn about 2 cm below the surface and about the same distance apart. They will tolerate sun or partial shade and because of their miniature nature they are often grown in pots. If grown in the ground ensure that they are not overgrown by nearby plants. Perfect for small rockeries.

Scilla (Squill). Blue, pink or white flowered spring flowering bulbs with 10–20 cm stems. Plant the bulbs 5–8 cm deep in autumn and a similar distance apart. Propagation is by bulb division. They are not fussy as to soil but prefer a spot where they get winter sun. They can be left several years before division.

> *S. bifolia* with blue, pink and white forms makes a nice display under deciduous trees or shrubs.

> *S. peruviana* requires a hot, sunny spot in summer to give best results.

> *S. verna* is a charming little bulb to 10 cm that could be grown to advantage in the rock garden or in a pot.

Snowdrops see *Galanthus*

Sparaxis (Harlequin flower). Showy freesia-like flowers on 30–40 cm stems in spring in various colours. Plant the corms in autumn 5–8 cm deep and about 10 cm apart. Propagation is by division of the corms in autumn. Will tolerate light shade. Suitable for containers.

Sprekelia formosissima (Jacobean lily). Summer flowering bulb of considerable beauty. The crimson flowers are carried singly on 30–40 cm stems. Plant bulbs with the neck at soil level and about 15 cm apart. Bulbs may be lifted and stored over winter if desired but it is better to leave them undisturbed until they become overcrowded. Propagation is by

division of clumps in late autumn. They are well-suited to container culture.

Sternbergia lutea (Autumn crocus). Bright, yellow, crocus-like autumn flowers on 15–30 cm stems. The foliage will remain green throughout winter and the bulbs become dormant at the end of spring. Plant bulbs 8–10 cm deep in groups 10–12 cm apart in January or February in a position that is normally hot and dry in summer. They will, however, flower satisfactorily if they get some water in the dormant period. Propagation is by division of the clumps while dormant. *S. sicula* is a smaller version of *S. lutea*.

Tigridia pavonia (Tiger flower, Jockey caps). Free-flowering bulbs with large vivid flowers on 30–60 cm stems; flowers appear in summer and autumn. Each flower lasts only one day but each stem produces a succession of blooms over a considerable period. Available in many colours. Lift in autumn, after the leaves die down, if division is necessary. Otherwise they may be left in the ground until overcrowded. Plant the corms from May to August, 5–10 cm deep and 15 cm apart. Propagation is by division, or from seed which takes only one or two years to reach flowering size.

Trillium (Wake Robin). This attractive plant does best in a rich moist soil in partial shade, mulched over the summer months. Flowers, generally in shades of pink, crimson, purple and white, are carried on up to 45 cm stems in spring. Rhizomes should be planted in autumn 5–10 cm deep depending on size and left to form clumps. Propagation is normally by division of the clumps. Production from seed is possible, but as seedlings will take 5–6 years to reach flowering size this is only for patient people.

T. grandiflorum with white flowers that slowly change to shades of pink is an attractive species worth a place in the garden. Other species are available from time to time.

Tulipa (Tulip). Spring flowering bulbs in a wide range with stems of 30–50 cm. Plant in late autumn (after mid-May) with the top of the bulbs 5–8 cm below the surface and 10–15 cm apart in a sunny well drained position. Mulch to keep cool. Planted at this time in Canberra you won't need to worry about chilling in the crisper as recommended in most guides although chilling tulips for a few weeks before planting can help in the production of longer-stemmed, larger blooms. Tulips are one of very few spring flowering bulbs which will benefit from occasional small amounts of a complete fertiliser during the growing period before flowering. Tulips are best planted in pots in a shady position until growth appears and then moved into a sunny position. Bulbs may abort flowers already formed if they become too warm. They should be fed again after flowering and lifted each year, once the leaves yellow, and stored in a cool, dry spot. Bulbs should be checked for any build-up of pests. Any that are soft should be discarded to keep remaining bulbs disease free.

Apart from the hybrids which appear every year for Floriade, there are a number of Tulipa species, ideal for rock gardens, which are available from specialist bulb growers. These are smaller tulips well worth growing in our climate. Many have the ability to multiply and to continue to flower when left in the ground.

T. aucherana Small starry pink flowers with a yellow centre.

T. batalinii A slender plant to 30 cm with flowers in the yellow to bronze colour range.

T. clusiana (the Lady Tulip) A very easy species to grow, white flowers are pink on the outer petals. The cultivar 'Cynthia' is yellow with deep pink outer petals and is highly recommended.

T. greigii Leaves of this species are always marked heavily with purple and the large flowers, usually in glowing shades of red, are held on short stems. A clump makes a strong impact.

T. fosteriana is similar to *T. greigii* but has shining green foliage. Many named cultivars are available.

T. praestans is a small plant with clusters of bright red flowers rather than the usual single flower to a stem. 'Fusilier' is a good cultivar.

Watsonia (Bugle lily). An easily grown bulb in a range of colours on stems 50–150 cm tall. Most flower in October–November but the near evergreen types flower in summer and autumn. Plant the corms in clumps 8–10 cm deep and 15–20 cm apart. Lift and divide clumps only when overcrowded. Excellent cut flowers. Some excellent hybrids are readily available and some species are available from time to time. *W. aletroides*, *W. marginata* and *W. beatricis* are worth growing in cold climates. Propagation is by division.

Zantedeschia (Arum lily, Calla lily). Spring and summer flowering in a wide range of colours. *Z. aethiopica* with large white spathes on 90 cm stems is the most commonly grown species. It does best in a moist to wet location and division of the clumps should be carried out in autumn. 'Green Goddess' with its largely green spathes is a popular form of *Z. aethiopica. Z. elliottiana* is a yellow form with white blotches on the leaves. *Z. pentlandii* is similar but generally regarded as superior to *Z. elliottiana. Z. rehmannii* with pink spathes is worth a place in the garden. Propagation is by division of the rhizomes which are then replanted 10–15 cm deep and 30–40 cm apart. The summer flowering species can be divided, when necessary, in early spring.

Zephyranthes (Zephyr flower). Dainty small flowers carried singly on 15–30 cm stems, several flowers to a bulb. *Z. candida* is a very hardy species with white crocus-like flowers on 15–20 cm stems in summer and autumn. Zephyranthes should be planted in clumps when dormant, 5–10 cm deep and 10 cm apart. They prefer a light sandy soil rich in humus. Replant only when overcrowded. Propagation is by division of the clumps. Suitable for containers.

A quick guide to some good bulbous species for Canberra

Name & common name	Planting season	Plant		Flowering season
		cm deep	cm apart	
Allium (Onion Flower)	Autumn	8	10	Late spring and Summer
Alstroemeria (Peruvian Lily)	Autumn - winter	10–12	30	Late spring and Summer
Amaryllis (Belladonna Lily)	Late autumn - winter	Neck at soil level	25	Late summer – early autumn
Anemone	Autumn	3–5	20	Spring
Babiana (Baboon Flower)	Autumn	15–20	10	Late spring
Bulbinella	Nov – Dec	Crown at soil level	In groups	Late winter & early spring
Canna	Winter – early spring	5	50	Summer & autumn
Chionodoxa (Glory of the Snow)	Early autumn	5–10	10	Early spring
Clivia (Kaffir Lily)	Autumn	Crown clear of soil	50	Late spring
Colchicum (Autumn Crocus)	January	5–8	10	Autumn
Convallaria majalis (Lily of the Valley)	Winter	5	15	Spring
Crocosmia (Monbretia)	Early winter	10	15	Summer
Crocus	Feb-March	5	10	Spring
Cyclamen	Late summer to autumn	9	In groups	Autumn to spring, depending on variety
Dahlia	Oct – Nov	8–10	75	Autumn

A quick guide to some good bulbous species for Canberra

Name & common name	Planting season	Plant		Flowering season
		cm deep	cm apart	
Dierama (Wand Flower)	Early winter	10	15	Summer
Eranthis (Winter aconite)	Jan-Feb	8	10	Early spring
Erythronium (Dog's tooth violet)	Autumn	8	10	Spring
Eucomis (Pineapple lily)	Winter	Top at soil level	30	Summer
Freesia refracta	Autumn	5	5–8	Spring
Fritillaria	Autumn	10	30	Spring
Galanthus (Snowdrops)	Autumn	8–10	Clumps	Spring
Galtonia candicans (Cape hyacinth)	Winter	5–10	20–25	Summer
Gladiolus	Spring to Dec	10–12	15–20	Summer – Autumn
Gloriosa (Climbing lily)	Oct	5–8	30	Summer
Hemerocallis (Day lily)	Autumn – winter	10	30	Summer
Hippeastrum	Winter	Neck above soil	30–40	Spring
Hosta (Plantain lily)	Winter	Crown at soil level	30–50	Spring & summer
Hyacinthoides (Bluebell)	Autumn	5–8	Clumps	Spring
Hyacinthus (hyacinth)	Late Summer	10–15	15	Spring
Hymenocallis (Spider lily)	Early spring	Neck at soil level	20, in clumps	Late summer
Ipheion uniflorum (Spring star)	Autumn	5	5	Early spring
Iris, Bearded	Early December	Top just above soil	40–50	Late spring
Iris, Japanese	Autumn	Top at soil level	30–40	Early summer
Iris, Louisiana	Late summer	5–8	30–50	Late spring
Iris, Californian	May – June	Just below soil level	40	Late spring
Iris, Siberica	Late winter	Crown just below soil	40	Late spring
Iris, Spuria	Autumn	3–5	40	Early summer
Iris, Stylosa	Early spring	2	40	Winter
Iris, Crested (I. Japonica)	Early December	Top just above soil	40–50	Ocotber
Iris, Dutch	Autumn	10–12	15	Mid-spring

A quick guide to some good bulbous species for Canberra

Name & common name	Planting season	Plant		Flowering season
		cm deep	cm apart	
Ixia (African Corn lily)	Autumn	5–8	8	Late spring
Kniphofia (Red hot poker)	Autumn – winter	10	50	Summer & autumn
Lachenalia (Cape cowslip)	Autumn	8–10	5–10	Spring
Lapeirousia laxa (Scarlet freesia)	Autumn	5	2–5	Early summer
Leucojum (Snowflake)	Mid-summer to autumn	5–10	5–10 in clumps	Late winter / early spring
Lilium	April – July	5–20 depending on variety	45 max, depending on variety	November – February
Lycoris (Spider lily)	Winter	Soil cover twice length of bulb	10	Autumn
Moraea (Peacock iris)	Autumn	5	5	Spring
Muscari (Grape hyacinth)	Autumn	10	10 in clumps	Early spring
Narcissus (Daffodils and Jonquils)	Autumn	Soil cover twice length of bulb	10–20 in clumps	Spring
Nerine (Spider lily)	Winter to early spring	Neck above ground	15	Autumn
Ornithogalum (Star of Bethlehem)	Autumn	10–15	15	Spring
Polygonatum (Solomon's Seal)	Autumn - winter	5–8	25–30	Spring
Ranunculus asiaticus	Autumn	5	15	Spring
Rhodohypoxis	Autumn	2	2	Summer
Scilla (Squill)	Autumn	5–8	5–8	Spring
Sparaxis (Harlequin flower)	Autumn	5–8	10	Spring
Sprekelia formosissima (Jacobean lily)	Late winter to early Spring	Neck at soil level	15	Summer
Sternbergia lutea (Autumn crocus)	Jan to Feb	8–10	10–12 in groups	Autumn
Tigridia pavonia (Tiger flower)	May – August	5–10	15	Summer and autumn
Trillium (Wake Robin)	Autumn	5–10	30	Spring
Tulipa (Tulip)	Late autumn	5–8	10–15	Spring

A quick guide to some good bulbous species for Canberra

Name & common name	Planting season	Plant		Flowering season
		cm deep	cm apart	
Watsonia (Bugle lily)	Autumn	8–10	15–20 in clumps	October – November
Zantedeschia (Arum lily, Calla lily)	Late autumn	10–15	30–40	Spring / summer
Zephyranthes (Zephyr flower)	Winter to early spring	5–10	10 in clumps	Autumn

CHAPTER 9: Irises

Glenn Sheldrick

Irises are one of the oldest plants in cultivation, found in texts, hieroglyphs and paintings dating back to antiquity. They are survivors and in times of water scarcity they have regained popularity, being amongst the hardiest, drought tolerant flowering plants in cultivation.

The genus is divided, according to growth habit, into three broad categories. These are bulbous, tuberous and rhizomatous. Only the rhizomatous and bulbous are in general cultivation and so will be dealt with here.

There are several specialist nurseries which supply a huge range of irises by mail order (colour catalogues or visit) and which are very reliable and reputable businesses.

All flowers in the Iris family have a basic form involving six petals. These come in two sets of three, called the standards and the falls. The standards were so named in the middle ages when this was a common term for a flag. They rise above the heart of the bloom like three small flags. The falls are so called because they 'fall' away from the heart of the flower like a small waterfall.

Bearded Iris (rhizomatous)

On each of the falls of a bearded iris, near the point where each joins the neck of the flower is a toothbrush-like section (the beard) which has colour qualities independent of the rest of the flower and which often adds character to the bloom.

This is a bearded iris named 'Beverley Sills'.

The bearded irises in cultivation have been developed over the last century or so with a number of related species used as the initial parents. The hybridisers' art is seen perhaps more clearly here than in any other modern plant family.

Bearded irises are grown from rhizomes (sections of stem) which run on or near the surface of the soil and produce a fan of flat, sword shaped leaves from the growing point. The leaves by themselves provide decorative greenery when flowering is finished.

Tall Bearded

These are the "Flag Lilies" that Grandma grew. If Grandma could only see the modern version — a colour range she never dreamed of!

Soil should be moderately rich, well drained and slightly alkaline. Most garden soils tend to be slightly acid and will benefit from the addition of a handful or two of dolomite to the square metre dug in thoroughly before planting the rhizomes.

After the new rhizome is separated from the main plant, trim off dead or broken roots with secateurs and trim the ends of the leaves to about 20-30 cm in an inverted 'V', leaving the centre leaves a little longer than the older outer leaves. Dying or badly damaged leaves should be removed as near to the stem as possible. If the plant has been out of the soil long enough to dehydrate (a week or longer) don't despair, soak the rhizome in a solution of fish emulsion fertiliser for 24 hours prior to planting. This applies also to mail order rhizomes, which often arrive looking a little sad. Plant new rhizomes either in early December or, for best results, in early autumn. Avoid dividing and replanting during the very hot months, as plants will not start to settle in and grow during this time.

Bearded irises are not lovers of greatly improved soils and if you are adding compost, it should be well dug in about a month before planting. Fresh animal manure or compost should not be allowed to come into contact with any part of the plant as rotting may be induced. These plants will in fact grow well in undeveloped soil provided drainage is good.

When planting, roots should be spread out, and the top of the rhizome left exposed on the soil surface. Rhizomes of a single cultivar should be planted 20–30 cm apart to form a clump quickly. If they tend to fall forward because they are a little 'top heavy', place a short stake in front of the fan for support until growth starts, at which time remove the stake completely. Clumps of different cultivars should be kept about 50 cm apart. If grown well the clumps will need to be

divided every 3–4 years: there will be plenty of surplus plants left over for friends or the school fete.

As near as possible, beds should be in full sun and with some shelter from strong wind. The beds should not be mulched as this may cause rhizomes to rot. Instead, regular weeding with a hoe or similar and a light dressing of complete fertiliser when active growth commences in early spring is all that is needed. If the spring is dry then a weekly watering will help when buds start to appear but generally the natural conditions will supply enough rainwater for the plants' needs.

Flowering from September through to November in the local climate (although some early flowerers have been seen in August), bearded irises can provide colour progressively if cultivars are carefully selected. Flower spikes carry from 6–15 or more buds and fill the 70–100 cm height range.

From very humble beginnings of flowers with thin petals, often heavily marked with veining, in white, yellow and dark purple shades has come the plethora of colour combinations we see today.

Blooms of one distinct colour are called 'self coloured'. This does not however include the beard which can be a variety of colours (and even more than one — blue tipped with yellow is often seen). This can lead to a huge range of subtle variations. For example, a white iris may have a beard colour of white, yellow, blue (light through to almost black), red, pink, orange and many subtle shades and combinations of these. This applies in most colours and makes the range almost limitless. Here the colours are dealt with without considering the effect of the beard.

The cultivars named below are a small selection of those proven to grow well in Canberra's climate.

Some suggested tall bearded iris

White	Skating Party (pure)
	Leda's Lover (creamy)
	Wedding Vow (pure)
Light to Mid Blue	Silverado (light – almost white)
	Victoria Falls (light blue)
	Full Tide (wisteria blue)
Mid to Dark Blue	Breakers (rich mid blue)
	Yaquina Blue (ruffled, mid)
	High Waters (blue-violet)
Violet-Purple	Titans Glory (rich purple)
	Dusky Challenger (purple)
Black	Hello Darkness (purple black)
	Witches Sabbath (dark purple/black, mustard bronze beards)
Orchid-Lavender	Mary Frances
	Entourage
Red/Burgundy (not a true red but many interesting shades)	Lady Friend (garnet rose)
	Loyalist (rich claret/wine)
	Mulled Wine (raspberry burgundy)
Brown	Café Society (golden tan)
	Tobacco Land (dark tobacco brown)
Orange	Hills District
Yellow	Opportunity (dandelion yellow)
	Bahloo (sulphur yellow)
	Gold Country (rich gold)
Pink	Beverly Sills (coral pink – best)
	Social Event (light to mid pink)
	Vanity (light pink)
Apricot-Peach	Goddess (light peach)
	First Movement (rich apricot)
Plicata – solid base colour edged, dotted or stippled in another colour — very striking	Rare Treat (cornflower blue on white)
	Jesse's Song (methyl violet on white)
	Classic Look (mid blue on white)
	Smoke Rings (lilac on cream)
	Queen In Calico (Brown on Cream)
Mixed Colours	Ride The Wind (standards white, falls mid blue)
	Alpine Journey (standard white, falls golden yellow)
	Aztec Burst (st white, f apricot)
	Mystique (st pale blue, f deep blue/purple)
	Edith Wolford (st yellow, f mid blue violet)
	Cheerful One (st creamy yellow, f yellow edged white)

fertiliser with a brilliant display in spring. They will also grow and flower well in pots or tubs with a regular feeding when in growth. Rhizomes can be planted at about 15 cm spacing. Pots can be moved to a less visible location after flowering has finished.

Median irises

These have followed the development of the tall and dwarf varieties, being largely the result of hybridisation of the two.

They are 40–70 cm in height and are generally much like their taller cousins in habit. They flower from the dwarf season through to the tall season (mainly September–October). They are useful to fill the gap between border and taller plants at the rear of the garden.

Pot culture is becoming more popular and these plants are well suited. Plant rhizomes with the heel to the edge of the pot and the fan of leaves to the centre. This allows for growth through the season toward the opposite edge with room for new side shoots. A teaspoon of 9-month slow release fertiliser on planting will ensure good growth. Potted median irises need replanting every two years unless the pot is very large.

They are generally available from specialist nurseries. Colour ranges parallel the tall bearded types.

Beardless irises

There are many species of irises in this category and only the more commonly grown have been dealt with here. Specialist literature should be consulted for information about other species.

A typical tall bearded iris, one of the easiest and toughest plants to grow.

Dwarf bearded

These are the miniatures of the group with general cultivation needs the same as above. The entire plant is a miniature recreation of its taller cousins and accordingly able to fit into much smaller spaces. The leaves are only up to about 15–25 cm long, the clumps developing in a tighter mass than the taller types with flowers in early spring (August–September) on stems up to 40 cm. The earliest flowerers are usually the smallest with the shortest stems.

Flower colours cover an amazing range with only true red not available (although red beards often occur). There are so many that it is not practical to recommend cultivars.

These are very forgiving border and rockery plants, which will reward a little effort and

Japanese irises (*I. ensata syn I. kaempferi*)

New hybrids are now available in white, pink, blue, violet, purple and 'beet' red, with flowers up to 25 cm across and on stems 60–120 cm in late November–December.

Plant in autumn with the tops of the rhizomes at soil level and 30–40 cm apart. Divide every 3 to 4 years as clumps become crowded. They will do well if grown in water pots or in pots placed in a pond during the active months and allowed to dry out during the winter when dormant. They are not bog plants and will eventually succumb if grown permanently in ponds or other wet conditions. If grown other than in ponds or water pots, they will need copious water from spring until flowering is completed in summer. They should be planted in humus-rich soil and will not tolerate lime in any form.

An *Iris kaempferi*.

Louisiana irises

A spring flowering iris bred from five wild species found in the Mississippi Basin. Leaves are more sword-like than bearded irises and many of the cultivars go into complete dormancy in the post-flowering period. Modern hybrids are available in a wide range of colours on stems 100–150 cm. They are moisture-loving plants and thrive in acid soils with high organic content. Ensure that they have plenty of water during the spring and early summer period, but reduced water in the dormant summer period. These are probably the most adaptable of all irises, growing successfully in a range of conditions.

These are plants which may be grown in pots in still water during the growing season provided the soil is rich enough to satisfy their gross feeding needs. They need about half the day of light and will even grow and flower successfully in filtered light under trees. They are often combined in beds with camellias.

Plant the rhizomes 5–8 cm below the soil and 30-50 cm apart in late summer. Replant only when too crowded (two years for more vigorous growers), using only the young vigorous rhizomes and discarding the old woody rhizomes from the centre of the clump. These are very fast spreading plants with long narrow rhizomes. An excellent cut flower.

Some suggested Louisiana irises.

Dural White Butterfly	Pure White
Dural Charm	Canary Yellow
Barcoo	Rosy Pink
Gulf Shores	Shorter Dark Blue
Gladiator's Gift	Rich Chocolate
Jazz Ballet	Violet, Ruffled, light rim — top award winner
Koorawatha	Rich Yellow — top award winner
Ocean Going	Mid Blue, lighter rim
Better Believe It	Yellow overlaid with reddish brown

Pacific Coast Hybrids (Californian iris)

A group of irises native to the west coast of North America which flower in early to mid-spring. They are available in a wide range of colours on stems 30–50 cm. Plant in May–June, ensuring that the roots do not dry out. They can be difficult to transplant successfully but are easily grown from seed. A semi-shaded area with a cool root run is essential to obtain best results. An excellent cut flower.

Two good Californian irises.

Come In Spinner	Clear butter yellow
Roy Davidson	Yellow with brown veining

English water iris (*I. pseudacorus*)

These have yellow flowers in early summer on 100–150 cm stems, ideally suited to wet conditions. Inclined to multiply rapidly. Plant in autumn with the top of the rhizome at soil level; in clumps with 30–40 cm between rhizomes

This is the 'fleur de lis' of fame as the French symbol of the 12th century. Overseas studies have recommended this plant as a natural means of combating water pollution and removing the ammonia produced by fish. It has a good root structure to hold the banks of ponds, lakes and rivers and grows well in part-shade.

Siberian Irises (*I. sibirica*).

A tall growing species with narrow grass-like foliage. Flowers are in shades of blue or white on stems 60–120 cm in late spring. Plant the rhizomes in late winter in clumps about 40 cm apart and with the crown of the plant just below soil level. Leave undisturbed for 3 to 4 years. Very hardy. An excellent cut flower.

Spuria Irises.

The modern varieties are hybrids bred from a number of iris species. Spring flowers in a wide range of colours on stems 60–120 cm. Foliage is thin, sword-like and up to 180 cm in height, clumps being very dense and up to a metre across.

Plant the rhizomes in autumn about 3–5 cm below the soil level in a soil rich in organic material. Water well when in bud and flowering but reduce the water over the summer period. They are best left undisturbed for a number of years as they may take two years to settle and flower. They can take over an area so are not recommended for small blocks.

Some good Spuria irises.

Bronzing	Violet Standards, Falls violet overlaid bronze
Goldmania	Pure Gold
In Depth	Dark blue/violet
Just Reward	Blue
Social Circle	Ruffled White

Winter flowering irises (*I. unguicularis syn. I. stylosa*).

Stems of only 15–20 cm but worth growing because they flower in winter. Cut foliage back to about 10 cm in late autumn so the flowers can be appreciated. Mainly in blue but white and pink forms are available. They tolerate partial shade.

Plant the rhizomes in early spring about 2 cm below the surface using relatively large divisions for best results. The plants are evergreen and soon develop into large clumps. Good for cut flowers but cut the flowers before they open fully.

Crested irises (Evansia)

These have a prominent 'cockscomb' like structure at the beginning of the inside of each fall petal. There are some subtropical species which are evergreen, but those which call temperate climates home are dormant in the colder months. They should be divided either immediately after flowering or in the autumn.

Dwarf crested iris (*I. cristata*) has broad strappy foliage, clear lavender blue flowers about 5 cm on 12 cm stems with a white crest. This one prefers some shelter from hot summer sun and will benefit from a good mulch of compost. The leaves continue growing after flowering (in spring) and will reach about 25 cm.

Iris japonica

This has foliage similar to tall bearded irises but the flower spikes of up to 60 cm are delicate and arching, bearing 30 or more small, lilac, orchid-like flowers with orange central markings. Each spike has many individual flowers that open over about 4 weeks in October. The flower spike can look very spectacular if trailed over a retaining wall or planted under camellias etc. Trouble free, but divide regularly for best growth. Requires some shade and soil should not dry out. *I. wattii* is very similar.

Dutch irises (bulbous irises)

The Dutch iris is undoubtedly the most popular iris for both garden and indoor decoration. It is a hybrid of a number of species and available in a wide range of colours that flower in mid-spring on 40–50 cm stems. Colour range is white, yellow, blue and combinations with bronze recently introduced.

The Dutch iris 'Lilac Queen'.

Plant the bulbs in late autumn 10–12 cm deep and 15 cm apart in well-drained, deeply dug garden loam. They will benefit from a light application of slow release fertiliser at planting and then feed them fortnightly with seaweed or fish emulsion from when growth starts until after flowering. They can also be grown in containers.

Best results are obtained by lifting the bulbs a few weeks after flowering and replanting in a different area each year. Bulbs left in will in most cases produce a larger flower the second year but are more subject to becoming virus infected or damaged while digging in the area. Virus attacks stems and foliage mainly and does not worry most people — flowers are normally OK.

After lifting, allow the stems to dry out almost completely in a cool dry area before removing from the bulbs. Bulbs should be dusted with Derris Dust® and sulphur before storing in a cool dry dark area until next autumn. Check the condition of the bulbs regularly and remove any that have deteriorated. Discard small bulblets after lifting, as they will not flower for about three years.

English iris (*I. xiphioides* syn. *I. latifolia*) flower later than the Dutch iris and have larger open flowers. Bulbs are also larger.

Iris ensata 'Peacock Dance'

Dwarf bulbous iris

The dwarf bulbous iris species are not as well known as their larger and later flowering relatives. This is a pity as they are not difficult to grow, have a good perfume, and flower in late winter when there is little else in bloom. *Iris reticulata* and *I. histrioides* and their cultivars are the ones most likely to be available locally or from mail order bulb companies which advertise in the gardening magazines.

The plants are small to about 10 cm and the flowers are very similar in structure to the better known Dutch iris. Colour is usually through the purple and blue spectrum though yellow is occasionally available in *Iris danfordiae*; this is unfortunately not as reliable in flowering as the others.

As they are small plants and easily lost in the garden, dwarf bulbous iris are best grown in pots and using a very free-draining potting mix. Plant them in autumn and place in shade till the plants commence growth when they should be moved to a sunny spot. The pots can be brought into a prominent position when flowering, including indoors for short periods so you can enjoy the bright flowers and the perfume.

After flowering, the leaves elongate. This is the time to fertilise with a low nitrogen type plant food and keep watered to build the bulbs up for the next growing season. Once the foliage has died down remove the bulbs and keep in a cool dry area until the next planting season.

Some that can be recommended are 'Harmony', 'Cantab' and 'Clairette' in the blue range and 'J. S. Djit' and 'Joyce' in purples.

CHAPTER 10:
Cacti and other succulents

Contributed by members of The Cactus and Succulent Society of the ACT Inc.
Plant list prepared by Brian Wray

With the advent of more water conscious times the use of succulent plants in landscaping has again become popular.

Succulent plants are native to all continents but until recently little has been written about their occurence in Australia. Most succulents come from arid climates, not necessarily deserts; indeed the number from true desert conditions is minimal. Many are found in mountainous places where the climate, while generally hotter, is not unlike Canberra's. Two things are common in all areas where cacti or other succulents occur and these are low but regular rainfall and good drainage. Cacti are found in the Americas from Canada to Patagonia in the Argentine and many other succulents come from those continents also. Noteworthy exceptions are the epiphytic types from tropical or sub-tropical forests, growing in similar circumstances to many orchids.

There can be great confusion between cacti and other succulents and many succulents are frequently referred to as cacti. A succulent plant is one which stores moisture in the stem (as in cacti and many euphorbias, the leaves (echeverias, sedums, crassulas, mesembryanthemums etc.) or in the roots. Cacti are a special group of succulents distinguished by the presence of aereoles over the plant body or along the ribs. These unique organs are the points where spines, hairs or wool, flowers and new stems originate. This is best described as a modified leaf axil (and would be the place where

Kalanchoe thyrsifolia 'Flapjack'.

leaves joined the body if there were any). The capacity to store water in the thickened stems or leaves has arisen in many unrelated families of plants and is a reaction to seasonal or prolonged dry conditions.

With a few notable exceptions most succulent plants can be grown very well in our climate. In nature, succulent plants grow mostly in sunny places with perfect drainage so that the plants quickly absorb rainfall and the soil dries out rapidly. With their shallow root systems, the plants take advantage of the occasional moisture to grow and to flower.

If you have a greenhouse the range of succulents that will thrive is increased dramatically and there are few that will not do well. Heating in winter is not necessary as most succulents, including cacti, go into a dormant state in the colder weather.

Preparation

Most succulents prefer the sunniest place in the garden where the sun shines virtually all day, certainly during the middle and afternoon portions of the day. The northern side of the home is generally the most suitable but the western aspect will also suit most plants.

The natural soils of the ACT are generally heavy and not consistent with the excellent drainage required for growing succulents. Even improved garden soil is generally quite unsuitable though some of the more hardy species will thrive.

Most of the plants likely to be grown here have come from climates where the rainfall is minimal and the plants will not tolerate wet roots resulting from poor drainage. With suitable preparation of the bed a good range of succulents can be grown.

The usual way to achieve perfect drainage outdoors is to construct a raised bed. There is no hard and fast rule as to the depth of soil required but the roots of the plants should always be perfectly drained. A range of materials can be used to build up beds with the limit being what appeals to the eye. Rocks, timber, bricks, concrete and the new retaining wall blocks may all be used. An edge will help prevent invasion by weeds – if weeds are allowed to seed, eradication may become a problem.

Many innovative materials such as coloured glass and contrasting pebbles of all hues are now being used to combine with succulent plants to provide striking combinations when landscaping around smaller areas such as courtyard blocks. The use of rocks on the surface is a matter of taste for the individual. The back may be built higher than the front

You can grow cacti and succulents in almost anything. These are growing vertically in a frame fashioned from old fence palings.

and the surface broken up into pockets which can be arranged at slightly different levels for good visual effect.

The growing medium is of utmost importance and fortunately the ingredients are readily available and reasonably priced in Canberra. The first and most important is coarse washed river sand. Test the material before purchase, taking a handful and pressing it tightly. If it moulds and does not break up when the pressure of the hand is released, it is unsuitable as it contains too much clay. The right grade of sand will stream from your hand when pressure is released. Coarse material such as decomposed granite or scoria may be incorporated to increase the open nature of the growing medium.

The other ingredient is compost, also readily available from many suppliers. Compost containing a little animal manure is suitable, provided it is well matured before use though mushroom compost contains too much animal manure and lime. A recommended mixture is 60% coarse washed river sand and 40% well rotted compost from which all rough, undecomposed material such as sticks should be removed. To that, add about a full handful of slow release fertiliser per square metre in the surface layers. You will find that there are as many recipes for the rockery mixture as there are growers e.g. some will add some well prepared garden soil but the above mixture has proved effective in Canberra over many years.

Outdoors – Planting and Watering

Frost can be a problem with many succulent plants but it has been proven that established plants are less likely to sustain damage than plants which have not had a chance to grow into their new locations. For this reason it is not wise to plant new succulents outdoors between the end of February and the end of September.

The main growing period for the majority of succulent plants grown outdoors in Canberra begins in October and extends to the end of February. During this time established plants will take regular watering but newly inserted plants should be left for two or three weeks to get their roots growing before watering. With the approach of the cool weather, they go into a resting state and shrink slightly. It is best to withhold artificial watering from the end of February till the end of September. This promotes a state of dormancy and they are hardier than when actively growing.

For protection during the resting period when growing outdoors, consider covering plants which are marginal under frosts. Bubblewrap, used for packing large objects for transport, may be suspended above the bed using any form of structure you can devise. This will not only protect against frost, but keep most of the winter rains at bay. Such a simple operation considerably expands the range of plants safely grown outdoors.

Do not use artificial nitrogenous fertilisers for succulents. Cacti and many of the Euphorbias do not have leaves and by using a fertiliser which will promote leaf growth, they tend to produce soft growth which is easily damaged in adverse weather.

In an established garden, if you wish to replace something or to put in a new plant, it is a good idea to remove the old exhausted soil and replace it with new soil to a spade depth.

With water conservation in mind, a large area, or even the whole garden, could be given over to succulents and xerophytes. If following this principle, first establish a framework of architectural plants, e.g cordylines, New Zealand flax, yuccas etc. These can then be interplanted with colourful succulents and tall column-like cacti for vertical effect.

Many less hardy plants, such as pachypodiums and aloes can be pot plunged for the summer and returned to shelter in autumn.

Container Growing

Large succulents or collections of succulents in containers in courtyard gardens, entrance areas and balconies can be very effective. Old boots painted in bright colours, cooking utensils, wheelbarrows or even paling picture frames can look very well, the only restriction being the imagination and daring of the designer. One such designer has been known to cover the roof of a small garden shed with protective material and chicken wire into which succulents have been planted.

Some people purchase nice specimens of cacti and succulents to use for indoor decoration instead of flowers. These plants will continue to look good with very little care and attention, and if in the end, they become a little pale and jaded, they can be put outside and will usually recover. Even if they were to die then you will still have had more value than from a short-lived bunch of flowers. The cost is comparable but the plant will last very much longer.

The potting mixture recommended for outdoor plants is fine. Perfect drainage is vital for potted plants, so put the compost through a coarse sieve, and discard any material which does not pass through easily. To a 20 litre bucket of this mixture add a handful of slow release fertiliser and a handful of old well-rotted cow manure. If using commercial cactus potting mixture, add half volume of coarse washed river sand to improve drainage and sieve out any coarse material. Plants should always be potted into a fairly dry mixture and preparing the potting mix in volume and storing it for later use allows it to mature and to dry before use.

Fill the pot to within 1 cm of the lip then cover the surface with a topping such as crushed brick, fine scoria or decorative gravel. This adds to the appearance, keeps the plant clean and slows surface evaporation. Newly potted plants should not be watered at all for about 2 weeks to allow damaged roots to heal and become active in their new home.

Newly obtained plants should be repotted into your own mix unless you know the supplier and trust their planting skills. The drainage times of different mixes will vary considerably, so it is wise to use a similar mix for all your plants so as to avoid drainage problems and rotting. New plants may also harbour pests so spraying is a necessary precaution. Some growers choose to dip the plant in the appropriate mixture in its original pot and allow it to dry for a time before repotting, while others dip roots and all in a solution of Confidor® or similar insecticide. Alternatively, the plant can be removed from its mix before dipping it completely in the spray mixture. The roots should be allowed to dry before repotting.

Some growers use rubber or other heavy gloves to handle cacti but spines can remain in the fabric to cause later injury. A spiny plant may be easily handled if the body of the plant is wrapped in several layers of paper, taking care not to damage the spines. You can also use long kitchen tongs to grasp the plant while potting. It is advisable to use some form of padding on the tongs to avoid damage to the plant. With a little ingenuity, cacti can be potted quite easily. Even very large plants can be rolled from their pots on to a bed of newspaper and the pot pulled away from the plant. After that the plant can be handled by the roots to get it into its new larger home.

Mealy bugs, scale insects and spider mites can all cause damage to the plants. It is better to keep the collection clean than to have to get rid of a bad infection of pests. Watch for the presence of ants which can be an indicator of mealy bug.

If you think that a plant has exhausted the nutrient content of its pot, a half strength

This low-maintenance garden was photographed at a Melbourne Flower Show but there is no reason why a similar garden could not be established in Canberra.

solution of low nitrogen fertiliser can be watered in during the normal watering program. Commercial slow release fertilisers may also be used but should be chosen carefully as most are high in nitrogen. In these circumstances it may be preferable to repot to the next largest size pot or, if the plant can be broken up, restart it in the same container. Carefully remove all of the spent mix by shaking the plant carefully or by using a blunt stick. Trim off any damaged roots if necessary.

Most succulent plants grow from spring till early autumn though the specialist may have some winter growers. Generally the one watering program can be followed for all plants through the year especially if one potting mix is always used. By September many plants will be in growth and light watering can be commenced with slightly increased frequency. By late October all plants can be watered well once weekly though this will be dependent upon the weather and how quickly the pots dry out. It is wise to let the potting mix become virtually dry before watering again. If the mixture is very free draining it is almost impossible to overwater

healthy plants during growth. When a vigorous plant fills its pot, the roots may slow the drainage rate so that is a signal to repot the plant. A fine light mist spray between normal watering, taking care to reach every plant, especially those in the corners, will help reduce the incidence of pests.

Watering of container grown plants should be tapered off in April/May. Canberra's cold climate sends the majority of succulents into a natural dormancy and many species need this period to mature growth and to prepare to flower in the spring. Some will flower before true growth commences. Dormancy is part of the natural cycle so we are fortunate in that our climate induces natural rest.

Propagation

The two simplest methods for increasing succulent plants are division and cuttings. Other methods do exist but will not be discussed in this book. Many succulents produce rooted offsets which should be left to dry in light shade for a day or two after separation and then potted up. This allows damaged roots to heal and reduces the risk of plants rotting.

Cuttings of most succulents are easily rooted. Cut surfaces may be treated with 'flowers of sulphur' to prevent rot or other infection before being placed in the rooting medium. The milky sap of some Euphorbia species is poisonous and for some people it is an irritant, so when taking cuttings, the sap should be washed away until the cutting ceases to 'bleed'. Wear gloves when handling any cuttings with milky sap. All cuttings should be allowed to dry for up to two weeks in light shade before standing the cuttings in a very sandy mixture. Most will strike very easily.

Old cactus plants, particularly cylindrical types such as some Mammillarias which have become weathered and unsightly at the base can be cut off and the top treated as a cutting and re-rooted to create a vigorous new plant. The procedure is a simple one which rarely fails.

Indoors, on the patio?

Many succulents are placed indoors and do not have sufficient light, and as a result they become pale, and their growth is long and thin. As sun-loving natives of arid places, any succulents grown indoors should always be near a north or west-facing window.

Good specimens can be grown in Canberra without a greenhouse, and this will usually mean locating them on a veranda or patio where there will be strong light but some form of frost protection, if only from overhanging eaves. The variety of species and cultivars available for this purpose is quite wide although there are some which prefer a lot of heat and do not like low temperatures and these plants should be avoided unless you can indulge them.

Growing epiphytic cacti

A number of cacti grow in tropical and sub-tropical forests, some on the forest floor while others are epiphytic—that is, they grow on the branches of trees. They do no harm to their host plant and draw their nourishment from the natural humus which accumulates on the branches and where branches join.

From these plants, a large variety of hybrids have been developed which have large flowers and a wide range of colours, especially in the Epiphyllums. These and

A collection of cacti and other succulents growing in Canberra.

the "Zygocactus" hybrids grow well in a sheltered location but need frost protection and more shaded conditions than other plants of the group.

The stems of Epiphyllums can reach more than a metre in length. They are flat and broad, usually with serrated edges, and are not leaves as might be thought. The name epiphyllum means "upon a leaf" referring to the flowers which come from areoles along the stem edges. These plants need a slightly richer potting mix with added peat or compost. A rest from watering after summer flowering is advisable but during growth they should always have a little moisture available. If drainage is good, this will not be a problem.

Outdoor Planting – Suitable plants

Members of The Cactus and Succulent Society of the ACT have been experimenting with rockery grown plants over many years to determine which plants will survive in our conditions. Fortunately, the Canberra climate has proved more suitable for outdoor planting than the coastal cities of Melbourne, Sydney and Brisbane as there are more hours of sunlight, less rainfall and lower humidity. The following list of hardy species is by no means exhaustive, but will indicate the variety of suitable plants.

Succulents

Aeonium sp. Although often damaged by frost, these plants are very decorative and root easily from cuttings. A little protection will normally see them through the winter, even wide roof eaves will do the job. Most popular is *A. arboreum* 'Schwarzkopf' with its rosettes of shiny red-black leaves.

Agave sp are hardy and decorative but larger species should be avoided. *Agave americana* (Century plant) and its variegated varieties are sometimes seen growing wild in the bush as garden escapees but are quite unsuitable for the garden because of their great size and the dangerous sharp leaf tips. More suitable species, which still carry spines, are *Agave echinoides, A. filifera, A. geminiflora, A. parrasana, A. parviflora* and *A. Victoria-Reginae.*

Aloes are a very large group of mainly African plants all of which make decorative plantings. Not all are winter hardy. Some reliable species are:

> *A. brevifolia* — stemless rosettes forming large clumps, with scarlet flowers.

> *A. humilis* which is clump forming with many soft fleshy spines
> *A. saponaria* — stemless rosettes with white-spotted leaves and orange flowers
> *A. spinosissima,* clump forming up to 1 m high and with orange red flowers
> *A. variegata*, stemless zebra striped leaves and red flowers.

Cotyledon. A group of African plants most of which are unsuitable for outdoor plantings, with two exceptions

> *C. macrantha*, a shrub growing to 1 m. It has large green leaves and umbels of bell-shaped red and yellow flowers
> *C. orbiculata*, a shrub to 1.5 m. Its leaves are covered in a hair-like wax giving a dazzling white effect. The flowers are red in umbrels.

A cotyledon growing happily in a pot.

Echeveria. A genus of mainly Mexican mountain plants, all rosette forming and mainly in shades of glaucous blue or even nearly black. Most species will survive outdoors, but not the large fancy leaved hybrids.

Haworthia sp are South African natives (mostly rosette type succulents) and as many of these grow naturally in the shade of shrubs they will do well indoors given sufficient light.

Mesembryanthemum group (Pigface) are excellent rockery plants. The group contains some very bright stunning flowered plants, mainly dwarf or sprawling. Also included here is the Australian native pigface.

Pachyphytum oviferum and *P. compactum* are excellent clumping plants with 'jelly bean' shaped leaves and are used to fill small spaces.

Sedums are often taken for granted in the garden, partly because they don't bloom until autumn, but also because they are so easy to grow and require so little care. Their thick, succulent leaves are able to withstand drought, they require little water and in Canberra, many of the larger forms are herbaceous and re-shoot into vigorous growth in spring. The flower buds form early and remain attractive well in winter as they age. Sedums have a variety of growth habits ranging from low spreading plants to large clumps as wide as they are high. The larger forms are generally herbaceous.

S. 'Autumn Joy' is a very popular herbaceous form, clumps reaching 80 cm x 80 cm and having pink flowers which age to a coppery-tan.

S. 'Bertram Anderson' is a tough drought-tolerant carpeting sedum, with coppery purple fleshy leaves which turn almost black by the end of summer, when showy heads of deep pink flowers are produced. A good basket plant. 10 cm x 30 cm.

S. *erythrostictum* 'Frosty Morn' is an herbaceous perennial with stout stems clothed with succulent, elliptic, grey-green leaves with white margins. In late summer to early autumn, it bears terminal heads of tiny pale pink flowers. If grown in rich soil, it flops.

S. *makinoi* 'Ogon' is drought and heat tolerant once established, though unlike other sedums, it does prefer a little afternoon shade on very hot days. It is thus best grown in a container where it will draw the eye with its brilliant yellow foliage. 10 cm x 30 cm.

S. 'Matrona' is a sturdy upright herbaceous plant with grey-green leaves and purple stems. Its long lasting flower clusters are pale pink and age to chocolate brown in winter. 60 cm x 60 cm.

S. *reflexum* 'Aureum' is a vigorous mat-forming evergreen perennial which displays yellow star-flowers freely through summer. 10 cm x 50 cm.

S. *spathulifolium* 'Purpureum'. A vigorous, evergreen plant with mat-forming growth habit. Fleshy stems bearing stiff, spoon shaped, silvery and reddish-purple leaves. Bright yellow star-flowers.

S. *spurium* 'Dragon's Blood' has succulent green foliage tinged with deep red. It is a dense ground cover 10 cm x 45 cm.

S. *rubrotinctum* 'Jelly Beans' has fleshy short rounded green leaves tipped crimson in winter clustered on short stems. Forms a quick ground cover and has yellow flowers in winter. Will grow in sun or part sun.

S. *rubrotinctum* 'Pink Jelly Beans'. Plump pink leaves clustered on short stems. Fallen leaves take root easily but new plants often revert to green. Bright pink in winter when dry. Sun/part sun.

S. *rubrotinctum* 'Aurora' Low cascading habit. Plump, oblong leaves are light green and heavily tinged pink. It's an attractive plant for rock gardens or containers.

Sedums are most reliable garden plants, particularly striking when in flower.

S. telephium ruprechtii 'Beth Chatto Form'. Low mounds of waxy blue-purple leaves from which creamy lemon flowers are produced in autumn. The flowers change colour with age to burnt bronze. It is herbaceous, sun loving and drought tolerant.

Sempervivum sp (House leeks) are very hardy rosette forming plants and like to grow with their roots in confined spaces between rocks. These are native to the scree slopes of mountains chiefly in Europe. They do not need much in the way of soil, often surviving on what blows or washes into the crevices they favour as homes.

Yucca sp are reliable but may grow too large growing for a small area. They have straplike leaves and spectacular spikes of white bell flowers.

Cacti

The cacti as a group are more suited to the avid collector than the landscaper, due mainly to their minimal body shape. All, however, have very spectacular flowers, and some have architectural growth forms which can be useful.

Cleistocactus is usually upright and column forming with narrow tubular flowes of red or yellow. *Cleistocactus strausii* (the Silver Torch cactus) with straight white spiny stems and thin, long red flowers is a desirable species. It gradually forms small clumps growing to 2 m.

Echinocereus sp with their spectacular flowers are an excellent addition to the garden. A large family of mainly hardy, clumping plants. Flowers mainly yellow or purple.

Echinopsis sp are hardy and include some very beautiful flowering hybrids. The family now includes the former Lobivia and Trichocereus species. They are usually globular and freely offsetting, forming a mound of plant bodies with age. Flowers range from white, yellow, pink, mauve, orange and red, tubular, often up to 10 cm across.

Gymnocalycium sp are generally hardy and if grown in a bright place they should flower. Flowers are mainly white or pink, occasionally red.

Lobivia sp are similar in habit and appearance to Echinopsis but flowers are smaller and more profuse. Colours are mostly red, white and orange.

Mammillaria sp are from a large genus of which not very many have been trialled outdoors in Canberra; however *M. celsiana, M. hahniana, M. elegans* and *M. geminispina*

do well and others are worth experimenting with. Flowers are generally small and appear in a ring around the top of the plant in spring, leaving a similar ring of red or purple berries. Plants are widely variable in form and habit.

Oreocereus sp occur on the slopes in the Andes and with their white wool and yellow spines make a spectacular addition, *Oreocereus celsianus* being the best. Columnar in habit, to 3 m. Morawetzia is now included in the family. *M. dowlzianus* is a good semi-trailing plant.

Parodia. This now includes Notocactus, a group with excellent flowers usually yellow at the top of the plants in spring. Most seem to be hardy in Canberra. Choice species are *P. leninghausii, P. magnificus, P. ottonis* and *P. uebelmannianus.*

Rebutia sp are small globular clump forming plants covered by a profusion of bright flowers in spring. All colours except blue.

Avoid

Conophytum sp (Cone plants) and *Lithops sp* (Living stones) are unsuitable as both need long periods of complete drought at different times of the year and will not survive a Canberra winter outdoors.

Opuntia sp including the prickly pear and related species as well as the cylindrical stemmed species are not grown in Canberra as a local regulation prohibits their transportation. In any case, their barbed spines make them extremely difficult to handle and they are not regarded as desirable garden plants.

> The Cactus and Succulent Society holds monthly meetings, usually at 10:30am on the second Sunday of the month.
> Phone 6286 2984 or 6258 7691 for details or write to PO Box 484, Mawson ACT 2607.

CHAPTER 11: Ferns

The ideal site for growing ferns in Canberra will provide protection from extreme hot and cold wind, frost and hot sun. This may be against a south wall or under shadecloth, though provided the above considerations are met, there may well be other suitable positions. Bear in mind that the ideal conditions for one fern may be unsuitable for another, so it is important to be aware of a plant's individual requirements, particularly in regard to light. Many ferns need bright light to do well.

The best soil for ferns will contain plenty of organic matter, and that should be reasonably deep, especially for tree ferns, friable, well-drained and moist. Addition of organic matter and sand to Canberra clay soils usually works very well if cultivated to about 20cm or so, and it is useful to place rocks to act as crevices for ferns to grow in.

Mulching is a good practice as it will reduce water loss in the soil and will keep the root zone cool. This is particularly useful for species which grow naturally on the forest floor. Mulch may consist of shredded eucalyptus leaves, pine needles, coir, old grass clippings and a variety of other materials.

Be aware of the natural environment of your specific ferns and try to mimic this. Moisture-loving ferns should of course be grouped together and grown separately to drier-land species, but for most fern species the best watering will be a good deep watering in warmer months to saturate the soil, easing off in winter. Water frosted plants to reduce damage, but apart from planting in a sheltered position initially, the only way to correct damage caused by dry heat and wind is to trim off affected fronds. Blood and bone or liquid fish emulsion are best applied during the warmer months when the plants are in active growth.

While generally pest-free, ferns occasionally suffer from the effects of snails and slugs, which enjoy the moist conditions preferred by ferns. Iron-based baits which are not a risk for household pets are now available, and there are a number of organic barriers which may be used to keep snails and slugs at bay. The Wingless grasshopper can also be a nuisance in some seasons, though as they thrive in the hot dry conditions of summer, regular watering of the area usually works as a deterrent.

Adiantum aethliopicum, Maidenhair. A soft, delicate-looking fern with long creeping wiry branched rhizomes. An easy fern to grow but resents poor treatment. Ideally requires dappled sunlight, protected from hot and dry winds, in moist well-drained area. Good rockery fern with prolific suckering. Resents uprooting or transplanting, especially from wild situation. Grows rapidly and will withstand extreme conditions.

Asplenium bulbiferum, Mother Spleenwort. A fleshy, medium to large ground fern with a tufted rhizome. Fronds are generally weeping to semi-weeping especially if growing out from a hanging basket. An easy fern to grow in containers both indoors and outside. Requires a very moist position protected from hot and dry winds. Grows best in partial to full shade. Very hardy.

Asplenium flabellifolium, Necklace Fern. A charming pendant groundcover with short creeping rhizomes. An excellent hardy fern suitable for semi-shaded moist banks, rockeries and as a semi-ground cover in association with other ferns or similar plants. While this fern looks delicate, it will actually withstand heavy frosts, fire and drought due to its ability to spread its rhizomes deep into rock crevices. Its proliferous bulbils ensure a quick and constant regeneration.

Asplenium australasicum (syn A. nidus), Australian Bird's-Nest Fern. This is a large epiphyte with a thick, fleshy, tufted rhizome and large fronds spreading in a rosette. It can be used as a container fern but is a hardy outdoor 'ground' fern for shady cool positions if protected from frosts and drying winds. As an epiphyte it obtains its nutrients from decomposing vegetable matter falling into the centre of the plant. If growing this plant in a container, place leaf mould and other plant debris into the centre of the plant to reflect what would happen in nature. Alternatively, use organic fertiliser applied the same way. If grown in the ground do not plant in heavy soil but preferably use a cymbidium orchid mix.

Asplenium trichomanes var. quadrivalens, Common Spleenwort. Densely tufted rhizome, short and thick; fronds 5–10 cm. This fern will grow in extremely exposed positions, but prefers to grow on limestone or with side dressings of agricultural lime. Spreads well if well mulched and watered frequently in hot months. An excellent rockery nook plant.

Azolla filiculoides var. Rubra Pacific Azolla. Resembles a floating moss-like carpet when growing densely. An easily grown pond surface free-floating plant ideal for providing shelter for pond life. Needs to be thinned during warmer months, as it can soon completely cover a pond surface.

Blechnum cartilagineum, Gristle Fern. Usually a small to medium sized ground fern, it is a remarkably beautiful plant. A hardy ground fern best grown from a small plant as it resents over-disturbance. Does well in reasonably deep shade but will withstand high light levels. Needs plenty of water and a well drained soil rich in organic matter or leaf mould.

Blechnum nudum, Fishbone Water Fern. Erect rhizome which will mature to a 50 cm high trunk; rhizome increases from stolons and erect spreading fronds are borne in a crown. A hardy fern which requires a very moist soil rich in organic matter. Will withstand full sun and hot conditions. Thrives if grown near a pond.

Blechnum patersonii, Strap Water Fern. Erect short tufted rhizome; long broad shiny brown scales; fronds strap-like and semi erect. Many plants growing together can resemble a reedy growth next to creeks. Easily grown in suitable conditions—rich soil, protected from hot dry winds, deep shade, deep leafy mulch, moist damp conditions.

Blechnum penna-marina, Alpine Water Fern. A good ground cover fern for boggy soils or damp pond edge sites. Spreads well, and prefers a shaded yet open situation. Withstands very low temperatures and has a dormant winter period. Will only generally produce fertile fronds in areas with cool to cold winters.

Cheilanthes tenuifolia, Rock Fern. Probably the hardiest fern growing in Australia, it is capable of withstanding drought, desiccation, bushfire and extreme temperatures. Quite

often it is a resurrection plant in "dead land" after drought or fire. While not widely grown, it has the potential to be an excellent rockery fern looking delicate but being hardy. It responds well to good watering and reasonably well drained soil. It prefers an open position with a little, to moderate, sunlight. It will recover well from a very wilted state. Resents disturbance of rhizomes.

Culcita dubia, Common Ground Fern, False Bracken. A tall feathery fern, it is easy to grow in bushland areas in and around coastal eastern Australia where it occurs almost as a weed. Withstands full sun, tolerates dry conditions and frost. Needs room to grow and spread — a shrub-like fern.

Cyathea australis, *Alsophila australis*, Rough Tree Fern. Grows a thick, tall, fibrous rough trunk suspending a full open crown up to 12 m high. The trunk at the base can grow up to 1 m in diameter, though more commonly around 25–30 cm. An easy hardy fern to grow provided the right conditions are maintained. It dislikes heavy frosts, hot dry winds and dry soil and should be given reasonable deep shade with plenty of water. Makes an excellent tub plant. A very attractive fern when young with masses of young fresh uncurling fronds in spring and autumn. Requires a well drained soil containing rich compost or leaf mould. Responds well in hot weather to overhead watering especially in mist form.

Dicksonia antarctica, Soft Tree Fern. A tall though often spindly (when old) tree fern with a massive base, up to 2m in diameter. (This can be variable as the fibrous roots growing down the trunk will cover anything close to the fern.) An easily grown fern which sometimes outgrows its intended position. Prefers a cool, moist, shady place with peaty rich well drained soil. Plenty of water should be provided as this fern requires large amounts especially during hot summer weather. Protect from severe frosts and hot sun. Good tub specimen and sometimes does well indoors in moist conditions. Grows in two main flushes spring and autumn when it will completely replace existing fronds with fresh new ones.

Doodia aspera, Prickly Rasp Fern. Tufted small fern from a short creeping rhizome. A tough yet very attractive and easily grown fern, ideal for protected rockery or shaded bank. Prefers plenty of water, shade, protection from frost, and a moist reasonably rich composted soil. Will tolerate even extreme conditions.

Marsilea drummondii, the Four Leaf Clover plant, is actually a fern for growing in shallow water in ponds or water gardens in a sunny position. This plant will suffer frost damage in winter but does recover well.

Marsilea mutica, Nardoo. Very long creeping rhizome with leaves resembling four leaved clover, arising separately along it, on stalks of up to 30 cm, or more. An excellent pond species for open sunny or shady protected spots. Will also grow well outside a pond if provided with very moist and cool, boggy soil. Lift and store in moist warmer conditions if grown in extremely cold areas. Replant or replace, if in container, during spring. A very vigorous growing plant. Extremely attractive and hardy.

Microsorium diversifolium, Kangaroo Fern. A strongly growing erect to pendant "climbing" fern growing from a strong thick long creeping rhizome covered with deciduous brown scales. One of the best container ferns available, especially in large containers. It is a very adaptable climbing fern for ferneries and cool shaded rockeries, or around flowing water and ponds. A hardy and trouble-free fern. Requires plenty of indirect light to grow well. Well drained rocky soil (plenty of peat incorporated).

Pellaea falcata, Sickle Fern. Fishbone-like fern arising erect from a short to medium creeping wiry rhizome. A very hardy attractive fern for bank, groundcover, rockery or fernery, such is the range of this fern. It requires a well drained mulched soil and although tolerant of dry conditions prefers moist cool positions. An easily grown self-perpetuating fern.

Platycerium bifurcatum, Elkhorn. An epiphytic plant which, in its natural habitat, would grow on rocks and trees. It is usually sold already affixed to a hardwood board, and here in Canberra it will need plenty of protection from frost on a sheltered verandah or the like.

P. superbum, Staghorn. A very large epiphytic plant with long, pendulous leaves which may reach 1.5 to 2 m long. As with *P. bifurcatum*, it is usually fixed to a hardwood board and will need plenty of protection from frost for it to grow at its best.

Polystichum proliferum, Mother Shield Fern. A spreading open crowned fern which forms a thick massive base. Fronds grow to 1 m x 0.3 m, light green when young, darker when mature. Possibly the easiest and one of the best garden ferns to grow. Extremely hardy, but requires excellent drainage. Will not tolerate boggy ground. Grows well in open warm positions or in semi-shade. As bulbil bearing fronds age they touch ground and thus the new plantlets grow and produce new ferns: self perpetuating.

Pteris tremula, Tender Brake. A soft green, tufted fern. Erect growing with multiple crowns in older plants. Easily grown in a wide number of different locations, if protected from strong hot winds and frost. Will grow in most soils provided they are mulched and contain reasonable levels of organic matter. A fast growing fern good for screening or mass display. The soft green lacy fronds wave gracefully in a light breeze. Very luxurious growth. Hardy.

Todea barbara, Austral King Fern. A primitive fern growing from a wide trunk like base on shallow fibrous roots. Multiple crowns form in older plants and can grow up to 1.5m tall. A hardy excellent tub fern for shady positions, where it stays a soft mid green colour. Slow growing and very unusual, this fern is amongst the most primitive ferns growing today. Not a deep rooting species, prefers moist, well drained, rich soil.

CHAPTER 12: Orchids

Lynne Phelan and Jane Wright

While there are more than 90 species of native terrestrial orchids that grow in the Canberra region, conditions in Canberra gardens are not suitable for growing epiphytic orchids from other parts of Australia and the world. The list of easily available terrestrial orchids that can survive Canberra's winters is quite small, but one species that is easy to obtain is the Chinese ground orchid, *Bletilla striata*, which dies down over winter and puts up an impressive show of purple flowers in summer. Treat it as a perennial in the garden.

For most people in Canberra, growing orchids means growing them in pots that can be situated indoors or outdoors in sheltered areas. The potting medium used is not ordinary potting mix but a bark mix or specially formulated free-draining orchid potting mix. These mixes are available from most nurseries.

To grow most orchids you need to create a growing environment that matches the needs of the plants. Fortunately, creating a growing area for a small collection of orchids can be achieved quite easily with almost no expense. Catering for a larger or more diverse collection usually means building a glasshouse so there are some costs involved in setting up and maintaining the right growing conditions.

Light

All orchids need light, moisture and fresh air. Without adequate light most orchid species will not grow strong enough to flower. When orchids are grown indoors they should be located in bright but not direct sunlight. Plants grown on windowsills or in sunrooms need to be positioned so that the direct rays do not burn the leaves, especially in summer. Outdoors, orchids can be grown on verandas, balconies, patios or even under trees provided they receive filtered sunlight for most of the day. A shade house with 50–70% shade cloth cover will suit most orchids in the warmer months. Plants grown outdoors are best placed on slats or stands to assist drainage and keep slugs and other nasties from entering the pot through the drainage holes. In winter, most orchids need protection from frost. With a small collection of orchids it is feasible to grow the orchids outside in the warmer months and move them to winter quarters as soon as frost threatens.

Water

Water is critical and more orchids are killed through overwatering than anything else. Orchids cannot tolerate 'wet feet' as the roots quickly rot and the plant dies. The medium should be kept just moist, not wet, and the frequency of watering depends on the water-retentiveness of the potting medium, humidity and air circulation. The best guide to watering is the 'scratch and feel' method. Scratch away the medium to the depth of about 3 centimetres and if it is moist then don't water.

Fresh Air

Very few orchids grow in nature where there is no air movement. Breezes blowing across the leaves help prevent rots as well as simulating a natural growing environment. Indoors, a circulating fan or evaporative cooler can be used to create air movement. Orchids grown outside benefit from natural air movements but should be protected from very strong winds that may blow pots over.

Fertiliser

In nature orchids obtain their food from decaying vegetable matter, animal droppings and from minerals and elements washed into the root zone. Special orchid fertilisers are available from nurseries and these should be used according to the directions on the packet. Avoid over-fertilising as this may lead to excessive growth at the expense of flowers. Many orchids require a 'rest period' when watering and fertilising are cut back or even stopped completely.

Potting or mounting

While most orchids will grow in containers some prefer to have their roots exposed and grow best when mounted on cork, bark or tree fern. In nature many of these orchids are epiphytic; that is, they grow attached to trees. Mounted plants need regular misting to prevent dehydration of the roots. When the plant reaches the edge of the mount it can be tied or wired to a new mount until the new roots have attached and then the old mount and back part of the plant can be cut away.

Orchids grown in pots should have just enough room for another 1–2 years' growth. Most orchids dislike being potted into too

One of the cymbidium family.

large a pot and may not flower until they have filled the spare space. Most orchids can be propagated by division though some make little plantlets that can be potted on. When repotting orchids, all the old potting medium should be removed from the roots and the dead and damaged roots cut away. Always use a sterile blade to avoid spreading diseases between plants. New medium should be worked carefully in around the roots and the plant staked and tied so that it is held firm while the new roots establish in the medium.

Pests and Diseases

Orchids are subject to many of the same problems as other plants but good culture can help to avoid them. Keep the growing area clean and tidy, always check new plants for pests before housing them with your collection and check plants regularly so that problems can be detected early. Care should be taken when using any insecticides and make sure you only use preparations labelled suitable for indoor plants. It's best to take your plants outside temporarily for any chemical treatment.

A beautiful phalaenopsis or moth orchid.

Conservation

In the wild many orchids are threatened with extinction through over-collecting or through destruction of habitat. Always purchase orchids from reputable growers and preferably plants propagated in greenhouses. Most traders know the origins of their plants so always ask and if they give evasive answers to your question take your business elsewhere.

Which Orchid?

There are 25,000–30,000 different species of orchids so the challenge is to avoid being carried away and to select only those for which you have the right conditions. The following orchids have been cultivated successfully in Canberra without the aid of a glasshouse using the indoor-outdoor

movement of plants to deal with the extremes of winter.

Cattleya. Both standard and miniature are suitable with the miniatures especially suitable for windowsill culture. They require filtered sunlight for most of the day and a minimum night temperature of 8–10°C. Allow the growing medium to dry out between waterings and give the plant a 'rest' from fertiliser after it finishes flowering until the new growths begin. Repot when the new roots are very small nubs, so that the new roots quickly establish in the new mix.

Cymbidium. Both standard (large) and miniature cymbidiums are suited to Canberra's cooler climate. During the growing season — spring to early autumn — grow outside under a tree or shade cloth with 50–70% filtered sunlight. Ensure they get lots of water and fertiliser so that they grow large and strong new pseudobulbs. Although these plants can generally tolerate temperatures almost to freezing, frost easily damages flower spikes, so put the plants under cover before the first frost. Reduce watering and feeding, and watch the flower spikes develop to bloom in late winter and spring. Repot after flowering is finished, every second or third year, making sure to leave at least 4 pseudobulbs together on each division.

Dendrobium, Dockrillia. These Australian natives are suited to culture in Canberra as, like cymbidiums, many will tolerate temperatures as low as 0°C provided they are protected from frost. *Dendrobium kingianum* and the many hybrids derived from it are especially attractive and rewarding plants to have in any collection. *Dendrobium speciosum* is a much larger specimen but is also tolerant of cold temperatures as long as it is kept dry. These plants put on a great and beautifully perfumed show in spring.

Australian terrestrial orchids

These little gems are remarkably easy to grow if you remember how they grow in nature. The easiest to cultivate are those that bloom in spring. The cycle starts when the underground tuberoid begins to grow with the first rains (or watering) in late summer. The plants grow through winter and send up the flowers in spring. As the soil dries out with the approach of summer, the leaves die down and the plant over-summers as a bare tuberoid in the soil. If you want to try these in the garden, it's best to start with local species, such as *Pterostylis curta*, and put them in the garden where you can mimic their natural surroundings – no additional

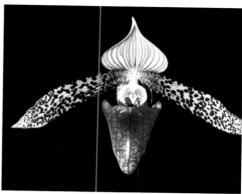

Paphiopedilum sukakulii, commonly called a slipper orchid.

water and only fertiliser that is suitable for native plants (if any). Beware of slugs and snails over winter. Growing them in pots is easier. Pot dormant tuberoids into a good native plant mix in a standard shaped pot, placing the tuberoids in the pot about 4 cm below the surface. Put chopped Casuarina or pine needles over the surface to protect the soil surface when watering. Water sparingly until the green shoots appear then keep moist through flowering. Water very sparingly through summer.

Paphiopedilum. Slipper orchids can be grown indoors where shade, temperature and humidity can be provided without any special

Pterostylis curta which is endemic to the Canberra area.

equipment. Good ventilation is important and placing the pots on gravel in a tray containing water will help keep the air around the plants humid, as will occasional misting with a fine spray of water. As these orchids have no pseudobulbs to store water, it is important not to let them dry out completely. These orchids generally appreciate annual repotting.

Phalaenopsis. The moth orchid is an excellent windowsill orchid (but not in direct sunlight) and flowers for 2–3 months. If you can grow African violets, you can grow moth orchids. Keep the potting mix moist, but not wet. In autumn, put your plants in a place where the temperature will drop at least 10 °C for about a week to encourage the formation of flower spikes. Once the spikes begin to grow, position the plant so that the spike grows towards the light in the way you wish it go and do not change that orientation, or the spike will twist.

Pleione

These orchids are also often available from nurseries in spring, when they are flowering from a leafless bulb. Although quite large, the flowers are short-lived and give way to the developing leaf. They should be given plenty of fertiliser and water and grown in semi-shade through summer. After the leaf dies down in autumn, set the pots aside and keep them dry until the new leaves and roots emerge in spring.

Of course, there are many other exciting orchids available to the hobby grower and this brief overview cannot possibly cover all you need to know about growing and flowering orchids successfully but help is at hand. The Orchid Society of Canberra meets each month from February to December with talks,

One of the pleione family.

library and a sales table. New members and visitors are always welcome. In addition to the monthly meetings the Society produces a newsletter and hosts an annual orchid show, field trips, beginners' workshops and various social events. Not only are you likely to meet new friends who share your interest but this group of fellow orchid growers is your best resource for good advice and information on growing orchids in Canberra.

For further information please refer to the White Pages under Orchid Society of Canberra Inc for the current contact phone number or the Society website at http://www.canberraorchids.org/.

Chapter 13:
African violets and other gesneriads

African violets remain a very popular flowering indoor plant. Discovered in 1892 in Tanganyika (now Tanzania) growing among shady rocky ledges, and initially known as the 'Usambara violet', it was later named saintpaulia in honour of its finder. The Saintpaulia is endemic to a small area in East Africa extending across northern Tanzania and part of southern Kenya from the Usambara Mountains to the coast. It is one of the best known members of the *Gesneriaceae* family, which also includes the Cape Primrose (*Streptocarpus*), the Goldfish Plant (*Columnea*), the Guppy Plant (*Nematanthus*), the Lipstick Plant (*Aeschynanthus*), Florists' Gloxinia (*Sinningia speciosa*) and Temple Bells (*Smithiantha*) amongst more than 150 genera.

Except where noted, the plants discussed in this chapter are suited only to indoors in Canberra.

Growing conditions

There are many misconceptions about growing African violets but the rule of thumb to remember is that these attractive plants prefer similar living conditions to those that most people enjoy in their homes. Optimum growing conditions for Saintpaulias are a temperature range of 15–26°C with moderately bright light so that they will flower well. They are, however, very adaptable plants and will grow quite well outside these parameters, although direct sunlight should be avoided as the rays of the sun will burn the leaves. If a plant is grown on a window-sill, a

Saintpaulia 'Coral Kiss'.

sheer curtain will provide sufficient screening from the direct sun. Insufficient light can be corrected with light from a fluorescent reading lamp placed alongside the plant.

Except for trailing African violets that produce stems that trail down over the sides of the pot, Saintpaulias should be grown as single crowned plants. Some cultivars occasionally produce an additional crown from a leaf axil causing the leaves to become very congested. To maintain the wheel-shaped symmetry of the plant these side-shoots should be removed as soon as they are noticed.

Watering

African violets like to grow in a moist mix but they are not bog plants – they do not like continuously wet feet. There are many ways to water an African violet but the main

Saintpaulia 'Precious Pink', a semi-miniature African violet.

thing is not to over-water the plant. Watering may be done by hand; either by standing in a saucer of water until the potting mix becomes damp or from the top using a long-spouted watering can that reaches under the leaves. Never leave the plant standing in water for any longer than necessary or it will develop root-rot.

Tepid water, or water that has been allowed to come to room temperature should be used for either of these methods. Cold water straight from the tap can cause marks to develop on the leaves. The time to water is when the top of the potting mix feels dry. Care should be taken that no water remains on the leaves or in the centre of the plant. If the plant is in strong light, water left on the leaves will burn the leaves while water left in the centre of the plant will cause crown rot.

Another method for watering is the wick method. A wick of wet synthetic material such as venetian blind cord or nylon stocking is inserted in the pot and allowed to draw water from a reservoir below the pot. Natural fibres should not be used for wicks because these rot with the constant moisture.

Pot size

Squat pots up to a maximum of 115–125 mm (4.5–5") should be used as using too large a pot will cause root rot. When re-potting, use a pot that is no more than about one-third the overall width of the plant. Miniature African violets only grow to 15 cm so they should not be grown in any larger pot than 50–55 mm while semi-miniatures only grow to 22.5 cm and will require a pot no larger than 75–80 mm.

Potting mix

Always use an African violet potting mix which should have a pH of 6.5–6.8. A mix that is too acid will cause brittleness in the leaves and tightness of the new growth in the centre of the plant.

Fertilisers

It is best to use a fertiliser formulated for African violets. A fertiliser with a very high nitrogen content will produce lovely lush green leaves but not many flowers. There are two forms of African violet fertiliser available. One is a powder, the other is a liquid. Both need to be added to water to make the required strength of fertiliser. Use whichever form you choose according to the manufacturer's directions. Too much fertiliser will cause fertiliser burn in the centre of the plant.

If the wick-watering system is used, fertiliser may be added to the water in the reservoir. In general, the liquid fertilisers are very suitable for this as they are usually formulated for constant feed. However, if using one of the powdered forms that are usually designed for application once a week, dilute the mixed fertiliser to one-eighth strength for use in a reservoir.

Columnea 'Early Bird'.

General care

Violets breathe through their leaves so brush the leaves regularly with a very soft paintbrush to remove dust and dirt, being careful to always brush in the direction that the tiny hairs grow. Brushing in the wrong direction causes tiny scars where the hairs break away from the leaf surface.

For an even symmetrical growth turn the pot one-quarter turn regularly (daily if possible). This will prevent a 'lean' towards the light.

Propagation

All gesneriads may be propagated from seed, cuttings and/or division. Gesneriad seed requires light to germinate and is best sown in a punnet that is placed into terrarium conditions until after germination occurs. When the plantlets are established the terrarium cover should be removed gradually to allow them to harden off. Plantlets should be potted up when large enough to handle.

Flowers of modern day Saintpaulias with their array of colours and patterns are far removed from the blue shades of the original species. To propagate African violets take a mature leaf, preferably from the third or fourth row of leaves from the centre of the plant. About 3½ cm from the leaf blade cut the stem from front to back at a 45° degree angle, insert it in potting mix and keep moist. Depending on the season and cultivar, plantlets should appear in 6 weeks to 3 months and may be potted up in small pots when they are large enough to handle easily.

Trailing gesneriads are best propagated by stem cuttings, while rhizomatous gesneriads usually produce several new rhizomes each growing season. Streptocarpus may be propagated by either division or by wedge-shaped leaf cuttings.

Streptocarpus 'Jealous Heart'.

Insect infestations

In the case of insect infestation remove all flowers and spray with a proprietary preparation suitable for use on house plants. Always spray from approximately 30 cm distance from the plant to avoid severe leaf damage. Infestation by cyclamen mite (a form of broad mite) is indicated by deformation of flowers and leaves together with greying tight centres, often with some webbing also in the centre. Treat such an infestation with a miticide. Cyclamen mite can spread through a collection very quickly so it is best to isolate and treat not only the affected plants but also other plants in their proximity.

Advice to the collector/exhibitor

New plants should be quarantined for 4–6 weeks before being introduced to a collection as should plants removed from the collection for showing. This helps to prevent the introduction of any pests or disease. Unhealthy-looking plants should also be quarantined until the problem has been treated.

Other gesneriads

Most of the other members of the Gesneriaceae family grow well with similar care to African violets. However the larger-growing members such as *Sinningia speciosa* (Florists' Gloxinia) and streptocarpus, as well as the basket varieties such as nematanthus, columnea and aeschynanthus require more fertilizer than African violets and grow better if an all-purpose slow-release fertilizer is added to their mix.

Due to its winter dormancy *Sinningia speciosa* (Florists' Gloxinia) may be grown in a sheltered position on a patio or verandah during summer.

Sinningias are natives of South America that grow from a tuber. They can vary in size from the smallest known gesneriad *Sinningia pusilla* that is only approximately 2 cm in diameter and requires to be grown in terrarium conditions to the much larger species such as *Sinningia cardinalis* and *Sinningia tubiflora* that can grow to 45 cm tall or more.

The smaller growing sinningias grow well in the same conditions as African violets and often do not go dormant, producing new growth as the old growth dies back after flowering. However the larger sinningias such as *S. speciosa, S. cardinalis*, and *S. tubiflora* die back in autumn. The tubers should be stored in their pots in a cool place during winter and repotted in fresh mix when new growth appears in early spring. Keep sinningias moist during the growing period but do not overwater or the tubers will rot.

Streptocarpus are fibrous rooted natives of South Africa. They will tolerate slightly lower temperatures than African violets but do not cope well with very high summer temperatures. They too like to be kept moist but not wet during the summer growing period.

The genus is divided into two sub-genera: *Streptocarpus streptocarpus* and *Streptocarpus streptocarpella. S. streptocarpus* are the strap leaf varieties commonly known as 'Cape Primrose' because of the similarity of their leaves in appearance to the English primrose. *S. streptocarpella* are very floriferous stemmed, usually trailing, varieties that are often sold in nurseries as 'Nodding Violets', although their tubular flowers are not really like violets except perhaps in colour.

Nematanthus are another fibrous rooted gesneriad. They are natives of South and Central America and will also tolerate cooler conditions than African violets. Trailing to semi-upright plants, they have glossy dark green leaves and glowing orange pouched flowers, hence the name of 'Guppy Plant'. They will tolerate some sun and are most suited to basket culture.

Aeschynanthus are fibrous rooted natives of Southeast Asia. Trailing plants that are best suited to basket culture, species may vary from very large to a more manageable medium size. They do not tolerate cool weather well, dropping their leaves when they become too cold. Their tubular flowers are in the red to red-orange range but not all species have the long tubular calyx that gives them the common name of 'Lipstick Plant'.

Columneas are trailing fibrous rooted natives of Central and South America that also drop their leaves when they become too cold. Their tubular flowers in orange to yellow tones generally have a slightly irregularly shaped corolla giving rise to their common name of 'Goldfish Plant'. Columneas make an ideal basket plant.

Smithiantha 'Copper King'.

Smithianthias are natives of Central America that grow from scaly rhizomes. Their wonderful velvety foliage may be a mixture of green tones through to rich burgundy. They are tall growers with spires of tubular flowers that give them the common name of 'Temple Bells'. Smithianthias have a period of dormancy during the winter months and like sinningias may be stored dry in their pots in a cool place until growth recommences again in the warmer weather.

Within the Horticultural Society of Canberra Inc. there is a group specialising in the culture of African violets and other gesneriads. They also display at the Society's Shows. The group meets monthly and you can find more information by checking with the Society.

CHAPTER 14: Climbing plants

Lyn Edwards

Climbers are a diverse group and bring an added dimension to the garden. They provide flowers and beautiful leaves at different levels, hiding unsightly objects, giving both shade and privacy from close neighbours and an interesting background to shrubs and other plantings.

Some plants climb using tendrils or twining stems, and require tying in to supports. Others, including ivy and Virginia creeper, attach themselves to walls using small rooting pads — these do damage to brickwork and painted surfaces. Care taken in the selection of a climber for the purpose intended can save many problems in the future. It is unwise to place climbers against an area requiring regular painting.

In this chapter we have concentrated on those climbers which are most attractive in the Canberra garden. Climbing roses are covered in the Roses chapter.

Planting and maintenance

Prepare ground for planting as you would for trees and shrubs. Dig over well and incorporate compost and manure. These plants will be in place a long time and good soil preparation will reward you with good growth. Construct supports before planting, tie in stems, and water well to settle the plants into their growing position.

Check ties regularly to prevent damage to stems and tie in new growth. Prune stems as required during the growing season and, as

with all plants, watch for pests and diseases and fertilise on a regular basis. Under eaves is a common place for climbers to be planted and in this situation artificial watering is a necessity as rain is unlikely to reach the root systems.

Pergolas

A strongly built pergola is the ideal position for the very rampant climbers such as ornamental grape, Virginia creeper, wisteria, and the Chinese trumpet vine. All provide good shade cover in summer, beautiful autumn colour and allow sun through in winter. Wisteria flowering in spring and the trumpet vine in summer are spectacular in bloom. This positioning also allows for good access for pruning to keep these strong climbers under control. Once the framework of the vines has been established shorten or remove new shoots to maintain shape. The beauty these plants bring to the garden amply rewards the care given.

It may seem a good idea to use fruiting vines on a pergola but the spraying necessary to keep fruiting vines such as grapes healthy, and messy dropping fruit, do not make for a pleasant place to enjoy the garden with family and friends.

Wisterias

Wisteria is well-known for its rampant growth and very beautiful, fragrant flowers. It is a wonderful plant but you need to be careful where you plant it and it should not be planted near walls, paths and drains. In time, the trunk will reach tree-like proportions.

It is available in two basic groups—the Chinese and the Japanese—though others do exist. All are hardy and a choice of cultivar depends on personal preference. All can be trained to make a beautiful standard by growing a single stem up a very strong support and training the top growth into an umbrella shape. Alternatively, you can twist several stems around a support which will eventually form a naturally grafted twisted stem. In either case, you will need to remove side shoots on the stem as they occur.

Pruning wisteria to achieve maximum flowering is a matter of timing. A few weeks after flowering the new long whippy growth should be removed — this will probably need to be done a few times during summer to keep it under control. During winter a second pruning, cutting back to about three buds on side shoots will help promote bud formation and flowering spurs. Fat oval flower buds are easy to distinguish from leaf buds which are narrow and pointed and produced on long annual growth. This is most apparent in late winter and pruning can be left until that time. This is a good time to tie in growth and also to check that existing ties are not strangling the plant.

Wisteria sinensis, the Chinese species, is the best known. It flowers early in spring on bare stems with small racemes of purple scented flowers; a lovely white version is also available.

W. floribunda, the Japanese wisteria, flowers along with its leaves and there are many very different cultivars. When established, some racemes of flowers can be a metre long. Colours are purple, pink or white depending on the cultivar and a double-flowered variety is also available. *W. f.* 'Macrobotrys' has metre-long racemes of fragrant purple flowers. *W. f.* 'Shiro Noda' has long racemes of white fragrant flowers. *W. f.* 'Honbeni' — long racemes of pink lightly-scented flowers. *W. f.* 'Flore-Pleno' — short racemes of double purple and lilac flowers. *W. f.* 'Shiro Kapitan' has short racemes of pure white and larger than usual flowers.

Clematis

This is a very large family which includes some Australian natives. There is a clematis for most situations and it is possible to have some type of clematis flowering all year including winter. Prepare your soil with lime and compost and dig well. Good drainage is necessary, but clematis prefer moist soil, with their roots shaded and with some support for the leaf stems to twist around so the stems can clamber up to the sunlight to flower.

Mulch well as in the wild these plants are nourished by leaf litter from the shrubs and trees they would be growing with naturally. All clematis need regular watering and fertilising and it helps to add water crystals to the planting hole.

Clematis napaulensis flowers in winter and then produces wonderful heads which will last for months. The plant is vigorous, summer dormant and then winter flowering.

The small flowered and species clematis should be planted at the level they have been grown at but the large flowered cultivars should be planted with the first node buried if soil depth allows that to be done. This gives the plant a point to regrow from if it happens to suffer from the disease known as clematis wilt at some time, and also allows for more stems to grow.

Clematis wilt may occasionally strike; a part or the whole plant will collapse suddenly without warning that all is not well. If this occurs cut the plant back and remove the diseased leaves. There is a good chance that new stems will be produced from the rootstock. This is most likely to occur if the plant has been deeply planted. It can take a considerable time for regrowth to appear so do not rush to remove the plant.

The small flowered and spring flowering varieties do not require pruning unless they are taking up more space than wanted; prune immediately after flowering if necessary. The large flowering cultivars are pruned back to a pair of low plump buds in winter to give maximum new growth to support their dinner plate sized blooms at a desirable height.

Spring flowering clematis

Clematis aristata, an Australian plant, is light and quick growing. It is frost resistant but needs a cool moist root run and good drainage. The leaves are slightly toothed and the flowers are starry white and abundant followed by fluffy seedheads.

C. armandii is a vigorous evergreen species with larger leaves and earlier flowers than other spring flowering clematis. The panicles of 5 cm wide flowers are white in *C. a.* 'Snowdrift' and palest pink in *C. a.* 'Apple Blossom'. The glossy deep green oval leaves are attractive all year. This species resents heavy pruning so is best left alone. A very beautiful and perfumed plant for a trellis or along a fence line.

The next five are ideal where a vigorous yet light-growing plant is desired.

C. macropetala is a smaller deciduous, mid-spring flowering species. The flowers are nodding and double; 'Markham's Pink' and 'Maidwell Blue' are delightful additions to the spring flowering range.

C. microphylla is a very slender fast-growing native plant both frost and drought-resistant

Clematis armandii flowers for quite a lengthy period in spring and has a wonderful scent.

with small narrow leaflets and masses of creamy white flowers in spring followed by fluffy white seed heads. Suitable for full sun to semi-shade in any soil provided the drainage is good. It is particularly attractive mingled with other plantings and on fences. It will never become invasive.

C. montana and its cultivars are the most frequently grown clematis in Canberra gardens. They are vigorous, deciduous late spring flowerers with white to deep pink blooms carried freely in clusters for a long period. There are a number of named cultivars including some semi-doubles. 'Freda', 'Tetrarose' and 'Elizabeth' are a deeper pink than the species and *C. m.* 'Rubens' has slightly bigger pale pink flowers. 'Marjorie' is a semi-double with a less formal flower.

C. spoonerii with its white flowers has growth and flowering pattern similar to *C. montana*; the flowers are a bright white.

Summer flowering clematis

Late spring into early summer sees the appearance of the species *C. viticella* and its cultivars and also the large flowered hybrid clematis, well known for their huge blooms in a vast colour range and combination of colours.

Clematis viticella is probably best grown scrambling through shrubs and trees and is suitable to grow with old roses, in particular in an informal garden setting. The blue to purple nodding bell-shaped flowers are borne in abundance and if pruned heavily after flowering will rapidly regrow and flower again in late summer. If half the vine is pruned heavily in winter and the other half left, the first flowering period can be extended greatly. Fine selections of *C. viticella* include 'Kermesina' red-flowered, 'Royal Velours' deep purple and the small double dusty purple 'Purpurea Plena Elegans'.

The greatly-hybridised, large-flowered clematis generally (and inaccurately) known as Jackmanii hybrids are a very mixed group and choice of a cultivar is a matter of choosing colour and form to personal taste. Try to see them in bloom before making a choice. They are available in a wide range of colours and

A large flowering clematis on a rustic fence.

in combinations of these colours and in large to very large double flowers. 'Nelly Moser', 'The President', 'Duchess of Edinburgh' and 'Vyvyan Pennell' are just a few garden worthy varieties. They are spectacular grown on a trellis, fences and up trees giving interest when spring blossom is long gone. After the first flowering cut them back, fertilise and water well for a second flowering. This group requires generous feeding, watering and mulching to give of its best. They benefit from hard pruning in winter.

Autumn flowering clematis

Clematis orientalis and *C. tangutica* are both light-growing, yellow flowered species. *C. orientalis* 'Bill MacKenzie' and the stunning deep yellow C. tangutica 'Golden Tiara' are currently the best of this group.

C. virginiana is a very vigorous deciduous species producing clouds of small white perfumed flowers in autumn, followed by the usual fluffy seedheads. This looks best climbing a tree or in a situation where it can grow without interference.

Winter flowering Clematis

Clematis cirrhosa and its varieties are small growing evergreen winter flowering clematis with small hanging bell shaped flowers. In a sheltered position on a wall they flower at a time few plants are in bloom, and also spot flower during summer. The species flower has cream bells and the variety *C. cirrhosa balearica* 'Freckles' has cream flowers with purple spotting inside and fern-like leaves. *C. c.* 'Lansdowne Gem' has deep red bells.

C. napaulensis is a very hardy vigorous summer–deciduous climber best grown up a tree or an arch with other plants to hide the tatty dead look of the vine in summer. In early winter this comes into its own when the new growth appears and the first of a long succession of its white hanging bells with long protruding purple stamens appear. It will continue to flower throughout the winter. It is greatly appreciated by the local bird life.

Some other plants for pergolas and other strong structures

Ampelopsis brevipedunculata, the Porcelain Berry, a member of the grape family, is grown for its turquoise berries, which have the look of cracked porcelain. A most attractive plant, growing 3–4 metres. Variegated leaved form available.

Campsis chinensis syn *C. grandiflora*, the Chinese Trumpet Creeper, is a very vigorous colourful deciduous climber with large clusters of orange trumpet-shaped flowers in summer. The glossy divided leaves produce superb autumn colour in reds, purples and bronze shades. It climbs by way of root pads and is therefore not suitable for painted surfaces. It flowers on new growth and can be pruned very heavily in winter, but once established, will produce sucker growth which should be removed. It is not affected by frost and is drought resistant.

Parthenocissus quinquefolia, the Virginia Creeper, with palm-shaped leaves in summer turns to brilliant scarlet in autumn and grows to fifteen metres. This plant and *P. tricuspidata*, cling to walls with rooting pads. It is very hard to remove these roots even after removing the vine itself and they are not suited to growing on masonry or painted surfaces.

P. tricuspidata, the Boston Creeper, has large oval-toothed bright green leaves changing to red and purple in autumn. It grows to a large size.

Vitis vinifera, the Ornamental Grape, is a strongly-growing deciduous vine with superbly coloured red foliage in autumn. It does not produce fruit in Canberra.

Annual climbers

Lathyrus odoratus (Sweet Peas) are probably the most commonly-grown annual climbing plant and rightly so. A row will provide large quantities of colourful fragrant flowers for garden display and for cut flowers for the home — the more flowers picked, the more will be produced. A position in full sun on a frame which the plants can twine around will give good results. The soil should be well dug and manured with compost and some garden lime incorporated a few weeks before sowing seed in autumn. Seedlings are also available.

L. latifolius, (Perennial Sweet Pea) is also an attractive plant for cottage gardens, scrambling up trees, through shrubs and on other supports. These do not have the perfume, shape or long stems of the annuals but are charming in their own right and are hardy low care plants.

Sweet pea 'Busby'.

Other annual vines worth considering are non-invasive members of the convolvulus family, *Cobaea scandens*, the Cup and Saucer Vine, and *Thunbergia alata*, the Black-eyed Susan. These can be perennial in milder climates but are grown as annuals in our area.

Native climbers
Light growing climbers

Clematis aristata and *Clematis microphylla* are covered in the earlier clematis section.

Hardenbergia violacea, Australia's wild sarsaparilla, is a strongly-growing twining plant which is sometimes used as a ground cover. It is both frost and drought tolerant, with oval leaves and sprays of purple flowers suitable for a sunny position with good drainage. Pink and white forms are available. The cultivar 'Happy Wanderer' is an excellent climbing form with larger flowers and can be used to cover a fence or a wall or to scramble over rocks and banks.

Sollya heterophylla (syn. *Billardiera heterophylla*), the Bluebell Creeper, is a small, frost hardy, evergreen creeper for sun or shade with dainty hanging bluebell flowers in spring and summer, followed by sprays of berries which turn blue as they ripen. Pink and white flowered forms are also available. This plant is very adaptable to soil conditions and can be used to cover fences, cascade down slopes, is excellent in large containers and can be clipped to make a compact shrub. It can also be grown in a hanging basket.

Large growing native climbers

The pandoreas with lush, glossy divided leaves and clusters of tubular flowers are large handsome climbers, capable of covering a carport or pergola. They require a soil enriched with compost, a position in semi-shade to full sun and ample moisture.

Pandorea jasminoides, the Bower Vine, has sprays of large pink trumpet flowers over a long period from spring through summer. The white cultivar 'Lady Di' is readily available and is more garden worthy than the species. It will need some frost protection when young and while it will tolerate frost when established, it does better in a protected site.

P. pandorana, the Wonga Wonga Vine, is a vigorous woody climber. The clusters of flowers are usually cream with red throats, though the colour can be variable, and are borne in profusion in spring. Several excellent cultivars are readily available. 'Golden Showers' produces masses of gold and brown bells in spring and 'Snow Bells' has pure white flowers in profusion in spring and summer.

Some other worthwhile climbers

Akebia quinata is a very commonly grown species and for good reason. It is light and gives excellent cover in a relatively short time. The five-lobed, soft green leaves are attractive and the vine will twist around any support. It is evergreen but does drop leaves in cold weather. The panicles of small chocolate-purple flowers carry a spicy fragrance in mid-spring through to summer. This plant is very hardy and will grow with little care.

Gelsemium sempervirens, the Carolina jasmine, is a light-growing evergreen twining plant with small glossy leaves. In late winter and spring this vine produces large quantities of small, bright yellow, trumpet-shaped fragrant flowers. Hardy.

Jasminum polyanthum aureum.

Jasminum polyanthum needs some protection from frost and can be controlled with a little pruning should it outgrow its situation. The plant is evergreen with beautiful long pink buds in large clusters unfurling to white strongly-scented flowers.

Lapageria rosea, the Chilean Bellflower, is a light twining evergreen vine with deep green, oval leathery leaves and has exquisite, bell-shaped flowers in white, pink or red which look as if they have been carved out of wax. New cultivars are being introduced with white flowers edged with pink or red. This plant needs a similar position to that of camellias — a slightly acidic soil with morning sun and shelter from hot sun and severe frosts. A slow grower, it may reach 5 metres in time. It is a good candidate for a pot on a sheltered balcony.

Mandevilla laxa, the Chilean Jasmine, needs to be protected from frost while young, against a warm wall being an ideal position. It is basically an evergreen plant with variable leaves which it can sometimes drop in cold weather. The flowers are large, white and star- shaped in clusters, their perfume reminiscent of gardenias and followed by 30 cm bean-like seed pods.

The blue potato vine, an especially attractive form of Solanum jasminoides.

Solanum jasminoides, the Potato Vine, is an evergreen fast-growing light climber with clusters of white flowers through summer. A blue-flowered form is now available. It is useful for quick coverage, is undemanding and can be clipped to shape. It has a place but it can get out of hand unless trimmed regularly, can self-seed and send up suckers.

Trachelospermum jasminoides, (Star Jasmine), is a hardy vigorous evergreen climber with dense glossy green or pink and cream variegated leaves with perfumed white starry flowers through summer. Slow to establish, but then, long-lived. Can be trained on single strand wires as a feature. Also useful where privacy is required due to its dense growth — a good choice for covering a fence or trellis.

A climber that is not recommended

Hedera — ivy has been grown extensively in the past but is no longer recommended because of its invasive nature. It layers easily, is unsuited for growing on masonry and painted surfaces and its berries are transported by birds, creating weed problems.

CHAPTER 15: General shrubs

Shrubs are woody plants, deciduous or evergreen, often multi-stemmed, but invariably long-lived. Evergreen shrubs provide permanent structure in a garden, especially in winter when deciduous plants are dormant. Consider also the advantage of permanent plant foliage against a house or fence, or where a division of garden space is required. They provide a whole range of features such as foliage colour, texture, flower colour and perfume.

In this chapter we consider some of a wide range of shrubs we know will do well in Canberra and similar climates. Other chapters deal with

» Roses
» Camellias, rhodendrons and azaleas
» Climbers
» Conifers
» Magnolias and related plants.

In the previous edition we included a chapter devoted to Australian plants. These plants are now included with the trees, shrubs, and annuals and perennials chapters.

By choosing from our plant lists, you will be able to have a garden for all seasons, with a range of shrubs to flower through the year, and others with colourful and interesting foliage or bark. Shrubs can be used in a mixed border along with small trees, herbaceous plants and bulbs. They also have an important role as hedges and for definition.

Hydrangea arborescens can produce very large flower heads and gradually expands by suckering. There are a number of cultivars but 'Annabelle' is the most commonly available.

In nature they may form the understory beneath large trees. A natural situation might well be partial shade in open, deciduous or mixed forest, a site ideal for growing camellias, magnolias or rhododendrons.

Most shrubs will tolerate a wide range of soil types, so long as the soil is well drained and reasonably fertile. Because shrubs are long-lived, ensure that the soil is well prepared before planting. It will be worth the extra effort. Read through the chapter dealing with planting techniques before you start planting.

Pruning

In general, plants which flower on last season's canes, eg abelias, forsythias, weigelas and kerrias will do best if cut back after flowering to give the developing new shoots room to grow. Plants which produce flowers on current season's growth usually flower towards the end of summer and are best pruned once the risk of frost is over in spring. Some special notes have been included for particular plants. Australian plants have a reputation of being easycare but they are no more so than any other plant and they will last longer and grow better with regular maintenance. Even their reputation for low water useage should be tempered by knowing where they grow naturally within Australia

Some shrubs especially suited to Canberra

The following list describes special features of each plant including its flowering period. Most plants recommended have no specific pests or disease, but where they do we have noted this in the list. Unless otherwise noted the plants are suited to open positions.

The list is not exhaustive and there are many other shrubs, varieties and cultivars which will grow satisfactorily in Canberra. Some of those found in older gardens have been superseded by superior cultivars and we have concentrated on the newer rather than the parent plants. In other cases there are varieties which will grow here but are very difficult to find in the garden centres: these have been left out. Some of the suggestions may be more easily found from specialist nurseries in the Southern Highlands, Victoria, Tasmania or from Australian plant specialists. The Horticultural Society of Canberra Inc. always aims to have some specially selected plants on sale at its four annual Shows.

Abelia grandiflora. Evergreen, 1–1.5 m. Compact with oval glossy green foliage, turning bronze-purple in late autumn–winter. The flowers are bell-shaped, white flushed

Abutilon 'Imp'.

pink. There is a golden form, foliage splashed with yellow, which turns reddish-gold in winter. Hardy, stands heavy pruning.

A. g. 'Sunrise' is a variegated form growing to 1 m.

A. schumannii is semi evergreen, 1–1.5 m. Compact with glossy green foliage, rosy-lilac bell flowers in arching sprays in summer–autumn. Stands hard pruning.

A. 'Kaleidoscope' grows up to 1m tall and 1.2 m wide. In early spring its leaves have bright red stems, lime centres and bright yellow margins. By summer, the yellow has turned golden, and in autumn and winter the foliage colour turns to shades of orange and red. White flowers in late spring, blooming well into autumn. A good container plant, or as an accent plant.

The softness and colour of Japanese maple leaves are wonderful from spring through autumn.

Abutilons (Chinese lanterns), native to tropical/sub tropical America, Asia & Africa, are very good shrubs to grow in a protected spot in the garden, eg on the east side of your house. They may be a little frost sensitive in newer gardens but are tough, hardy, easy care plants with low water requirements once established, and with a lengthy flowering season from early spring through to end of autumn. Then you can give them a good prune in readiness for the next flowering in spring. This will keep them from becoming leggy. There are many different cultivars ranging in size from 0.5 m to over 3 m tall and wide, in colours of yellow, orange, white, pinks; and variegated flower and foliage types. Some named cultivars include A. 'Imp', 'Ashford Red', 'Red Emperor', the dwarf 'Halo', 'Red Goblin', 'Yellow Gem' and 'Boule de Neige'. They are propagated easily from cuttings taken at any time of the year.

Acacias. There are many wattles available. We have concentrated on smaller Australian types that will do well here. Many in the list have interesting leaf shapes and are grown for this rather than their flowers. Once established, all are frost tolerant.

Acacia baileyana (Cootamundra wattle) is a weed in the Canberra area and is not recommended.

Acacia buxifolia, Box leaf wattle, grows to about 3 m, with a spectacular display of brilliant yellow flowers from spring to summer. It will tolerate frost and some dryness. Grow in well-drained soil in a sheltered position and prune regularly to maintain the desired size.

A. boormanii, Snowy River wattle, a shrub to 4 m with fine grey-green foliage and fragrant lemon flowers in spring. The birds love it and it tolerates dryness. It is inclined to sucker.

A. cardiophylla (Wyalong Wattle) is a free flowering shrub native to the Mallee areas of NSW. It grows 1.5–2.4 m, and flowers in spring. It has weeping, fine foliage. There is also a prostrate form.

A. cognata 'Limelight'(River wattle) is a dwarf shrub growing to between 0.5 and 1 m high and 1 m wide, grown for its beautiful foliage. It prefers part shade, is an ideal low informal hedging plant or tub plant, and responds well to pruning. There is a range of similar cultivars. They are useful plants if nursed through the initial year of frost sensitivity.

A. cultriformis, the knife leaf wattle, grows to 3 m. Profuse bright yellow globular flowers in late winter on attractive grey green pendant foliage make this a valued addition to the garden. It is drought resistant. A prostrate form 'Australflora Cascade' is ideal for spill-over on banks or for a feature plant in a tall pot.

A. leprosa 'Scarlet Blaze' has flowers more reddish than usual. It looks best on a ridge as its branches tend to be a bit floppy. Best not to let it encroach on paths.

A. podalyriifolia (Queensland silver wattle), a tall shrub to 5 m with silver grey phyllodes and large globular fragrant yellow flowers in spring. While it's a little frost sensitive when young, mulching and good drainage will help.

A. pravissima (Oven's River Wattle') probably should be classed as a tree at 6m high x 6m wide. It is quite hardy and tolerates dryness. Its dull grey foliage is an attractive feature. *A. p.* 'Golden Carpet' is a prostrate form to 40 cm high which can spread to 5–6 m. and is ideal for banks and rockeries. Profuse yellow flowers in spring.

A. vestita, (Hairy wattle), a tall shrub growing to between 3 and 4 m. It has a weeping habit

Regardless of a bit of drizzle, wattles brighten every Canberra winter and spring.

and attractive grey-green phyllodes. Masses of bright yellow ball-flowers in spring. It will tolerate most soils, some dryness and frosts. It can be used as an informal hedge, as a screen plant or as a low windbreak.

A. 'Little Nugget' is 1.2m high and 1m wide. It flowers late winter/early spring with clusters of yellow flowers. Tolerates full sun or part-shade and withstands heavy frosts.

A. 'Ruby Tips'. A small to medium shrub with small globular golden flowers and bright red new growth. It prefers moist, well-drained gravel and can adapt to heavy clay. Likes dappled shade through to full sun. It is frost tolerant and is moderately drought resistant. This plant will sucker but that is no pitfall, for with age, it will provide an effective dense ground cover.

Acer (Maple). Maples range from tall trees to diminutive shrubs, and it is the latter which are discussed here. These deciduous plants are cherished for their very attractive palm-shaped spring foliage, soft leaves through summer, brilliant autumn colour and the tracery of their winter branches. A few cultivars also have brightly coloured bark.

The small-growing Japanese maples are deservedly very popular foliage plants for the more established garden where protection can be given from hot dry summer winds. They are best grown in a position giving morning sun and afternoon shade. The shallow fibrous root system needs a moist well-drained soil kept mulched to prevent drying out.

They are also excellent for pots and can be kept as pot specimens for many years provided some attention is given to replacing potting soil every few years during winter, and they are given light pruning and fertilising.

The foliage is easily scorched by hot winds and the variegated leafed cultivars in particular are susceptible to sunburn. Scorching not only spoils the look of the plant during summer but also means the loss of the autumn display of colour from yellow to oranges and reds. Placing a small water feature or birdbath close by will provide needed humidity in summer.

Weeping maples are cultivars of *Acer palmatum dissectum* grafted at varying heights onto *Acer palmatum* stock; this gives good choice of heights from a few centimetres to 2 m to suit individual requirements. Shorter grafted plants are capable of weeping down a shaded bank very attractively.

The leaf shape and colour varies dramatically depending on the cultivar. They are heavily divided in differing patterns, and colour varies from red to deep purple through greens to pink and cream variegations. In time the branches will spread considerably and light pruning may be needed to keep to the size and shape wanted.

The following is a short list of cultivars but many others are available.

Acer palmatum dissectum 'Beni shidare variegata'.

Acer palmatum dissectum atropurpureum 'Inaba shidare' has the deepest purple leaf colour available and will tolerate quite a deal more sun and has a faster growth rate than others. The leaves keep their colour and do not 'bronze' during summer. If there is space for only one this is very highly recommended. Excellent red autumn foliage.

Acer p. d. 'Tamukeyama' also has lovely purple coloured leaves and a very good weeping habit. Good orange autumn foliage.

Acer p. d. 'Red Filigree Lace' has the finest cut leaves and needs more shade than the above to prevent scorching.

Acer p. d. 'Ever Red' — while the name describes its year-round foliage colour, in autumn the leaves turn rich scarlet and its spring foliage is purple-red but it is the attractive silvery pubescence of the new growth in spring which sets it apart from other cultivars at that time.

Acer p. d. 'Filigree' has pale green leaves overlaid with minute flecks of pale gold along the veining of the leaf. This plant requires more shade than darker coloured cultivars.

Acer p. d. 'Flavescens'— green leaves which will tolerate more sun and has yellow autumn foliage.

Acer p. d. 'Beni shidare variegata' has very beautiful, heavily variegated soft leaves in green, pink and creams. Shade is essential to prevent severe scorching and loss of leaves prematurely. Orange autumn foliage.

Upright Maples. The small upright-growing named Japanese maples also add vertical interest with beautiful leaves, not as divided as the dissectum group but with differing shape and leaf colours as well as good autumn foliage colouring.

Acer palmatum 'Chishio'is a very slow growing twiggy shrub. The spring foliage is pink to red, changing to green during summer, and in autumn orange to red shadings. Grows to about 4 m.

Acer p 'Butterfly' grows to about 2 m with green leaves bordered in cream. It is fairly sun tolerant and has good autumn colour.

Acer p. 'Senkaki', growing to about 2–3 m, has green leaves giving good yellow autumn colour and the extra advantage of bright red bark in winter.

Acer p. 'Ukigomo' (Floating Clouds). Growing slowly to 2–3 m, this is one of the most outstanding variegated varieties, the leaves being marked in varying ways. The least variegated leaves are green with pink shadings, some with white and pink spotting on a green background many pure white or pink. Early morning sun only and good protection from wind is essential for good performance. N.B. as a young plant this will have quite a large percentage of plain green leaves which should not be removed, the coloured leaves develop as the plant matures.

Acer japonicum 'Aconitifolium' (Fernleaf Maple) grows slowly to 3–4 metres. This has a cascading growth pattern with the 'snowflake' shaped leaves colouring superbly in autumn, as do all *A. japonicum* cultivars. Lovely in a shady area.

Acer j. Aureum (Full Moon Maple). The large pale gold leaves are very attractive and will light up a shady area. With slightly cascading growth, this can grow larger than most of the small maples.

Acer rubescens 'Summer Surprise' is a shrub growing to approximately 4.5 m high and wide when mature, with branches and twigs striped with green. Leaves are green with abundant white and pink variegations.

Aucuba japonica 'Variegata' (Gold Dust Aucuba). Evergreen, 1–2 m. Leaves are spotted with yellow. Foliage can be scorched black by hot sun and wind so it prefers semi-shade, but is nevertheless tough and resilient and tolerates frost, neglect and heavy shade. Female plant has drooping, clustered red berries. A great plant for Canberra.

Azaleas see the Chapter on Camellias, rhododendrons and azaleas.

Banksia. A family of Australian shrubs which do very well in Canberra. There is a growing number of improved cultivars.

Banksia ericifolia (Heath Banksia) is a tall shrub to 6 m with a spread of around 2 m. Heath-like foliage and erect torch like flowers during winter and early spring, usually orange.

Banksia ericifolia.

Some forms are deep orange/red to burgundy and others pale yellow. It's a good cut flower and source of nectar for honeyeaters. There is a dwarf compact form at 1 m high and 2 m across which flowers from autumn right through to spring.

B. spinulosa (Hairpin Banksia). A hardy shrub varying in size from 1 m to 3 m. It has long narrow leaves and flower torches with colours varying through gold, orange red or brown and appearing from autumn to mid spring. A good cut flower and attracts bird with its nectar. Dwarf forms are available. Prefers well-drained soil and some moisture. Will flower in filtered shade and is frost resistant.

Bauera rubioides (the River Rose), is a variable Australian shrub which can be up to 2 m wide and from almost prostrate to 1 m high with showy rose-pink flowers in spring and summer. Will tolerate shade, full sun or frost so long as it is well-drained.

B. sessiliflora, (the showy Bauera or Grampians Bauera) is an open shrub to 2 m high and 2–4 m across with masses of magenta flowers closely packed along the stems in spring and early summer. It is frost hardy. Mulch well to retain moisture and prune lightly after flowering to keep compact.

Berberis (Barberry). Plants are usually thorny and are grown mainly for foliage or berries, or as a dog-deterring hedge in the front garden. Masses of yellow or yellow-orange flowers in spring. They prefer a sunny position. There are over 400 species, for example:

B. sargentiana (Sargent Barberry), evergreen, 2 m. Large narrowly elliptical thorny green leaves turning reddish-bronze in autumn and winter. Yellow flowers, blue-black berries.

B. thunbergii 'Aurea' is a multi stemmed plant suitable for hedging or for feature planting. 50 cm to 180 cm height with yellow spring flowers and golden foliage. A tough hardy, fast growing plant. 'Golden Glow' has lemon-yellow leaves.

B. thunbergii f. *atropurpurea* (Purple Japanese Barberry). Deciduous, 1 m. Leaves deep red to copper-purple, yellow flowers, red berries.

B. thunbergii f. *atropurpurea* 'Helmond Pillar' is a mid-sized deciduous shrub (2 m x 2 m) with upright stems bearing red-purple leaves that turn brighter red in autumn. It bears small, yellow flowers and has red berries in autumn. This plant needs little regular pruning, but to renovate old plants, remove the oldest stems at the base and cut back all branches to healthy young shoots.

Boronia. The following boronias are quite frost tolerant in the ACT but all require perfect drainage and moisture. All are Australian plants.

B. heterophylla (Red boronia), a compact shrub which grows to 1–2 m. It has hanging magenta bells in spring.

B. megastigma (Brown boronia) A low shrub to 1 m with sweetly fragrant flowers in late winter and spring. The brown boronia prefers light shade and has a reputation for being short-lived. Even if grown as an annual, it is well worth the effort. There are a number of cultivars with varying flower colours, and all are scented.

B. serrulata (Native rose) grows to 1 m with vivid pink cup-shaped perfumed flowers in spring. It comes from sandstone country and requires good drainage and moisture, though it is quite frost hardy.

Brachysema celsianum syn *B. lanceolatum* (Swan River pea). A low growing Australian shrub to 1 m high with bright red pea flowers. This plant is another which requires good drainage, but is well worth growing. Though it prefers full sun it will tolerate partial shade and most frosts.

Buddleia (Butterfly Bush, Summer Lilac). Hardy fast growing large plants with showy flowers in summer, suitable for most soils. They need a sunny position. Require an annual hard pruning to prevent woodiness.

B. alternifolia is a 2.4 m evergreen shrub from China. Long arching branches carry along their full length dense clusters of small rosy-mauve scented flowers. Prune after flowering to keep good appearance and within bounds.

B. davidii (Butterfly Bush) Deciduous, 2–4 m. Most common of the buddleias. Large dense spikes of fragrant lilac flowers, long pointed leaves, whitish beneath. A number of cultivars have been introduced, eg 'Veitchiana' which has improved colour and habit, 'Pink Pear' mauve pink, 'Isle de France' deep violet,

'Royal Red' rich red-purple, 'Black Knight' close to navy blue, 'White Bouquet' and 'White Cloud' white.

B. salviifolia (Sage Leaf or Winter Butterfly Bush). Evergreen, 2–3 m. Large plumes of mauve fragrant flowers at the top of square stems, long pointed wrinkled leaves, greyish beneath. It flowers in late winter and early spring.

Buxus (Box). Compact small dense shrub, glossy leaves, slow growing. A good small specimen plant or as a low hedge. Responds well to clipping.

B. sempervirens (Edging Box). Evergreen, 1 m, hardy with small glossy leaves. *B. s.* 'Marginata' (Variegated Box). Evergreen, I m. Similar in growth habit to above — leaves with yellow markings.

B. s. 'Suffruticosa' is evergreen, I m. Compact and with dense foliage, it may be clipped to form a very low hedge.

Callicarpa japonica (Japanese Beauty Berry). Deciduous, 1–1.5 m. Pale pink flowers in clusters in early summer, small violet berries, and oval pointed leaves spotted beneath. Lime loving plant.

Callistemon. The genus *Callistemon* is now included in *Melaleuca* . There is a large range of bottlebrushes available with new colours and sizes continually being introduced. Make sure that any plant you buy can handle our frosts. With all bottlebrushes, after flowering, prune to just behind the dead flower to promote new growth and flowers for the following year.

M. citrina (syn. *C. citrinus*) forms are tolerant of varying soils and positions, and are able to tolerate heavy frosts. 'Anzac' is a low growing compact shrub to 2 m with soft green foliage and white bottlebrush flowers in spring and autumn. 'Endeavour' is compact, growing to 3 m with masses of red flowers in early spring and autumn. It is a good cut flower.

M. pallida (syn. *C.* pallidus) (Lemon bottlebrush). To around 3 m, it is frost tolerant and grows well in most soils but prefers full sun. Lemon-coloured flower spikes in summer.

The following two are now treated as separate species: *M. paludicola* (syn. *C. sieberi*) and *M. pityoides* (syn. *C. pityoides*). *C. sieberi* (syn. *C. pityoides*) (Alpine bottlebrush) is hardy and available in several forms. The alpine form is compact to about 1 m tall with small dense cream flowers in summer. It is very hardy and though it prefers a moist soil, it will tolerate dry conditions. It should be pruned after flowering to encourage compact growth. Another form grows as an erect shrub to about 2 m. Yellow flower spikes in spring and summer. It is best in moist soils but is frost hardy.

M. 'Cherry Time'. This plant is a hybrid between *M. citrina* and *M. subulata*. Glossy leaves and bronze new growth. Vivid clear cherry-coloured flowers, attractive to birds. Weeping shrub to about 1.8 m by 1.5 m.

M viminalis 'Captain Cook'. A very popular bottlebrush which grows to 2 m high. It forms a dense compact shrub with small leaves consistent with its height. Flowers are red and produced at the end of the branches. Main flowering period is spring with a reduced show in autumn.

Melaleuca 'Burgundy Jack', to 3 m high and 2 m wide, has burgundy-violet flowers in late winter and spring with a second flush in autumn. It tolerates drought, is frost hardy and tolerates a wide range of soil types. Can be used for medium height screens or hedging. Prune regularly to encourage dense growth and to promote new bronze-coloured growth.

M. 'Hannah Ray' is a weeping small tree to 5 m with grey-green foliage and red flowers in spring, sometimes repeating in autumn.

M. 'Kings Park Special', a hybrid large bushy shrub to 4 m. Its branches are slightly pendulous and masses of bright red flowers appear in spring and early summer. Extremely hardy, withstanding dry periods and heavy frosts. An excellent specimen plant. Use it as either a screen plant or in a tub.

M. 'Little John' is a dwarf (25–30 cm all over) red bottlebrush with blue-green foliage, and produces masses of flowers in summer. It is excellent for rockeries and for mass planting.

Camellias see the Camellias, rhododendrons and azaleas chapter.

Ceanothus edwardsii (Edward Ceanothus). Evergreen, 2–2.5 m. Small glossy deep green leaves, deep blue flowers in dense clusters, fast growing and flowering in spring. The deep blue of the flowers is the principle reason for growing this plant.

The most common form is *C.* 'Blue Pacific'. Sometimes subject to dieback. Prune after flowering to keep a compact form. Bees love this plant.

C. 'Blue Sapphire' has arching growth and is covered in small, very dark, glossy green leaves. The whole mound is covered with deep blue flowers in spring. Sun loving, tough and drought tolerant 1 m x 1.5 m.

C. 'Joyce Coulter' is a low growing shrub making a dense evergreen dark green groundcover 60 cm or more tall and 3 m across. In late winter and spring it has 10–15 cm heads of gentian blue flowers. Best in a sunny position but water a few times when first planted to help settle it in.

C. 'Blue Cushion' has abundant pale blue flowers in button-like clusters from late winter until mid spring. Dark glossy evergreen serrated leaves form a dense ground cover some 90 cm tall by 2 m across.

C. x delilianus 'Gloire de Versailles' is a 19th century French hybrid between deciduous *C. americanus* and the evergreen *C. coeruleus* from Mexico. Later to flower than the Californian species it has a long flowering season. 10-15cm long panicles of light blue flowers from December until April. Burnt orange seed heads are a bonus. Cut back about a third each winter. 2 m x 1.8 m.

C. 'Yankee Point' (Yankee Point Californian Lavender). Another ground cover ceanothus making arching mounds of dark green, relatively large evergreen leaves. In early spring dusty white buds develop into 5 cm long panicles of china blue flowers. It is both frost hardy and very drought tolerant. 0.9 m x 2.5 m.

Chaenomeles (Flowering Quince, Japonica). Deciduous, dense compact shrub, flowering late winter/early spring. Fruit may be used for jelly and instant ikebana for those who aren't great with flower arranging!

C. japonica (Dwarf Flowering Quince). Deciduous, 1 m. Dwarf habit more rounded than the common *C. speciosa*. Flowers reddish-orange, shiny coarsely toothed leaves. Free flowering and fruiting. The great attraction of this plant is the flowers which appear in late winter. Named cultivars have advantages in that they are less likely to sucker.

C. speciosa (Flowering Quince). Deciduous, 2 m. Spreading shrub with spiny branches, dark glossy green leaves, red flowers.

Chimonanthus praecox brings flowers and lovely scent to the winter garden.

There are a number of very good cultivars, for example *C. s.* 'Apple Blossom', single white with rosy pink centre; and *C. s.* 'Nivalis Single', pure white.

Chamelaucium uncinatum (Geraldton Wax) grows over a wide area of the sandy plains north of Perth. Despite its origin, this long-flowering outstanding shrub is grown extensively in Australia and overseas as a cut flower, and many different forms have been introduced ranging from pure white through pinks, mauves and purples and combinations of colour. Constant tip pruning will keep the plant as a dense shrub of 1.6 x 1.6m. Without pruning it may grow leggy, reaching up to 5m. It prefers well drained soil in partial sun, and is quite drought tolerant once established. In Canberra, the plant will usually be sold during flowering in winter. It may be at risk of frost damage, if planted then, due to having been grown in a softer climate. You can overcome this by keeping the plant in its pot until later in spring when it can be planted out with safety. Geraldton Wax is also a useful plant for pots and hedges.

Chimonanthus praecox (Allspice or Wintersweet). Deciduous, 2–3 m. Grown mainly for the fragrance of its brownish yellow flowers which are produced while the plant is leafless in mid to late winter. A very good plant for Canberra's winters.

Chionanthus virginicus (Fringe Tree) is very hardy and requires little water beyond the initial first year of growth. It grows 3 m high by 2 m wide and has masses of white flowers with strap shaped petals. It flowers spring to summer.

Choisya ternata (Mexican Orange Blossom). Evergreen, 1–2 m. Compact shrub with deep green glossy leaves and fragrant white flowers similar to orange blossom, mostly in summer. May be used as a hedge plant. Occasionally subject to caterpillar attack.

Cistus (Rock Rose). A genus of hardy shrubs which prefer a sunny position. Do not prune hard. Many species and hybrids are called rock roses. Most flower over a long period. They are lime tolerant. There are many attractive cultivars, offering a range of flower colours from white through to red in summer.

C. albidus. Evergreen, 1–2 m. Rosy-lilac or magenta flowers, yellow at base of petals. It has oblong hairy net-veined leaves and white woody stems.

C. salviifolius (Gallipoli rose) is a form grown from plants collected from the Gallipoli Peninsula. It has large single white flower with gold stamens and small woolly sage-like leaves. The plants can be grown in pots or in the garden, but need full sun and good drainage. Grows 60 - 90cm. C. salviifolius 'Prostratus' grows to 120cm wide as an evergreen mat and in late spring has small white golden centred flowers which look like single roses. Good for spilling over a retaining wall.

Clethra. A family of deciduous shrubs or small trees grown for their flowers which have a resemblance to lily of the valley. They have scented flowers from late spring to summer. While these shrubs are often planted near water to prevent erosion, they do not require continual moisture and once established adapt to a regime of weekly watering with ample mulch. All grow as a spreading mound with some suckering.

C. alnifolia 'Hummingbird' is a dwarf form at 1m x 1.2m with glossy leaves and white flowers. C. a. 'Ruby Spice' can grow a little larger and has dark pink, fragrant flowers.

C. delavayi has long flower trusses and good autumn foliage.

Coleonema (Diosma). Compact free flowering shrubs with heath-like foliage. All require regular shearing three or four times a year to encourage dense growth, to keep their shape and to encourage flowering in late winter and spring.

C. album (White Diosma). Evergreen, 1–1.25 m. Compact shrub, scented heath-like foliage, masses of small star-like white flowers.

C. pulchrum (Pink Diosma). Evergreen, 1–1.5 m. More upright growth than C. album. Masses of small pink flowers.

C. p. 'Sunset Gold' (Golden diosma) is evergreen, 0.75 m. Very compact dense foliage, bright butter yellow. Deeper colour in colder weather. Pale pink flowers.

Convolvulus cneorum A small grey-leaved shrub growing to 0.9 m high and 1.2 m wide with profuse white flowers in summer. A very hardy plant which tolerates frost and drought.

Coprosma repens (Looking Glass Plant) is an evergreen shrub 2.5–3 m which grows in most soils and sites. Deep green glossy leaves and tiny white flowers, clusters of berries which turn from green to orange. Its tough leaves are frost tolerant and also ideal for exposed locations where wind or salt spray are a problem.

C. repens 'Picturata' has variegated leaves with a central yellow blotch. *C. repens* 'Variegata' has leaves with a broad yellow margin. *C. repens* 'Copper Shine' has round shiny leaves tinged bronze. *C.* 'Yvonne' grows to 1.5 m round with dark glossy brown/black leaves.

Conifers See the Conifers chapter.

Cornus (Dogwood). This genus has a wide range of shrubs and small trees. They are grown for their spring flowers (bracts), autumn foliage or winter bark. Many will eventually become small trees unless pruned heavily. C. alba and C. stolonifera, which are grown for their coloured stems should be cut back heavily after flowering in spring, but are generally too demanding of water to work well in Canberra.

C. alba (Tartar Dogwood). Deciduous, 2–3 m. Vigorous spreading shrub, oval green leaves, autumn foliage, coral red branches in winter. Best colour in cooler areas and in a damp site.

C. florida (White Flowering Dogwood). Deciduous, 2–4 m. Tiny true flowers

surrounded by large showy white bracts, reddish tinged autumn foliage. Will tolerate pruning after flowering.

C. f. rubra (Pink flowering Dogwood). Deciduous, 2–3 m. Similar growth habit to *C. florida* but the bracts are in pink shades, showing deeper pink in exposed areas, red autumn foliage.

C. stolonifera 'Flaviramea' is deciduous, 1.2–1.8 m, with bright greenish-yellow shoots. Moist conditions required for optimum growth.

Correas. A family of rounded Australian shrub to 2 m with grey-green rounded leaves which flower in autumn. It is very hardy and is tolerant of most soil types so long as the drainage is good. It flowers best in full sun and is frost resistant. Can be grown as a hedge or screen plant and is attractive in a tub.

C. alba x 'Mallee Pink'. Masses of bird attracting pink flowers in winter. 2 m high by 2 m wide. Vigorous and quick growing. Requires well-drained soil. Cut back after flowering to keep compact.

C. baeuerlenii (Chef's Cap Correa), a rounded shrub to 2 m. Its green/yellow flowers in autumn and winter resemble a chef's cap. It grows well in most well-drained soils and responds to watering in dry weather. Tip pruning is advisable to keep growth compact. It is suited for screening or as a tub plant. If you rub the leaves they smell of Juicy Fruit chewing gum.

C. lawrenciana (Mountain Correa). A taller shrub at 3 m with green bell flowers between autumn and spring. It prefers a cool, moist, well-drained position with some shade but will tolerate frost and snow. A good choice for a screen or fence cover.

Correa 'Canberra Bells', Canberra's centenary flower.

C. pulchella ranges from prostrate to 1 m high and 3 m across. The pendulous tubular flowers appear from autumn through to spring, and range through pink, orange, red and sometimes white. It likes a well-drained soil. Tip prune to encourage bushy growth.

C. reflexa (Native Fuchsia), a variable shrub ranging from prostrate to 3 m high and flowering from autumn through to spring. The flowers are usually pendulous and yellow, green, pink or red with green tips. 'Fat Fred' is a large-flowered form with broad red flowers with greenish-yellow tips. It prefers a well-drained moist site with filtered sunlight. Tip prune after the main flowering to encourage compact growth and more flowers.

C. 'Dusky Bells', an excellent shrub for Canberra's conditions, it grows to 60 cm high with deep pink flowers from autumn through to spring. It is frost resistant and as it flowers through winter, it is a very welcome addition to a Canberra rockery, or as a ground cover. Can also be grown in tubs.

C. 'Marian's Marvel' is an open grower from 1 to 2 m tall by up to 3 m across. It has tubular bell flowers between March and September which are pink with pale green tips. It prefers shade or filtered sun and needs good drainage. It is frost hardy, but a little extra water may be needed during protracted dry periods.

C. 'Wyn's Wonder' Grows densely to 0.75cm tall by 1m – 1.2m wide and has olive green leaves with distinct cream margins. Long rose-pink bell flowers with flared tips and soft pink interior. Plant in full sun to light shade and good drainage.

Corylopsis spicata (Winter Hazel). Deciduous, 2 m. Bushy shrub with broad roundish leaves, yellow flower bells in drooping short chains, fragrant. It flowers before the leaves appear in spring, followed by red berries.

Corylus avellana (Hazel). Deciduous, 3–4 m. Dense mass of stems with roundish toothed leaves, paler beneath, short male catkins, sweet edible nuts. Cross-pollination required for a good crop of nuts. There are a number of varieties available.

C. a. contorta (Harry Lauder's Walking Stick). Deciduous, up to 2 m. All the shoots and branches are twisted and contorted in corkscrew fashion. Likes shade in summer.

C. maxima purpurea (Purple-leaf Filbert). Deciduous, 2–3 m. Attractive shrub with deep purple leaves spring and summer.

Cotinus coggygria (Smoke Bush). Deciduous, 3–4 m. Large shrub, roundish green leaves which turn to brilliant colours in autumn. The tiny flowers in large trusses become a smoky-grey mesh of fine hairy threads carrying the seeds. There are named, improved varieties.

C. coggygria var. purpureus 'Atropurpureus' Leaves green, but flower spray is rich red-purple.

C. coggygria 'Rubrifolius'. Purple-leaved Smoke Tree. Leaves are deep purple, red in autumn, flower spray is reddish also.

C. coggygria 'Golden Spirit' has lemon-yellow leaves. Its new foliage is outstanding. It is best planted where it will receive light shade in the afternoon to prevent leaf burn. Autumn tones of pink-orange to red and yellow.

C. 'Grace'. An outstanding cultivar with richly coloured purple leaves that mature to blue-green and are very large, with 25-30 cm panicles of pink blooms. The autumn color is excellent.

Cotoneaster. A large genus of evergreen and semi-evergreen shrubs with long lasting berries. See the Weeds Appendix.

Crowea exalata (Small Crowea) another Australian shrub to 1 m high and 1 m wide with bright pink star flowers along the stems in summer through to autumn. Likes a well-drained soil with some shade, and requires some extra moisture during dry periods. It is frost resistant. Prune after flowering to encourage bushy growth.

Cytisus. Shrubs with stiff wiry stems, small leaves, pea-shaped flowers.

Dampiera diversifolia is a spreading Australian shrub up to 2 m across with small toothed leaves and a suckering habit. Masses of brilliant blue-purple flowers in spring. Requires a well-drained moist soil and a little shade. It is moderately frost-resistant and is ideal for rockeries, banks, walls, tubs or hanging baskets.

Daphne. The daphne family (Thymelaeaceae) comprises about 50 species of evergreen and deciduous shrubs. They are some of the most sweetly scented garden shrubs, forming roundish bushes with dark green leaves.

The daphne we usually grow (*D. odora*) is especially renowned for its highly scented flowers, though some in the genus have no fragrance. On the whole, daphnes are neat compact plants, well-suited to a rock garden, and at home with camellias, rhododendrons and similar plants. What the small flowers lack in size, they often make up for in quantity, for many species produce showy heads of blooms in shades of white, cream, yellow, and pink during winter or spring.

Daphne species vary in habit and may be erect, rounded, or spreading, but the majority

Daphne odora, the perfume of spring.

are neat, compact evergreen shrubs. The deciduous plants have less heavily-textured foliage. The showy rounded heads of small flowers open from mid-winter to late spring, depending on the species, and are usually in delicate shades of white, cream, yellow, or pink and *D. genkwa* has lavender flowers. The fruit that follows the flowers may be very colourful, ranging through white, pink, red and purple.

Daphnes generally prefer moist, cool, humus-rich, well-drained soil, and are best placed where the plant will receive morning sun and protection from the hot afternoon sun. Once established, the plant will need to be mulched well and the roots undisturbed. Small-leafed species prefer better lit conditions, while larger-leaved species need some shade from the hottest sun.

Maintenance consists of a simple trim to shape after flowering, or better still, pick

some sprigs of daphne and fill your home with perfume. At the same time you will be giving your plant the tip pruning it needs to keep growing well. The plant can be fertilised at that time with a good all-round fertiliser.

There are a few things that can go wrong:

» Sometimes daphne can suffer root rot as a result of over-watering, and that will cause the leaves to hang down and look particularly sad. Gardeners tend to indulge daphne by watering it, but better to ignore it sometimes and allow it to dry out between watering. Keeping the plant mulched will help keep the roots cool. If the leaves of your daphne are pale green and hang down, then this can also be an indicator that it needs some fertiliser.

» If the leaves are bright yellow, that can be an indicator of an iron deficiency, remedied by a foliar spray of sulphate of iron.

» If over or under watered, daphne can become stressed and that's when insects such as scale will move in. Scale insects are small shelled creatures that appear on or beneath the leaves, and on the stems. Make a habit of checking your plants regularly. If you find some on the daphne, but not too many, then they can be squashed, but if they have built up their numbers, then you should spray with a horticultural oil to smother them. Check a few weeks later, and if the shells have not become papery and dry, give the plant another spray.

» Daphne virus used to be common but proper hygiene and better plant propagation methods by growers means that you will rarely see a modern daphne with virus. It can still be possible if you take cuttings from an affected plant.

Here's a short list of daphne, starting with those more readily available and ending with some which are well worth growing. Some occasionally appear in garden centres, and the Horticultural Society often has some of the more unusual daphne plants for sale at its Shows.

Daphne odora – One of the best known and most desirable of all flowering shrubs. It is native to Japan and China and is an evergreen, growing to between 1 and 1.5m.

D. odora 'Marginata Alba' – Has yellow-edged leaves and a delightful scent. *D. odora* 'Alba' has pure white, scented flowers. The leaves of *D. odora* 'Aureomarginata' have a thin margin of creamy yellow.

D. x burkwoodii. A hybrid between *D. cneorum* and *D. caucasica*, it has light pink fragrant flowers in small dense clusters on a compact bush of 60-90cm. *D x burkwoodii* 'Variegata' has pale yellow leaf margins.

D. genkwa – Native to China and deciduous, it has lilac flowers along leafless branches in early spring and grows to 90cm. In acid soils it will need extra lime to thrive. A compact form is sometimes available.

The daphnes that follow are available through the wholesale nursery Yamina Rare Plants, and sometimes a few of these will appear on the Society's plant stalls, so keep your eyes peeled!

D. bholua is an upright evergreen to semi-evergreen suckering shrub to 2m or more with sweetly scented flowers which fill the air with perfume in early winter. The flowers are reddish-purple in bud, opening white. *D. bholua* 'Jacqueline Postill' has larger flowers, which are more pink and showy than the species. Another winter bloomer with outstanding perfume.

D. cneorum (the Garland Flower). A suckering dwarf shrub displaying very showy bright pink scented flower heads in spring. Neutral to acid soils. *D. cneorum* 'Variegata' is a vigorous form with cream-edged leaves and bright pink scented flowers.

D. collina - Slow growing dwarf form with glossy rounded leaves and beautiful rose-purple scented flower heads in spring.

D. longilobata – An evergreen shrub to 2m with open growth, narrow leaves and scented white flowers in summer.

D. mezereum – A small sturdy deciduous shrub which has massed purplish flowers on leafless stems in early spring. Lime should be added to acid soils for best results.

D. x napolitana. A compact shrub, usually less than 1m, with narrow leaves and rose-pink scented flowers in spring or summer.

D. pontica. A small shrub with large dark green, shiny leaves, spidery yellow-green flowers and a spicy scent. This daphne grows well in dense shade.

D. sericea – A small shrub with narrow leaves, pale pinky-mauve scented flowers and orange fruit.

Deutzia. A deciduous shrub to 1 m flowering in late spring. Should be pruned immediately after flowering to maintain compact plants. There are many good cultivars, with white or pink flowers.

Diosma see Coleonema.

Dodonaea viscosa 'Purpurea' (Purple Hopbush). Evergreen, 2–3 m. A fast growing shrub with purple foliage, sometimes sticky. Copper red seed capsules are 3 winged.

D. procumbens (Creeping Hop bush) is endemic around Canberra. It has a small white flower and can be used as a ground cover, in a basket or to hang over rocks. It needs very little water. The reddish fruit are an attractive feature.

D. sinuolata is a spreading shrub which grows to between 1 and 2.5m high and 2m wide. It has ferny divided foliage and decorative brick-red fruits appear on the female plant. An attractive plant once established.

Edgeworthia papyrifera syn *E. chrysantha* (Chinese Paperbark, Yellow Daphne). Deciduous, 1–2 m. An open shrub whose dark green leaves appear after rounded heads of small tubular white and yellow perfumed flowers. These become obvious from mid-winter, continue well into spring, and appear on independent short stems off main growth giving an interesting sight in late winter as flowers open. As the flowers can be damaged by heavy frost it is best planted under the canopy of taller deciduous trees or in a similar protected area. There is an attractive orange flowered form, but perhaps these plants are for collectors.

Elaeagnus pungens. Evergreen, 2.5–4 m. Large dense shrub, sometimes thorny, leaves silvery beneath. Small fragrant white flowers in autumn followed by reddish brown berries. The variegated forms are best.

E. angustifolia 'Quicksilver' has silver leaves and is a very pretty feature plant.

E. p. 'Aurea' has gold markings whereas *E. p.* 'Frederici' has silver markings. Suitable as a fast-growing hedge.

Epacris impressa, (Native Heath) is Victoria's original floral emblem. A frost-resistant small shrub to 1 m with sharp pointed leaves and narrow bell flowers along the stems in late winter through to spring. These may vary

Dodonea sinuolata. This photo was taken in September.

from white to pink or red. The plant prefers moist well-drained soil. Prune after flowering for compact growth.

Eremophila (Emu Bush). Relatively new to cultivation, these plants are increasing in popularity. One significant reason is their low water use and ability to withstand long dry periods, at the same time producing masses of flowers. While some of the eremophilas originate in Western Australia and might be considered hard to grow here, garden centres are now offering grafted forms to make it easier to grow these. There are many eremophilas, however, that do not need to be grafted to do well in our soils , so check your Australian plant sources. Whether grafted or not, many eremophilas will do very well here.

E. nivea grows in most soils, including heavy clay, but does best in full sun. It responds well to pruning directly after flowering. Without pruning it can become leggy. Annual pruning will keep it compact. Though often offered in Canberra as a grafted plant, *E. nivea* can be propagated easily from cuttings taken when the new spring growth has hardened off in summer. Keep foliage on cuttings dry to avoid fungal problems. 'Gubburra Bells' is an improved cultivar with larger flowers.

Eremophilas are becoming justly popular in Canberra. This is *Eremophila glabra* 'Kalbarri Carpet'.

E. glabra is a small shrub growing to 1m high and wide. It prefers a warm airy site, and its flowers can be green, yellow, orange or red. Prune to maintain dense foliage.

E. glabra 'Kalbarri Carpet' is a ground cover growing to 0.3m high and 1.5m wide, with striking silver foliage which has proved to be extremely drought and frost hardy. Its foliage combines with bright yellow tubular flowers in spring and summer to create a stunning living carpet of at least 1 square metre. Tip prune to keep the foliage dense.

Erica (Heath). A large genus of mainly South African shrubs. There are over 600 known varieties, plus many garden hybrids and seedlings. A number of varieties are worth planting in this area, from very dwarf to over 2 m high. Flowers, which appear through winter, are white, pink, red, mauve and various shades of these. It is best to buy when they are flowering so you can see what you are getting. Give them a good clipping after flowering. Poor drainage can cause loss of the plant.

Eriostemon see Philotheca

Escallonia. A genus of hardy free flowering evergreen shrubs, small to medium sized leaves, usually glossy dark green with finely serrated margins. There are a number of hybrids which are becoming popular as a hedge.

E. iveyi. (Hybrid). Evergreen, 2.5–3 m. Compact growth, glossy deep green leaves, dense clusters of white flowers in late spring, will stand clipping. Better as a specimen plant than as a hedge.

E. macrantha (Common Escallonia). Evergreen, 2–3 m. Fast growing shrub with deep green glossy leaves and rose-pink flowers in late spring, sometimes sold as *E. rubra.*

E. 'Hedge with an Edge' is an attractive dwarf plant, an alternative to a box hedge, growing to approximately 30 cm.

E. 'Pink Pixie' is another good hedge, about 80 cm all round. Glossy green leaves and pink bell-shaped flowers through summer.

Euonymus (Spindle Tree). Evergreen, 2.5–4 m. Large shrub which can be used as a specimen or is excellent as an evergreen dense hedge with deep green shiny oval leaves and attractive pinkish-red berries which split to show an orange seed.

E. alatus, 3 m, deciduous. Has broad wings of corky tissue on the stems and brilliant red leaves in autumn. Demands to be seen. E. a. 'Compactus' is about 1.5 m by 1.5 m, ideal for the smaller garden. Good autumn colouring of light red.

E. fortunei tend to be ground hugging or small mounded plants. Can be cut for indoor decoration.

E. f. 'Silver Pillar' is evergreen, 30 cm. Undemanding, slow-growing, for a sunny position. Handy for a small area. It is variegated, but remove any green bits.

E. f. 'Emerald 'n' Gold' is evergreen, 50 cm. Gold margined, changing leaf colour through winter and at its brightest in the coldest weeks. A foolproof plant.

E. japonicus 'Albo-marginatus'. Evergreen, 1–1.5 m. Leaves with narrow white margins on a compact bush.

E. j. 'Argenteo-marginatus' has wider irregular margins.

E. j. 'Aureo-marginatus' leaves have broken margins of yellow-gold.

Winter flowering *Acacia podalyriifolia.*

E. j. 'Aureus' has roundish leaves with patches of deep yellow.

E. j. 'Aureus Tricolor' has leaf edges tinted pink as well as the gold marking. A very attractive compact shrub. Remove all green shoots.

Exochorda x macrantha 'The Bride'. Deciduous, 2 m. A very pretty plant, at its best in spring, with pendulous white flowers. Very hardy. With age, can become rangy, and it's better to prune after flowering each year to maintain dense growth.

Feijoa sellowiana (Pineapple Guava). Evergreen, 2.5–3 m. Elliptical leaves, dark green above silvery beneath, attractive crimson and white flowers in early summer. Fruit stay green and ripen after falling to the ground. Can be eaten raw or used for jam. Plant will tolerate partial shade. A very pretty cut flower for January.

Forsythia (Golden Bells). Attractive early spring-flowering shrub, masses of bright yellow flowers. There are a number of hybrids and cultivars. *F. x intermedia* 'Lynwood Gold' is deciduous, growing to 2–2.5 m and is one of the best. Prune each year, immediately after flowering, removing the oldest canes. Flowers in early spring.

Fothergilla gardenii. Deciduous, 1 m. Autumn leaves of bright red, orange and yellow. Requires acid soil. Full sun encourages better autumn colour and more flowers, which are small and bottlebrush-shaped.

F. major. Much like the above, but a larger plant, at 3 metres.

Fuchsia. A large genus of plants of many types and varieties, mostly deciduous here. Most need protection in Canberra. Some of the hardier varieties can be grown outside all year round in protected positions. Do not cut back the old growth until after the heavy frosts have finished as the old foliage protects the plant from damage. Best to buy them in flower. Many are suited to pots or baskets.

Gardenia. Evergreen shrub with single or double very fragrant white, cream or yellow flowers. Best grown on protected patios or courtyards. Good for pots, in an acid mix. Keep moist.

Garrya elliptica (Catkin Bush). Evergreen, 2–3 m. Attractive late winter flowering shrub with elliptical grey-green leaves. The plant has long drooping silver-grey catkins, which are long lasting. Be aware the catkins on the female plant are shorter and open so a male plant is preferable. Propagate by cuttings from the male plant. The new cultivars 'James Roof' and 'Evie' are improvements.

Genista. See Appendix 2 for a weed list.

Grevillea. Grevilleas are diverse Australian plants and range from small prostrate shrubs to large trees. The large flowered types you see in Sydney and on the South Coast do not grow here. Increasingly however, attractive cultivars suited to Canberra are being introduced to the market.

G. iaspicula 'Wee Jasper Spider Flower'. This grows from 1.5–3 m tall in limestone soil. It is very hardy and adaptable, suited to free draining soils in a semi-shaded situation. Produces abundant flowers from May to November, cream and pink in pendulous clusters. Very attractive to native birds.

G. lavandulacea (Lavender Grevillea). A variable shrub ranging from almost prostrate to 1 m high. Though foliage is also variable, some forms have narrow grey leaves like lavender. Flowers are pink or red in winter and spring. 'Billy Wing' is a semi-prostrate plant with grey leaves and deep pink flowers. 'Tanunda' grows to 1 m with silvery-grey leaves and deep pink flowers during winter and spring.

G. rhyolitica 'Deua Flame'. Medium shrub to 1.5 m with a similar spread. Produces bright red flowers almost continuously, with peak flowering in August to October. Native to Deua National Park and grows inland from Moruya. Frequents moist gullies and also steep rocky ridges to an elevation of 600 metres above sea level. Requires a well drained soil and is reasonably frost-tolerant.

G. rosmarinifolia 'Rosy's Baby', small spreading shrub 80 cm to 1 m high by 60–80 cm wide with pink and cream bird attracting flowers which hang along the stems in winter to summer. High frost tolerance. Tip prune after flowering to promote bronze new growth.

G. *sericea* (pink spider flower), a shrub to around 1.5 m. It produces pink spider flowers year round, though its best show is in spring. It tolerates frost and likes a sunny well-drained position. Prune to encourage compact growth.

Grevillea x gaudichaudii, a good ground cover shrub which will spread up to 3 m or more. It has dark red new growth and dark red toothbrush flowers in late spring to summer. It will grow in most well-drained soils and prefers a sunny position. It is frost resistant and requires very little pruning except to control wayward branches.

G. 'Lady O' is a spreading shrub 1–1.5 m high by 2 m across. It has dark green leaves and bright red flowers for most of the year. Highly frost and drought tolerant and responds well to pruning.

G. 'Misty Pink' grows to 3 m with beautiful silvery green leaves and large pink flowers in spring and autumn. Tolerant of most soils so long as it is well-drained, and will tolerate either dry or moist conditions. It will withstand frost. Prune off old flower heads to stimulate flowering. A spectacular plant.

Hakea laurina (the Pin-cushion Hakea) is a strikingly beautiful plant originating in south-western Australia, but grown widely all over Australia and in other countries. In Italy and America its uses include street and hedge planting. It will grow to a large shrub 2.5 m or up to 5 m as a small tree. It prefers an open site with light well-drained soil with regular water. It can be frost tender in the new tip growth made during autumn and some may be lost each winter, unless sheltered by trees, and as a safeguard, it is helpful to cover young plants each night during winter until they reach around 1 m. Flowering starts

Hakea 'Burrendong Beauty'.

towards the end of April, is at its best in July in a mild winter and ends towards the end of August, although in an extremely cold winter flowers are held back and reduced in size. The rounded pin-cushion flowers are soft red, with projecting long styles, white to pale pink on ageing.

H. sericea (Silky Hakea) is a quick growing shrub with needle-like leaves and showy white scented flowers in July/August. Due to its spiny foliage, it can be used as a deterrent barrier, or alternatively, grown where it cannot be brushed against in the garden. In light, watered soil it will grow at least 5 m in seven years, with stiff growth, the heavy branches arching at the tips. There is a scent of honey or almonds from the flowers. It prefers good drainage.

Hakea 'Burrendong Beauty' originated as a hybrid seedling at the Burrendong Arboretum in NSW. It is a sprawling ground cover shrub growing to 0.5–1 m high by 1.5–3 m wide with arching branches, small grey leaves and conspicuous reddish-pink and cream flowers in autumn and winter. It grows in most soils and is both frost and drought tolerant. As with all hakeas, it should be pruned every two or three years to promote bushy growth.

Hamamelis mollis (Chinese Witch Hazel). Deciduous, 2–3 m. Interesting shrub for winter. Fragrant spidery yellow flowers in winter before leaves appear. Leaves roundish oval. An expensive shrub, but well worth having for the winter flowers and scent. Newer varieties may have orange or red flowers. Needs a fair bit of moisture for best performance.

Hebe (formerly known as Veronica). Hardy, compact evergreen plants. Most hebes need little or no pruning, though the larger-leaved types are prone to damaged stems. These can be safely cut back anytime in the growing season. Dead-heading of old flowers is well worth the effort, and if your particular plant becomes straggly, then cutting back fairly hard to new shoots lower down the stem will rejuvenate it.

H. x andersonii. Evergreen, 1–1.5 m. Very compact bush, glossy green narrow leaves. Spikes of violet blue flowers fading to whitish.

H. buxifolia (syn. *H. odora*). Evergreen, 0.5–1 m. Very compact bush, glossy small elliptical green leaves, clusters of white or pale pink flowers, sometimes blue tipped. Will tolerate wet conditions.

H. Wiri Series. These are small plants developed at the Auckland Botanic Gardens, up to 1 m, with smaller leaves than the others and come in quite a range of colours. Most attractive. Hard pruning is the key.

H. 'Emerald Green' is an especially attractive hybrid. It is very compact and neat, almost an alpine plant, with deep green whipcord-like growth. It could be mistaken for a conifer. Ideal for a pot or in a courtyard garden.

Hibiscus syriacus (Syrian hibiscus or Rose of Sharon). Deciduous, 2–3 m. Hardy shrub with

Hibiscus syriacus double form.

green toothed leaves, summer flowers single or double, mauve, pink, lilac blue and white. Will tolerate reasonably dry conditions. Some very attractive named varieties.

Hydrangea A very useful and versatile family of shrubs and a couple of climbers, mainly deciduous in this climate. Height can vary from 50 cm in the dwarf cultivars to the tall self clinging climbers which once established can cover several metres. Flowering can take place from late October until early March. With the exception of roses and oleanders, hydrangeas are perhaps the only shrub to provide colour continuously through summer.

Most hydrangeas in our gardens are cultivars of *Hydrangea macrophylla*. Flower colour of this species can be controlled in most older pink and blue cultivars by controlling the pH of the soil in which they grow. In general, most plants in Canberra will become pink if untreated. To maintain or introduce blue colouring add aluminium sulphate or blueing tonic or powder regularly from July to October and water well. It can take several years to obtain the desired effect and treatment must be continued if colour is to be maintained. Similarly, to maintain or intensify pink colouring add lime regularly to the area and

Hydrangea macrophylla 'Ayesha' whose flowers differ quite a bit from the normal mophead.

use fertilisers high in phosphorus which will neutralise the aluminium and iron in the soil.

White flowers will not alter regardless of soil conditions, but will colour around the edges as flowers age on the bush. New red cultivars also will not change completely but can lose some intensity in acid soil.

The macrophyllas are very good cut flowers, but for best results cut them with a long slanted end, in the cool of the evening and leave in deep water overnight before arranging. Use only mature flower heads as immature flowers will not develop further or keep well. Flowers dry well and can be used for several months in this form. Flower heads left on the bush can become quite attractive as they age, taking on many different colours from the original, making them useful for early winter indoor decoration when other flowers are scarce. Foliage of some cultivars colours well in autumn and early winter and remains until heavy frosts arrive.

Plant in protected semi-shaded areas away from the hot afternoon sun for best results. While plants will grow in full shade, this restricts flowering and the plants can become spindly. Hydrangeas need moisture in early

years, but once established they will cope with less frequent watering. Leaves will droop in the heat but pick up overnight.

Pruning should be carried out in winter, and like roses they perform best on new growth. So where possible completely remove canes more than three years old from the base of the plant to encourage new buds to develop. Canes which flowered last season should be shortened to just above a set of plump double buds low down in the bush. From these buds come the next flower stems. Single buds low down in the bush are growth buds and pruning to these will produce a stem which ends in a flower bud. This may not flower until the next season, but forms the structure for the future.

New firm canes which have not flowered should be left untouched if the terminal bud is in good condition. Otherwise just tip prune these as they should produce early flowers while the new flower stems develop from lower down. Immature weak growth, old leaf litter and snails should be completely removed from the base of the plant.

Dwarf cultivars (such as *H. macrophylla* 'Pia') flower on new flower stems from the base of the plant and then tend to die out, so all stems which have flowered should be completely removed. Finally, lightly cultivate the area, mulch and apply snail bait to protect new growth as it appears. Keep these plants moist at all times.

Hydrangeas make good tub or pot specimens for areas away from hot afternoon heat and wind. They can be taken indoors for short periods while in flower then returned outdoors. They may be propagated readily from softwood cuttings in early summer or hardwood cuttings in winter.

As they mature many hydrangea flower heads change their colour and gradually take on an 'antiqued' hue. Later they can be dried and used indoors over winter.

Many species and cultivars are available, some with tiny fertile flowers surrounded by, or interspersed with, larger sterile flowers with showy petal-like sepals. Others comprise almost entirely large sterile flowers. All of the following, except the second last, are deciduous.

H. arborescens 'Grandiflora', 2–2.5 m. Upright, bushy with broad oval leaves, large rounded heads of white sterile flowers. This spreads gradually by suckers and flowers on the new season's growth.

H. aspera (normally we see members of the Villosa group), 2 m. Upright growth with colourful peeling bark in autumn, broad domed heads of small pinkish fertile flowers with a ring of large sterile mainly white flowers. One of the last to flower.

H. macrophylla, 0.5–2.5 m. This species includes the most commonly-available hydrangeas and is divided into two main groups. First, the mop top cultivars with mainly sterile large rounded ball-like flowers, in Europe referred to as Hortensias. Good examples are 'Blue Bonnet', 'Tosca' with creamy salmon frilled foliage, 'Red Emperor'

deep red, 'Alba' pure white which will become pink around the edges if left on the bush after maturity. Second, the Lacecap cultivars with open flat heads of tiny fertile flowers surrounded by larger sterile flowers. Good choices are 'Blue Wave', 'Bluebird', or 'Veitchii' (white-flowered). 'Libelle', a lacecap, is thought by many the best white hydrangea.

H. paniculata, 2 m. Large creamy white conical flowers which turn pink with age. Large oval leaves. Prune hard if you wish to promote larger flowers. The most common cultivar has been *H. p.* 'Grandiflora', known in the USA as a Peegee hydrangea. More cultivars of *H. paniculata* are becoming available, for example 'Kyushu' and 'Unique', and these tend to hold their flowers more erect. All flower on the new season growth and handle sun better than the *H. macrophylla* cultivars.

H. petiolaris (Climbing Hydrangea), 6–7 m. Self-clinging woody plant, small white lacecap flowers with bright green foliage.

H. quercifolia (Oak-leaf Hydrangea), semi-deciduous, has conical white flowers on new season growth, turning deep pink with age. Large oak-like leaves on colourful woody stems which shed bark in autumn. Foliage colours magnificently in autumn with red, yellow and finally deep red-brown lasting for many weeks in sheltered areas. Will accept more sun than many other varieties. There is a very good double form called 'Snowflake'.

H. serrata is somewhat similar to *H. macrophylla* but with smaller and often more delicate foliage and flowers. Good for a pot in a sheltered spot.

Hypericum. Attractive small to medium shrub, various leaf shapes and colours. It has masses of flowers in early summer, followed by red berries which turn black as they age. Remove oldest canes after flowering to promote new growth.

H. x moserianum 'Tricolour'. Evergreen, 0.5 m. Leaves green edged with pink and white, yellow flowers. Great winter foliage.

H. patulum 'Henryi' is semi evergreen, 1–1.5 m. Compact bush, oval pointed leaves, large yellow flowers, green stems.

H. 'Hidcote', a semi evergreen hybrid, 1–1.5 m. Similar growth to *H. p.* 'Henryi'. Larger flowers and probably the most free flowering variety. One of the best.

Ilex (Holly). A large group of evergreen and deciduous shrubs which, if not controlled, will in time grow into small trees. Best in our climate are evergreen cultivars with a range of foliage and berry colours in winter. Foliage in most cases is stiff and spiny when mature. Slow growing, they make good feature, screen or tub plants. Prune to shape in early years and maintain by trimming mid-spring — pruning in autumn will reduce the amount of berries left for winter. Birds appear to attack the berries only in years when other food is scarce. If you have any concerns about this aspect, choose *Ilex x altaclarensis* and *I. crenata* which do not produce berries. The following are evergreen.

Ilex aquifolium (English or Common Holly). Both green and variegated forms are very reliable, with glossy leaves. Need pruning often in early stages to direct growth in the desired direction.

I. a. 'Ferox', 2–7 m. Tall upright growth, very spiny dark green glossy foliage, red berries in winter, new growth almost purple.

I. a 'Golden King', 2–7 m. Variegated glossy green foliage heavily overlaid cream to yellow. Very spiny and does not have a lot of berries.

I. a. 'J.C. van Tol', 2–6 m. Green foliage, red berries and very few spines.

Jasminum A large group of evergreen and deciduous plants including semi-climbers and climbers, some fragrant.

J. mesnyi (Primrose Jasmine). Evergreen, 2–4 m. Long arching branches, short side shoots, three to five narrow leaflets. Fragrant semi-double yellow flowers. Semi-rambling habit.

J. nudiflorum (Winter Jasmine). Deciduous, 2–3 m. Slender dark green branches, semi-rambling habit. Needs support and should be trimmed to maintain control. Valued for its cheery yellow flowers in winter when flowers are scarce.

Kalmia latifolia (Mountain Laurel or Calico Bush). Evergreen, 1–2 m. Attractive shrub with narrow elliptical leaves, saucer shaped flowers in spring on previous year's growth. Requires well-drained moist cool acid soil. Best suited to a shaded, protected position. There are some improved cultivars.

Kerria japonica (Kerria, Japanese Rose). Deciduous, 1–2.5 m. Slender branching canes and deep yellow spring flowers with prominent stamens. Very hardy and will tolerate shade. Suckers readily.

Kolkwitzia amabilis (Beauty Bush). Deciduous, 1.5–2.5 m. A compact shrub with arching branches, oval pointed, wrinkled leaves and masses of light pink bell flowers. One of the best spring flowering shrubs.

Kunzea baxteri, from Western Australia, is a spreading shrub to possibly 3 m with a cascading growth habit and bright red bottle brush type flowers from late winter through spring. Requires a well drained position with full sun and regular pruning to keep it bushy.

Kunzea ericifolia 'Snowman'. A slow-growing plant with dense, dwarf habit. 30 cm wide and 50 cm high, dark green foliage and white flowers in spring. High frost tolerance. Fertilise in spring and autumn and trim lightly three to four times per year.

Lagerstroemia indica (Crepe Myrtle). Deciduous, to 2 m. Although generally thought of as a tree, there are now some very good dwarf cultivars, grown for their flowers in late summer and autumn colours. Flowers range from dark red through to white. Prune in winter to encourage new growth as they flower on new wood. These dwarf cultivars can be used for low hedges and as a feature plant. Very drought tolerant, lovely flowers and smooth shiny bark. A good plant for Canberra conditions.

Lechenaultia. These very attractive plants from Western Australia produce strikingly coloured flowers including the vivid blue *L. biloba*. As they need perfect drainage they are at best short lived. Only for the experienced enthusiast.

Leptospermum. Cultivation of the Australian Tea-tree is easy as plants are adaptable to a wide range of conditions and some will even tolerate poor drainage. Ranging from tree forms to small shrubs and with profuse flowers over a long period, they might well be considered a good choice for your garden. A frequent pest in Canberra is the webbing caterpillar which feeds on the leaves of most of the small leaf species, creating patches of webbing on the plant and filling that webbing with its droppings. It results in defoliation

and sometimes, the death of the plant. The webbing is unsightly, and unless you are prepared to remove the affected areas or to use some form of control regularly, there are other plants which may suit your needs while being relatively trouble-free.

There are a number of newer cultivars becoming available from Bywong Nursery, a local wholesale nursery, and these seem to handle pests better. 'MesmerEyes' and 'Rudolph' are two fine examples of this range.

Leucophyta brownii, previously Calocephalus brownii (Cushion Bush), from the coasts of southern Australia. Evergreen, 1 m. Small rounded intricately branched plant with silver grey foliage, small yellow flowers spring and early summer. Something a little different. Highly recommended plant for a sunny well drained position. Frost and wind tolerant.

Leucothoe fontanesiana (Pearl Flower, Switch Ivy). Evergreen, 1.5 m. White racemes of lily of the valley flowers in spring on graceful arching stems. Glossy leaves. Stems and leaves have an interesting fleshy appearance and there is a variegated form available.

Ligustrum (Privet). See Appendix 2 for a weed List.

Lonicera fragrantissima (Winter Honeysuckle). Semi-evergreen, 2–2.5 m. Long slender arching branches with fragrant creamy white flowers in winter. Inclined to sucker.

L. nitida (Box-leaf Honeysuckle). Evergreen, 1–2 m. Glossy small ovate leaves, small fragrant creamy flowers, blue-purple berries. A plant for a low hedge or shaping which is sometimes marketed as 'Oz Box'.

L. 'Silver Beauty' is a semi-deciduous shrub with silver variegation which grows to 1 m and tolerates heavy pruning. Remove any growth reverting to green as it appears.

Lophomyrtus x ralphii 'Crinkly' or 'Krinkly'. Evergreen, 1.5 m. Small red to brown foliage darkening in winter. Very useful in floral art and much sought after colour in the garden. Tiny cream flowers in early summer.

L. 'Little Star' 0.6–1 m, is a small leaved, rounded shrub, variegated with pink tones. Rich colour in winter. Occasional clipping will help. Cold hardy.

L. 'Black Stallion' is similar in leaf and shape, but with striking dark burnished foliage.

Loropetalum chinense (Fringe Flower). An evergreen rounded shrub with heart-shaped leaves, hairy branches and masses of creamy-yellow spidery flowers in late spring growing to between 1–2 m. Requires a sheltered position with some moisture and mulch. L. chinense 'China Doll' is a purple-leaved form with deep pink flowers.

Magnolia see the chapter on Magnolias and related plants.

Mahonia aquifolium (Oregon Grape). An evergreen shrub with glossy dark green spiny leaves turning bronze-red in winter and massed yellow flowers in late winter-spring, followed by blue-black berries. Grows to 1–1.5m and is very hardy and tolerant of most positions.

Melaleuca thymifolia (Thyme Honey Myrtle). Attractive Australian shrubs to about 1 m with small neat foliage. The delicate flowers along the stems, in either white or pale mauve, are reminiscent of lace and bloom through spring and summer. Prefers a sunny, moist position

Osmanthus fragrans. The flowers have a wonderful scent.

but once established, is tolerant of drought and frost. A good container plant.

Michelia see the chapter on Magnolias and Related Plants.

Micromyrtus ciliata, native to the Canberra area, is a hardy but variable prostrate shrub. It will reach no more than 20 cm by 1.5 m across, while the erect form will grow to 1 m by 1 m. It requires a well-drained position. Has tiny leaves clothing each stem with a profusion of tiny white flowers over a long period which redden as they age.

Nandina domestica (Sacred Bamboo). Evergreen, erect shrub growing to 1–2 m. Bamboo-like stems with finely divided leaves. Its new growth can be bronze-red, and it has sprays of white flowers in summer followed by red berries on the female plants. Valued for autumn and winter colour, it is suitable for shady areas and is also a good pot specimen. With age, its rhizomatous root system can become a nuisance and must be controlled.

N. d. 'Nana' a dwarf, compact variety growing to 0.5 metre. Its foliage changes to bright red in winter and it is an ideal tub or pot specimen.

Neillia sinensis to 3m x 2m and *N. thibetica* (syn. *N. longiracemosa*) 1.5 x 1.2 m. Both are deciduous with interesting lobed leaves and bell-shaped flowers held in slender racemes in pink or white. They need a fertile soil and are very frost hardy.

Nerium oleander (Oleander). A hardy summer flowering evergreen shrub growing to 2–3 m which will tolerate dry conditions. There are many cultivars, both single or double and a colour range across white, pink, red and salmon. There is also a variegated variety with yellow margined leaves. A very tough plant.

Osmanthus Evergreen, 1–3 m. A slow-growing trouble-free plant which is generally not fussy where it is grown, but is valued for its tiny but extremely fragrant white flowers which, according to the variety, may appear in late winter or from mid to late spring.

O. delavayi 'Pearly Gates' and *O. delavayi* 'Heaven Scent' both grow to 1.5 m and have fragrant white flowers in late spring.

O. fragrans, 3 m, can be trained as a small tree or grown in a large pot. Small white or cream fragrant flowers appear intermittently in spring and autumn, some flower in late winter. *O. f. aurantiacus* has a similar habit and flowering pattern but has apricot flowers.

O. heterophyllus is a large shrub with holly-like leaves. Growing to 4.5 m high and wide, sometimes used as a hedge. Flowers again are small, inconspicuous, white and fragrant in early summer. A second lot of flowers may appear in autumn. *O. h.* 'Purpureusa' is similar to the species, but has dark purple holly-like leaves. *O. h.* 'Variegatus' is one of the best variegated plants, slow-growing and trouble-free. It grows to 1–1.5 m but does need a

Lophomyrtus x x ralphii 'Black Stallion' is a small shrub grown for its striking foliage.

sunny position for the best colour. Its tiny flowers have a lovely perfume.

O. serrulatus grows to 3 m with small white fragrant flowers in spring.

Paeonia suffruticosa (Tree Peony). A deciduous shrub growing to between 1–2 m. There are many cultivars, mainly slow growing with large compound leaves. Flowers are single or double in colours of almost black through red, pink, mauve and white. There is a yellow flowered form, a hybrid of *P. lutea*. All need protection from wind but are a delight in a garden.

Persoonia pinifolia (Pine-leaf Geebung) from eastern Australia is a large shrub to 3 m. It has attractive bright green soft conifer-like foliage with bright yellow flowers. It grows in a lightly shaded location with good drainage. It does well in fairly dry conditions and is frost-resistant.

Phebalium glandulosum has cream to yellow flower clusters in spring. Mulch well for a cool root run. Grows to 1 m.

P. squamulosum, yellow flowers in spring. A medium shrub to 2 m which prefers moist soil. A variegated form is sometimes available.

Philadelphus (Mock Orange). A large group of hardy shrubs, mainly deciduous, generally with fragrant flowers in late spring. Flowers have four petals and many stamens in the centre.

P. coronarius, a deciduous shrub growing to 2–3 m with small creamy white flowers. There is a form with leaves light yellowish in spring, turning to green-yellow. It does require protection from hot sun and wind.

The hybrid *P.* 'Virginal' is also deciduous and grows to 2–3 m. It has upright growth, large leaves and fragrant semi-double or double flowers. It flowers best on second-year wood so it should be pruned immediately after flowering. *P.* 'Manteau d'Hermine' only grows to 75 cm with dense, compact growth and has small double white ball flowers.

Philotheca myoporoides (formerly *Eriostemon myoporoides*) (the long leaf wax flower). Another Australian shrub to around 2 m with dense growth and aromatic leaves. Pink buds open to white waxy star flowers from winter to spring. It can be grown almost anywhere in the garden from full sun to part shade, and so long as the drainage is good, it will grow in most soils. It is frost resistant. Prune lightly after flowering to keep the plant bushy. It can be used as an informal hedge or screen and makes a pretty container plant.

Photinia A group of mainly evergreen shrubs, suitable as specimen, hedge or screen plants. Can be shaped.

P. glabra 'Rubens' (Red-leaf Photinia). A large evergreen shrub growing to between 2 and 3 metres, with new growth coloured crimson to reddish-bronze, turning green as it ages. Regular clipping or pruning will promote new growth. Clusters of buds, with smoky appearance, and small white flowers.

Philadelphus 'Virginal' should be pruned immediately after flowering as the new flowers will be on the previous year's wood.

A popular hedge plant, (its flowers are a nuisance for hayfever sufferers). Since it is pollinated by flies, for some sites there are better choices, eg coprosma, euonymus, Sasanqua camellias, pittosporum and callistemon.

Physocarpus opulifolius is a hardy quick growing deciduous shrub to 2.5 m all round. It has clusters of white flowers in spring, rich orange autumn colour, and the bark peels in winter to a shiny bronze. It needs little water and is frost hardy.

P. o. 'Luteus' has yellow leaves in spring and these turn yellow-green in summer.

P. o. 'Purpurea' has red brown leaves and pink flowers.

P. o. 'Diablo' has deep burgundy foliage and pink flowers. Leaves turn bronze-red in autumn.

P. o. 'Dart's Gold' has golden yellow foliage in spring which fades to a distinctive chartreuse-yellow during summer. White flowers and good golden orange autumn colour.

Physocarpus opulifolius 'Dart's Gold' in its autumn colour.

Physocarpus opulifolius 'Diablo'.

Pieris. A small attractive evergreen shrub with profuse small flowers in late winter and colourful new growth in spring. It is a plant for the shady or semi-shaded areas with a cool, moist, well-mulched root zone. It requires an acid soil and will not tolerate lime. It grows well under deciduous trees, around and mixed with camellias, rhododendrons or azaleas. Extra water may be needed. Prune lightly after flowering to encourage new colourful foliage which continually changes colour as it matures. Slow-growing in this climate, which can be an advantage.

P. forrestii, 2 m. A dense shrub with large oblong glossy dark green foliage, large terminal sprays of pearly white flowers in spring, frost hardy. *P. f.* 'Chandleri', 2 m is an Australian cultivar, with showy spring growth changing from copper-salmon to apricot to cream and finally green. *P. f.* 'Wakehurst', 2 m. New growth in early spring is brilliant fiery red, later changing to pink then cream-yellow and finally dark green.

P. japonica (Lily of the Valley Bush), 0.5–1.5 m. Amongst the best small shade-loving, frost-hardy shrubs for this area. Incorporate some well-matured compost or good potting mix into the top soil before planting (rather than bringing heavy clay to the surface) and keep moist at all times. Many good cultivars are available with a range of different flower and foliage colours, and may be used for indoor flower arrangements. Lightly prune flower trusses out of plants after flowers finish in spring to encourage the colourful new growth.

P. j. 'Christmas Cheer' has deep green foliage which is copper-red when young. Its stems are red to brown and its flowers rose- pink at the tips. *P. j.* 'Shojo' has mid-green foliage with light green stems, new growth red to yellow, flowers pink and most prolific. It is more upright in growth than some other cultivars and a great specimen plant. *P. j.* 'Forest Flame' has deep green foliage, new growth red to pink then creamy white. Flowers have a hint of pink fading to cream. Good slow growing shrub with upright growth. *P. j.* 'Dorothy Wykoff' has lighter green foliage sometimes with slight cream edging, new growth pink to yellow, flowers creamy turning white. Growth is spreading rather than upright. *P. j.* 'Valley Valentine'. Bushy evergreen shrub displaying pendant clusters of deep rosy-red flowers in spring. Height and spread will reach 1.2m–1.5m in 10 years. *P. j.* 'Variegata' has green foliage, heavily and consistently edged with white.

The spring flowers of *Pieris japonica ryukyuensis* 'Temple Bells'.

Qualup Bells must have good drainage.

Its edges are bronze-yellow when young. The shrub has yellow-green stems and white flowers, with spreading growth.

P. j. ryukyuensis 'Temple Bells' (syn *P. ryukyuensis* 'Temple Bells') is slightly quicker growing than the listed *P. japonica* cultivars and has larger flowers. It needs some protection from very heavy frosts so is best situated under the canopy of taller trees and shrubs. Deep emerald green foliage, new growth light green to apricot then bronze red, flowers cream to white.

Pimelea physodes (Qualup Bell). While this small frost-tolerant shrub is endemic to Western Australia it grows well in Canberra to about 1 m high and wide. Give it a well-prepared sunny site to which coarse sand has been added to enhance drainage. The small flowers occur in clusters at the ends of the branches and are enclosed by leafy bracts. These bracts may be yellow, green, red or purple in colour and give the appearance of a large pendant bell-shaped flower. They have a long flowering period from late winter through to spring, and in WA have become a valued plant for the cut flower industry. In Canberra, Qualup Bells have traditionally been sold as a grafted plant while in flower. After the first

flowering, your plant should be lightly pruned to encourage bushy growth and regularly each year once the flowers have aged. The Qualup Bell is a useful plant for rockeries and tubs, but remember always that good drainage is the key.

Pittosporum. A large group of evergreens which range from small compact shrubs to small trees. They are grown for their outstanding foliage and as an excellent hedge or screening plant. Not all are suited to our climate so take care if purchasing plants outside of your local district. Those listed are quite frost-hardy and will thrive in full sun or partial shade, with a wide range of size and foliage variation available. With many new and interesting cultivars being released regularly the choice is extensive.

They may be grown as specimen plants to give a variation of colour throughout the year, they make good tub plants or can be used as hedge or screening plants. May be pruned to size or shape as desired but for best results, prune twice a year in late spring and late autumn. Older plants, grown sparse with age, can be rejuvenated with heavy pruning and commensurate watering. All have inconspicuous small brown to black flowers in late spring, which in some cases are lightly fragrant. Will grow well in most soil types, but it should be well-cultivated before planting. Keep plants well-watered until established and though they will look better with regular water, they can tolerate less water once established.

P. argentea nana 'Shorty' 1 m. Compact low growing grey-green plant, keeps shape well with minimum pruning. Slow growing compared to other cultivars, suited for a low hedge, tubs or smaller areas.

P. eugenioides 5 m. Large fast growing shrubs which will grow into small trees if left uncontrolled. *P. e.* 'Variegatum' is a popular shrub with pale variegated lemon-scented foliage. Watch for any stray growth which appears unvariegated and prune out immediately. *P. e.* 'Variegata Purpureum' as above, only with pink to purple mixed with the variegations.

P. tenuifolium includes most of the popular readily available cultivars for most areas in any garden. Choice depends on the use to which the plants are to be put. *P. t.* 'Cathy' 3 m has striking light cream variegations on the leaves. *P. t.* 'Green Pillar' 1.5 m, is a rounded slow-growing plant with mid-green foliage and is well suited to tub growth or in smaller areas. *P. t.* 'Irene Patterson' 3 m, is a rounded dense plant with mid-green mature foliage which is heavily overlaid speckled-white on new growth. Honey-scented purple flowers in late spring. *P. t.* 'Limelight' 4 m, is tall growing with oblong, brightly variegated, lime-green foliage. A good quick screen or hedge plant. *P. t.* 'Pixie' 1.5 m, a very small rounded shrub with silver-green foliage and fine black to purple branches. It shapes well and is a fine tub plant. *P. t.* 'Silver Magic' 3 m,

has tall upright growth with small grey-green leaves which are overlaid with silver and pink. A great specimen plant, particularly in semi-shaded areas. *P. t.* 'Silver Sheen' 3 m is quick-growing with small silver-green leaves on dark stems. Possibly the best screen and hedge cultivar. Prune regularly and often for good results. *P. t.* 'Sunburst' 3 m has light green leaves which are heavily veined with yellow on black stems. *P. t.* 'Stirling Mist' 3 m . Silver white tipped margins on foliage and black stems. Foliage is moderately dense, giving it a very pretty effect. It is a good feature plant and useful for indoor decoration. *P. t* 'Stirling Gold' is similar but has gold leaf margins. *P. t* 'Variegatum' 2 m has upright growth, with neatly variegated green and cream leaves on dark stems. *P. t.* 'Tom Thumb' 0.5 m. A dwarf, small leaf cultivar with foliage maturing deep brown to purple.

Prostanthera. The mint bushes are deservedly popular Australian shrubs as they are fast-growing, flower when small in blue, purple, red, yellow and white and are pleasantly perfumed. Mainly small to medium-sized shrubs depending on species tending to be short lived but nevertheless worth growing for their beauty and fragrance. Most prefer light shade. Good drainage is essential. Tip prune frequently for best performance. Smaller species are ideal for containers and as rockery plantings. There are many frost-resistant varieties and the following are readily available. There will likely be more species on sale as grafted plants become more readily available.

P. lasianthos, the Victorian Christmas bush, is a fast growing tall shrub (up to 5 m), with white terminal flowers and orange and purple dots in the throat around Christmas.

P. ovalifolia. There are a number of cultivars of this available. One form is dwarf but most are plants to 2 m tall. Leaves may be grey, variegated or with purple tonings. Purple flowers are produced profusely in spring.

P. rotundifolia (Round Leaf Mint bush). Generally well shaped shrub with grey-green leaves to 1.5 m and masses of lilac flowers in spring. This is suitable for hedging but needs moisture in summer and good drainage. Prune lightly to keep in shape. *P. r. var rosea* is a dwarf form flowering very heavily in spring, flowers mid pink in colour.

Prunus glandulosa 'Alba Plena' (Double White Bush Cherry). Deciduous shrub to 1–1.5 m with double white flowers in spring and tiny red fruit. Birds spread the seeds and they can become a nuisance, as it is also inclined to sucker.

P. g. 'Rosea' Deciduous, 1–1.5 m. Single pink flowers and red fruit. Produces long wands of flowers which are good for cutting. *P. g.* 'Roseoplena' (Double Pink Bush Cherry). Deciduous with leaves turning red in autumn. Grows to 1–1.5 m. and has double pink flowers in spring.

Pyracantha. See Appendix 2 for the weed List.

Rhaphiolepis x delacourii (Indian Hawthorn). An evergreen shrub to 2–2.5 m. Its broad oblong leaves are reddish-bronze when new, turning to green as they age. Large heads of pink flowers in spring and autumn followed by black berries. A very nice hedge plant.

Rhododendron see the Camellias, rhododendrons and azaleas chapter.

Rosmarinus officinalis (Rosemary). Evergreen, 1–1.5 m. Dense compact shrub, grey-green aromatic leaves. Makes a very

nice low hedge and responds well to clipping. There are forms with blue, white or pink flowers. Also a prostrate form, creeping and growing to 15–30 cm.

Sambucus nigra (European Elder). Deciduous, 3–4 m. Large shrub with large leaves of five leaflets, white flowers and shiny black berries which have traditionally been used for elderberry wine. There is a variegated form with creamy white margins, a golden form, and a new bronze-leaved cultivar.

Scaevola, Australia's Fan flowers, are small spreading shrubs, frost resistant and excellent plants for garden culture.

S. aemula (Fairy Fan flower) is available in a number of named cultivars and grows to 50 cm and spreads to about 1 m. Spring flowering, the leaves are small and shiny green with interesting fan shaped flowers in pale lilac through to purple, depending on variety. Grow in well drained soil with summer moisture, in sun or light shade. Choose the cultivar to suit your garden.

Spartium junceum. See Appendix 2 for the weed List.

Spiraea japonica 'Anthony Waterer' Deciduous compact shrub to 1 m with narrow leaves and flattened heads of carmine flowers. It will flower over long periods if the dead flower heads are removed. There are many other attractive cultivars.

S. prunifolia 'Plena' (syn *S. p.* 'Flora Pleno', Bridal Wreath Spirea). A compact deciduous bush to 1–2 m with slender arching branches, oval oblong leaves, masses of small double white flowers in spring on previous year's wood and orange-red foliage in autumn.

S. thunbergii (syn. *S. gracilis*) (Thunberg Spirea). Deciduous, l–2 m. Smaller type, slender branches and narrow leaves with masses of single white flowers in small clusters. Bright orange-tinted foliage in autumn.

Stachyurus praecox Deciduous, 2 m. Arching branches with racemes of yellow bell flowers in late winter. Easily grown in moist soil with plenty of compost and a little shade. *S. chinensis* 'Magpie' is a smaller variegated plant.

Symphoricarpos albus (Snowberry). A compact deciduous shrub to 1.5 m with pendulous branches and inconspicuous flowers followed by large, long-lasting white berries. It will tolerate shade but sometimes suckers.

Syringa (Lilac). Deciduous, 1–3 m. A group of popular plants, with mostly fragrant flowers, dark green leaves and various leaf shapes. There are many cultivars available, flowers single or double, colours white, pink, mauve, lavender and purple. It is advisable to buy grafted stock to avoid suckering. Lilacs appreciate limed soil and a little extra water in summer. Prune immediately after flowering.

Telopea. Australia's waratahs grow into open upright shrubs from 1.5 to 3 m. The large flowers appear from late spring to early summer. There is a white form as well as the usual red. New cultivars seem to be easier to please in the garden. Requires good drainage above all else. It will grow in shade or full sun if well mulched and kept watered. Growing in a large container is worth considering.

T. mongaensis (Braidwood Waratah). A hardy shrub which grows from 1.5 m to 2 m and has large red flowerheads in late October

The flowers of a stachyurus appear on the bare stems in late winter.

to summer. It requires good drainage, and will tolerate either full sun or shade so long as it has a cool well-mulched root run with adequate moisture. It is frost hardy. Cutting the flowers will promote bushy growth.

T. 'Braidwood Brilliant'. An upright and compact multi-stemmed shrub to about 2 m when mature. Flowers are brilliant red, and while it is less showy than the NSW waratah, *T. speciosissima*, its flowers are larger than those of *T. mongaensis*. It flowers for 2–3 weeks during October and is well-suited to the colder regions when given protection.

T. 'Errinundra White', a white flowered selection of the species *T. oreades*, is a small tree. Flowers are borne in large terminal white racemes in spring and early summer. It is frost hardy, though moisture and good drainage are vital.

Tetratheca ciliata (Pink Bells). Small upright growing Australian shrubs to 30 cm with pink pendant bell flowers in late winter through spring. Grow in well-drained soil with light shade. A small attractive plant for the rockery, general garden or a container.

Thryptomene calycina (Grampian Heath Myrtle) grows to about 1 m and the arched stems are covered in small white flowers in winter and spring. Used extensively in floral arrangements. This is moderately frost tolerant when established. Needs light well drained soil. Plant under trees for protection from sun and cold.

Veronica See Hebe.

Viburnum. A very large genus of evergreen and deciduous shrubs, varying in height and size. Ideal as specimen, hedge or windbreak plants. Some have autumn colour, others are grown for their perfume or flowers. There is a wide range of evergreen, perfumed varieties; and a group with large snowball flowers. With such a broad range, you should choose your plants to meet your special needs. They like moist, well- mulched soil. Some examples:

V. burkwoodii Semi-evergreen, 1.5–2.5 m. Open shrub with narrow, oval deep green shiny leaves, fragrant white flowers. Requires regular pruning to keep reasonably compact. Extra water may be needed until well established.

V. carlesii Deciduous, 1–2 m. More compact than *V. burkwoodii*. Downy grey-green oval leaves, clusters of pink buds opening to very fragrant white flowers, black berries, and autumn colours.

V. farreri (syn. *V. fragrans)*. Hardy deciduous shrub to 2.5 m. Scented flowers, white heavily flushed pink, in winter.

V. macrocephalum (Chinese Snowball Tree). Deciduous, 2.5–3 m. Large spreading shrub, oval leaves, large snowball white flower heads, slight autumn colours. *V. macrocephalum* 'Sterile' (Snowball Tree) is a deciduous shrub growing to 3 m. with globular clusters of sterile greenish flowers turning to pure white.

Viburnum farreri with its scented winter flowers.

V. odoratissimum 'Emerald Lustre'. Evergreen shrub to 4 m with small fragrant white flowers in spring.

V. opulus (Guelder Rose). Deciduous, 2–3 m. Hardier than *V. macrocephalum*. Three-lobed green leaves colouring rich red in autumn, large heads of snowball white flowers, orange-red berries. There is a dwarf form, *V. o.* 'Nanum' which grows only to 0.5 m.

V. plicatum. Branches more horizontal, about 1 m all over. Pure white flowers, in an upward facing cluster. V. p. 'Molly' is a dainty specimen 1 – 1.5 m. with soft pink upward

This is *Viburnum plicatum* 'Molly' a shrub to show off most of the year. Following the pinkish flowers in spring, the shrub has an attractive shape all summer and then good colouring for autumn.

facing flowers. *V. p. tomentosum* 'Lanarth' is an attractive cultivar with good autumn colour, large single white flowers followed by attractive small red berries.

V. tinus. Evergreen to 3 m and has been used widely in Canberra as a hedging plant. Fine whilst in flower, but other viburnums have better flowers, leaves and shape.

Weigela. Attractive group of flowering shrubs growing to about 3 m. There are a number of hybrids and varieties, all with masses of bell-shaped flowers in spring. Fairly undemanding of siting in the garden with colours of white, pink and dark red. There is a variegated form with silvery-cream and green leaves and pale pink flowers. May need extra water in harsh times.

Westringia 'Wynyabbie Gem'. An Australian shrub to 1.5 m, which is frequently used as a screening and hedging plant. Very hardy, frost and drought-resistant, it will grow in the harshest conditions. The leaves are small and neat in grey or deep green. Flowers are mauve and present for most of the year. Prune to keep in shape and to invigorate. It is a very good Australian plant for topiary purposes.

W. 'Glabra Cadabra' A hardy hybrid which makes an ideal screening plant at 1.5 m x 1.5 m. Its violet-lilac flowers appear late winter through to spring. It should be pruned after flowering to encourage a dense habit. Responds well to pruning and if trained as a formal hedge, can be pruned twice a year.

Xanthorrhoea at the Australian National Botanic Gardens.

Frost hardy, tolerates dry conditions, but is also OK for coastal planting. *W. fruticosa* 'Morning Light' (Coastal rosemary) is a variegated form with cream edged leaves and white flowers in spring through to summer. It grows to 1 m x 1 m.

Xanthorrhoea australis (Grass tree). This is a very slow growing plant, and hence an established plant can be an expensive. It is nevertheless excellent for landscaping and good in a container. An old plant may have a trunk 2 m tall. The trunk is bare with a grassy skirt crown. The small white flowers are produced around a tall spear-like stem from the crown. Grow in a well-drained sunny position and light soil. Frost resistant and once established is drought-tolerant. Highly recommended for its 'presence'. Grows naturally around Canberra.

CHAPTER 16: Roses

John Woodfield revised by Chris Ryan

Roses are one of the most versatile, hardy and sought after plants we can enjoy in our gardens. Whether you are a dedicated specialist or the newest home gardener, with the help of modern hybridisation techniques, you can find a rose to suit most situations.

Before you start, think what you want to achieve — learn about rose characteristics before choosing a rose. Depending on the position you choose, the space available and your plans for nearby parts of your garden you might choose on the basis of perfume, colour, hips, height, appearance of the stems, ability to cover an arch or perhaps the ground. Some roses flower only in spring but have great perfume for those few weeks, and that may well be something you would prefer to flowers over a longer period but with less perfume. Some roses provide a wonderful display in the garden, but make poor cut flowers. Choose what suits you best as there is a tremendous variety.

We have not tried to describe every type, variety or cultivar available so the suggestions at the end of the chapter are some reliable roses for this climate. There are some hundreds of new releases each year, and some may be even better than this edition's recommendations.

Members of the Horticultural Society conduct annual rose pruning and culture demonstrations and are continually trialling new roses for the Canberra environment. You can find more about forthcoming demonstrations from the Society's web pages.

The best position

Plant your roses where they will receive as much sun as possible. This will encourage good growth and development of flowers all over the plant. Not all gardens can provide the ideal situation, so aim to place roses where they will receive most sunlight, free from overhanging trees, tall shrubs and dense shade from buildings and structures. Some roses, for example, English Roses (David Austin), will tolerate a little shade and in fact prefer a little protection from the hot afternoon sun. Usually we plant roses in winter when trees are bare. Try to imagine the shade those trees will cast in summer; and how far that shade might extend in say, five years time. As the garden grows ensure that roses are not robbed of their direct sunlight, for the canes will become long and the quantity and quality of flowers will be greatly reduced.

Some protection against our hot winds in late spring and summer helps, but should not be so dense as to stop air circulation through the plants. Poor air circulation in humid conditions will encourage the spread of fungal diseases. Worse in our conditions is the lack of air circulation in midsummer heat waves, which causes heat concentration at and near ground level. This heat build-up can stop growth completely. Affected canes will quickly turn yellow and often show blackened scorch marks low down. Few of these canes ever fully recover their vigour. Newly planted roses can be lost to heat if the problem is not noticed soon enough. Some shallow rooted annuals or perennials planted among the roses can help dissipate this heat, but don't let them become too tall or overgrow the base of the plants. Thick mulch will help, particularly if not allowed to dry out.

Preparing the bed

Preparation of an area specifically for roses should begin some months before planting if possible. The aim is to have an area with plenty of organic material well worked into the soil, and well drained by being raised above surrounding ground levels.

There is a belief that roses prefer clay soils, but we need to work with it. Clay soils will compact, preventing air and water penetration and this restricts the growth of fine fibre roots. It is these fine roots which take up water and nutrients for growth and development of your rose. The clay is found mainly in lower levels of the soil and, if disturbed, should be thoroughly mixed with the top soil, adding plenty of organic matter.

Do not dig holes below the level of the existing garden into solid clay as this will cause sumps which will not drain in times of heavy watering or rain. This causes the root

An arch of roses such as these need a good support if they are to be kept tidy. They are about to be mulched using bales of lucerne.

system to rot. Far better to raise the level of the surrounding area to accommodate the rose to the depth required for its roots, using organic matter to help raise the level. As a rule of thumb, the worked soil should be approximately 45 cm deep, and a liberal application of gypsum will be beneficial.

If you are planting among other shrubs and plants in an existing garden ensure the area for any roses is well prepared as a rose can remain in that position for many years, and thorough preparation will help maintain its health and vigour.

Planting your rose

When you buy a rose treat it as an investment. Chapter 24 has some extensive advice on planting trees and shrubs but in this chapter we concentrate on some aspects which are especially important for roses.

Planting time is anywhere from early June through to early September for bare-rooted roses and August is the ideal time. Sometimes you will find plastic-wrapped roses on the shelves as early as April, but this is far too early for planting in Canberra.

Yet another approach to rose growing is this ferocious looking plant. It is *Rosa sericea pteracantha*, grown mainly in shrubberies for the appearance of the new stems and thorns. A floral artist's delight.

Container or potted roses are advertised as ready for planting at anytime. While this is possible, the dormant winter period is ideal. Any potted roses which have become pot bound will need to have their roots teased out, so that they can be planted similarly to bare rooted roses.

June will see bare-rooted roses start to arrive in local garden centres and other outlets and from interstate specialists, if ordered. Early selection from local outlets will give you every opportunity to obtain good vigorous clean plants. Reject any plants with broken stems, showing signs of die back or having dried out excessively, showing signs of too much early growth or if the bud graft is not firmly attached to the understock.

Sometimes packaged plants are sealed in plastic containers and are in very advanced growth. Reject these if it is early in the season as extreme frosts may kill this early growth and plants often do not recover. Plants from interstate will have some form of protection on the root system to prevent them from drying out; this may be in the form

of a gel, peatmoss or damp straw. They will also be tied together rather tightly to allow for smaller packaging and enclosed in plastic sheeting sealed with adhesive tape inside a large cardboard box. If you are not ready, or the weather is too bad for planting, these will normally be quite happy left in their packaging for up to a week. Leave the unopened package in a cool dry area such as the garage or shade house.

After carefully unpacking roses remove any ties, check labels are well attached and inspect all plants for broken or damaged stems. Trim any damaged stems to just above a firm undamaged bud, and shorten any damaged roots. Be particular with the bud union to check it is not fractured from the rootstock as it is not very strong in young plants — handle all plants by the rootstock for the same reason.

Some roses are worth growing just for their autumn hips. This is thought to be *Rosa moyesii* 'Geranium', growing among perennials and other shrubs.

After unpacking, soak the plants in a bucket of water for at least two hours. Up to 20 ml of seaweed or fish emulsion in the bucket has a good effect. Carry plants to planting position in water; do not allow roots to dry out at any stage.

Before starting to plant bushes mark out the area to get spacing correct (see the next section) and plant the centre of the bed first so you do not have to walk over or through those already planted. Dig a hole for each plant deep and wide enough to take the root system well spread out, so the bud union will finish at or just above ground level — this will give a much better supported plant on our windy days than those planted higher as recommended in some publications.

Spread a quarter cup of nine-month slow release fertiliser into the soil at the bottom of the planting hole. Good results are being experienced with a couple of handfuls of rose fertilizers such as Sudden Impact® and Seamungus®. Form a firm mound of soil in the centre of the hole and spread the roots over and down on the mound. Make sure the ends of the roots are facing down to help prevent suckers forming from the root system. Back fill the hole with soil, firming by hand only, to about two thirds of the depth of the hole and gently fill the hole with water. This will help settle the soil around the roots and remove air pockets. If drainage is correct the water will drain away in less than two hours and then the hole should be back filled to ground level. No further water will be required for at least two to three weeks and then only if rain has not fallen.

The next job is to prune the canes back to just above a good firm bud. New roses, regardless of where they are purchased, are trimmed only for easy transportation. They are not prepared specifically for their needs in our climate where growth will not start for some weeks. Failure to prune new canes can cause die back rather than encourage new growth, and this can lead to loss of canes or even the newly planted rose. This initial pruning is likely the most important point for a new rose grower to remember.

New roses should not be fertilised heavily with chemical fertilisers until well established. A quarter cup of nine-month slow release fertiliser spread evenly around the drip line once growth really starts, followed by a good mulch will see most plants through their first year, as long as moisture is kept up and plants are not allowed to dry out for long.

If you don't have enough time to finish planting or if the ground has not been prepared ready for planting, you can 'heel in' your roses for some weeks in a protected spot in the garden. This should be close to a fence, garage or other area protected from severe frost, but not where plants will become too warm on sunny days, so areas facing south-east are best. Open a shallow trench and place roses a hand span apart at an angle in the trench with the bud union or graft well above ground level. Back fill the trench to ground level and water well. Plants can then be removed as required, handling below the bud union. As plants are already separated the remaining plants are not disturbed when each plant is removed.

Stem or tree roses, including weeping types, need staking at the time of planting. Stakes are most important. Best of all is galvanised water pipe covered with a length of plastic waste pipe or electrical conduit; treated wooden stakes may be used but will deteriorate much sooner than steel and may allow the plants to be blown over just as they are at their peak. Weeping types will need a rose wheel or similar circle fitted at the top of the stake to help spread the head out to form a crown from which canes cascade downwards.

The bud union on all stem roses, when planting is finished, should be just clear of

The David Austin rose, 'Wildflower'

the top of the stake. Drive the stake in to approximate depth before planting starts, positioning it on the west-north-west side to protect the stem from the summer sun. The top of the mound in the planting hole should be about 15 cm below ground level. Support stems loosely around the stake while planting, and adjust the length of the stake carefully before making the final tie near the top of the stake. Two screws or clips should be fitted to the support under the top tie to prevent it slipping down. This top tie is the most important and the only one required. It should be checked and replaced regularly. If this tie breaks the stem will tip over from ground level and can be raised again. However, if the rose is also supported by a tie in the middle there is a chance the top heavy rose will break at mid-point. Ties must not cut into and damage the bark, as the bark carries water and nutrients from the soil to the head of the rose. Ties should be durable and strong such as leather or soft plastic, and you should check them at least every time the plant is pruned.

Spacing the bushes

Before planting consider the normal growth patterns expected from each plant so as to avoid having to move plants later. If possible, leave more space than recommended, as this will help with air circulation and make maintenance and removal of flowers much easier. This spacing information is sometimes found on labels, but it is better to seek specialist information from your local garden centre or local growers. They will enjoy passing on their knowledge.

In general, bush and shrub roses should be given at least one metre between plants. Miniatures need up to half a metre and can be used around the borders as highlights, also in rockeries and are very useful when grown as stem or standard roses above groundcovers and low growing annuals and perennials.

New groundcover and modern shrub roses need at least 1.2 m in all directions and are more effective planted with several in a group. Some ground cover types will root and sucker where they make contact with surrounding soil, so these may need to be kept in check to avoid spreading beyond the desired area. Climbers, ramblers, pillar and some tall growing David Austin roses all need something to support their canes as they grow and should be planted 30 to 40 cm away from such supports to allow weeding, feeding and growth of new canes to take place without difficulty.

Vigorous climbers need solid permanent support 4 to 6 metres in width, and to a height that suits your garden. Their canes should be trained to these supports so they grow into a horizontal fan-like position, encouraging flowers to develop along the canes. Canes left vertical will flower only at the very tip. Ramblers need support to train them to areas with enough room to wander over and through the garden, flowering as they cascade over and through structures, fences and trees. Some ramblers only flower well in spring, but growth will continue through the warmer months. Oldest canes and growth in unwanted areas should be pruned out after flowering in late spring.

Pillar roses, including newer patio types, have much more controlled growth while still having climbing characteristics and will cover areas up to 2 to 3 metres wide. They can be trained over or through archways, fences and similar structures, and are well suited for smaller gardens with restricted areas. Remember, before planting any type of climbing rose that they vary greatly in vigour, and can get out of control very quickly so need constant attention. Many flower only in spring but the bush has to be maintained at all times, so do your homework before purchasing any of these to avoid later disappointment.

Replacing a rose

To replace a rose first remove the rose and surrounding soil down to the level of the lower roots and for about 50 cm all around, making sure all existing roots are removed. Refill the area with new soil and organic matter for preference or, if the surrounding area has been heavily mulched over recent years, backfilling the hole with the top 5-6 cm of soil from the surrounding area and incorporating some extra, well-decayed organic material will be acceptable. Avoid bringing soil from other areas of the garden which may be harbouring harmful soil fungus — such as areas where potatoes, tomatoes or dahlias have been growing.

The blue flower in the foreground of this rose bed is *Veronica spicata*. It is easily increased by dividing the plant in spring or autumn.

Roses in containers

Roses may be grown in pots or containers very successfully, but a few precautions will need to be observed and maintained in our climate. The container should reflect the size of the fully-grown plant if you plan for it to remain in the container for any length of time. Plastic pots suffer from extremes of temperature, from freezing in winter to boiling in summer, if pots are not protected at extreme times. A double pot (place your pot within a slightly larger pot) overcomes this to a degree. Wooden casks or well-glazed earthenware pots are more reliable and attractive in the long term.

Container grown roses can be moved to different areas to highlight that position if only for a short time. Large containers can now be attached to a base with castors to make moving them about much easier. Growing in containers for the first year also allows you to evaluate the rose before planting permanently. Potted plants of course will at times require extra watering and may also require anchoring to a support in very windy weather as the plant grows.

Roses need good drainage and the mix needs a good proportion of organic matter. Add to each container the recommended amount of water retention crystals or water regularly with a soluble form as directed. These products help keep the soil in good condition and allow better water and nutrient retention while not interfering with drainage. The only fertiliser required at planting time is about a quarter of a cup of nine- month slow release. Spread half of this over the area a few centimetres below the planted root area and the rest evenly on top. Plant with the bud union just on top of the soil level in the

Rosa 'Pierre de Ronsard'. There are cultivars of this with deeper colours but the original seems to do best in Canberra.

container — the soil should be approximately 5 cm below the top of the container when planting is complete.

After planting, mulch the container well, preferably with one of the cube or pellet forms of lucerne now available. These break down slowly and naturally with almost the perfect ratio of N:P:K required for good healthy rose growth. As buds begin to form a soluble fertiliser of seaweed or fish emulsion will increase flower size and keeping quality. These materials smell for about twenty-four hours so maybe should not be used if you have visitors arriving.

Mulching your beds

Mulch and compost are discussed in some detail in Chapter 5. For better, easier maintenance of roses it is very important that you apply a mulch of organic material in early spring. Do it before plants put on too much growth, to make the job easier. Mulch should be at least 7–8 cm deep and be maintained throughout the growing season. Keep the soil in good condition by lightly cultivating through the mulch regularly, keeping water content constant. Light cultivation helps decomposing mulch fully mix into the soil to improve and maintain its physical condition, allowing ready water penetration to facilitate nutrient absorption and subsequent growth. Mulch helps maintain lower soil temperatures, restricts weed growth, and reduces watering through reduced evaporation.

Lucerne mulch in any form is the superior mulch for roses and for most other plants. Lucerne, as it breaks down, releases the vital major nutrients of nitrogen, phosphorus and potassium in the right combination to stimulate and promote growth. Lucerne may be obtained in cube form, chopped and bagged or in bales. Cube or chopped are most easy to handle, but can be rather expensive if you have a large area. Baled lucerne is available from many local outlets such as garden centres, farm produce stores and at times can be purchased direct from growers straight from the paddock. Second or third cut bales are best if available, as first cut bales often contain more weed seed than later cuts. Bales need to be opened out and spread evenly over areas. Earwigs like to live in mulch and will move from there to your blooms, but Vaseline spread around the stem of your roses will discourage them. Weeds are easily removed from mulched areas when they first appear and before they produce seed.

Fertilisers

Fertilisers are the subject of Chapter 26. Fertilise your roses once the soil starts to warm up and roses are beginning to come into early growth, around late September, and taper off by the end of April. Nothing is gained by applying fertiliser during winter dormancy. In well-mulched, well-prepared soil fertilising

and watering can be reduced, though all plants will still need a continual supply of food for growth and good flowering.

A wide choice of fertilisers is available. Best are those with an N:P:K analysis high in potassium (K). Fertilisers may be organic or chemical, soluble or dry and for best results a combination of all works well. Many fertilisers are designed and marketed specifically for roses and should be applied at no more than the recommended rate as excess is only wasted and could upset the chemical composition of the soil.

A cup of dolomite per square metre worked into the topsoil each winter will help keep the soil in good balance, enabling plants to take up most available nutrients in the soil

Watering in a dry season

Watering is most important for carrying nutrients to the roses through foliage and root system. A deep watering twice weekly will give better results than watering regularly with a hand held hose. Roses should not be allowed to become dehydrated at any stage. Overhead watering can promote spread of fungus but is not a problem as long as it is not done late in the day at times of the year when foliage will remain damp overnight.

We are fast learning to manage on less water. Roses are proving very tough plants and will survive the harshest of droughts. They may not flower so abundantly or be as large as they are during times of plentiful rainfall, but they will survive with occasional watering through the hottest part of summer so long as the water gets down to their roots. There are various ways to do this, with a dripper system or by digging in a plastic pot or agricultural drainpipe as close to the roots as you can and filling this with water from a hand-held hose or watering.

Even newly planted roses will survive on little water if the ground they are planted in is well prepared. The bed needs to be raised from the surrounding area, dug over well with plenty of organic matter added. A couple of handfuls of Seaungus® will ensure the rose gets off to a good start. Newly planted roses have grown very well without any additional water during extreme summer heat.

Pests and diseases

The main section on pests and diseases is Chapter 28. Here we just cover the experiences of some local rose growers.

Many growers prefer not to use chemicals and are quite successfully using good cultural methods, common sense and vigilance. Firstly, do some research and ensure that you choose healthy disease-resistant roses. Some roses are known to develop fungal problems, mostly during autumn, so check and see what looks good at that time. If you do find black spot, mildew or rust on your plants, then these problems can be reduced by introducing drip-irrigation, by removing diseased leaves from plants, and at the same time applying a little fertiliser to encourage new growth. By checking your plants regularly you can find and squash insects such as aphids, thus stopping the increase of numbers before they reach plague proportions.

Despite your best efforts, roses still experience some disease and a few pests, but in our climate, they should recover quickly and are trouble free for much of the time. After identifying a problem, select the least toxic solution for effective control. Use sprays

as directed on the container, wear protective clothing at all times and check for more details on pests and diseases in Chapter 28.

Fungal problems such as black spot, mildew or rust may appear in humid conditions; hot days and cool nights encourage these problems. Prevention is much easier than cure with most fungal diseases. A preventive clean-up spray of lime sulphur or a copper spray after pruning and planting during winter dormancy may help. There are many products designed specifically for roses to minimise fungal problems. Use them regularly throughout the season and for best results vary the types of spray as rose diseases and pests tend to build up immunity.

Some people use home remedies with some success, and while growers will vary the content slightly, it is basically 20 ml each of bi-carbonate of soda, bleach and household detergent mixed well into five litres of water and applied liberally during the early growing season: 30 ml of white oil or pest oil may be added which will also repel some insect pests. After rain, another application will be necessary.

Insects that normally give most trouble in this area are aphids, thrips, hibiscus beetles, twospotted mites (red spider), caterpillars and earwigs. Katydids, looking like fat green grasshoppers, can sometimes be a problem.

Aphids normally are at their worst in early spring on juicy new growth and can also attack new growth in late autumn. Thrips are often in plague numbers during the time of hot winds in November-December. When thrips are in plague proportions it is almost impossible to prevent damage to light coloured roses. Heavy rain will temporarily reduce numbers.

The large flowers of 'Just Joey'.

Hibiscus beetles, like thrips, are much worse in some years than others. Some control is being claimed with new low toxicity systemic sprays. Beetles affect light coloured flowers more. Two-spotted mites also are normally at their worst in hot dry conditions. Watering underneath foliage will help control, but in bad years a systemic spray may be needed. Predatory mites are available from a number of suppliers — see the website for The Australasian Biological Control Association Inc at http://www.goodbugs.org.au/. They help by feeding on the two-spotted mites but are of little use if you are using heavy spray programs, as many sprays will also kill the predatory mites.

Good eyesight and strong fingers can often control caterpillars and katydids early in the morning. Rolled up leaves are a good indicator of caterpillars — this is where they hide before moving into flower buds and destroying them. Katydids are not normally in great numbers but they can ruin flowers very quickly. The most effective insecticides if caterpillars become wide spread are those containing carbaryl. Biological controls are also available (eg Dipel®), but must be used while caterpillars are young to be effective.

Earwigs can be controlled by finding their hiding places, usually dry sheltered areas, and physically destroying them. Rolled up newspaper left in the garden overnight will attract them and they can be shaken into a bucket of hot water next morning.

While our climate is usually reliable it can vary, particularly in springtime with cold frosty or wet nights extending into October and beyond. This causes many buds not to open or become a balled up mess; those that open may produce deformed blotchy flowers. There is little you can do to rectify this, but remove the affected buds down to just above the next plump bud on growth of at least a good pencil thickness and wait for the weather to warm up. This will produce a nice flush of flowers from mid December to early January, and these are often among the best of the year.

An increasing problem is damage to new shoots by birds. They have tended to attack the bushes during early spring and later in autumn, and recently damage has continued through the season. Gardeners have attempted to prevent the damage by scarecrows of different types, plastic bags or foil ribbons, compact discs, netting, artificial snakes, foul tasting sprays, but have had very little reliable success.

Watershoot or sucker?

Almost all purchased roses, regardless of type, will have been budded onto a virus-free rootstock. This budded area is known as the bud union or bud graft. Because it is from this area that the growth of the new plant comes, this must be protected and encouraged at all times. This new growth is referred to as basal or water shoots. The removal of these shoots or canes as they age or suffer dieback encourages the development of water shoots and is the main reason to prune regularly.

Sometimes growths come from the rootstock, below the bud union. These are known as suckers and should be removed quickly by cutting completely away on the stem or cut a section of root growth out with offending sucker — the remaining root system should be pushed downwards to discourage further sucker growth.

You can distinguish suckers from watershoots because they will have foliage distinct from the actual rose. Do not just trim these suckers, as they will quickly regrow to the detriment of the desired plant. Remove them at their origin cleanly. Suckers if allowed to flower often confuse new gardeners, as the flowers can be attractive, but quite different to the rose you bought. Suckers on stem or weeping roses can occur above ground anywhere below the bud union and should be completely removed as soon as first noticed. Roses under stress will produce suckers.

Pruning

Pruning stimulates new vigorous growth on productive wood and encourages new water shoots to develop, producing more and better blooms. Constant regular pruning will maintain the bush for many years. A few general pointers follow, but if you are unsure as to how to tackle this task watch for advertisements of pruning demonstrations by the Horticultural Society or others in July each year.

Late winter is the best time for major pruning of roses in our climate, preferably in August.

» Remove old unproductive wood, weak spindly growth, dieback and crossing canes which restrict air circulation through the bush.

» Cut away cleanly without leaving short stubs as dieback and disease can ensue. A sharp pruning saw or large loppers may be required for this job. Do not damage remaining canes while carrying out this task.

» Remaining canes and branches that have flowered throughout the season are then shortened by about a third.

» Final cuts on the remaining canes should be made 1–2 cm, or alternatively the thickness of the stem above a mature bud. The ideal bud is one facing outwards or at least into a clear space, but certainly not across the centre of the bush. The angle of the cut should be 45 degrees, sloping away from the bud so that water will be shed away from the new growth as it develops from the bud. Always use sharp secateurs.

» New water shoots which appear in late autumn and have either not flowered or flowered only at the very tip should be tip pruned as they will still be soft and immature.

» These canes may need staking in springtime to avoid wind damage. Branches will develop on these canes in spring and the very top growth may then be removed down to a firm branch after the first flowering.

Where canes are broken or showing signs of dieback, prune out the affected areas at any time by shortening or removing the cane completely. Do not postpone the job until winter.

Whether cutting flowers for use or just removing spent blooms from bushes, always

This hedge of 'La Sevilliana' is about 50 m long and seems to be in flower all summer.

prune to just above a good mature bud on growth of at least a good pencil thickness. This will promote continuous flowering on the recurrent varieties.

Summer pruning should be slightly heavier than that carried out when removing spent blooms throughout the year. Remove any weak unproductive growth. Good autumn flowers will follow summer pruning in late January to early February. Most repeat flowering types will then produce another flush of flowers in approximately fifty to sixty days. While this timing is reasonably reliable it can vary from plant to plant and is altered to some degree by extreme heat, wet weather or the timing of summer pruning.

The above pruning techniques apply to large flowered or hybrid tea roses. The

basic principles can be transferred to most other types with good results; however the following modifications may help newer growers gain confidence.

Miniatures need to be pruned lower. Make sure all dead growth is completely removed. They produce most and best flowers from new growth.

Stem roses depend on new growth coming from above the point where the flowering part has been budded to the stem. Be very careful not to cut below this point.

Climbers should not be pruned heavily for the first two years to allow a framework of canes to develop. Limit pruning in early years to removing dead wood and weak growth. As plants develop remove oldest unproductive canes and position new canes in a fan-like shape. Remaining canes should be shortened at the extreme ends back to productive looking growth and positioned back on their support. Shorten branches which have flowered back to two buds off the main cane.

Recurrent flowering old fashioned, historic, modern shrub and ground cover roses should all be kept tidy by removing all dead, unproductive and immature canes together with those going in the wrong direction or becoming too crowded. Remaining canes should be shortened to remove any unproductive and weak growth at the tips. Branches which have flowered off these canes last season should be pruned to a firm bud just off the main canes, removing all spent flower heads.

Weeping stem roses, ramblers and some old fashioned or historic roses which flower only in spring should have main pruning carried out after spring flowering. This will allow new growth to develop in autumn ready for flowering next spring. Winter pruning of these types should be limited to removing any dead canes and removing excess growth.

Renovating an old rose

The dormant season is the time to renovate an old overgrown rose by drastic pruning. In Canberra, this means in late July or early August. Follow any renovation by clearing away grass and weeds and loosening the soil around the plant; and then feed and mulch in spring.

For very badly neglected roses, hard cutting back is the simplest, though sometimes risky, method. At worst it will kill a rose that would very likely have lingered only a little longer anyway.

» Saw away dead wood and stumps at the base of the plant.

» Remove any very old, unhealthy or spindly stems, cutting back to the point of origin.

» Cut remaining older main stems back to a strong new shoot further down, cutting cleanly across the stem.

» Shorten the remaining strong healthy stems to reduce the overall height of the bush to about half. Cut a range of heights.

Selecting roses

Choice of types, variety, cultivar or colour is a personal decision as gardens are designed by their owners for different reasons. Make sure you do some research before selecting roses. The following explanations may help, but are by no means complete in detail.

Type refers to the classifications which roses fall into. There are now three main overall classifications, which are then subdivided again within each classification and into climbing or non-climbing, recurrent or non-recurrent flowering. Classifications in the main are:

Wild Roses, which include the true species and some hybrids closely resembling the species.

Old Garden Roses which include Gallica, Damask, Centifolia, Moss, Alba, China, Tea, Portland, Bourbon, Hybrid perpetual, Scots, Sweet Briar, Ayrshire, Laevigata, Sempervirens, Noisette, Boursault and are often referred to as historic roses.

Modern Garden Roses include the plants most gardeners use today, the result of hybridisation to combine the best of other types. Within this classification are Hybrid teas (now referred to as Large flowered

Rosa 'Friesia', one of the most dependable of the large-flowered yellows for Canberra, although this one has attracted a few thrips. Light coloured roses are more prone to thrips but Eco-Oil provides some protection.

roses), Floribunda (now referred to as Cluster flowered roses), David Austin or English roses, Patio or dwarf cluster flowered, Polyantha, Modern Shrub, Ground Cover and miniature roses.

Standard roses (now referred to as Stem or Tree roses) are usually advertised with their length of stem, roughly the length of stem above the ground after planting. Choose your stem roses carefully as stems budded with vigorous or tall growers can be easily damaged by winds. Miniature, dwarf cluster flowered and new carpet roses are better choices for stem roses in Canberra. Weeping stem roses are restricted to ramblers and climbers which flower well when hanging down, but many of these are not recurrent so one day of bad weather can destroy your display for the year. Some hybrids now being used for weeping stem roses overcome the problem of once a year flowering to some degree. Some of these have only a semi-weeping habit but are very attractive throughout the year at different times.

Large flowered roses

Large flowered (or Hybrid Tea) roses make up a significant proportion of roses planted in Canberra. They produce an abundance of large double flowers on long stems, and most are recurrent flowering when grown as bush roses. Large flowered cultivars usually grow from 1 m to 1.5 m high and should be planted at least one metre apart. Again, this group is subdivided into decorative or garden, exhibition and dual purpose.

Garden or decorative cultivars usually bloom in profusion, have only around twenty or so petals which open quickly, but hold well in the open stage, whether cut for indoor use or left on the bush for decorative effect.

Exhibition cultivars have many petals, often over fifty, and at times may not perform well in our climate in early spring, but for much of the year will produce well formed blooms which will hold their shape and appearance for some time, often not reaching the full blown stage before the petals fade.

Dual purpose cultivars are just that — a good mixture of the other two groups, usually of good form opening well, yet holding well for several days before becoming full blown. Dual purpose roses make good specimen blooms with a little disbudding when colour starts to show in the top bud of a head. It is from this group that almost all exhibition roses come in our climate.

Some reliable large flowered roses:

Red

Avon Large dark red. Holds colour well, highly fragrant, best in warm area. Tall growing.

Christian Dior Top exhibition rose, fragrant red flower with lighter colour on underside of petals.

City of Newcastle Lovely dark red prolific bloomer, nice perfume, reliable grower, good exhibition rose, one of the better newer roses.

Grand Amore Medium sized red blooms on long stems

Kardinal Perfect form, blooms early, keeps well, repeat flowers quickly. Low growing.

Legend Dark red cluster flowered rose, reliable grower

Mr. Lincoln Fragrant, dark velvet red, great full bloom rose. Tall upright growth.

Olympiad Bright medium red, unfading, mostly one bloom per stem.

Papa Meilland Dark red, very fragrant. Tall growing. Watch for mildew in cool weather.

Sir Harry Pilkington Blood red with darker edged petals in spring and a sweet fragrance. A reliable rose.

Timeless Inside petal light red and outside deep pink, slight fragrance. Tall growing.

Vital Medium red, long stems, keeps well, repeat flowers well.

Pink

Bewitched Clear salmon pink flowers on long stems. Holds colour in summer heat and strongly fragrant.

'Julia's Rose'.

Duet Two tone rose-pink, very reliable, grows like a cluster rose but with larger blooms.

Esmeralda Fragrant, two-tone mid-pink flowers with deeper colour towards centre. Very healthy. Tall growing.

Katherine McCredy Single flower in shades of pink to salmon pink in spring, clusters in summer. Fragrant.

Maria Callas Very fragrant vivid bright pink, becomes full-blown quickly, lasts well on bush.

Mondiale Dark salmon pink, lighter cream at the centre with slight fragrance. Very tall growing and trouble-free.

Peter Frankenfeld Dark pink, healthy, reliable in all weathers, light fragrance, a good choice.

Pink Silk Fragrant mid-carmine pink with a high centre and many petals, a good exhibition flower.

Queen Elizabeth Clear pink, reliable rose for garden or cutting, light fragrance and very tall growing.

Silver Lining Fragrant rose pink tipped with silver, white base petals, healthy. A reliable rose.

Yellow/Cream

Ashram Bright old gold, good healthy foliage, slight fragrance.

Diamond Jubilee Buff yellow, strong fragrance, slow to open in spring.

Elina Lemon to pale cream, fragrant and tall growing. A reliable rose, useful at all stages from bud to full bloom.

First Gold Well shaped bright yellow on long, almost thornless stems. An excellent cut flower.

Glorious Clean yellow with good stems, excellent foliage and repeat flowering.

Golden Gate Intense yellow, holds form well, a good cut flower. Tall growing.

Helmut Schmidt Pure yellow, very few thorns and light fragrance. A low grower.

Safari Bronze yellow, medium-sized fragrant flowers which hold their form well.

Spirit of Peace Dark apricot cream to buff, very fragrant, vigorous, tall-growing rose.

White

Class Act White cream with bright stamens, multi-flowered heads like a cluster rose. A low grower.

Escimo (syn. Eskimo) Very good cut flower. Lasts well, both on the bush or when cut.

Grand Finale Ivory white with sweet fragrance, high centred blooms with long stems. A tall grower.

Karen Blixen Pure white, large well-formed flowers with a strong fragrance.

Pascali White sometimes tinged with pink in cool weather. A reliable and healthy tall grower.

Polar Star Cream white with a hint of green, holds its form well. A healthy tall grower.

Pristine White fragrant blooms shaded with pink in cool weather, profuse flowers and healthy.

Tineke Pure white flowers with plump pointed buds, does best in a warm position. Vigorous.

Apricot and copper shades

Brandy Golden apricot, fragrant blooms with golden stamens and glossy mahogany foliage.

Cubana Light apricot, medium well-formed, wavy petals, a good cut flower. Tall growing.

Joyfulness Apricot flushed golden yellow fragrant blooms with long stems. Repeat flowers and is tall growing.

Just Joey Copper orange tone, wavy frilled petals with a sweet fragrance. A good tall growing rose.

Valencia Old gold copper, large full-petalled fragrant blooms on long stems. Tall growing.

Whisky Peach apricot, large ruffled fragrant blooms. Tall growing. A delight in the garden.

Orange

Alexander Bright vermilion, fragrant flowers. Blooms early and is quick to repeat flower. A good tall growing rose.

Corvette Orange red, long strong stems, well-formed, long lasting blooms.

Duftwolke (syn. Fragrant Cloud) Coral orange, a well-formed, reliable rose. Likes a dry area.

Laura Orange with golden reverse, prolific medium flowers. A show stopper.

Mauve

Blue Moon Lilac lavender, usually one flower per long stem, sparse foliage. Tall growing and fragrant.

Charles De Gaulle Warm lilac, fragrant, well-formed flowers. It dislikes damp conditions. Low growing.

Paradise Fragrant, silver lavender-edged carmine to red flowers, attractive at all stages. A healthy rose.

Stainless Steel Soft lilac fragrant blooms. A classic show form on long stems and keeps well. Tall growing.

Vol De Nuit Deep mauve, fragrant blooms with good repeat flowering.

Bi- or Multi-Colour, Different

April Hamer Blooms are fragrant, pale base with apricot pink tones. A good Australian-bred rose.

Baronne E. De Rothschild Deep pink-red with white base. A good full fragrant bloom.

Brigadoon White cream and pink tones, slow opening fragrant flowers last well.

Diana Princess of Wales White/lemon apricot pink fragrant blooms. A tall, healthy, vigorous rose.

Double Delight Creamy white blooms edged with carmine red which fades in the heat. Has great fragrance.

Gemini Coral over cream, lovely bud shape, highly recommended for all.

Honey Dijon Warm golden brown changing to honey lemon depending on the weather. Healthy foliage, fruity fragrance and a good cut flower.

Ian Thorpe Terracotta red, almost continuously flowering

Moonstone Porcelain pink over white, good exhibition rose, lovely bud shape.

New Era Yellow fragrant blooms overlaid with red, holds its colour well in all conditions.

Princess of Monaco Prolific fragrant blooms in ivory flushed clear pink. A reliable tall growing rose.

Royal Dane Orange copper fragrant blooms with red outer petals, something different and reliable. Tall growing.

Signature deep pink over lighter reverse, good for exhibition but slow to repeat flower.

Cluster roses

Cluster roses, also called Floribunda roses, provide some of the most colourful, healthy and reliable roses for garden display and indoor decoration. Almost all will repeat flower in around forty five days if trimmed back as each flowering is finished. The flowers come in clusters and are quite spectacular when several of the same colour are massed together.

More even development of the flowering cluster may be obtained by removing the main centre bud when it first starts to show colour. Normally this will result in the rest of the cluster opening together and more evenly. Height is variable between cultivars so some research is needed if planting any amount together. Planting space between bushes should be between 0.75m and 1 m.

Red

Cathedral City Brilliant orange-red with dark green to red foliage.

Europeana Deep crimson fragrant flowers with dark foliage.

Evelyn Fison Deep red fragrant flowers with green foliage.

La Sevilliana Vermillion red, repeat flowers. Light fragrance, a good hedge rose.

Marlena Crimson red with attractive yellow stamens.

Moulin Rouge Fragrant scarlet red blooms with upright tall growth.

Pink
Bridal Pink Fragrant pale pink flowers. A low grower.

Elizabeth of Glamis Fragrant salmon pink flowers with dark foliage.

Kalinka Fragrant porcelain pink early flowers. Almost thornless.

Pink Parfait Fragrant pastel pink. A low grower.

Sexy Rexy Fragrant shell pink with camellia-like flowers. Low growing.

Shady Lady Fragrant rose pink with shading ivory centre. Tall growing.

Sir Cliff Richards Clear pink, very popular rose, tall grower. Healthy foliage and good repeat flowering.

The Fairy Deep pink polyantha with miniature flowers, late to start, but then seldom without flowers. Many uses and makes a very good stem rose. Low, spreading growth suited to spilling over walls or as ground cover.

Yellow and Cream
Friesia Bright yellow fragrant flowers. Does not fade, even in hot weather.

Rosa 'Graham Thomas', a strong growing David Austin cultivar.

Gold Bunny Soft gold fragrant flowers. Low grower.

Golden Girls Soft yellow, a healthy bush seldom without flowers.

Nana Mouskouri Cream to almost white fragrant flowers. Tall growing.

Victoria Gold Golden yellow with fine red edges in cooler weather.

Yellow Simplicity Bright yellow fragrant flowers. Tall upright growth.

White
Iceberg Pure white fragrant flowers. Tall growing. A good rose for all conditions.

Margaret Merril Clear white fragrant rose with red stamens. Tall grower.

White Spray Fragrant white rose with light cream centre. Tall growing.

Mauve
Angel Face Deep mauve fragrant bloom with wavy petals. A Low grower.

Blueberry Hill Large blousy lilac blooms on a medium bush.

Burgundy Iceberg Dark burgundy red with sweet fragrance. As good as white Iceberg.

Love Potion Deep lilac fragrant blooms with ruffled petals. Low grower.

Bi-Colour

Hannah Gordon (syn. Raspberry Ice) White fragrant flowers, flushed and edged with light cherry red and dark green foliage.

Red Gold Fragrant gold flushed red.

Seduction Fragrant white flushed pink, colour more intense in cloudy and cool weather.

Woman's Day Creamy white blooms, flushed and edged pink to rose pink.

Orange and Apricot

Apricot Nectar Buff apricot. A taller grower, healthy and fragrant.

Brass Band Clusters of fragrant apricot blooms with yellow reverse. Medium bush.

Orangeade Clear orange, fragrant flowers with upright tall growth.

Orange Silk Fragrant orange vermilion. Tall growing.

Warrior Fragrant orange red blooms. A low grower.

Different!

Julia's Rose Café au lait with a hint of lavender. A low grower.

Hot Chocolate Fragrant rich orange red blooms shading to brown, different every day.

Victoriana Smoky salmon and pink fragrant blooms with wavy petals. A low grower.

Vesper Fragrant apricot brown blooms. A low grower.

Rosa 'Mary Rose' is one of the most popular of the David Austin roses, named after Henry VIII's flagship which was raised just before the release of the rose.

Thornless roses

Where space is restricted and there may be danger of passers-by being hooked on thorny climbers, then consider planting a thornless rose. These are not common, but those that are available are becoming popular:

Crépuscule A repeat flowering climbing rose with fragrant apricot flowers.

Honorine de Brabant Has few thorns, striped pale pink to dark pink flowers, with a main flush of flowers in mid-summer but seldom out of flower. Classed as a tall shrub, this could be grown as a small climber.

Kathleen Harrop Pale pink spring flowering and suited to climbing either on an arch or a frame, rather than against a wall, where black spot may be a problem.

Madame Plantier A large shrub which could be trained as a climber. It has clusters of white, pendulous sweetly-perfumed flowers in spring only.

Pinkie, climbing. A modern polyantha rose which repeat- flowers.

Reine des Violettes Well worth growing as a shrub rose for its pretty violet quartered and spicy scented blooms which repeat flower.

Renae A repeat flowering pale pink climber with distinctive bright stamens and some scent, suited to growing on pergolas. Also available as a stem rose. A vigorous healthy rose.

Vielchenblau Flowers over a period with a small, violet bloom and as the flowers age, the plant presents an attractive range of shades through to lilac.

Zéphirine Drouhin Cerise pink, spring flowering and suited to climbing either on an arch or a frame, rather than against a wall, where black spot may be a problem.

David Austin or English Roses

These roses have a diverse range of colour, flower form, fragrance and bush form. There is a never ending supply of new releases, most of which combine the form and fragrance of old world roses with the repeat-flowering characteristics of modern cultivars. Height and spread vary greatly so details should be checked before purchase. Taller cultivars may need to be grown together or given support for best results.

These plants should be treated as large flowered roses as far as care throughout the year is concerned and should be planted one to one and a half metres apart, depending on the expected spread. With such a range of flower form and colour available the following recommendations are but a sample of what is available. All are fragrant. The indications of height and spread are still only approximate and can vary according to their siting.

Ambridge Rose 75 cm x 75 cm. Apricot pink becoming paler towards the outer edges.

Claire Rose 1.2 m x 1 m. Blush pink fading with age. Large, many petalled rosette sprays.

Crocus Rose 1.5 x 1.5 m. Lovely cream prolific flowerer with large clusters of blooms on arching branches, a lovely decorative rose

Evelyn 1.8 m x 1 m. Apricot-yellow. Large open shallow cup shaped blooms. One of the most fragrant.

Golden Celebration 1.5 m x 1.2 m. Rich golden yellow, large cup shaped blooms and arching canes.

Grace Pale apricot fully double flower, a good branching shrub that repeat flowers well. A small grower.

Graham Thomas 1.5 m x 1 m. Deep golden yellow, medium cup shaped blooms with arching canes. Can be used as a small climber.

Heritage 1.5 m x 1.5 m. Soft pink paling on edges. Well-placed petals provide a shell effect.

John Clare 1 m x 75 cm. Deep pink, informal cup shape. Prolific bloomer, reliable.

Leander 3 m x 2 m. Deep apricot blooms. Can be used as small climber. Best in summer.

Mary Rose 1.5 m x 1.5 m. Rose pink, loose petalled old rose form. Most reliable.

Moulineux 1 m x 75 cm. Rich yellow. Short upright growth, good repeat flowering.

Pat Austin 1.2 m x 1 m. Bright copper with copper yellow reverse, large cup shape.

Radio Times 1 m x 1 m. Fresh pink well-formed rosette trusses, gently arching canes.

Tamora 1 m x 75 cm. Deep cup shaped apricot, reliable low grower. Good in mass planting.

Teasing Georgia Soft yellow, large flowers, sweet scent, very tall grower, ideal for a pillar.

The Dark Lady 1.5 m x 1.5 m. Exquisite dark purple quartered bloom. Could be a good pillar rose.

William Morris 2 m x 1.5 m. Apricot pink, well-formed rosettes. Makes a good small climber.

Winchester Cathedral 1.5 m x 1.5 m. Snow white frilly double blooms, scented, medium growth.

Patio Dwarf Climbers

These are starting to make their mark in the rose world, growing with canes of just over two metres tall and bushing out nicely to fill a column or arches. They can also be used as a climber in smaller gardens. They have masses of dwarf-sized cluster flowers just slightly larger than miniature roses. Some recommendations are:

Edith Holden 3 m x 2 m. Tan brown to orange. Unique colour, ideal for pillar or tripod.

Patio Pearl 2 m x 1 m. Pale pink with golden stamens. A prolific healthy small climber.

Pillar Box 2 m x 1 m. Bright vermilion red. Tall upright growth.

Modern Shrub Roses

An ideal selection where a mass of colour is required over a long period with minimum maintenance. Good for hedges or back drop planting, while still very useful as a specimen feature anywhere in the garden. Most of

Rosa 'Altissimo' is a climber with magnificent brilliant flowers.

these plants are very tall and hardy, ranging from 1.5 m to 2 m tall, with a spread of over one metre. They should be planted at least 1.2 m apart.

While some removal of spent heads will help the repeat flowering process, these hardy plants will normally repeat flower fairly quickly without help. Once plants are fully established they should not require any extra support particularly if a number are grown together. Two recommendations are:

Hanza Park 2 m x 1 m. Lavender to lilac pink. Continually in flower, makes good hedge.

Sally Holmes 2 m x 1.2 m. Large trusses of white tinged pink single flowers with golden stamens.

There are a number of new plants from the French nursery Delbard which look promising. Their suitability for Canberra is still being assessed. Check that your choice is fragrant.

Miniature Roses

So called because of the size of their flowers, these are very reliable and will fit in almost any garden landscape, large or small. Bushes need to be regularly cut back to solid growth after flowering to encourage the next lot of flowers on new growth. Growth habit can vary greatly between cultivars, so check before selecting. Miniatures are good as stem roses, since they are not troubled with the wind as much as other roses. Miniature roses also come in climbing forms. Some suggestions are:

Double Joy Fragrant dusty pink flowers. A low grower.

Figurine Porcelain white flushed pale pink, fragrant flowers.

Gidday Buttercup yellow flowers.

Green Ice White with a touch of pink, centres develop a green hue as the flowers age.

Heartbreaker White to cream base flushed and edged deep pink fragrant flowers.

Holy Toledo Apricot-orange with a yellow orange reverse and a touch of red. A low grower.

Jean Kennealy Pale apricot pink fragrant flowers. Tall growing.

Magic Carousel Creamy white fragrant flowers edged vivid red with golden stamens. Tall growing.

Minnie Pearl Light pink flowers with a pale cream base.

Petite Follie Fragrant vermilion flowers with carmine reverse. Tall growing.

Red Beauty Deep red fragrant flowers with yellow base.

Starina Bright red with gold to yellow reverse, low grower.

Ground Cover Roses

New cultivars offer an outstanding range of colours which, when planted in groups, make spectacular displays over long periods without a lot of attention. Repeat flowering takes place readily, giving a splash of colour for most of the flowering season. Trusses of flowers are too short for cut flowers, but can brighten a dull corner in the garden. Weeds may be a problem growing up through the bushes, but if the area underneath is heavily mulched early in spring the weeds will pull out easily if removed when first seen. Plant them about 1.2 m apart.

Old fashioned, or heritage shrub roses

Old Garden Roses cover such a wide range development over the years that one should look for specialist publications on the subject before purchasing plants. Some of the plants listed here are modern roses with old characteristics.

Buff Beauty Hybrid Musk Rose, 1939, has fragrant apricot flowers, repeat flowering, colouring more intense in autumn. An arching shrub to 1.8 m.

Cornelia Hybrid Musk Rose, 1925, fragrant pale pink flowers with a touch of apricot — repeat flowering, an arching shrub or small climber to 1.8 m.

Felicia Hybrid Musk Rose, 1928, pale pink fragrant flowers in summer repeating through to autumn, when flowers attain an apricot tinge — an arching shrub or small climber to 1.8 m

Fritz Nobis 1940, flowers once only but with a wonderful flush of soft pink flowers in early summer and bright red hips in autumn – a large shrub or small climber to 1.8 m.

Fru Dagmar Hastrup A rugosa seedling from 1914 suitable for low (1 m) high hedges with single pink continuous flowers and crimson hips.

Gruss an Aachen 1909, a fragrant creamy-pale apricot pink bloom which fades to creamy-white. Suitable for very low hedges at a height of 0.5 m.

Madame Isaac Pereire A Bourbon rose of 1881 with repeat flowers. A large shrub growing to 2 m with deep pink, strongly-fragrant flowers shaded with magenta. Ideal for the pillar or trellis.

Mutabilis Probably introduced to Italy from China in 1894 – a single repeat flowering rose. A large shrub growing to 1.8 m and can be used as a small climber. The plant will carry flowers of many different hues from buff yellow through pink to carmine, and is spectacular.

Penelope Hybrid Musk 1924 – a fragrant rose with repeat clustered pale pink flowers fading to white. 1.2 m.

Finally, some Climbing, Rambling, and Pillar Roses

Altissimo Clear deep red single fragrant flowers with bright yellow stamens, repeat flowering.

Albertine Attractive dark pink buds with salmon pink to apricot fragrant blooms for about three weeks in late spring. Very vigorous.

Black Boy Dark crimson fragrant blooms, repeat flowering. Bred in Australia by Alister Clark.

Blossomtime Two-tone pink fragrant blooms, repeat flowers.

Crépescule Apricot fragrant blooms with very few thorns and repeat flowering.

Gold Bunny Soft-gold fragrant blooms, repeat flowering.

Iceberg Fragrant pure white flowers, repeat flowering.

Lorraine Lee Fragrant apricot to coral pink flowers, repeat flowering. Bred in Australia by Alister Clark.

Pierre de Ronsard Fragrant creamy white flushed pale pink to carmine blooms, repeat flowering. Well worth growing, but its heavy blooms tend to hang down so grow it on a frame or arch where you can appreciate its beauty.

Royal Gold Fragrant golden yellow blooms, repeat flowering. One of the few hybrid tea roses which is only available as a climber.

CHAPTER 17:
Camellias, rhododendrons and azaleas

Neil Mitchell and Brian Usback

Camellias, rhododendrons and azaleas have always been popular garden shrubs because of the dependability of their colourful blooms, ease of cultivation and a wide range of available varieties. While these plants may not be considered ideal choices for times of drought, if you have shady and protected areas in your garden, then camellias, azaleas and rhododendrons are very useful in invigorating an otherwise dull and gloomy location, especially given that they do not have to be in bloom to be attractive. Consider also that with good mulch and ample compost, such plants may actually use less water than the traditional Canberra lawn. This chapter offers some easily followed suggestions that will help you succeed in growing them.

Cultural requirements

These plants prefer a position with semi-shade or filtered sunlight; an arc facing from north–east through to south–west would normally provide the necessary protection from the hot afternoon sun. That is, unless the plants are labelled as sun-hardy, the shaded side of your house or a shady place in the garden is desirable. Some additional shelter is necessary to restrict frost damage to the blooms of pale flowered cultivars. This can be provided by trees or by locating the plants near the protection of eaves. Frost damage is a concern when the bushes are small; as the plant grows it will provide its own protection for a greater percentage

of its blooms. Later blooming varieties of rhododendrons and azaleas are more likely to escape the frosts.

Proper drainage ensures healthy growth. If the garden beds are relatively flat, beds are best raised with good soil to a level which would provide a soil depth of at least 20-30 cm. The soil should be neutral or preferably slightly acid (pH 5.5 to 6.5). Rhododendrons and azaleas are particularly sensitive to lime, so only add lime or dolomite if the acidity level is too low. Gypsum and compost may be added to improve drainage.

Environmental considerations

With our recent history of watering restrictions, it is reasonable to ask why one would grow exotic plants such as these. Here are a few observations. Unlike some introductions from Mediterranean climates or Australian species which are not local, these plants are not invasive and will not become

One of the *Camellia japonicas*, called 'Black Tie', showing a typical formal double flower shape.

weeds. With care given to mulching and weeding, watering can be done once weekly except in extreme conditions. Camellias (and magnolias) become deeply rooted with time, so they develop a little more drought resistance than azaleas and rhododendrons. However, the latter are always useful for the extended flowering season that they can offer. In summary, be guilt free in growing exotic garden plants.

Planting

There is general advice on planting, transplanting and pot culture of trees and shrubs in a later chapter so only some special points are given here.

Camellias, rhododendrons and azaleas are all sold as container plants and may be planted into the garden at any time of the year. Avoid, if possible, the extreme times of the year that will place the plants under undue stress, particularly late spring and summer when plants will dry out excessively, and severe winter cold snaps when the ground can be frozen for days on end.

These plants are all surface rooting - they should never be planted deeper into the garden than they were in the pot. Planting too

deeply is one of the most frequent reasons for poor growth and can lead to loss of plants through root rot.

Camellias can be spaced at least 2 m apart and should be at least 1 m away from a house wall or a fence. For a hedge, the spacing can be 1 m apart. Rhododendrons and azaleas are very variable in size so be guided by the plant label. Where water is in limited supply, grow your drought-sensitive plants together and limit their numbers. In general, azaleas are not a problem for foundations or pipes.

Camellias can readily be transplanted — see the later chapter for general advice. If it is unavoidable to transplant at the 'wrong' time of year, consider completely defoliating the plant and protecting it with a temporary shade cloth shelter.

Camellias, rhododendrons and azaleas all do well in pots, but cope poorly with 'wet feet' so do not stand your pots in saucers of water.

Pruning

If you wish to prune then do it after flowering unless you are prepared to lose next season's show.

Camellias may grow to the size of a small tree but they can be kept in check by pruning immediately after flowering, or as flowering is declining, but before spring growth commences. Prune and thin to control size and shape to keep the plant to the desired size. Dead wood, weak spindly growth, crossing, and low growing branches, should be removed to let in light and air. Long unproductive wood can be cut severely. Quite impressive growth often results.

Rhododendrons and deciduous azaleas can be pruned in a similar manner and cutting

The single flowers of 'Wirlinga Bride', a miniature flowered camellia hybrid, bred in Australia. The flowers are fragrant and the bush has an attractive weeping shape.

Moisture, food and mulch

In general, these plants are from temperate woodlands and appreciate mulch more than the heavy use of fertilisers, but retention of moisture through Canberra's dry summer is vital. The proper watering of camellias, rhododendrons and azaleas will be helped by using moisture-retentive soil, and the application of humus material to the top of the ground around the bush will help to conserve moisture and keep the roots cool in summer. The humus material could be well-made compost, pine needles, leaf mould, cow or sheep manure, spread at a depth of about 8 cm around established bushes and about 4 cm under small plants.

Drought has been a recurring phenomenon for the past twenty years. Well-established camellias have demonstrated more drought hardiness than rhododendrons and azaleas but, even so, they appreciate a good soaking at least weekly in hot, dry weather and at least monthly in dry winters. Azaleas should not be left to remain dry for more than a few days at any time.

While these plants will flower and grow quite well with adequate moisture and mulch, the general health of the plants and the size of the blooms may be improved by the application of fertilisers. The best time to fertilise is early spring, with a small follow-up in mid-summer. Suitable fertilisers can be either organic, such as cow or sheep manure, or inorganic, such as ready mixed Camellia and Azalea foods or complete general purpose fertilisers. When using fertilisers, it is important to follow a couple of general rules, fertilising only when the soil is moist and spreading it evenly under the bush but not against the main stem. Too much fertiliser will damage a plant and may even kill it.

of blooms is beneficial. Spent flower heads of rhododendrons are easily twisted off the plants. Evergreen azaleas can grow quite large if not pruned, and can be clipped to shape with shears, preferably after flowering. In general, the spread of rhododendrons exceeds the height quoted on the plant's label. Therefore, unless a very large shrub or tree is wanted, select lower growing varieties or control the growth from the outset.

If camellias, rhododendrons and azaleas are not pruned after flowering, they will often set seed. In the case of camellias, fruit may be seen on single and semi-double cultivars. The fruit may resemble small apples or be round and covered in brown felt in the case of some hybrids. The fruit may be cut off.

Gordonia yunnanensis

Pests, diseases and other problems

Camellias are generally trouble-free. Young plants may suffer more than older ones from caterpillars. Aphids can distort young growth and scale is occasionally seen. In late spring, old camellia leaves are often shed — this is a normal occurrence. Viruses in camellias are generally benign but they can cause variable yellow spotting or mottling of the leaves and white spotting or mottling of the petals. There is nothing you can do about this.

Rhododendrons and azaleas are subject to attack by mites or lacewings (causing a silvery scaring of the leaves) which is controlled with Confidor® or other systemic insecticides and, in wet seasons, are also subject to petal blight. Petal blight tends to vary with the seasons, being worse in wet springs. No reliable fungicide is available. Evergreen azaleas normally shed some leaves in autumn and this is not a sign of stress.

Leaf burn, appearing on plants that experience direct sunlight, is a sign of inadequate watering. Plants should not be allowed to dry out, though not watered to the extent that waterlogging results.

Camellias to grow

The most commonly grown camellias in the colder climates are cultivars of *C. sasanqua*, *C. japonica*, *C. reticulata* and the hybrids of these and others. The major advantage of the sasanqua type is that it will tolerate a greater degree of sun than other camellias and is thus more versatile as a general garden plant. In addition sasanquas flower mainly in late autumn and early winter and are a welcome source of colour in the garden.

Camellia flower forms are quite varied but the main types are single, semi-double, informal double (including roseform and informal double/paeoniform), formal double and anemone (or elegans) form. A wide range of colours is also available but the darker colours perform best as they have blooms that are less easily discoloured by frost or sunlight.

Choosing a camellia depends on personal taste and there is a very large range to choose from. It is best to see the plant flowering before making your choice. The plant label will indicate the season of bloom. In general, early to mid-season bloomers are of better value in Canberra for they will bloom longer. A wide range of cultivars suitable for colder climates is listed below.

Miniature Camellia hybrids

Small leaves and a clustered flowering habit are features of miniature flowered hybrids. Most of these are fragrant. Bear in mind that the plants grow in time to a large size. Exceptions include 'Baby Bear' and 'Baby Willow' – they remain small.

Camellia species

Local garden centres sometimes offer species camellias. *C. sinensis, C. grijsii, C. yunnanensis, C. trichocarpa, C. fraterna, C. rosiflora, C. pitardii, C. lutchuensis, C. tsaii* and *C. saluenensis* do well here, taking a fair amount of sun. All of these produce single flowers.

Camellia relatives that are worth trying

Gordonias are evergreen shrubs that flower with the sasanquas in autumn. They have large, white sasanqua-like flowers but are a little too frost-tender to be grown in the open. Several species and varieties are now offered.

Cleyeras are evergreen shrubs with fragrant flowers in summer. They make good low hedges. *Cleyera japonica* has deep green leaves and *Cleyera fortunei* has variegated leaves and pink coloured new growth.

Franklinia alatamaha is a deciduous shrub that blooms in mid-summer. It produces good autumn colours but dislikes our low humidity. Try it in a sheltered spot. Similar comments apply to the lovely Stewartias (Stuartias) that have attractively coloured trunks with peeling bark.

Suggested Camellias

Camellia sasanqua

White to light coloured
Fuji-no-mine Informal white. Low growing.

Fukuzutsumi syn. Zerbes Single white with pink edge.

Mine-no-yuki Peony to formal form. White, low growing.

Setsugekka Single to semi-double, white, tall and open.

Star Above Star Semi-double, white with lavender pink edges. Winter to spring blooming.

Pink to red
Bert Jones Semi-double, silver pink.

Bonanza Semi-double to peony, deep red.

Chansonette Formal double, deep pink, lavender overtone.

Edna Butler Semi-double, silver pink.

Exquisite Single pale pink.

Hiryu syn. ***Camellia vernalis*** Semi-double, scarlet, winter blooming.

Kanjiro (incorrectly, **Hiryu**) Semi-double, cerise, silvery centre of petals. Tall.

Jennifer Susan Rose form, pale pink, spreading.

Lucinda Peony, pink, tall and spreading.

Marge Miller Informal double with lavender rose flowers. Low, spreading growth.

Plantation Pink Single pink, tal.l

Camellia japonica 'Moshio' is an all time favourite. It has a semi-double bloom.

Paradise Belinda Semi-double to anemone, cerise to light red, large flowers. Tall.

Paradise Joan Semi-double to informal, Bright red flowers.

Showa-no-sakae Semi-double to rose form, lavender pink, spreading habit.

Shishigashira Semi-double to informal double, rose red, low growing.

Tanya Single, light red. Low, spreading growth.

Yuletide Single deep red with golden stamens. Compact, slow.

Camellia reticulata (including hybrids with reticulata parentage)

These are typically large flowered, vigorous growing, sun hardy and bloom from late winter to late spring. The flowers usually have wavy petals. The choice from garden centres is usually limited to just a few that are easily propagated. To acquire more unusual varieties, you will need to visit a specialist nursery.

Shades of pink

Arch of Triumph Informal. Deep pink to wine red.

Buddha Semi-double. Bright pink.

Captain Rawes Semi-double. Deep rose pink, very late bloomer.

Dayinhong (syn. Shot Silk) Informal double. Bright pink, lavender shaded.

Dream Girl Semi-double to informal. Bright rose, early bloomer.

Flower Girl Semi-double. Deep rose, early blooming. 'California Dawn' and 'California Sunset' are similar.

Camellia sasanqua 'Chansonette'.

Francie L Semi-double to informal. Deep rose. Open growing, hanging leaves.

Howard Asper Semi-double to loose informal. Salmon pink.

K.O. Hester Semi-double to loose informal. Orchid pink.

Lasca Beauty Informal to semi-double. Soft pink. Glossy leaves. Attractive plant.

Leonard Messel Semi-double. Rose pink.

Mouchang Single to semi-double. Salmon pink.

Royalty Single to semi-double. Deep rose.

Show Girl Semi-double. Mid-pink, very early blooming.

Valley Knudsen Semi-double. Orchid pink.

Winter's Own Informal double. Mid-pink. (A variegated form is available).

Red

Dataohong (syn. **Crimson Robe**) Semi-double to loose informal. Bright red.

Dr Clifford Parks Semi-double, anemone or informal red. Highly recommended.

Ellie Rubensohn Semi-double to rose form. Rosy crimson.

Miss Tulare Informal double. Bright red to rose red.

Nuccio's Ruby Informal double. Dark red.

Robert Fortune (syn. **Pagoda**) Formal double. Bright red.

Purple Gown Rose form to formal double. Purplish red, slow growing.

William Hertrich Semi-double to informal double. Deep cherry red, large.

Bi-coloured
Alaskan Queen Semi-double. White to blush pink.

Damanao (syn. **Comelian**) Informal double. Red blotched white.

Lady Pamela Semi-double to informal double. White, pink edge.

Suzanne Withers Semi-double to informal double. White with pink edge.

White Retic Semi-double to rose form. White to blush pink, late bloomer.

Camellia japonica and some of its hybrids.

You will be spoiled for choice. Some 'tried and true' cultivars follow.

Shades of pink
Akashigata (syn. **Lady Clare**) Semi-double. Deep pink (also a variegated form, 'Oniji').

Anticipation (hybrid) Informal double. Deep lilac pink.

C.M. Wilson Anemone. Silvery pink.

Debbie (hybrid) Informal double. Rose pink.

Demi-Tasse Hose-in-hose semi-double. Peachy pink, small flowers.

Doctor Tinsley Semi-double. Salmon pink.

Donation (hybrid) Semi-double. Orchid pink.

Easter Morn Semi-double. Pale peach pink.

Edith Linton Semi-double. Pink, shading to silvery pink.

E.G. Waterhouse (hybrid) Formal double. Light lavender pink (also a variegated form).

Elegans Anemone, rose pink (also a variegated form).

Elegans Supreme Anemone. Deep rose pink with deep serrations.

Elsie Jury (hybrid) Informal double. Rounded bloom, bright lilac pink.

Gay Pixie Informal double. Light orchid pink with darker stripes. Open growth.

Georgia Rouse Informal double. Vivid mid pink.

This is 'Fircone variegated' a sport of 'Fircone'.

Guilio Nuccio Semi-double. Rich coral rose (also a variegated form).

Laurie Bray Semi-double. Pale pink, intensifying with age.

Magnoliiflora (syn. **Hagoromo**) Semi-double. Hose-in-hose blush pink.

Margaret Waterhouse (hybrid). Semi-double. Light rose pink.

Mary Phoebe Taylor Loose informal double. Light rose-pink with upright spreading growth.

Nicky Crisp Semi-double. Pale, lavender pink. Long blooming. Compact, slow grower.

Otome Formal double. Small. Pale pink.

Phillipa Ifould Formal double. Peach pink.

Prince Fredrick William Formal double. Rose pink.

R.L. Wheeler Semi-double. Rose pink (also a variegated form).

Spencer's Pink Single. Light pink wavy petals, early.

Spring Sonnet Informal double. Pale pink with cyclamen edge. Slightly fragrant.

Susan Stone Formal double. Blush pink.

Twilight Formal double. Light blush pink. Blooms need protection.

Waterlily (hybrid) Formal double. Lavender pink.

William Bull Formal double. Rose pink.

Wynne Rayner (hybrid) Semi-double. Lavender pink.

Red

Black Lace Formal double. Deep red, late blooming.

Bob Hope Semi-double. Deep red. Sun hardy plant. Recommended.

C.M. Hovey Formal double. Deep red.

Emperor of Russia Informal double. Deep rose red (also a variegated form).

Grand Slam Semi-double to anemone. Glowing red.

Great Eastern Semi-double. Deep rose red, purplish in heavy soil.

Jamie Semi-double. Bright red.

Kramer's Supreme Peony. Turkey red, fragrant. A shy bloomer when young.

Midnight Semi-double to informal. Dark red.

Moshio Semi-double. Hose-in-hose pure red.

Prince Eugene Napoleon Formal double. Red with darker veining.

Red Red Rose Formal double. Bright red, high centred blooms. Late.

Susie Fortson Formal double to Semi-double. Blood red.

Takanini Informal double, anemone. Deep purplish red. Open growth. Very long blooming.

Camellia japonica 'Lovelight' is one of the best whites but to be at its best it needs protection from early morning sun while frost is on the flowers.

The Czar Semi-double. Light crimson, purplish in heavy soil.

Wildfire Semi-double. Fiery red.

White to light coloured

Brushfield's Yellow Anemone. Antique white, primrose petaloid centre.

Elegans Champagne Anemone. White, creamy petaloid centre.

Kamohonami Single with white, cupped bloom. Early bloomer.

Lovelight Semi-double. White. Must have protection for good blooms.

Margarete Hertrich White formal double.

Nuccio's Gem Formal double. White.

White Nun Semi-double. Large white flowers. Blooms need protection.

Bi-coloured

Betty's Beauty Informal double. White, edged orchid pink. Replaces 'Betty Sheffield Supreme'.

Blushing Beauty Formal double. White centre to blush pink outer edge.

Desire Formal double. Ivory white shaded pink.

Elegans Splendor Anemone. Blush pink edged white.

High Fragrance Informal double. White to soft pink deeper pink at edge of petals. Fragrant. Rampant grower.

Margaret Davis Informal double. Creamy white, brilliant rose edge.

Nuccio's Jewel Peony. White shading to orchid pink.

Nuccio's Pearl Formal double. Pale pink shading to orchid pink.

Roma Risorta Formal double. Pale pink streaked and flecked rose pink.

Shiro Chan Anemone. White, pink at base of petals. Needs protection.

Tabbs Formal double. Crimson, marbled white.

Camellias with miniature flowers

These have miniature flowers but are not small growers. They are of the species *Camellia japonica*.

'Magnoliiflora', also known as 'Hagoroma'.

Baby Sis White, occasional pink stripe. Single.

Bokuhan (syn. **Tinsie**) Deep ruby, white petaloids. Anemone.

Fircone Blood red semi-double.

Little Red Riding Hood Formal double to peony, deep crimson.

Man Size White, anemone.

Pearl's Pet Rose red. Anemone.

Tootsie Chalk white. Formal double.

Miniature Hybrids

All bloom from late winter to spring with clustered flowers unless otherwise stated.

Baby Bear Single soft pink. Slow, compact growth.

Baby Willow Single pure white. Slow upright growth.

Blondy Anemone form, white, fragrant. Open growth.

Bogong Snow Anemone form, pink bud, white petals, fragrant. Weeping growth.

Gay Baby Semi-double, deep purplish pink flowers. New foliage is dark purplish bronze. Open growth.

A mix bed of camellias, evergreen and deciduous azaleas.

Camellia 'E.G. Waterhouse' is an Australian-bred plant.

Mandy Semi-double, soft pink, fragrant flowers. Open, weeping growth.

Night Rider Semi-double, very dark red flowers borne singly. Purplish red new foliage. Compact grower. 'Black Opal' is similar with slightly larger flowers.

Paradise Little Jen Informal, soft pink flowers with sasanqua fragrance. Very long blooming season. Weeping growth.

Snowdrop Single, fragrant white flowers, flushed pink. Long blooming. Weeping growth.

Tiny Princess Soft pink, informal, fragrant flowers. Weeping habit.

Wirlinga Gem Single. Pale pink. Early blooming.

Wirlinga Princess Single to semi-double pinkish white flowers. Fragrant. Open, spreading growth.

Wirlinga Bride Single white flowers, pink in the bud. Fragrant. Attractive foliage. Weeping growth.

Yoi Machi Single, open white flowers, pink in the bud. Fragrant. Long blooming season. Attractive foliage. Upright growth.

Camellias with small flowers

These plants have small flowers but are not small growers. A few to consider are:

Bob's Tinsie Almost pure scarlet. Anemone.

Dolly Dyer Scarlet, rose form.

Grace Albritton Light pink, deeper edge. Formal double. ('Tammia' is indistinguishable.)

Kitty Formal double white with blush border.

Roger Hall Long blooming red formal double.

Rhododendrons to grow

Rhododendrons are divided by botanists into two broad groups (one of which includes all of the azaleas and most of the large leafed rhododendrons) but the gardener need only remember that one subgroup, the vireyas (tropical rhododendrons), is completely unsuitable for cold climate gardens. These require a glasshouse over winter in this climate. There is a huge choice of rhododendrons, extended further by related plants such as kalmias.

Evergreen Azaleas

In previous editions, we included lengthy lists of azaleas for your reference, but because gardeners usually select their plants in bloom, we have dropped the list this time.

Where azaleas are intended to create a landscaping impact, plant masses of just a few varieties in order to achieve uniform flowering times and growth habits. Azaleas are technically rhododendrons, but distinguished in ordinary speech as azaleas or 'small leafed rhododendrons'. There are some distinct groups such as kurume azaleas (which have small flowers and can be kept low and spreading), satsuki azaleas and indica

Azalea 'Alphonse Anderson'

types (both of which flower in late spring with larger flowers than kurumes).

Kurume azaleas are evergreen shrubs 30–90 cm high (often taller if unpruned), early to mid-spring flowering and, with many small flowers, the whole plant is covered. They look good in mass plantings (e.g. island beds or wide borders) and can take a fair amount of sun, if watered. They are best pruned with shears or they become untidy. The colour range is white through lavender and rose to red shades. It is best to choose plants in bloom so that you can be sure that they will suit your planting scheme. Many cultivars have Japanese names but others have been hybridised elsewhere. Include them in your Japanese garden.

Satsuki azaleas are late spring flowering and slow growing. They have rather large, single blooms. They can be trimmed to resemble boulders, a technique used in their country of origin. Include them in your Japanese garden.

Indica azaleas are evergreen shrubs growing 50–180 cm with spring flowers and a few later. Include them in a Chinese style garden.

A truss of flowers from a rhododendron.

Deciduous (Mollis) Azaleas

These shrubs have spring flowers and colourful autumn foliage and are often fragrant. Well-suited to cool climates, they flower in interesting sunset colours. They require a sunnier position than evergreen azaleas as they are susceptible to mildew. There are some supposedly distinct groups such as mollis, Knap Hill, Exbury and Ghent. All of these can grow to be quite large but a few more compact growers are available. Buy them when in flower.

Low Growing Rhododendrons

These are useful in borders and in small areas. They are often better performers than evergreen azaleas. *Rhododendron yakusimanum* and its hybrids are worth looking out for — they have interesting trusses of flowers and velvety silver or rust coloured growth under the leaves. The plant label may refer to the cultivar as a "Yak hybrid".

Large Rhododendrons

The tall growers in the accompanying lists will often become tree-like. For a truly tree-sized plant, grow the species *Rhododendron arboreum* (including *Rhododendron delavayi*). It comes in a range of colours from white to fiery red.

Suggested Rhododendrons

Rhododendrons — Large leafed hybrids

Sizes and flowering times given in these lists are approximate in this area, under normal conditions and culture. Tall plants may become tree-like after many years. Rhododendrons will often spread widely when grown in sunny conditions.

Pink to red

Alice Deep pink fading to rose pink. Medium, flowering Oct.

Albert Schweitzer Mid pink. Tall, flowering Oct.

Anna Rose Whitney Rose pink, florets up to 100 mm. Tall, flowering Oct–Nov.

Betty Wormald Soft pink, purple spots. Medium, flowering Oct.

C.B. van Nes Scarlet fading to lighter shade. Medium, flowering Oct.

Earl of Athlone Rich blood red. Medium, flowering Oct.

Furnival's Daughter Bright pink, dark blotch, fragrant. Tall, flowering Oct–Nov.

Jan Dekens Mid pink, large frilled. Tall, flowering Nov.

Jean Marie de Montague Brilliant red, compact. Medium, flowering Oct.

Lamplighter Clear red, large flowers. Tall, flowering Oct.

Mrs Charles Pearson Orchid pink, brown spots. Tall, flowering Oct.

Mrs E. Stirling Blush pink, frilled. Tall, flowering Oct.

Mrs G.W. Leak Soft pink, brown purple blotch. Tall, flowering Sept–Oct.

Pink Pearl Rose pink, fading to blush. Tall, flowering Oct–Nov.

Sir Robert Peel Rosy red. Medium, flowering Sept–Oct.

Unknown Warrior Bright scarlet, large. Medium, flowering Sept–Oct.

Apricot
Mrs W.C. Slocock Apricot. Low growing, and flowering Nov.

Unique Apricot buds opening cream. Medium, flowering Oct. **Bruce Brechtbill** is a deeper coloured sport of Unique.

Mauve to Purple
Blue Peter Pale lavender blue, deep blotch. Medium, flowering Oct–Nov.

Countess of Athlone Rich mauve, small yellow blotch. Medium, flowering Oct–Nov.

Purple Splendour Deep purple, black blotches. Low, flowering Nov.

Van Nes Sensation Soft lilac, large, fragrant. Medium to tall, flowering Oct–Nov.

White to light coloured
Harvest Moon Creamy white, carmine blotch. Tall, flowering Oct–Nov.

President Roosevelt White with red edging variegated foliage. Medium, flowering Sept–Oct.

Princess Alice White, very fragrant. Medium, flowering Oct.

White Pearl Blush pink turning to white. Tall, flowering Oct–Nov.

A mature rhododendrum in all it's spring glory.

Rhododendrons suitable for rock gardens and low plantings

The foliage and growth habit is quite different from the larger growing varieties, they add interest to the garden. The heights given are only approximate in the average garden.

White to light coloured
Alison Johnstone Small cream flowers changing to light apricot, dense habit. 1 m tall, flowering Sept–Oct.

Snow Lady Pure white. Dwarf, flowering Sept.

Mauve to purple
Augfast Small lavender blue flowers. 1 m tall, flowering Sept–Oct.

Blue Diamond Small mid blue flowers. 1 m tall, flowering Sept–Oct.

Rhododendrum 'Cilpinense'

Blue Tit Small smoky blue flowers. 1 m tall, flowering Sept–Oct.

Florence Mann Smoky Blue. 1 m, flowering Sept–Oct.

Ocean Lake Small lilac blue flowers. 2 m, flowering Oct.

Pink to red
Bow Bells Loose trusses, soft pink edged, deep pink. Low growing, flowers Oct.

Bronze Wing Soft pink flowers with burnished foliage. Grows to 1 m and flowers Oct.

Cilpinense Bluish pink bells. 1 m tall, flowering Aug–Sept.

Fragrantissimum Large loose white bells tinged pink, very fragrant. 1.5 m tall, flowers in Oct–Nov.

Scarlet Wonder Scarlet red. Semi-dwarf, flowering Oct.

Seta Tubular, white-rose pink margins. 1 m, flowering Aug–Sept.

Suave Blush pink-white, trumpet, very fragrant. 1 m, flowering Sept–Oct.

Gold to apricot
Broughtonii Aureum Low bushy plant, golden-yellow flowers and bronze foliage. 1 m tall, flowering Oct.

Crossbill Slender leaves, tubular apricot-yellow flowers. 1.5 m tall, flowering in Aug.

Denise Small growing, apricot-yellow with small red blotch. Flowers in Sept–Oct.

Eldorado Deep yellow, loose trusses. 1 m tall, flowering Oct.

Mary Flemming Small lemon flowers. Semi-dwarf, flowering Sept–Oct.

Rhododendron relatives

There are some very attractive relatives of the rhododendron that are worth trying. They require conditions similar to rhododendrons. Kalmias, pieris and arbutus are discussed more fully in other chapters.

Kalmias are low to medium evergreen shrubs with attractive clusters of flowers in shades of pink to white or lavender. They have particularly beautiful flower buds.

Pieris are shrubs that produce drooping sprays of fragrant lily of the valley–like flowers in spring. The new growth is usually a bright coppery-red. Variegated leaf forms are frequently offered.

Oxydendrons resemble pieris but grow to the size of small trees and have deciduous leaves that colour intensely in autumn. They will take full sun if well watered.

Arbutus are evergreens, often with interesting bark and edible fruit and good drought and sun tolerance.

CHAPTER 18: Conifers

Peter Ellerman

In simple terms, the name 'conifer' refers to those trees and shrubs which do not have showy flowers and which bear their seeds in cones. It includes major groups such as the pines, cypresses, spruces and firs. Also generally included are the ginkgo and yew families, although their seeds are borne in small fruits, rather than cones. Most conifers are evergreen but there are some exceptions, including the European Larch, Swamp Cypress and Dawn Redwood. Conifers can be found in nature across the world, but most particularly outside the tropics and in the Northern Hemisphere. They range from forest giants such as the sequoias of North America to small, stunted alpine shrubs such as the microcachrys of the Tasmanian Highlands.

In most cases the wild species grow much too large for home garden use, however there are thousands of smaller cultivars (cultivated varieties) that we can use. The great majority of these cultivars have come about because of either seedling variation, or 'sports' (naturally occurring vegetative mutations) or witches' brooms (abnormalities with extremely congested foliage due to another type of mutation or because of insect or viral attack). The best of these have been selected and propagated by growers for garden use. In addition, we can use alpine species which have a naturally dwarf habit due to the extremely harsh conditions they have to endure.

Growing Conditions

Conifers are in general full-sun plants, although some golden-foliaged and variegated forms can suffer from burning of the foliage tips in hot summers, and can therefore benefit from some light shade at this time. Their great advantage to Canberra gardeners is that they are almost all extremely cold tolerant, and will shrug off the worst Canberra winters with ease.

Although they will do best in improved, well-drained soils, conifers are reasonably tolerant of soils which have a high proportion of clay and are less than perfectly drained, which again commends them to Canberra gardeners. They do require attention to watering in hot periods as they do not give warning of stress by wilting, like broad-leafed plants, and when the visible signs appear it may already be too late to save the plant. Where moisture is likely to be unreliable, the junipers and callitris are the most hardy conifer groups.

If necessary most varieties can be moved while young to a new site. Thus, if a planting looks like becoming overgrown, and provided the plant is no more than, say, 1.5 metres tall, it can be moved by two or three people to a new site with the following method. In winter, and preferably when the site is quite moist, dig a trench around the drip-line of the plant and spade in underneath from all sides until all the roots are free. Wrap the root ball in hessian or some other material and move it to the new site, replanting at the same level and watering in thoroughly with a seaweed-based product. Provided the plant does not dry out over the next twelve months, it should survive without any trouble.

Uses of Conifers

The conifers include trees both evergreen and deciduous, shrubs of every imaginable shape and size, and a great variety of groundcovers. They are equally suited to formal and informal garden designs, make great specimen plants, can be used for screening and windbreaks, as hedges, and for narrow garden areas, and make excellent tub plantings. The inclusion of a variety of conifers in a mixed planting will provide strong all-year focal points around which other more seasonal plants can play. The many varieties of dwarf conifers are ideally suited to rockeries and small areas, and are excellent choices for smaller blocks and town houses.

Conifers offer a wide variety of colours and textures, many of them changing with the seasons.

Considering their many attributes, conifers have been a relatively under-utilised group of plants in Canberra gardens in recent times. Perhaps this is because they do not 'flower', at least not in the showy way we associate with other plants. However, experienced gardeners know that it is the contribution that a plant makes to the landscape over the whole twelve months of the year that measures its worth, and by this test conifers rate very highly, because of the enormous range of colours, shapes and foliage types that they encompass. Colours include green, grey-green, blue-green, blue, yellow and bronze, as well as varieties with cream, yellow or gold variegations. In some varieties, greens change to reddish-brown in winter cold, or golds become more intense. Shapes range from completely prostrate through all sizes of buns, globes and cones to very large pyramids and columns. Foliage can be soft and feathery, hard, prickly or thread-like, often with interesting layered or book-leafed arrangements.

The final attribute of conifers that should be mentioned is their longevity. It is quite normal for a conifer to reach 50 years of age without losing its shape or appearance, while some varieties have been known to reach 100. This should obviously be taken into account when deciding where to plant them.

Pruning

If careful attention is paid to their mature height and width when selecting where to plant, most conifers should require very little pruning. Where it is necessary, perhaps to restrain growth or increase bushiness, it should be restricted to the last year's growth only. Conifers are unlikely to shoot from old wood. Pruning can be done at any time of year, but is best in late winter, before new growth commences. Conifers with fine foliage can be trimmed with shears, but those with coarse foliage or with layered or fan-shaped foliage are best pruned with secateurs, care being taken to choose the point of cutting so that it is hidden by other shoots around it. The central leaders of pyramidal specimens such as spruces and firs should never be touched, as it will destroy their symmetry.

Particular thought should be given before planting any of the taller-growing conifers as hedges, as they can grow rapidly and quickly get out of control. Canberra's streets are full of examples of such hedges which have been neglected and become maintenance nightmares or misshapen eyesores. Ensure that there is adequate access from all sides to enable pruning to be carried out, and be prepared to pay for a professional to carry out the work at least twice a year. Also, commence trimming at a height and width which is comfortably below the maximum height, as even the best-kept hedges tend to creep upwards and outwards over the years.

Note that when a conifer grows against another plant, the part of the conifer touching that plant will die off, and even if the adjoining plant is removed, it will leave an unsightly scar for some years. Therefore, in managing a garden that includes conifers, it is best to prune so that plants do not overcrowd each other, or to move some plants before this can occur.

Pests and diseases

Conifers are relatively free from pests and diseases, however the following problems may arise.

Spider mites, which suck sap from the needles and turn them greyish or brownish in colour, are particularly active in hot, dry weather. The needles may die and be shed. Small trees may be sprayed with a miticide as soon as the infestation is seen.

Aphids may suck sap from needles and shoots and produce honeydew, on which black sooty mould grows.

Green larvae of the cypress pine sawfly chew needles and can defoliate tips of shoots in quite a short time, causing them to wither. The larvae can be picked off by hand but are difficult to see. Small trees can be sprayed with an insecticide.

The larvae of various bark beetles feed under the bark of some conifers, causing dieback of trunk or branches. The tiny holes on the trunk are caused by the adult beetles emerging after pupation. Dead branches should be removed and the tree watered and fertilised regularly. Severely injured trees may need to be removed.

A fungal disease, cypress canker, causes dieback of certain Cypress varieties, in particular Monterey Cypress (*Cupressus macrocarpa*) and its cultivars. This causes splits in the bark and oozing of resin from branches and trunks. Whole branches and trees eventually die. Infected trees should be removed and the area replanted with a different species.

Flammability

Many mature conifers such as pines, cypresses and Callitris are highly flammable, due to their small leaves and high resin content and the fact that they have a large amount of dry wood under their green exterior. Consider potential fire risks before you plant these close to houses or other structures.

Recommended varieties

Thousands of named conifers are now available. The following are lists of varieties which have proved reliable in the Canberra climate and which should be reasonably available from garden centres in the region.

Note that the heights given are for plants grown under average conditions over a period of ten years. As mentioned above, conifers can live for a very long time, so the mature size could be twice this amount or more.

Groundcovers

Juniperus communis 'Depressa Aurea' 30 cm. Bright yellow spring foliage turning more bronze with age.

J. conferta (Shore Juniper) 30 cm. Fresh green foliage, very quick-spreading.

J. horizontalis (many varieties) 10–30 cm. Green or blue-green foliage, often with purple tones in winter.

Shape, colour and texture!

J. x media 'Gold Coast' 50 cm. Low, spreading bush; bright golden new growth.

J. pingii 'Prostrata' 15 cm. Lime-green new growth, turning to light green.

J. procumbens 'Nana' 10 cm. Blue-green, prickly foliage.

J. sabina 'Tamariscifolia' 30 cm. Mid-green foliage.

Small

Abies balsamea 'Hudsonia' 40 cm. Bun-shaped; new growth light green, turning to deep green later.

Chamaecyparis *lawsoniana* 'Aurea Densa' 50 cm. Oval-shaped; golden foliage. *C. l.* 'Filiformis Compacta' 70 cm. Globular; fine, thread-like, blue-green foliage. *C. l.* 'Minima' 70 cm. Globular; dense green foliage. *C. l.* 'Minima Aurea' golden yellow foliage. *C. l.* 'Minima Glauca' blue-grey foliage.

C. obtusa 'Kosteri' 80 cm. Pyramid; layered, mid-green foliage. *C. o.* 'Nana Aurea' 80 cm. Narrow-topped pyramid; bright golden yellow foliage, tinged bronze in winter. *C. o.* 'Nana Gracilis' 70 cm. Broad-based pyramid; deep-green foliage.

C. pisifera 'Baby Blue' 1 m. Cone; blue foliage. *C. p.* 'Filifera Aurea' 1 m. Weeping mound; golden, thread-like foliage. *C. p.* 'Filifera Nana' mid-green foliage. *C. p.* 'Plumosa Flavescens' 50 cm. Globular; creamy-yellow foliage changing to green. *C. p.* 'Squarrosa Intermedia' 50 cm. Globular; compressed, blue-grey foliage.

Cryptomeria japonica 'Globosa Nana' 1 m. Globular; mid-green foliage. *C. j.* 'Vilmoriniana' 50 cm. Globular; light-green foliage turning bronze in winter.

Juniperus *communis* 'Compressa' 50 cm. Narrow, miniature spire; grey-green foliage.

J. squamata 'Blue Star' 40 cm. Wide bun; intense blue foliage.

Picea glauca 'Alberta Globe' 30 cm. Near-perfect globe; compact mid-green foliage. *P. g.* 'Albertiana Conica' (Dwarf Alberta Spruce) 80 cm. Perfect cone; mid-green foliage.

Pinus mugo (Dwarf Mountain Pine) 90 cm (but very variable). Bun-shaped; dark-green foliage.

Thuja *occidentalis* 'Rheingold' 70 cm. Bun-shaped; pinkish-gold foliage turning bronze in winter.

T. orientalis 'Aurea Nana' 80cm. Rounded cone; golden foliage turning orange in winter.

Medium

Chamaecyparis *lawsoniana* 'Silver Queen' 2 m. Broad-based pyramid; silvery, greenish-white foliage. *C. l.* 'Stewartii' 3.5 m. Pyramid; golden foliage, drooping slightly at the tips.

C. obtusa 'Crippsii' 3 m. Broad pyramid; golden foliage.

C. pisifera 'Boulevard' 2 m. Rounded pyramid; blue-grey foliage.

Another Abies, this time *Abies koreana aurea* with its striking dark blue cones.

Cryptomeria japonica 'Elegans' 3 m. Narrow pyramid; soft, green foliage turning rich bronze in winter.

Cupressus sempervirens 'Swane's Golden' 2 m. Pencil-shape; yellow-gold foliage.

Juniperus *chinensis* 'Pyramidalis' 2 m. Rounded pyramid; prickly, grey-green foliage.

J. virginiana 'Skyrocket' 3 m. Narrow column; blue-grey foliage.

Thuja occidentalis 'Smaragd' 2.5 m. Narrow cone; dark-green foliage.

Tall (for very large blocks, acreages, parks)

Callitris *endlicheri* (Black Cypress Pine) is a native conifer endemic to this area. It has very dark green foliage and grows up to 10 m and 4 m wide. This tree tolerates poor soils.

C. glaucophylla syn. *C. hugelii* (White Cypress Pine) is suited to inland districts. It grows to 15 m with a width of 10 m. It is very drought resistant and fast growing but, due to its ultimate size, should only be considered for very large blocks or farm sites.

C. rhomboidea (Port Jackson Cypress Pine) grows to between 5 m and 7 m with a width of between 2 m and 3 m. It has grey-green foliage but needs more moisture than *C. endlicheri*. Useful as a large tub plant.

Cedrus *atlantica* (Atlas Cedar) 5 m. Erect tree; horizontal or slightly weeping grey-green branches.

C. deodara (Himalayan Cedar) 5 m. Pyramidal tree; glaucous green foliage weeping at the ends of the branches.

Cupressocyparis leylandii 'Castlewellan Gold' 6 m. Fast-growing, dense tree; green-gold foliage. *C. l.* 'Leighton Green' has dark-green foliage. *C. l.* 'Naylor's Blue' has blue-green foliage. All are very hardy and can be used as large hedges.

Cupressus *sempervirens* 'Stricta' 4 m. Tall pencil-shape; dark green foliage.

C. torulosa (Bhutan Cypress) 4 m. Tall spire with a bulbous base in colder climates; dark-green foliage.

Larix decidua (European Larch) 5 m. Deciduous pyramid; fresh-green growth in spring, turning golden-yellow in autumn.

Picea *abies* (Norway Spruce) 2.5 m. 'Christmas-tree' shape; dark-green foliage.

P. pungens 'Koster' (Koster's Blue Spruce) 2 m. Pyramid; blue foliage.

Thuja *occidentalis* 'Pyramidalis' 3 m. Tall, narrow spire; deep-green foliage.

T. plicata 'Zebrina' 3 m. Pyramid; lemon-yellow, variegated foliage.

A young Wollemi pine at the Botanic garden.

Wollemia nobilis (Wollemi Pine) 3 m (in a pot). 'Living fossil' believed extinct until rediscovered in Wollemi National Park in 1994. Somewhat temperamental in cultivation, requiring good drainage. Best suited to container growing. As yet unproven for long term cultivation in Canberra.

CHAPTER 19:
Magnolias and related plants

Neil Mitchell

Magnolias are amongst the showiest and most admired of spring and summer flowering shrubs and trees. They are suitable for planting as single specimens, as part of a shrub border or in large containers. Many would be grown for their fragrance alone. Not all magnolias are suitable for the Canberra climate but the species, hybrids and cultivars suggested in this chapter should give satisfactory results.

The magnolia family is amongst the most ancient of flowering plants. Magnolias would be worth growing for this reason alone.

To the gardener, magnolias fall into three broad groups: deciduous magnolias, evergreen magnolias and related species. As the cultural requirements for all groups are similar, this aspect is discussed first.

Cultural requirements

Please refer to the chapter on Camellias, Rhododendrons and Azaleas. Magnolias come from the same environments (indeed, they will be found growing with these other plants in the wild) so, if you can grow camellias or rhododendrons in your garden, you should be able to grow well at least some of the magnolias.

Although they are a little more lime-tolerant than camellias and rhododendrons, magnolias do not differ in their need for plenty of water and mulch in our climate. Magnolias will also take to life in a container but most will eventually outgrow even a large tub. In

general, magnolias are not for small gardens or for planting near walls or foundations. Smaller growing exceptions are mentioned in this chapter.

Pruning of magnolias should be limited to removing crossed branches and the removal of low forks (to ensure a single, straight trunk). Careful shaping of the young, growing plant is a worthwhile investment. Magnolia branches should be cut so as to leave a short spur. Small leaved michelias can be clipped to form hedges. Heavy pruning is best done in winter. Any resultant watershoots (soft, vigorous branches that emerge from the edge of the wound) should be rubbed off

A special note on Climate

Most books on magnolias are written for Northern Hemisphere readers and references to "hardiness" refer to winter hardiness, the ability to withstand extremes of low temperatures that are never experienced here. The two main climatic problems encountered in Canberra are spring frosts and typically hot and low-humidity summers.

Strong winds may damage magnolia blooms and cause branches to be lost, a risk that should be borne in mind when siting forms that grow to the dimensions of trees.

Spring frosts

These present two problems. First, early flowering deciduous magnolias and early blooming michelias can suffer flower damage. Planting near an evergreen tree or near a house will offer some protection, as the lowest temperatures are closest to ground level. As the tree grows it will be less affected by the problem. Choosing cultivars and species that bloom late is good practice.

The second problem is the danger to young deciduous magnolias from severe frosts in late winter and early spring. When the sap is rising and a young plant is just breaking into growth, the plant can be extremely vulnerable to a severe frost and to prevent damage, a deep mulch of straw and a temporary shelter should be erected until the plant has come into leaf. After several years, there is no need for such precautions.

Lack of summer hardiness

This is a long term problem for some deciduous magnolia species. Protection from north-westerly winds (e.g. plant on the south-eastern side of a house or a windbreak of evergreen trees), a healthy root system and deep watering will help. A healthy root system will be encouraged by adequate soil preparation, occasional use of fertilisers and good general care. The cultivar lists in this chapter mention summer hardy magnolias and warn about less hardy forms.

Summer hardiness is less of a problem for evergreen magnolias, michelias, manglietias and liriodendrons.

Magnolias to grow

Deciduous magnolias

This group is divided into two subgroups that are quite distinct from the point of view of a gardener — those that flower before or with the leaves; and those that flower after the leaves have formed. Although deciduous, autumn colour is generally not a feature.

Deciduous Magnolias that bloom in spring before or with the appearance of the leaves

These are amongst the showiest of all flowering plants. The beauty of the flowers is magnified because the leaves are either very small, or absent at the time of flowering.

Magnolia stellata — the Star Magnolia — is the plant anyone can grow in ordinary garden conditions. Most clones produce fragrant multi-petalled white flowers in early spring (pink flowers in the case of *Magnolia stellata* 'Rosea'). The plant grows in a slow, regular manner to make a medium sized shrub. Good named clones include 'Royal Star', 'Waterlily' and 'Rosea Massey'. The last will become a large shrub. If you only have a small garden, then *Magnolia stellata* is the species to grow.

Some excellent and hardy hybrids have been bred from the star magnolia and are listed below:

'Pristine' – a tall upright shrub or small tree with multi-petalled tulip-shaped fragrant, pure white flowers. It may rebloom in summer. 'Suishoren' is similar. Both have *Magnolia denudata* as the other parent.

Magnolia x loebneri is a cross between *Magnolia stellata* and *Magnolia kobus*. *Magnolia x loebneri* varieties make small trees that bear, usually early in spring, fragrant flowers like those of *Magnolia stellata*. Notable forms include the pink flowered 'Leonard Messel' (all others are white flowered), the very fragrant and large growing 'Merrill' and the multi-petalled 'Ballerina'. 'Gold Star' is a newly available yellow flowered hybrid of *Magnolia stellata*.

Magnolia x proctoriana is a fragrant, white flowered hybrid between *Magnolia stellata* and *Magnolia salicifolia*. It is an alternative to the *Magnolia x loebneri* cultivars.

Magnolia liliiflora is undoubtedly a hardy deciduous magnolia for this region. Its deep purplish-red flowers are scented and appear with and after the leaves, with frequent reblooming throughout the summer. Height 3–4 m with a tendency to grow as a wide, multi-stemmed shrub. The unnamed clone has narrow flowers, pale within and the named clone 'Nigra' has very dark flowers inside and out. As a number of clones are sold as 'Nigra', not all of which are as dark, buy your plant when in bloom or take cuttings or layers from a good plant. 'Holland Red' has flowers that are slightly brighter in colour than those of 'Nigra'.

Magnolia liliiflora has produced many excellent and hardy hybrids. Prominent amongst these are the following recommended ones:

'Heaven Scent': not fragrant, unfortunately. It is a narrowly upright small tree that will spread, in time. The flowers are also narrowly upright, with 12 petals that are pale inside, blushed rose over pale pink outside.

Magnolia 'Heaven Scent'.

'Jane' is distinguished by its very fragrant flowers, red-purple on the outside and white on the inside. It blooms in late spring and makes a good tub plant.

'Pinkie': a spreading, large shrub with tulip-shaped pink flowers in spring. The flowers are as close to clear pink as is obtainable in magnolias.

'Royal Crown': will make a medium tree in time. Large, waterlily shaped flowers that are deep purplish red outside, paler within.

'Star Wars': very large rose pink flowers with paler tones within, cup and saucer shaped, on a plant that will become a small to medium tree. 'Star Wars' is the hardiest and best *Magnolia campbellii* hybrid for Canberra.

'Susan': upright, narrow medium shrub with deep purplish flowers for a few weeks in spring, later than many spring blooming magnolias.

'Vulcan', with large deep purplish-red flowers, is from a similar parentage, so should be summer hardy but it needs shelter when young.

'Ricki' is an upright, narrow medium shrub with deep purple flowers in spring. Late blooming.

The most famous hybrids of *Magnolia liliiflora* are of the group known as *Magnolia x soulangeana*. This plant is well known to most gardeners. Its virtues include the production of enormous numbers of blooms (inherited from one parent, *Magnolia denudata*) and the capacity to bloom while still a small plant (inherited from the other parent, *Magnolia liliiflora*). Young plants can be extremely vigorous. The plants grow to the size of small trees and tend to spread with age. Young plants may need frost protection. Cultivars differ in flowering time, so it is possible to choose several for a succession of bloom. The following are recommended:

'Etienne Soulange Bodin' is the familiar prototype, usually sold simply as *Magnolia x soulangeana* which is a pity, since unnamed seedlings are also sold (quite lawfully) as *Magnolia x soulangeana*. 'Etienne Soulange Bodin' is one of the world's showiest plants, bearing innumerable tulip-shaped flowers that are warm rose pink outside and paler within. It blooms relatively late, missing some frosts. Buy it in bloom to be sure.

'Alexandrina': vigorous, early blooming, white with purple at the base of each petal. The early blooming habit means that all blooms could be lost in the event of a heavy frost. Has a tendency to rebloom.

'Brozzonii': fast, upright grower with fragrant, narrow, elegant white flowers that have a rose coloured line up the outer surface of each petal. Late blooming.

'Deep Late Pink': small, purplish-rose flowers. Blooms late.

'Lennei': large, dark, purplish bowl-shaped flowers, paler inside. Vigorous and spreading growth, suitable for large gardens

'Lennei Alba': a cross of 'Lennei' back to *Magnolia denudata* with flowers like *Magnolia denudata*, though unlike the former, the flowers have a fine rose pink line up the outer surface of each petal and it is much hardier and later blooming. It is much used by hybridisers. Young plants will need protection from frost.

'Picture': a vigorous, upright grower with very large, pale flowers with a marked purplish rose band down the outside of each petal. Has a tendency to rebloom. Much used by hybridisers.

'Rustica Rubra': deep, reddish-purple flowers are fragrant. An untidy, rampant grower.

Other magnolia hybrids which flower before the leaves develop and that are worth trying include the creamy yellow flowered 'Elizabeth', 'Butterflies' and 'Yellow Lantern', and the very large white flowered 'Milky Way', 'Manchu Fan', 'Sayonara' and 'Tina Durio'. All of these are tree-like.

Deciduous Magnolias that bloom in spring and early summer after the appearance of the leaves

These plants have a quieter beauty, chiefly bearing white flowers for a few weeks or longer. Most are not summer-hardy and all require protection from hot north-westerly winds.

Magnolia x thompsoniana is semi-deciduous, with creamy, fragrant flowers in late spring and early summer. Large glossy leaves and spreading habit.

Magnolia sieboldii – only for a sheltered spot, this medium shrub has drooping, fragrant, cupped white flowers with red stamens.

Only one recent hybrid within this category is recommended — the golden flowered 'Yellow Bird'. The fragrant flowers appear with and after the leaves for several weeks. It will eventually grow to tree size. It is quite hardy. 'Woodsman' is similar but has oddly coloured flowers in a mix of purple and yellowish green.

Evergreen magnolias

Only a few species are suitable for Canberra, all of them hardy. They bloom in summer.

Magnolia grandiflora is a large tree that is worth growing if you have room for it. The unnamed clones that are usually offered lack indumentum (velvety rust-coloured growth on the underside of the leaves) under its light green, slightly twisted leaves. It has an open growth habit and can take 5 years to begin blooming. The flowers are large, white and fragrant and are produced from late spring to early autumn. Only a few named varieties are available in this country:

'Exmouth' (more correctly, 'Compact Form') has good brown indumentum, blooms by about five years of age and is long blooming. The compact growth and indumentum make it more attractive than the above. It will become a large tree. 'Saint Mary' is similar.

'Warner's Compact' is reluctant to bloom and should be avoided.

'Little Gem' blooms as a small plant. It will

be successful as a tub plant for some years and its narrow upright growth habit makes it useful in smaller gardens. Leaves and flowers are smaller than the other forms. Flowering starts in summer and will continue until heavy frosts. It is the parent of 'Kay Parris' which is of a more open growth habit but still compact.

'Cairo' resembles unnamed clones but has deeper green leaves.

Magnolia virginiana, a smaller tree or large shrub which may be semi-deciduous, has leaves with bluish white indumentum underneath and bears fragrant flowers like those of a small *Magnolia grandiflora* but the petals are narrower. This is a good selection for small gardens

Magnolia delavayii is a large shrub to medium tree that would make a striking specimen. It is worth growing for its leaves alone — they are bluish- green, tend to droop and are large, resembling *Ficus elastica*. The fragrance of the large flowers is most noticeable in the evening.

Magnolia coco is like a small Magnolia grandiflora with drooping white flowers that are fragrant at night. It will be unlikely to exceed 1.5m in height and makes a good tub plant.

Magnolias that are not recommended for Canberra

Magnolia denudata is only marginally hardy, especially as a young plant. Some deciduous species lack summer hardiness and/or spring hardiness. These include, *Magnolia wilsonii, Magnolia campbellii, Magnolia sargentiana, Magnolia sprengeri,* and *Magnolia dawsoniana*. Hybrids of these species that share the same weaknesses include: 'Phillip Tregunna', 'J.C. Williams', 'Como', 'Caerhays

'Elizabeth', one of the magnolia hybrids.

Belle', 'Kew's Surprise', 'Sweetheart', 'Felix Jury' (a.k.a. 'Felix') and 'Princess Margaret'. Of these, 'Sweetheart' is an upright grower with large, rose pink flowers. It is worth trying if you have mature trees nearby to provide some shelter.

Related plants

Magnolias have a number of interesting relatives. A few grow well in Canberra. These are the michelias, the liriodendrons and one species of manglietia.

Michelias. These have now been reclassified (renamed) as magnolias by botanists. At the moment they are still being sold under the name michelia. The forms offered in Australia are evergreen shrubs or trees that produce numerous flowers along the leaf axils of the branches (not just at the tips of the branches, as in magnolias). They are all summer hardy but the spring blooming species and cultivars may need some bloom protection, particularly for the first few years. The michelias are generally notable for their glossy to waxy leaves and for the perfume of their flowers. In some cases, the fragrance is best late in the day or at night. *Michelia figo* 'Port Wine' apart, these horticulturally meritorious plants are too little known.

Michelia figo is known as the Port Wine Magnolia ('Port Wine' is the name of the clone that is commonly grown in this country). This species is a compact grower that eventually becomes a large shrub. It can be clipped, making it suitable for hedging and use in courtyards. It copes well with being grown as a container plant. It is notable for its strongly fragrant flowers that are produced for months in late spring and summer. Several clones are now available:

'Port Wine': the commonly grown form. The flowers never open fully and are dark purple, paler within, smelling of port wine and bananas. Recommended.

'Lady of the Night' has larger leaves than the above with wider opening flowers that are brownish yellow.

'Coco': similar to the above but not as frost hardy. Not recommended.

'Compact Form': large yellow flowers, mainly in spring, smelling of ripe bananas. A small grower, ideal for containers. Previously sold (wrongly) as *Michelia compressa*. Recommended.

Michelia doltsopa is a large, eventually wide-spreading tree that flowers heavily in mid-spring. The flowers are pure white. Some forms have a very good scent. Unnamed plants are often seedlings that may take over ten years to flower. A named clone 'Silver Cloud' has a wonderful fragrance and is a heavy bloomer, but is too frost tender to be grown here. It could be grown in a conservatory over winter, as a tub plant.

Michelia x foggi is a hybrid of the above two species. It is like a vigorous form of *Michelia figo* with larger leaves and flowers, paler flowers and a tendency to be semi-deciduous.

Several clones are offered:

'Bubbles': white, edged pink flowers. Slight fragrance but good growth.

'Allspice': similar to 'Bubbles' with good foliage, noticeable scent.

'Mixed Up Miss': creamy white flowers with a pink edge. Fragrance is closer to *Michelia figo*. Recommended.

'Touch of Pink': large, white flowers with a fine, pink edge. Exquisite and powerful fragrance like that of its parent *Michelia doltsopa* 'Silver Cloud'. Large glossy leaves. A little less cold hardy than the other two clones but worth protecting when young.

Michelia yunnanensis (now reclassified as *Magnolia dianica*) is a vigorous, open growing large shrub or small tree with white flowers in early spring, finishing as other michelias commence. Its flowers are frost hardy but are not highly fragrant. Excellent as a shrub, as a specimen plant and it could also be espaliered. The unnamed clone is especially suited to this purpose due to its open growth habit. A number of named clones are offered, such as 'Paradise Perfection' and 'Scented Pearl' (which is not remarkably fragrant).

Michelia maudiae is a small tree that has glossy green leaves. It covers with very fragrant flowers that resemble a smaller version of the flowers of *Magnolia grandiflora*. Young plants may lose flowers to late frosts. Highly recommended, it is a better choice than *Michelia doltsopa*.

Do not try to grow *Michelia champaca* or *Michelia x alba* – they do not tolerate frost.

LiriodendronsThese are large deciduous trees that flower in late spring and early summer, with and after the appearance of the leaves. There are two species both of which grow here. They tolerate waterlogging much more than their relatives, the magnolias. They are also completely hardy. The leaves resemble saddles in shape and they colour briefly to a clear butter yellow in autumn before turning brown, then falling.

Liriodendron tulipifera (the Tulip Tree) is the species to grow but only in large gardens. The typical form offered would be a seedling plant that grows vigorously to become a large, pyramidal shaped tree after about ten years. Its eventual height will easily exceed 15 metres. The fragrant flowers are like tulips in shape, greenish yellow outside and yellowish to orange (at the base) within. Seedling plants can take seven or more years to bloom. There are several named clones available in this country:

'Fastigiatum': a narrow upright form that is useful where space is limited. Not a prolific flowerer.

'Aureomarginatum': a lovely, broadly pyramidal growing clone that grows a little more slowly than the typical form. The leaves are margined yellow, most noticeably so in spring and early summer. A reliable bloomer.

The flower of the Tulip Tree.

'Glen Gold': an Australian seedling of the above with golden young leaves that mature to lime green. Needs some shade to avoid leaf scorch.

Liriodendron chinense is the other species that is sometimes available. Its flowers are less showy (lacking prominent orange markings) so it is not recommended.

Manglietias

Most species are tropical and subtropical plants that are closely similar to magnolias (botanists regard the differences in the leaf petioles and the number of seeds per carpel as significantly different from the magnolias) but only one species is known to be hardy here.

Manglietia insignis is a lovely, evergreen large shrub or small tree, suitable as a specimen plant or in a shrub border. Leathery leaves, flowering at the tips of branches in summer with pink tipped white flowers to about 7.5 cm diameter that smell of melons. Can be grown in a tub for some years.

CHAPTER 20: Trees

Revised by Ivan and Joy Colaric

The selection of trees for the home garden needs to be carefully considered as they are the largest of our cultivated plants and, as many are long lived, they may have a profound effect on other plants and structures within the landscape. It is important therefore to ensure that your garden can accommodate your trees without causing problems to the house foundations, driveways, paths, pipes and neighbours' amenities.

Trees in your garden can perform a number of functions besides the production of flowers and fruit.

They can shelter outdoor living areas from the hot summer sun, divert and slow windflows, create areas of privacy and block out unsightly views, along with providing a habitat for birds and creating areas suitable for the cultivation of plants requiring wind, sun and cold protection.

Most new home blocks in the Canberra area are smaller than those of the earlier years of the city's development. That coupled with the fact that houses are often larger, results in there being little space for a garden. Fortunately there is also now a wider range of species and cultivars available which will suit the dimensions of a smaller garden.

A number of evergreen and deciduous species suitable for the Canberra area are listed at the end of this chapter. There are many others that are also suitable and, if you are unsure of which trees would be best suited to your requirements, seek advice from

The Horticultural Society of Canberra and qualified personnel at nurseries and garden centres.

Conifers and magnolias are listed in specific chapters.

Planting

A later chapter covers the planting of trees and shrubs. However, there are a few special points to keep in mind with trees. Because of their size, in siting trees on the block ensure that they are not planted directly under powerlines or immediately above sewerage and water pipes. Trees planted from containers generally benefit from a light teasing of the roots and loosening of the soil root base immediately prior to planting.

The watering needs of trees deserves serious consideration in order to maintain health and vigour in times of prolonged water restriction and drought. As well as being the backbone of your garden, the amenity a tree provides is a valued consideration. Many trees are slow growing and a mature, well-grown specimen is a great asset to the overall value of your home.

Newly-planted trees are most vulnerable when they are establishing their root system. Once established, probably after more than one complete year of successful growth, watering the young tree can be reduced. In times of drought, priority should be given to ensuring that the root zone does not dry out and though the tree's need for moisture is diminished in cool and cold weather, it should not be completely ignored. Most established trees will survive with reduced watering, providing their root zone is well-mulched and when they are watered, they are given a deep soaking. Two or three drippers or a soaker hose which encircles the trunk in the region of the root zone can be a very effective method of watering a mature tree. Similarly, using a manual posthole digger to dig two or three holes into which you can then insert lengths of agricultural pipe will ensure the water gets down to the root zone where it is needed.

Well mulched trees will make better progress during the establishment period than those that are left to compete with surrounding weeds and periodic drying out of the top soil. The mulch should be at least 8 cm deep, but not heaped around the trunk as that may cause 'collar rot', a decaying of the living bark at ground level.

Do not use polythene film under the mulch for, while it restricts the natural evaporation of soil moisture, it also prevents moisture and nutrients from reaching the root area. There is also a tendency for the trees to create a shallow root system where polythene is used.

If there is room in your garden a Gum tree can add wonderful bark and form.

Fertilising

Fertiliser may be added at planting time providing it does not come into direct contact with the plant's root system but it's better to fertilise when the plant shows signs of active growth. There are many fertiliser types specifically formulated for trees and woody shrubs. Amongst these are slow release fertilisers which give up their nutrients over a long period and are ideal for promoting controlled growth during a full growing season.

As soon as a tree (other than the fruiting types) is reasonably well established, say after two to three growing seasons, it should not require annual dressings of fertiliser as it will normally gain sufficient nutrient from that given to lawns, shrubs, flowers and groundcover species in the garden.

This group of young elms displaying their autumn colour is a public planting in Macquarie.

Staking

It may be necessary to stake some trees at planting time; these are generally the taller deciduous plants and advanced evergreens. With smaller trees it may only be necessary to lightly prune the crown to allow wind to flow through it.

Research over recent years has revealed that young nursery trees will not develop strong anchorage roots if the tree is too firmly tied to its stake, therefore, it should be tied so that the crown has some movement.

The ties should be inspected regularly during the growing season for firmness, and to ensure that the ties are not cutting into the bark of the tree.

Where staking is necessary place the stake firmly in position prior to planting to avoid possible root damage.

Pruning

General

Allow only one main trunk or leader to develop in a tree, especially in larger species. Excess main leaders may present a problem as the tree ages, causing splitting or loss of large limbs in wet or windy weather. An alternate arrangement of limbs along and around the main trunk is ideal.

Little or no pruning will be required at planting time other than to remove damaged branches or twigs. Most young trees are pruned at the nursery prior to sale.

The main objective of pruning is to establish a strong framework which will carry the tree's future branching system and the first step would be to remove dead, diseased, or injured wood. Next, branches that are crossing or rubbing together should be removed to allow light and air to penetrate the canopy and to prevent a tangled mass within the interior of the tree.

Specific purpose

In some circumstances pruning is used to train growth to fit a set of special conditions, and it is here that the natural form of the plant can be altered quite markedly, eg espaliering, which is the technique of training plants along a fence or wall using wires or plugs to attach the plant's branches.

Trees may also be trained as hedges by the removal of the terminal growth at a desired height followed by regular clipping during the growing season.

Some species such as ornamental prunus are often pruned quite severely to encourage heavy flowering.

It is advisable to check with your nurseryman or an experienced gardener before attempting to prune a tree if you are not familiar with its growth habit.

Trees in containers

Certain trees may be grown in large tubs or pots and utilized as temporary screens or placed on a patio or porch to provide colour and shelter.

Nurseries now also carry a range of trees trained as standards, which are well suited to courtyard gardens and containers.

Many conifers are also well suited to containers and can provide a living Christmas tree each year.

The tub or pot size should be as large as can be conveniently managed so as to allow the plant to reach a reasonable size. It is helpful to use a pot that is wider at the top so that the plant can easily be removed and worked on.

Depending upon the species cultivated it is possible to keep them for many years by re-potting into fresh potting mix every few years, as they become 'pot bound' with massed roots. A light root pruning will be required before re-potting. Use a good quality, free draining potting mix, preferably with water retaining granules if you intend growing plants in containers for the long term.

Some trees recommended for Canberra

With a few marked exceptions, all the trees do best in an open position. Magnolias and conifers are covered by their own chapters.

Acacia. There are many Australian wattles available. We have concentrated on smaller trees that will do well here. Some have interesting leaf shapes and are grown for this rather than their flowers. All are frost tolerant and evergreen.

Acacia baileyana (Cootamundra wattle) is a Proclaimed Weed in the ACT.

A. covenyi (Blue Bush), grows to a height of 3 to 6 metres depending on situation, i.e. soil, climate, locality. Frost tolerant and native to Southern Tablelands of N.S.W. Commences flowering in August and continues into September. Adapts well to a wide range of soils and climates.

A. iteaphylla (Flinders Range Wattle). Many forms of this wattle are available and the eventual height can vary from 3 to 6 metres. It can have a weeping or upright growth habit and the perfumed flowers appear from April to July with attractive seed pods after flowering. This species is widely planted

Maples provide a wonderful range of colour and leaf shapes, varying from a spring flush, through the mature leaves of summer to autumn foliage. On the left is *Acer* 'Esk Sunset' and on the right the spring foliage of one of the Japanese Maples.

at the Sculpture Garden of the Australian National Gallery. Inclined to be a little frost tender in early stages of growth and may need some protection in exposed sites. Prefers a dry situation in well-drained soil.

A. pendula (Weeping Myall or Boree), a small tree to 10 m. Its silver pendulous foliage falls almost to the ground and it is well worth a place in the garden. It is drought resistant, but curiously the flowers are quite inconspicuous and appear irregularly.

A. pravissima (Ovens wattle), a large shrub or small tree at 7 m with bright yellow globular perfumed flowers in spring. It has high frost tolerance. Prune to shape in early spring and late summer. Tip prune regularly to encourage new golden growth. Feed with control release low-phosphorus fertiliser in early spring and late summer.

Acer (Maple). In this chapter we are concerned with the larger trees. Smaller plants such as the weeping Japanese maples are covered by the shrubs chapter.

A. campestre albo-variegatum (Variegated Hedge Maple). A hardy tree 5 m high with a rounded form and butter yellow autumn foliage.

A. griseum (Paperbark Maple). Grown for its attractive coppery peeling bark and beautiful burgundy autumn colour. It will grow slowly to 9 m.

Acer japonicum. Grows 4–5m, rounded shape. Autumn colour. Wind protection is needed.

Acer negundo 'Esk Flamingo' is occasionally grown as a small tree but usually grafted onto a standard, which can still grow to around 5 m. With leaves smaller and daintier than *A. negundo*, they are variegated pink and white, the variegation being particularly noticeable in spring, with young growth coloured red. As with most plants being grown for a particular feature, it is best to see your plant before purchasing and know that it is displaying the feature. Some specimens have been disappointing, while others are spectacular.

A. palmatum (Japanese Maple). 3–7 m high with irregular shape. Autumn colour. Many cultivars available. Shelter from hot winds.

A. platanoides 'Crimson Sentry'. Attractive purple red foliage, growing up to 7 m with a spread of 4 m. Can be used for small yards and courtyards. Golden-brown autumn foliage.

A. rubrum (Canadian Maple), 15 m, varied shape. Good autumn colour. Hardier than *A. palmatum*. Many good smaller cultivars available.

A. saccharum 'Goldsphere' is a dense column form with brilliant autumn foliage. Grows up to 10 m and spreads to 4 m.

Agonis flexuosa (Aust. — Willow Myrtle, Willow Peppermint). A weeping small tree to 6 m with a spread of around 7 m. Small white flowers clustered along stems in spring. An ideal specimen tree. Once established it will tolerate dry conditions and will withstand heavy frosts. *A. flexuous* 'Nana' is a dwarf form of agonis with striking red new foliage. *A. flexuosa* 'Variegata' is a slow growing shrub to 3 m with cream and pink foliage.

Albizia julibrissin (Silk Tree), 5–8 m high with a spreading crown. Pink flowers in early summer. Fast growing but short lived. Prone to borers but this can be controlled to an extent by cutting off affected branches. Seeds readily.

Allocasuarina littoralia is an Australian evergreen tree growing up to 10 m and is considered hardy. It has fine needle-like leaves and deeply furrowed bark. Fast growing when young. The sound of wind moving throught allocasuarinas is an interesting feature for many.

A. torulosa (Forest Oak) is a hardy Australian tree which grows between 8 m and 12 m. A slender upright tree with fine, weeping foliage and deeply furrowed bark, it makes an interesting specimen. Female flowers are red and male spikelets a rusty colour.

Arbutus Menziesii (Pacific Madrone) is a larger evergreen growing to 7–12 m, dome shaped. White flowers, yellow to orange fruit, and handsome colourful bark.

The bark of the Paperbark Maple, *Acer griseum*.

A. unedo (Irish Strawberry Tree). An evergreen growing to 5–8 m with a spreading dome. White flowers and fruits in autumn. Slow grower, long lived, attractive bark.

Azara microphylla (Vanilla Tree) is an evergreen growing in a slender shape to 5 m. Small vanilla-scented flowers in spring. Handsome bark.

Betula pendula 'Dalecarlica' (Cut-leaf Birch) 10 m, weeping shape. Yellow autumn colour. Needs wind protection. Other cultivars are available. 'Barossa Evergreen' holds its leaves throughout winter until the new growth appears.

Catalpa bignonioides (Indian Bean Tree) grows to 10 m with a rounded shape. Prominent white summer flowers, attractive bean-like pods. Some wind protection helps. Other cultivars are available.

Cercis siliquastrum (Judas Tree) grows to 4–5 m and is multi stemmed with rosy-purple flowers covering trunk and limbs. *C. siliquastrum* 'Alba' has white flowers in summer. A slow grower.

C. canadensis 'Forest Pansy' (Red Bud) 10 m, rounded shape. Attractive claret foliage and rich autumn colour. Tiny fuchsia pink flowers appear along the branches in early spring. A popular feature tree.

C. chinensis 'Avondale' is a very showy small tree, up to 3 m high and 2 m wide, with pink-mauve flowers in spring and golden autumn foliage. It prefers a slightly acid soil and a good mulch.

Cornus capitata (Himalayan Strawberry Tree) is a slender evergreen growing to 6 m. Yellow spring flowers, autumn fruit. Shelter from hot winds and water in summer.

Cornus florida (Dogwood), which is deciduous, has a cone shape and grows to 4 m. Pink or white flowers available. Shelter from hot winds and give filtered light.

Cydonia oblonga. Quinces grow to around 4 m high and wide, and produce well in cool climates. They are a compact tree, sometimes rather twisted in growth with soft foliage and attractive white-pink tinged solitary flowers followed in autumn by large golden yellow fruit, many of them on the tips of long annual growth. Such features make the tree a good ornamental as well as fruiting tree. Whether grown for its fruit or sheer beauty, the quince makes a good subject for espalier work, and is a fine inclusion in Asian-style gardens.

If the fruit is left on the tree until it is ready to drop, it develops a strong pleasant aromatic fragrance.

A mature white Dogwood arching over a front garden.

Quinces grow best in deeper heavier soils with good moisture retention but in pockets of alkaline soil will readily show yellowing associated with iron deficiency. Water them regularly during the growing season. Fruit production can be increased with a cross pollinator but one tree will set fruit quite well. As the fruit are usually borne singly on the ends of shoots the delicate skin can be damaged by wind.

Davidia involucrata (Handkerchief or Dove Tree) 12 m, conical. White flowers late spring. Prefers shelter from hot winds.

Diospyros kaki (Chinese Persimmon). Grows 6–8 m with a short trunk and spreading branches. Brilliant autumn foliage and colourful, edible fruit. A good specimen to brighten a winter garden.

Eriobotrya japonica (Japanese Loquat) is an evergreen, 6–7 m tall and a wide habit. Creamy white flowers in autumn. Edible yellow fruits in spring.

Eucalyptus. There is a very large range of eucalypts, most far too large for the garden. Some are particularly liable to drop branches. There are also a few smaller varieties with attractive flowers although some are susceptible to disfiguring insect damage.

Many species of Eucalypts are classed as Mallee types and would be well-suited for Canberra gardens. The Mallee types produce a number of stems from the base of the plant (lignotuber, an enlarged woody structure). You can encourage the proliferation of stems by removing the main stem at ground level (coppicing). Other small eucalypts can also be encouraged to grow this way. Retaining 4 or 5 shoots of a proliferation of growth will make an attractive feature tree. Eucalyptus foliage in florists' shops is produced by this method.

You might consider using *E. gillii, E. polybractea, E lansdowneana* and *E. crucis* in this way.

Eucalyptus leucoxylon (Red-flowered Yellow Gum). A small tree, often multi-stemmed,

The flowers of *Eucalyptus leucoxyon*. The bark and shape of this tree is attractive throughout the whole year.

flowers from late winter through to spring. In spite of its common name, the flowers vary from white, pink to red and are very attractive to birds. It is extremely hardy, with attractive bark and is tolerant of drought, wind and frost.

E. pauciflora 'Edna Walling Little Snowman', a selected dwarf form of snow gum growing 4–7 x 3–4 m, with a smooth creamy white trunk, an open pendulous canopy of grey green leaves and masses of cream flowers.

E. stellulata 'Aemon' Little Star (Black Sally). A small multi-stemmed mallee 3–7 m high by 2–3 m across. Its stems are olive green to gold and it has cream flowers in midsummer through to early winter. It has high frost tolerance and thrives in full sun or light shade in moist clay. This plant is ideal for a small garden, with its trunk and blossom a feature.

Fraxinus excelsior 'Aurea' (Golden Ash) 10–12 m tall and broadly domed. Yellow bark, black buds, golden foliage in autumn. For medium-large gardens.

Fraxinus oxycarpa 'Raywoodii' (Claret Ash) 12–15 m, rounded and with burgundy autumn foliage. For large country gardens only.

Ginkgo biloba 'Fastigiata' (Maidenhair Tree) 15 m, columnar habit. Lime green foliage turning yellow in autumn. Plant the male form only. Ideal for large gardens or in narrow spaces where homes are multiple storeys. There are variegated forms.

Gleditsia triacanthos 'Sunburst' (Golden Honey Locust) 10 m, horizontal branching habit. Bright yellow leaves in spring turning pale green in autumn. Water regularly in summer. 'Ruby Lace' has reddish young foliage turning bronze in autumn.

Hakea laurina (Pincushion Hakea). A tall Australian shrub or small tree which may

The Golden Ash is a great plant for Canberra's autumns, but only in a large garden. This one is in the grounds of Government House.

reach 5–6 m. It has bright red ball flowers, with cream styles protruding all around like pins, which appear in autumn and winter. It will grow in a well-drained soil in full sun. It is frost-resistant, though sometimes new growth may be damaged. Nevertheless it is worth growing for its spectacular flowers.

Hoheria populnea (New Zealand Lacebark), an evergreen growing 6–10 m tall. White flowers in summer. Requires protection from hot winds, and regular water in summer.

Koelreuteria paniculata (Golden Rain Tree) 10 m, horizontal habit. Foliage turns yellow in autumn. Large brownish papery capsule fruit. This tree has a dense surface root system and is best planted in an area where there will be no cultivation around its trunk.

Lagerstroemia indica (Crepe Myrtle) 3–6 m, vase shaped. Panicles of white, pink, red, mauve flowers in summer. Foliage turns yellow in autumn. Many cultivars available.

'Betchel Crab Apple'

Some are prone to mildew in humid weather. Very attractive bark in winter.

Magnolia see Chapter 19: Magnolias and related plants.

Malus floribunda (Japanese Crab Apple) 3–5 m, broadly domed. Pink-white flowers in spring. Red fruit in autumn. 'Golden Hornet' has flowers red in bud, opening white and then yellow fruits. 'Gorgeous' has single white flowers in spring and crimson fruit in autumn. Both grow 3–5 m all round. Many other crab apple cultivars are available. They all do best with shelter from hot winds.

Malus ioensis 'Plena' (Bechtel Crab Apple) 3–5 m, broadly domed. Semi-double, soft pink flowers in spring. Does not normally set fruit

Malus spectabilis (Chinese Crab Apple) 3–5 m, broadly domed. Single to semi-double rose-red buds opening to blush. Spring flowering.

Malus x purpurea 'Eleyi' (Crab Apple) 3–5 m, broadly domed, has wine red flowers in spring, purple foliage. Purple red fruits.

Melaleuca (Paperbark). A very large Australian family of plants, melaleucas are fast growing small trees and ornamental shrubs from small to large in size. The papery bark peels readily

from the trunk of some of the larger species. Many have toothbrush flowers similar to bottle brushes whereas others have the look of the finest lace. Very good plants for difficult situations, there are plants within this group for damp situations while many are drought and pollution tolerant.

M. armillaris (Bracelet Honey Myrtle). A small tree or large shrub to 3 m with bushy growth and flowering heavily in spring and autumn with small 'bottlebrush' flowers suitable for screening, hedging or as a small street tree. Will tolerate poor drainage and is quite frost-resistant. Needs regular pruning.

Nyssa sylvatica (Tupelo) 10–15 m, spreading, branching. Brilliantly coloured foliage, scarlet-orange. Requires moist soil. Slow grower.

N. sylvatica 'Autumn Cascade' is a weeping form with larger leaves than its parent. It too needs a moist soil.

Olea europa (Olive) evergreen, growing to 7 m with a rounded shape. White flowers in summer, green or black fruit. Good evergreen screen.

Parrotia persica (Persian Witch Hazel) 8–10 m, wide spreading habit. Brilliant autumn foliage of apricot, crimson and gold. Relatively slow growing.

Paulownia tomentosa (Royal Paulownia) 8–10 m, rounded. Mid-spring mauve-violet flowers. Generally fast growing but not long-lived. The large leaves require it to be planted with some shelter. Needs water but is proving to be more resilient than might be expected of such a large-leaved plant. It is unsuitable for small blocks.

Pistacia chinensis (Chinese pistachio) 4–5 m, rounded. Foliage colours in autumn to red and yellow-orange. Drought-hardy,

Ornamental pears in autumn colour. Photo courtesy of Sherry McArdle-English.

relatively slow-growing. A very good small tree for Canberra.

Prunus varieties may require a little shaping and pruning in the early years, but this should be confined to early shaping only. Pests do not generally worry them but in some years the pear and cherry slug will attack their leaves. Dry soil or vacuum cleaner bag contents thrown over the leaves of small trees will deter the slug. Flowering peaches are generally regarded as being high maintenance in that in addition to their need for pruning immediately after flowering, they require spraying with copper or lime sulphur at autumn leaf fall and at early bud swell to control the fungal disease peach leaf curl. Green peach aphids may attack them in some seasons.

P. blireiana (Double Cherry Plum) grows to 6–8 m, rounded shape. Double rose pink flowers in spring. Purple foliage. *P. moseri* is similar with paler pink flowers.

P. campanulata (Formosan Cherry) 6 m, rounded. Rosy-red bell-shaped flowers in winter and early spring. Autumn coloured foliage. Suitable for smaller gardens.

P. mume (Flowering Apricot) 6 m, rounded. Single or double rose pink flowers in late winter. Also available as a weeping standard.

P. persica (Ornamental Peach) 6 m, rounded. Cultivars available in shades of white, pink, red flowers in spring. Should be pruned after flowering. Subject to peach leaf curl disease.

P. serrula (Tibetan Cherry) 8 m and rounded. Mahogany red bark, white flowers in spring. Worth growing for the beauty of its glossy 'varnished' bark alone.

P. serrulata 'James Veitch' (Japanese Flowering Cherry) 6 m, rounded. Double

Prunus serrulata 'Mount Fuji' in spring. It's worth growing for the bark and autumn leaves alone.

pink flowers in late spring. Ample summer watering required. Many cultivars available.

P. s. 'Mount Fuji' has double white flowers in spring and autumn foliage. Beautiful small tree, best where sheltered from hot winds.

P. s 'Tai-Haku' 6–8 m, rounded, with single white flowers in spring is a stronger grower than *P .s.* Mount Fuji.

P. subhirtella 'Pendula Rosea' (Spring Cherry) is grafted on a standard. Single shell pink flowers in spring. Beautiful weeping habit.

P. x yedoensis (Yoshino Cherry) 6–12 m, arching branches. Small white flowers in early spring. Flowers are almond-scented.

Pyrus calleryana (Callery Pear) 7 m tall with a branching habit. Drought tolerant with white flowers in spring. There are many cultivars available.

P.c. 'Aristocrat' is an attractive ornamental pear. A fine shade tree growing to 11 m x 7 m with dark green foliage and variable autumn colour but mainly yellows to reds. Abundant white flowers in spring. Best in full sun.

P.c. 'Bradford'. This ornamental pear features rounded leaves, a prolific floral display and good autumn foliage, growing to 12 m x 9 m. Pyramidal when young, becoming broader with age.

P.c. 'Capital' is a narrow, fastigiate form with a height of 11 m x 3 m and dark green leaves changing to reddish–purple late in autumn. Abundant white flowers in spring. Best in full sun. Disease resistant.

One of the flowering apricots, *Prunus mume*

P.c. 'Glen's Form' has a dense habit and attractive foliage. It grows to 11 m x 6 m with dark green leaves that turn gold, plum and burgundy in autumn. It is excellent for sites where lateral space is restricted. It is conical and dense and less resistant to wind damage than many ornamental pears. The cultivar 'Chanticuleer' seems to be identical.

P.c. 'Winter Glow'. An attractive ornamental pear growing up to 15 m x 5 m. It has beautiful autumn foliage of flame red, and holds its leaves well into late winter. In early spring pink eyed white blossoms appear.

P.c. 'Red Spire' grows to between 8 and 10 m high and 7 m wide. It has brilliant autumn foliage as its glossy green leaves turn to shades of crimson and burgundy in autumn-winter. Its clustered flowers are white, tinged with pink. It prefers an open position in well-drained soil.

P. salicifolia 'Pendula' (Silver Pear) 8 m, arching branches. Silvery-grey foliage, insignificant white flowers. Has a willowy habit and small leaves.

P. ussuriensis (Manchurian Pear) 12 m, rounded habit. Small white flowers in spring. The foliage colours in autumn. Prefers a well-irrigated site. Brittle stems are prone to cracking and falling.

Sapium sebiferum (Chinese Tallow Wood) 6 m, spreading shape. Red and gold foliage in autumn. Good specimen for small gardens.

Sapium sebiferum, the Chinese Tallow Wood.

Tamarix parviflora (Early Tamarisk) 4 m, spreading. Deep pink flowers in spring. Prune after flowering. Hardy. Large shrub-like growth.

Tilia cordata (Small-leaved Linden) 10–15 m tall, rounded shape. Foliage clear yellow in autumn. Best sheltered from hot winds. Not suited to dry sites. Large gardens only.

T. americana 'Bailyard' is a fine feature tree growing to 12 m high and 9 m wide. A rounded tree with large textured, deep green leaves turning golden yellow in autumn. Cream-yellow fragrant flowers in spring born in clusters.

Ulmus glabra 'Pendula' (Weeping Wych Elm). Weeping habit, grafted on standard. Foliage colours yellowish in autumn. Good specimen tree. Attractive weeping habit.

Ulmus parvifolia (Chinese Elm), 13–15 m, rounded shape. Foliage colours yellow in autumn. A graceful tree with open spreading crown and attractive bark but for large gardens only. Seeds readily.

CHAPTER 21:
Making the most of your cut flowers

Keith Brew and Marie Lenon, revised by Chris Ryan

Fresh flowers

Picking flowers

Some flowers keep better if cut when the flowers are still very much in the bud stage and just starting to show colour e.g. roses, lilies and gladioli. Others such as poppies, daffodils and dahlias are better cut when they are more mature. A little experimenting will soon prove which method is best. All will be best if cut in the early morning before sunrise or late in the evening after sunset. Always take a bucket of clean water when cutting and place stems immediately into it. Stems may be recut under water as an added precaution. Leave flowers in deep water for at least an hour and preferably longer before attempting to arrange them. This water can have added to it one teaspoon of household bleach to prevent bacteria, sugar for food and vinegar to help the uptake of water.

Treatment of cut flowers

Most flowers respond well to having the bottom of their stems placed in shallow boiling water for thirty seconds and then being transferred back to deep cold water. When using the boiling water treatment care should be taken to protect the bloom from steam, paper can be used to provide a temporary screen. Soft-stemmed flowers such as daffodils, agapanthus and arums do not appreciate this type of treatment.

Stems of woody plants such as protea and banksias keep better if the stems are split, scraped and cut at an angle before placing

A lovely vase of Australian flowers and foliage. These have a long vase life.

in water to help the uptake of water. Most flowers with woody stems use a lot of water, especially for the first two or three days after cutting.

Grey foliage plants such as lamb's ear, wormwood etc. do not like having their leaves wet, unlike most other foliage plants which benefit from being totally immersed overnight. Some flowers such as hellebores, violets, euphorbias, viburnums, lilacs and hydrangeas benefit greatly if fully immersed for several hours. Hydrangea and lilac should have most of their foliage stripped before treatment.

Conditioning each type of flower in a different bucket helps. Do not overcrowd buckets and keep them in a cool position. Daffodils, jonquils and tulips should not be placed with other flowers immediately after cutting as their secretions can cause other flowers to collapse prematurely. They may be safely added to mixed arrangements after a few hours.

A mixed display of delphiniums, daisies, roses and native roses with palm foliage, all in a plastic bowl.

Flowers that develop bent necks usually have an air lock in the stem and are unable to absorb water properly. Re-cutting the stem under water and leaving them in deep water in a cool spot for a couple of hours may help.

Most flower stems absorb water best if cut between nodes or joints particularly with carnations and hydrangea. It had been believed that crushing the stem of some flowers such as hydrangeas would assist in the uptake of water. Crushed stems will block up very quickly with bacteria and prevent the flower from drawing up water. Sharp-angled cuts are best as they allow the stems to absorb water more efficiently.

Before arranging flowers cut at least a couple of centimetres off the stems with sharp secateurs and be sure to remove any leaves that would be below water level in the vase. These leaves on the stems will quickly decay shortening the life of flowers if left in the water.

Make sure vases are perfectly clean as stains in vases are usually bacteria that will get to work blocking water uptake of the flower stems. Difficult stains may be removed by filling with water to which a few drops of household bleach has been added. Soak for a while before washing clean.

Clean water is important to cut flowers. Water can be changed every day or a preservative used and changed every other day. There are a number of floral preservatives on the market or you can use a mix of your own similar to that used when cutting flowers. A quick easy preservative for vases can be made from 300 ml of lemonade (not diet), 300 ml of clean water and half a teaspoon of household bleach.

Buying cut flowers

Look for bright fresh looking flowers that are just starting to open and avoid flowers that have been standing in the sun or have been exposed to car exhaust fumes. Flowers with yellowing leaves on the stems or with slimy stems have been in water for quite some time and are unlikely to be satisfactory. As soon as possible put them into a deep container of water without fully unwrapping and leave in a cool place to revive. Cutting the stems under water may also help the uptake of water.

Making the most of your flowers

Check the water in vases every day and top up or change as necessary. Remember woody stem flowers can be very thirsty.

Flowers will not keep long if placed in full sun near a window or in a room that is overheated. Strong draughts will also dry out flowers quite rapidly. Do not place your flowers next to the fruit bowl as ripening fruit give off ethylene, a natural ripening agent that will age flowers prematurely. Remove flowers as they age or die to maintain the overall fresh look; a few fresh flowers look better than a vase overcrowded with half dead flowers. Be aware also that some cut flowers will produce an unpleasant strong odour as they age in the vase.

Dried materials

Without too much trouble a number of natural flowers and foliage can be collected and dried for use when fresh material is in short supply. Some dry naturally in the garden, some need to be hung to dry while others are better if given a little more help. The following is a brief outline of some of the materials and methods to help. Most of the plants referred to will be found in the general text but some may not have been included because they are not fully frost hardy or are considered to be a weed as they self-seed freely.

The following can be hung in bunches upside down or stood in a container in a warm airy position.

» *Achillea clypeolata* — the spreading root system of other types of achillea can become invasive.

» Agapanthus and garlic heads; these may be left to dry on the plant after which they may be used in their natural dry state or spray-painted for a different effect.

» Hydrangea; great range of colours and flower types, some are best left on the bush until autumn when many in

protected areas change colour again as autumn tones take over.

» *Moluccella laevis* (Bells of Ireland), but can suffer frost damage.

» Statice; a wide range of vivid colours available, pick before colour starts to fade.

The following foliage can also be hang-dried with success.

» Carrot leaves give a soft lovely look to arrangements.

» *Cotinus coggygria* (Smoke Bush) looks like smoke and softens the outline of arrangements.

» Maize (sweet corn) seed heads and husks; husks take on the appearance of crepe paper.

Nature can play a big part and often does most of the work. Some flowers dry colourfully in the garden while seed heads and grasses dry crisp on their stems and need very little attention once picked. Some materials worth considering follow, but many others can be used and are only limited by your imagination and experimentation.

» Bluebells and grape hyacinths can be left on the plants until they start to dry then pick and stand in a wide container to allow air to surround the stems to complete the process.

» Clematis will give a good range of colour from purple to pink, cut early enough the large fluffy seed heads will dry well.

» Dianthus (garden pinks) should be picked before they are fully open, store in a dark place to keep their colour.

» Dianthus (Sweet William) picked before flowers fully open will dry into balls of soft colours.

» Globe artichokes flowers dry well and turn creamy yellow. Globe thistles should be cut when just starting to open as left any longer they will fall apart as they dry.

» Gourds should be dried in a hot airing cupboard or similar warm area for three months before painting with clear varnish and make great and interesting features.

» *Lunaria bienni* (Honesty, Money plant) should be cut when there are still two layers of brown skin on the seed pods. Rub these layers off just before using in arrangements. Self seeding of this plant can be a problem.

» Thistles (Scotch, cotton and teasels) are great in arrangements.

Another drying treatment makes use of glycerine or antifreeze. Leaves treated this way will take on a permanent sheen.

The best time to carry out this process is in mid-summer while plants are still absorbing moisture. Houseplants and evergreens can be treated at any time if in good condition. The process can take from a few days to three or four months. The result can be soft and supple and not as brittle as with the hanging or natural process.

Prepare material by removing all damaged and blemished leaves. Scrape off any bark and split the ends of woody stems for about five centimetres.

With glycerine use one part to two parts of very hot water. For woody hard stems boil the water and use immediately.

Antifreeze — use equal parts with hot water shake or stir until thoroughly mixed. Boil water for hard stems and use immediately.

An ikebana arrangement of Japanese maple and camellias.

Place either mixture in a container so that it will cover about five centimetres of stem. Glycerine is quite expensive but can be reused if stored in a sealed container. The following are some of the materials that can be treated with these methods.

» Aspidistra; immersion gives better results.

» Beech; cut when fully mature, before they have dried out on the tree.

» Camellias turn deep brown with glossy leaves.

» Fatsia; evergreen leaves turn mid-brown in glycerine and dark brown with antifreeze.

» Gum leaves turn a pale grey-mauve.

» Ilex (Holly); treat leaves and berries together, spray berries with hair lacquer.

» Ivy; long sprays are best and berries can be preserved.

» Laurel leaves turn almost black. Antifreeze is best.

» Maidenhair fern can be preserved at any time because it is evergreen.

» Maple sprays of different types provide a wide range of colours, light to very dark.

» *Moluccella laevis* (Bells of Ireland); preserve and then hang them upside down.

» Mountain ash — sprays of leaves and berries form a dramatic combination of nut brown and orange berries may be sprayed with lacquer.

» Oak leaves and acorns preserve well.

» Raspberry; cut young perfect leaves, which turn dark red with silver underneath.

» Rhododendron; sprays of leaves and tight young buds turn a lovely brown.

» Rosemary stems turn silver-grey; the leaves normally retain scent.

» Silver birch cut with catkins on the twigs, shades vary from yellow to deep brown.

» Viburnum leaves turn dark brown on top with an olive brown underside.

Guidelines for flower arrangers

If you would like to know more about flower arranging or floral art a good start would be to visit one of the Horticultural Society's four annual Flower Shows. On display at the shows is a wide range of traditional to modern styles in classes for the Novice, Progressive, A Grade and Open categories and the results are always inspiring. Information on floral arranging can be gleaned from the exhibitors or stewards who are usually on hand at the Shows and are more than happy to discuss their work.

Detailed information for exhibitors is included in the Show Schedule rules for each show and the Horticultural Judges and Exhibitors' Show Manual, both publications produced by the Horticultural Society and available by contacting the Show secretaries on (02) 6255 1371 or the website www.hsoc.org.au.

There are two flower clubs in Canberra:

» The Floral Art Guild of the ACT Inc. The Guild meets on the second Thursday of each month at 7.30 pm at the Uniting Church Hall, Yarralumla. These meetings are very informal, a short business meeting, a demonstration and a critique of members' monthly themed designs followed by supper. Annual activities include arranging displays for the Royal Canberra Show, Canberra Quilters Annual show, weekend workshops and seminars, friendship mornings & afternoons and demonstrations annually at Floriade. For more information see the HSOC website.

» The Canberra Flower Club meets on the second Tuesday of each month at the Downer Community Centre at 10 am. These meetings also are an informal gathering commencing with a roll call, a quick meeting, sales table, demonstrations, inspection of members' arrangements followed by morning tea. An annual activity is an event called Flowers and Music at one of Canberra's Overseas Embassies. Guests are treated to a wonderful evening of music surrounded by beautiful flower arrangements designed by members. For more information see the HSOC website.

For those interested in floral art and trying their hand at exhibiting, the following publications provide good guidelines/references: The Handbook of the ACT Judges School for Floral Art. In 2006 the guidelines were superseded by a national manual published by the Australian Floral Art Association (AFAA). The new guidelines include the more advanced contempory styles. Website: www.ausfloralart.org.au.

For a range of interesting and informative floral art websites with very good photo galleries refer to:

www.wafloralart.org.au

www.nswfloralartassociation.org.au

www.floralartssocietyvictoria.org.au

www.fasnz.org.nz

For the beginner/novice the various sites maintained by Chrissie Harten (for example, www.thegardener.btinternet.co.uk) are excellent.

There are some very good colourful magazines produced for the interested floral designer. These include Floral Design www.floraldesignmagazine.com; Fusion Flowers www.fusionflowers.com and The Flower Arranger www.nafas.org.uk/flowerarranger.

Further information may also be sought from the Canberra Institute of Technology's Solutions Calendar of Courses.

PART D: The kitchen garden

Canberrans are growing a lot more of their own vegetables and fruit. And, self-sufficiency is largely achievable in the Canberra area.

This part of the book covers the principles of growing vegetables, herbs and fruit. We tell you how to do this without the use of artificial pesticides, fungicides and fertilisers.

Once you learn the principles for developing a healthy soil and the watering techniques, discussed in Part B, you will be well on the way to an organic garden.

CHAPTER 22: Vegetables

Bronwyn Beechey, revised by Graeme Davis

Whether it is potted tomatoes in the courtyard or a variety of vegetables in a permanent plot, the Canberra climate allows a range of summer and winter vegetables to be grown successfully. This chapter will tell you what vegetables grow well in the climate, how to care for them, and, importantly, when to plant them to maximise crops. The information is a consolidation of vegetable growing experience and expertise from the Horticultural Society's members in Canberra over many years. It provides tried and true advice to give you the best chance of successfull, vegetable growing in Canberra.

Growing your own vegetables has many benefits. First, it allows you to experiment with vegetables and varieties not available in the shops. Second, you can choose to avoid artificial fertilisers, pesticides and genetically modified varieties. Third, it can give you pleasure to serve them fresh from the garden. Fourth, vegetable plants look good in the garden too. They can be colourful, like rainbow chard, or decorative, like a chilli plant in fruit in a courtyard.

Different approaches to growing vegetables

Broadly, there are two approaches to vegetable growing — conventional growing using inorganic fertilisers and pesticides; and organic growing using natural fertilisers and pest management systems with a view to maintaining the natural ecosystem. While some may follow one method or the other, vegetable gardeners often choose elements of both, depending on the climate, situation and the growing conditions of that particular season.

This chapter is generally aligned with the organic methods of growing vegetables.

Conventional growing

In conventional growing the focus is on the plant. Water-soluble inorganic fertilisers provide nutrients for the plant, but do not benefit the soil. Plants are protected from pests and diseases by artificial pesticides and fungicides, which may kill pests and beneficial insects and soil microorganisms alike. Moreover, conventional growing is not greatly concerned with the soil and its immediate and future health, the relationship between the naturally occurring parts of the growing system, and wider ecosystems.

In this combination vegetable garden and chook run the contents of each partition are gradually moved around the structure during the year. Contact the Society for more information about this approach, or look at strongbuild.com.au.

Organic Growing

In organic growing the focus is on feeding the soil, which in turn nourishes the plant. Plants gain nutrients from soil that has been enriched with organic matter, and organic matter improves soil structure, an essential factor for healthy plant growth.

Healthy plants stand the best chance of resisting pests and diseases. A fertile, well-prepared soil is the most important factor in growing healthy plants. Other contributing factors in promoting healthy plants are; crop rotation, choosing the best time to plant for the climate, choosing the most suitable location in your garden, and effective and timely watering.

Organic pest management comprises companion planting, controlling slugs and snails and encouraging natural predators. If pests are still a problem, pest controls such as garlic spray, pyrethrum, Derris Dust® and Dipel® can be used. Such control measures would only be considered necessary if pests are actually present, and are destroying an unacceptable amount of the crop. The severity of pests and diseases will vary from season to season depending on climatic and other conditions, so a control measure required one year may not be necessary the next. For pest control advice, see Chapter 28.

One of the keys to effective growing of vegetables organically is to keep everything in balance. This goes for the soil where every effort is made to avoid shocking the system with too much of any one thing. The aim is to create an environment where the soil microbes and worms can keep doing their jobs effectively. Artificial fertilisers can create a sudden excess of nutrient to the potential detriment of a healthy soil. So too can adding too much animal manure. On the other hand, green manure crops and organic mulches which break down over several months help build up the soil organisms.

Balance is also the key in keeping pests at bay. Often more damage is caused by trying to eliminate a pest than would have been caused by leaving nature to do its thing. Sometimes nature needs a helping hand while the natural predators catch up. For example, red spider mite is a destructive pest but there are natural predators that can reduce it to a minor issue. Unfortunately most of the sprays we have used in gardens for the last 60 or 70 years are more likely to kill the natural predator than they are to kill red spider. One option when you see red spider is, rather than spray, to wet the underside of the leaves every day for a week or two. Red spider hate this and do not multiply as fast, giving the natural predators time to get established.

So, rather than think about how to get rid of something or make something grow faster, why not think about what is required to maintain or re-establish the system balance?

Best sites for growing vegetables

The amount of sunlight is the prime consideration in where to plant vegetables — they need at least six hours of full sun a day (except a few vegetables such as leeks and summer lettuce which will tolerate some shade). Also, when choosing a place for the vegetable plot consider that you will need to dig over the soil and incorporate organic matter without disturbing other plants' roots, divide the area into several small beds for crop rotation purposes, and make paths for easy access without treading on the garden. Beds one to two metres wide are an easy size to work with.

In an established garden vegetables need to be grown away from the root zones of trees and shrubs to avoid competition for moisture and nutrients. Disturbing tree roots by digging around them will most likely cause problems with suckers growing from the roots. Building a raised bed on grass or even concrete may be the solution if vegetables cannot be incorporated into existing garden beds. In a new garden it is often a good idea to keep a sunny area next to a fence for vegetables as the fence can be used without much work to support climbing vegetables.

An option to consider for both new and established gardens could be the prefabricated corrugated iron raised beds that are now available from a range of sources. These can be a convenient height and size for most gardeners, reducing the need to bend down to tend the vegetables. A root barrier can be put under these beds to keep out the tree roots.

As well as a dedicated vegetable plot, vegetables may be grown in the flower and shrub garden. It may be that the flower garden receives the longest hours of sunlight in the day. Plants with interesting foliage, like the ferny tops of carrots, can form a decorative row along the front of the flower garden. Also, perennial vegetables that stay in the ground for several years can be grown in a general garden bed.

Vegetables in containers

Many vegetables grow well in containers, and some dwarf forms are bred specifically for container growing. Vegetables that can do well in pots are tomatoes, capsicums, cucurbits, and 'cut and come again' leaf vegetables. An advantage in growing lettuce in pots is that the pot can be moved into a shaded position out of the hot afternoon sun.

The growing medium in the pot needs to be well drained. Pots tend to dry out in hot weather, so please pay attention to watering to maintain evenly moist soil. Wetting agents, double potting or covering the outside of the pot with foil can help prevent the pot from drying out. Also, avoid placing pots in positions that become very hot, like against a solid brick wall as the reflected heat will burn the foliage, dry the soil and damage the roots. Pots need to be in a place where there is reasonable air circulation.

Soil preparation

The preparation of the soil before planting is vital to the health and success of vegetable plants. Fertile soil with a good structure will allow a plant to grow to its full potential, to produce well, and to withstand pests and diseases. The key to providing such a soil is to improve the humus content by adding organic material. Canberra soils are not naturally well supplied with humus. Organic matter is usually added in the form of animal manure, compost and green manuring. Autumn leaves, well broken down, are also useful. Also, when initially preparing the soil take the opportunity to remove any stones, tree roots and perennial weeds. Concientously removing perennial weeds such as couch grass will save much work in subsequent years. If the topsoil is fairly shallow try not to bring the heavier clay sub-soil to the surface.

Humus, which is produced from the decomposition in the soil of organic materials, is essential in the creation of a soil with a good structure. Soil structure is the network of soil crumbs and the spaces between them. Humus is the key agent in crumb formation. It combines with mineral particles in the soil to form tiny but stable crumbs of varying sizes. Crumbs are separated by spaces, the larger spaces contain air, and the smaller ones hold moisture. Soils with a poor structure set hard after rain or watering. Additionally, water-holding capacity is reduced, aeration is poor and, even if adequate nutrients are supplied, plants do not grow well.

Organic matter is also an important source of nutrients to the growing crops. Soil bacteria break down the organic matter into humus and this improves soil fertility. Earthworms are enormously beneficial in the soil as they kick-start the process of converting organic matter into humus. From the humus, three elements essential for plant growth, nitrogen, phosphorus and potassium are released in forms the plant can use.

Which vegetables and where?

Competition between crops

Vegetable plants that have a heavy need for nutrients will compete with other plants for those nutrients. Many home gardeners have found that a tomato crop can be markedly reduced when grown adjacent to sweet corn. The roots of the sweet corn will compete more successfully for the plant nutrients than the tomato roots.

Tall plants, such as broad beans, climbing

peas and beans, sweet corn and tomatoes should be grown on the southern side of vegetable beds, or against a fence. If you grow them on the northern side, the shade created by the tall plants will affect crops such as carrots, onions and dwarf beans, which need a lot of sun.

Companion planting

Companion planting is a pest management method. It relies on using a companion plant to repel pests on other plants, to encourage beneficial insects, or to provide beneficial growing conditions for the other plant. The repelling action may occur because pests dislike the companion plant because of its scent, or the companion plants' leaves or shape disguise the other plant. A beneficial growing effect may occur because the companion plant produces a chemical that promotes growth in the other plant. For example, legumes are well known for providing nitrogen to the soil, so planting them near crops requiring high levels of nitrogen such as lettuce and spinach is beneficial.

Crop rotation

It is best to use a crop rotation system, aiming to rotate the various vegetable families around different areas of the vegetable garden. Different crops grow roots at different levels and make varying demands on the plant foods in the soil. Crop mixing aims to make full use of the soil's resources. For example, vegetables such as cauliflower, potato, tomato, pumpkin and sweet corn, have heavy nutrient requirements and others, such as carrot, parsnip and onion have less nutrient requirements. Consequently these 'follow-on' crops do best in beds previously used

for heavy feeders. Furthermore, crops of the same family are subject to the same diseases and crop rotation will help to reduce trouble from diseases and viruses, particularly those that may survive in the soil from previous years. Try to fit an unrelated crop between two crops from the same family whenever possible. For example, peas and beans could be followed by one of the cabbage family and in turn by a root crop such as carrots.

Rotations are often worked on a four or six year basis; however, in a small intensively planted garden it may be more realistic to observe a two or three year rotation period. Rotations are not inflexible codes, but it is important to follow three principles. First move vegetables around keeping in mind the various vegetable families. Second incorporate legumes, and third grow some green manure crops.

Which vegetables, which season?

The temperature and available water dictate which vegetables can be grown in an area. In Canberra frost largely governs what vegetables can be grown and when to plant them. Available water can be a limiting factor in years when water restrictions apply.

This section provides a general guide to vegetables to grow in Canberra and their season. The cultural notes for individual vegetables that follow provide more detailed information on planting and harvesting times.

Warm weather vegetables

The last frost, usually in October, and the first frost, usually in April, limit the growing season for warm weather vegetables.

Nevertheless, the five to six months between October and March is long enough for a large range of vegetables to grow well and produce successfully. Of these, good results are usually obtained in reasonable soil from zucchini, beans, tomato, sweet corn, silver beet, radish, cucumber, potato, and beetroot. None of these have particularly specialised soil and care requirements. Other crops, such as carrots and cabbages have particular soil and growing needs, and successful results will usually require a little more time and effort.

Successive crops of the quicker maturing summer vegetables can be grown, extending the harvest period. Some plants such as tomatoes and zucchini can become less productive at three to four months old or can be damaged by pests or disease. A second round of plants will give a better chance of healthy plants giving good crops well into autumn.

On the other hand, some vegetables such as capsicum, chilli, pumpkins and eggplant take most of the warm weather season to grow and ripen, and only one planting is possible. This group needs to be planted at the right time to give them the best opportunity to grow and produce before the cool weather arrives.

Cool weather vegetables

Canberra's cool weather suits frost-tolerant vegetables. For example, cauliflower and broccoli prefer cooler growing conditions and do not grow well in the warmer months. Also carrots, parsnips, turnips and swedes are sweeter for having been exposed to frost.

The cooling of the air and soil temperatures in autumn causes plant growth to reduce markedly in April. The single most important step in growing vegetables through autumn and winter is to get them actively growing before the onset of the cooler weather. This means that seedlings must be planted by mid February — if they do not get the chance to grow in February and March they will never catch up. Onions are an exception — plant seedlings in late winter and early spring and harvest in summer. Seeds, except peas and broad beans, will not germinate in cold weather.

Vegetables to harvest most of the year

Some vegetables can be planted in spring, summer and autumn for harvesting most of the year round. A few vegetable seedlings such as lettuce, radish, beetroot and silver beet can be planted every few weeks from mid-September to February. Even though these vegetables will grow through the autumn and survive into winter, the last plantings before winter need to be in February. This is so that the plants can become established before the cold weather starts. Seedlings of even frost-tolerant plants will not grow in cold weather, but fully-grown plants will survive the cold to provide modest harvests into winter.

Selecting a variety

Selecting vegetable varieties usually involves a choice between a recently developed hybrid, a conventional variety, and possibly an heirloom variety. New hybrids have been developed with specific features and can be exceptionally vigorous plants producing high yields of excellent quality vegetables. A hybrid plant's features can include disease resistance, ability to set fruit in adverse conditions, tastier produce, and compact plant growth. Conventional varieties have usually been on the market for quite a few years and are tried and true. Heirloom varieties are generally only available as seeds from specialist mail order companies but occasionally you will find them on sale in Canberra.

Seeds

Seeds allow you to experiment with a larger range of vegetables and many more varieties than are offered as seedlings. Heirloom varieties and the latest 'must try' hybrids are generally only available as seed. Garden centres and supermarkets carry the range of seeds offered by the major seed companies, but for something a little different or unusual try experimenting with the wider number of varieties offered by the mail-order specialists. Many of them advertise in the popular gardening magazines. Also, some vegetables are best grown from seed, because transplanting can damage roots or cause a seedling to go to seed.

Seed packets specify the time it takes for a plant to reach maturity. However cold snaps, irregular watering or poor soil can limit growth and cause set backs that add to the time to maturity. A hint when sowing seeds is to put some extras in at the end of the row. When they reach the seedling stage they can be used to fill in vacant spots in the row where a seed has failed to germinate.

For information on growing plants from seed see Chapter 26: Hints on growing your own. In addition, some vegetable specific techniques can be used.

Peas, broad beans, dwarf beans, climbing beans, sweet corn.

In the late autumn and early spring germination of seed can be quite slow and losses higher than in warmer weather. To overcome this, pea, broad bean, dwarf bean, climbing bean and sweet corn seeds can be pre-germinated ready for planting in the garden. To do this, place the seeds between layers of paper towelling (or other absorbent material) and keep it moist and warm until the seeds germinate. Germination by this method normally takes only a few days at which time the seed can be sown, root down, in the garden. Do not let the roots grow to more than one cm before planting out as they damage easily and can get tangled in the towelling.

Carrots, parsnips.

The soil in which seeds are germinating needs to be constantly moist and the hot dry weather in Canberra can pose problems because the soil dries out quickly. Summer-sown seeds that take several weeks to germinate, like carrots and parsnips, are especially at risk because the soil has to be kept evenly moist the whole time. To stop the soil drying out place shade cloth or other suitable covering like hessian over the seeds once they have been sown, but remove the covering as soon as the seed germinates. Seed tapes are useful.

Seedlings

Many gardeners find purchased seedlings easier and more convenient than seeds, especially when only a few plants are required, eg zucchini, pumpkin. Some plants, like capsicum, also benefit from a start as a seedling because the seed will not germinate until the soil is quite warm. Seedlings ensure that the plant gets a start at the right time, and that enough of the summer growing season is available for fruit production and ripening.

Seedlings generally give quicker results, but sometimes not by much. For example, cucumber seed sown in summer grows to seedling size in about a week. Seedlings will also take about a week to get established and start to grow well after transplanting.

When buying seedlings avoid those that have dried out, as they will not always recover with any vigour. Soak the seedlings in a weak solution of liquid fertiliser (seaweed ones are good) overnight before planting them.

Caring for growing crops

Watering

Most vegetables need consistent watering to maintain steady growth. Severe fluctuations in soil moisture reduce the yield and can also cause damage to the crops; e.g. blossom end rot of tomatoes is principally due to wide fluctuations in soil moisture. Deep wetting of the soil encourages the roots to go deep instead of searching the surface for moisture. Encouraging an extensive root system results in the plants being able to use all the goodness from the soil.

How much water and watering techniques
When seeds are germinating they need evenly moist conditions. Therefore water the planting ground in advance, and then once or twice a day to maintain evenly moist soil. Likewise, when transplanting, the soil needs to be moist. Water the seedlings gently and frequently until they become established. For established vegetable crops, in the absence of good rain, water regularly and deeply about once a week or perhaps more frequently in hot, dry weather. Growth is checked once they start to wilt.

Different types of vegetables benefit from water at different growth stages. The critical time for watering fruiting vegetables such as tomatoes, cucumbers, peas, beans etc, is when the plants are flowering and the fruits start to swell. Heavy watering at this time increases the yield. Root crops need regular watering for steady growth, but too much water encourages lush foliage rather than root development. They require more water in the later stages as the roots begin to swell. As water mainly stimulates leaf growth, leafy vegetables such as brassicas, lettuce, spinach, silver beet and zucchini require consistent amounts of water throughout growth.

The rate of water loss from the soil depends not so much on evaporation but on the leaf area of the plant. This means large leafy plants will need more water than those with smaller leaf surfaces. Wind greatly accelerates water loss, so if windy conditions persist, more frequent watering will be required. Early morning or evening watering avoids the high levels of evaporation that occur in windy weather and the hotter parts of the day.

With established plants, direct water at the base of the plant. Where plants are spaced far apart, water a circular area around each, leaving the soil between them dry to discourage weeds. This method also keeps the foliage dry, which helps to reduce insects and disease. Watering systems, such as drippers or porous soaker hose placed under mulch, minimize evaporation and deliver water right at the root zone. A piece of pipe can be sunk in to the ground next to large plants such as tomatoes, and the plant watered directly at the root zone below the surface by placing a hose in the pipe inlet. However irrigation equipment may have to be relocated each season to cater for different plant sizes and spacing if using a crop rotation system.

Mulching

Many gardeners use organic mulch to cover the soil around vegetables. Mulch adds to the nutrient level of the soil, it suppresses the growth of weeds and makes any weeds that do grow easy to pull out. The benefits and types of mulch are many. See Chapter 5 for a full discussion on mulching.

Weeding

The vegetable garden needs to be kept weed-free, whether or not it has been mulched. Weeds compete for moisture, food and sunlight. Furthermore, they are host agents for pests and diseases, and should be removed where possible. Weeding should be thorough, ensuring that no weeds are left to produce seed. The old adage 'One year's seeding, seven years weeding' is certainly true.

Weeds are more readily killed when the soil is dry, so it is better to allow the soil to dry out after watering for a day or two before weeding is done. If the weeds are thick, close to crop plants, or in closely sown rows of vegetables such as carrots, hand weed between the plants. Do not leave weeds on the surface — they may re-root and grow again, or if they are in flower they can set seed.

Cultural notes for vegetables suited to Canberra

The following pages give brief cultural notes and growing requirements for the more common vegetables that are reliable in Canberra's conditions. They assume a good fertile soil, prepared the way suggested in the Soil Preparation section in this chapter. If a vegetable has a different soil requirement it is stated in the notes for that vegetable.

At the end of the chapter is a planting and harvesting calendar for the most common of the vegetables grown in Canberra.

Artichokes

Globe Artichoke: Globe artichoke is a perennial, thistle-like plant with large deeply cut leaves, growing to a metre tall and a similar width. They are impressive plants and make quite a statement in the garden. They are best grown from offshoots or suckers from good plants, rather than from seedlings. Globe Artichokes need heavily fertilised soil and lots of water. Plant the suckers in mid–late winter in a spot about a metre in diameter. Divide them every 4 to 6 years in late winter. They are very attractive to snails.

Globe artichokes are a fine ornamental plant as well as good eating.

Pick the flower heads in spring when they are fully developed but before the thickened fleshy scales begin to open.

Jerusalem Artichoke: Jerusalem artichokes are a type of sunflower that grows to 2 m tall. The crop grows readily in any soil but you will get more evenly shaped tubers in lighter soils. Select the smoothest tubers for planting; they will produce less knobbly tubers that are easier to peel. Plant the tubers in late winter or early spring 12–15 cm deep in rows 90 cm apart allowing 40–45 cm between tubers. The tubers are ready for harvest in autumn when the plants begin to turn yellow. Be sure to dig out all the tubers, as Jerusalem artichokes will become a weed unless kept under control.

Asian Greens

The common connection between these leafy greens is that they are all Brassicas (members of the cabbage family). Centuries of breeding and interbreeding throughout Asia have resulted in a diversity of shapes, sizes and names that are very confusing to westerners. The secret as a gardener is to be adventurous because all of these greens are easy to grow and can provide a range of tasty leaves suitable for cooking or salads throughout the year in Canberra gardens.

Sowings in early spring, late summer and autumn work best as all the plants tend to bolt in hot weather. The plants mature fast and must be harvested quickly once mature so small regular sowings are necessary.

As with all members of the cabbage family the plants are susceptible to attack from cabbage white butterfly. They are best covered with fine mesh to exclude the pests.

The table opposite is a simplified summary of this large group of vegetables. There is actually a continuous spectrum from the hard, ball shapes of Bok Choi through to the leafy open mustards so the boundaries are somewhat arbitrary.

For more information consult Joy Larkcom's definitive book "*Oriental Vegetables*" (John Murray 1991).

Asparagus

Asparagus is a long-lived plant that is best in a spot or a bed to itself where it can remain undisturbed for many years. To make the crop worthwhile thorough preparation of the soil and annual fertilising are essential. To prepare the soil dig it very deeply adding plenty of animal manure or compost and lime, as asparagus plants dislike acid soils.

The usual method is to grow the plants from roots, called crowns. Plant in winter to early spring about 20-25 cm deep. Place the crowns about 30 cm apart with the roots downwards and carefully spread out. Cover with about 10 cm of soil at first and water. As the plants grow, gradually fill in the holes. Spears will grow in October and November. Don't cut them in the first year but make every effort to promote good growth. If the plants are vigorous a light cutting can be made in the second year and gradually increased in later years. After the cutting period is over encourage top growth by watering and feeding.

In winter dig the beds over, being very careful to avoid damaging the crowns, and work in a thick cover of manure or compost and extra fertiliser if desired.

Some Asian vegetables

Type	Varieties	Description
Heading	Bok Choi Michihili	Tight headed 'Chinese cabbages' that can be tall and cylindrical or more barrel shaped. Best planted in February to give good tight heads that hold well into winter. Earlier sowings tend to bolt. Use: Best cooked – stir fried or steamed
Bunching	Pak Choi (white stemmed, green stemmed & baby) Tatsoi	Distinguished by the thick edible stem. All of the plant is edible including the flower stalks. Best sown in spring and autumn. Use: Mature plants are best cooked, young leaves are suitable for salads
Loose Leaf	Komatsuna Senposai Mustards (Green Wave, Red Giant)	Extremely hardy, open leafed types. Can be sown any time from very early spring through to late autumn. The leaves are picked one or two at a time at any stage of growth (the same as silverbeet). Some varieties are mild and tender, others more pungent and peppery. Use: Leaves are cooked as you would silverbeet.
Flowering	Hon Tsai Tai (purple) Kailan (Chinese Broccoli) Choi Sum (flowering Pak Choi)	Grow summer and autumn. Stems, including leaves and flower buds are harvested and the plants left to regrow. Use: Cooked
Salad	Mizuna (serrated leaf) Mibuna (straight leaf)	Thin stemmed Japanese salad greens. Can be grown any time from early spring through to late autumn. Use: The tender young leaves and stems are delicious raw.
Baby Leaves	All of the above (and more!)	A few short rows of closely spaced seed planted every two weeks throughout most of the year will provide succulent cut and come again salad greens when the plants get to between 10 cm and 15 cm tall.

Beans

Broad beans: Broad beans are a hardy crop and valuable in spring before other beans are ready. Cole's Dwarf Prolific, Early Long Pod and Broad Windsor are all good varieties, the latter two being much larger than Cole's Dwarf Prolific. Sow them from late April to July but germination is very slow in June and July. Sow the seed about 5 cm deep and about 15 cm apart, with 75–90 cm between rows. Flowers formed during the frosty weather are unlikely to set pods but, in the spring, you can encourage setting by pinching the tops out of the plants. Pick the pods when the seeds are fully formed and show a black 'eye' but before they commence to harden. Younger pods can be eaten in the same way as Dwarf beans. Rust, a fungal disease which produces brown powdery spots on leaves can occur on broad beans, mostly towards the end of the crop.

Dwarf beans, Climbing beans: Dwarf beans and climbing beans (which take a little longer to mature than dwarf varieties) both come in many varieties: green, yellow (wax) or blue-podded. Good varieties are many but for ease of use go for the completely stringless varieties. Some of the newer types like Jade and the Sword types (from mail order specialists) do very well in Canberra.

Dwarf and climbing beans are very frost tender and may be damaged by low temperatures even if not frosty. The seed will not germinate well if the soil is cold and growth under low temperatures is generally weak and liable to disease. Sow when spring temperatures commence to rise, and then make successive plantings until late January for a continuous supply of beans from December to April. Be careful not to let the seed come into direct contact with fertiliser otherwise the seed may rot.

Dwarf beans should be sown in rows about 30 cm apart, allowing 7–10 cm between seeds. The depth of planting depends on soil type and the time of the year. In cold soils 5 cm is deep enough, especially if the soil is heavy, but as the soil heats the depth can be increased to about 7.5 cm. As the plants grow hill them lightly to prevent wind damage but take care not to damage the roots. Climbing beans need more room than the dwarf varieties. They need to be grown on a support, such as a trellis, a tripod, or a large mesh frame supported by stakes. The seeds should be spaced about 10 cm apart.

Regular and thorough watering is essential, particularly when flowering commences. Dryness can cause many flowers to fall or can result in very poor pods. Night hosing will help the flowers set and also reduce the effects of red spider. The pods should be picked regularly as soon as large enough to eat. This will encourage longer cropping in the plants. The main pests affecting dwarf and climbing beans are two-spotted mite and bean spider mite. Mites produce sandy mottling of leaves and webbing.

Scarlet runner beans: This is a different species from the Dwarf bean and is a perennial, but the general cultural requirements are identical to those of Dwarf beans. It is more of an ornamental, producing many racemes of bright scarlet flowers but the pods can be eaten like Dwarf beans if picked while young and tender. It crops best in autumn.

Beetroot

Beetroot is a must in the home garden for summer salads. Beetroot leaves are also edible, and are highly nutritious. The young leaves can be used in gourmet salad leaf mixes. A new variety, Hybrid King, seems to do very well.

Sow the seed 8–10 cm apart, about l–2 cm deep in rows 35 cm apart. You can take care to place seed 8–10 cm apart when sowing, or scatter it and later thin the plants to 8–10 cm. Beetroot seeds are clusters of 3 or 4 seeds in a corky case, so need thinning after they have germinated. When the plants are about 7–8 cm high thin them to one seedling in each spot and pull some soil around the plants left, to prevent them from falling over. Thinnings can be transplanted to form additional rows, or to fill in vacant spots within the row. Beetroot is not generally subject to pests or diseases but occasionally grubs attack the leaves. Use beets while young as they become woody with age.

The Brassica family

This family includes more kinds of vegetables than any other group. It includes Brussels sprouts, broccoli, cabbage, cauliflower, Chinese cabbage, kohlrabi, kale, mustard, white turnips and swedes. This section covers the kinds grown for their above-ground parts as they have common cultural requirements. All demand a high level of soil fertility and will not do well in acid soils.

Brassica crops generally do best in cooler months and are planted to mature in the autumn, winter and spring. Good cabbage can, however, be grown during the spring and early summer.

You can grow winter brassicas such as broccoli, Brussels sprouts, cabbage and cauliflowers on a continuous cropping basis by selecting the right varieties. The time of sowing is critical and you cannot catch up time - all crops should have started to grow actively by early March, as growth slows after this. As summer crops will already occupy most space at the time of sowing, sow seed for winter crops in a seedbed, preferably an open sunny area. Alternatively, buy seedlings in late January and plant in medium sized pots, transferring them to the garden in March when space is available. This will minimise transplant shock and the plants will continue to grow without check when they are planted in the garden.

Brassica crops all have the same diseases and pests. Occasionally downy mildew can occur on brassicas, but generally diseases are not prevalent as long as crops are rotated and there is good garden hygiene by early removal of any diseased crop residue. However pests are common and can be problematic. These are the velvety green caterpillars up to 30 mm long of the cabbage white butterfly, cabbage aphids (slatey-grey in colour) and snails and

Tuscan kale. You can cut leaves from this gradually over the season and the plant will continue to grow happily.

slugs. Control these pests as soon as you see them, otherwise they will cause severe damage. Marix cloth (or a similar product) is very useful for protecting your plants against most pests. Drape it over the plant, or over a support such as a tunnel made out of irrigation pipe bent over with the ends pushed into the ground.

Broccoli

For growing requirements see information under the Brassica family heading.

One of the best and most productive vegetables for a small garden. The most commonly grown is the calabrese type. The main terminal shoot in the centre of the plant will produce a large head and after this is cut the plants will continue to produce smaller lateral heads for several weeks. Another type of broccoli is the romanesco type, which has numerous yellowish-green conical groups of buds arranged in spirals. It takes a little longer to mature than the calabrese type, but otherwise has the same growing requirements.

Brussels sprouts

For growing requirements see information under the Brassica family heading.

Brussels sprouts produce over a long period of the autumn and winter. With Brussels sprouts, it is better not to fertilise until the plants are carrying a good crop of sprouts. They are very prone to slatey grey cabbage aphid infestations.

Cabbage

For growing requirements see information under the Brassica family heading.

Sugarloaf, Savoy, Superette and Ballhead are good winter types, maturing in that order. Red cabbages are very hardy and are also a winter type. In early spring you can sow seed of Sugarloaf or Superette in seedbeds for seedlings to be transplanted later for cropping in December. Successive plantings may be made up to the end of December or early January.

Capsicum (also called peppers)

Capsicums need conditions similar to tomatoes. Red capsicums are ripened green capsicums, but there are also varieties that are yellow or blackish/purple when mature.

Capsicum seed will not germinate in soils below 20°C, and for this reason it is best to buy seedlings, rather than sow seed. Capsicums resent the cold, so seedlings should not be set out in the open before November as they will not grow until the soil has warmed up. Capsicums take three months to mature so there is little opportunity for successive plantings.

A banana capsicum.

Chillies are closely related to capsicums and have the same growing requirements. The degree of hotness varies according to the variety and can be affected by the climate. Hot weather produces hotter chillies, and they also become hotter and sweeter as they ripen.

Carrots

Carrots are one of the most useful crops for the home gardener especially where space is limited. Even a small plot of carrots can yield a substantial quantity over quite a long period. Western Red is one of the best long varieties, Chantenay types are better varieties for shallow soils and there are some good new hybrids.

Carrots need a good soil that has been thoroughly dug to at least 20–25 cm. If the soil is not worked deeply distortions may occur. Avoid green or animal manures or any fertilisers for a few weeks before sowing otherwise forking or hairy roots may develop. Keep fertilisers from coming in contact with carrot roots.

To spread the harvests over a long period sow just a small spring crop in September, followed by a larger crop in November, then the main winter-maturing crop before early January. A sowing in late January will produce a good crop of smaller carrots.

Carrots are best grown from seed, sown in a warm soil where they are to grow. Sow them in rows 30–35 cm apart. Make shallow drills about 1 cm deep and 10–15 cm wide in finely raked soil. Cover the seed with 1 cm of fine soil. With such shallow sowing the surface of the soil dries rapidly, particularly in hot weather, so frequently watering with a fine spray is required for a good rate of germination. After the initial watering when the seed has been sown, cover the sown

area with shade cloth to keep the soil surface damp and reduce the number of waterings each day. Remove the shade cloth as soon as the young seedlings begin to emerge to prevent the small seedlings from becoming spindly.

To grow good carrots plants must be thinned and this can be done in two stages, thinning first to about 3 cm apart as soon as the plants are 5–7.5 cm high and finally to about 6 cm apart. If sown in wide drills as suggested the plants can be staggered in the row thus giving a greater number of plants per row. Thinnings at the second stage can be used as baby carrots. Carrots must be watered regularly to avoid wide fluctuations in soil moisture. If allowed to dry out and then given plenty of water the roots tend to crack.

Cauliflower

For growing requirements see information under the Brassica family heading.

Cauliflowers demand high fertility and good culture. If you give them proper attention and use a mix of the many varieties available you can produce cauliflowers for several months. Snowball is a fast maturing variety for autumn use. Four varieties, Phenomenal Early, Deep Heart, Main Crop and Paleface are good winter varieties, maturing in this order. The very early varieties do not seem to do as well as the later ones in cold climates.

Chinese cabbage

For growing requirements see information under the Brassica family heading.

This plant is like a large Cos lettuce, but with a crisp watery texture and mustard-like taste. It has pale green leaves gradually becoming pale yellow closer to the heart, and long, broad, white ribs. Best sown direct in January or February and grown quickly in very rich soil with ample water at all times. The plants should be thinned to about 30 cm apart. Early spring sowings could be tried, but they tend to bolt to seed from spring plantings.

Cucumbers

For growing requirements see information under the heading Cucurbit family.

Fresh cucumber is a crisp and refreshing salad vegetable. Cucumbers grow and produce fruit quickly in warm weather; the plants also need plenty of water, and should never dry out. A good range of different types of cucumber is available as seedlings, or you can grow them from seed. Cucumbers should be spaced about 1–1.5 m apart each way in clumps of 2 or 3 plants. If using seed, sow several seeds in each 'hill' to ensure that 2 or 3 good plants will result. They are best grown on a trellis or frame to save space and allow air circulation through the bush helping to prevent early fungal attack on the foliage, which retards the crop yield. Gherkins are a type of cucumber grown for pickling. They are grown in exactly the same manner as cucumbers but, for crispness, must be picked regularly when the fruits are only 4–7 cm long.

The Cucurbit family

These are all summer growing vegetables, which need warm conditions for best results. Cucumber, button squash and zucchini can be ready in 8–10 weeks from planting seedlings or sowing seed, while pumpkins, winter squash and melons need a long growing season and can be unsatisfactory in Canberra if the summer is cool and short.

All will do best in a raised circular bed with lots of compost with a bank around the perimeter of the bed. The bank will help retain water right where it is needed. This sort of bed is traditionally called a hill. As a group cucurbits require well-prepared and fertile soil with ample supplies of organic matter. Some people like to grow their cucumbers and pumpkins on a trellis so that the fruit hangs from the vine. This produces long straight cucumbers and protects the fruit from snails and slugs.

Cucurbit seed will not germinate in cold soil and if you want to get the crops started early it is best to sow in pots or in a protected seedbed for later transplanting with the minimum of disturbance to the roots. If sowing direct where the plants are to grow, or planting seedlings, wait until the end of October or even later if the spring weather is cold.

Pests rarely trouble Cucurbits, but at the end of summer they invariably succumb to powdery mildew, especially in wet summers or if they do not have sufficient air circulation and sunlight.

Eggplant

Eggplants are closely related to tomatoes and need much the same climatic conditions and cultural practices. The larger fruiting varieties take longer to mature and are more susceptible to check by cool weather than are tomatoes so they need a warm spot in the garden. Set out seedlings in early November. There are many types and colours available. The fruits are ready when they become highly shiny. Newer varieties may take less time to mature.

Eggplants come in a variety of colours and sizes.

Garlic

Garlic is an easy crop to grow in Canberra and can easily be grown in among other vegetables or ornamental plants.

Garlic is normally planted from March through to September or October. Most do best planted late March or April. They like a good well drained soil but not one with fresh manure. Break into cloves and plant pointy end up a few cm below the ground and 10 cm apart. The garlic is harvested in early to mid summer when it can be dried and stored. There are a number of varieties available and all should grow well in Canberra. Try a few and find the one you like the best.

There are not many problems with garlic other than the occasional attack of aphids in spring or, if it is wet and cold, downy mildew and rot can sometimes occur. Leaving the crop too long in the ground can encourage rotting.

Leeks

Leeks are easily grown and have the advantage over onions of being tolerant to shade. You can grow two crops in Canberra. For the main crop sow seeds or plant seedlings in September for autumn use,

and for a second crop, sow or plant in late December for spring use. A good friable soil, rich in organic matter is needed, with a good dose of lime.

Sow the seed in a seedbed; when the seedlings are 25-30 cm high, dig them out, shorten the leaves and roots leaving a stem at least 20 cm long with short roots about 5 cm long.

To obtain the white fleshy stem at maturity, use a tapered bottle to make vertical holes about 25 cm deep and place the seedling in the hole; drop a small amount of fine soil in the hole to cover the roots. The hole can be left open to give the upper part of the seedling access to sunshine. The hole will eventually fill up with soil when the bed is watered. The holes for the seedling should be 15–20 cm apart on a zigzag pattern in rows. Three such rows in an area half a metre wide and one metre long will grow approximately 25 leeks to maturity.

Lettuce

For good results you must give lettuce the very best conditions in the garden. Keep the plants growing rapidly at all times — they need lots of water. Lettuce is very attractive to slugs and snails; it helps to keep boundaries of garden plots weed free so that snails and slugs are not given a hiding place. Occasionally downy mildew and bacterial rot can occur on lettuce.

There are many varieties of lettuce, different colours, leaf shapes and textures, and with different seasonal preferences. By growing a range of varieties you can be sure of having good lettuce for much of the year. Butterhead and Mignonette are good varieties for spring and autumn use. Oakleaf and Cosmo types will tolerate warm early summer temperatures. Yatesdale is an excellent late spring and early autumn variety while Great Lakes sown during December until mid-January is the best variety to resist the hot weather. Smaller types of lettuce grow well in pots.

Melons (Rockmelons and Watermelons)

For growing requirements see information under the heading Cucurbit family.

Rockmelons take a long time to mature and need hotter, drier weather than is normal in Canberra. Rockmelons should be planted in hills about 1.3 m apart each way. Due to the short growing season only early varieties of cantaloupe or netted skin varieties should be grown and these should occupy the hottest part of the garden for best results. The late casaba types are less satisfactory than the cantaloupe types as they need an even longer growing season.

Watermelons need a long growing season and for home gardens the small-fruited earlier varieties are best. These should be planted in hills 1.75 to 2 m apart each way. In general, watermelons do not mature until autumn.

Onions

Onions grow best in open sunny situations; they do not grow well in shade. The soil should be in good condition for the seedlings as onions are shallow rooted plants.

If using seed the time for sowing is critical—early (white, salad onions) and mid-season varieties should be sown in a seed bed in April until early May; keeping varieties (e.g.

cream gold) should be sown in May until June. Seed sown late will produce a smaller sized crop. The seedlings should be ready for transplanting in late August to September. If using seedlings purchase them in late August to September either in punnets or in bunches wrapped in damp paper. For best results do not plant earlier than August as early planted onions often run to seed.

The seedlings should be planted 5–7 cm apart in the row and the rows 30 cm apart. 'Top and tail' the plants by reducing the length of the stem to about 12 cm and the roots to about 6 cm. The seedlings should not be planted deeply as most of the bulb is formed above ground level. Spread out the roots and just cover with loose soil to prevent blowing over. Seedlings can be planted leaning over, supported by a low ridge (about 2 cm high) along the row on the windward side. They will stand upright within a week or so.

Keep them free from weeds and water regularly. Cultivation should be shallow to avoid root damage. Stop watering as the bulbs approach maturity, which is when the tops turn yellow and some fall over. The bulbs should be harvested before the tops die off altogether - over-mature onions will not keep well. Pull the bulbs, tie them in bunches and hang in a dry well ventilated place to allow them to dry out completely. They can be cleaned of roots, leaves and loose scales, being careful not to strip the bulbs. They are best stored on wire-netting trays or hung up in plenty of ventilation.

Onions are generally free from diseases and pests but in wet or humid years downy mildew can cause some trouble. Crop rotation is the best answer as sprays do not easily control the problem.

Shallots: The shallot or eschallot is closely related to the onion. It is a perennial that seldom produces seed. The bulbs separate during growth into a number of cloves attached to a common base plate. Shallots need similar attention to onions. Divide bulbs into single cloves and plant them about 15 cm apart in rows 25 cm apart in late autumn or early spring. Shallots may be used green as a spring onion or allowed to dry out in the same way as onions.

Parsnips

Parsnips require the same cultural treatment as carrots but, being even deeper rooting, it is more important to have the soil very thoroughly and deeply prepared. The seed takes longer to germinate than carrots and care is needed to keep the surface moist. Seed must be fresh.

As parsnip tops are large and shade other rows try to space rows further apart than you would carrots, or use some method to stop the tops falling over other crops.

Parsnips take a long time to mature and there is little scope for successive sowings. Best results will be achieved from sowing about November–December. When the plants are 5–7 cm high thin the strongest plants to 10–12 cm apart.

Peas

There is no vegetable more delicious than fresh garden peas, but it is not always the easiest crop to grow and it takes a good deal of room to give a substantial yield. A moderately rich soil is desirable and peas will generally do well after a leaf crop that has been heavily manured.

Sow the seed 5 cm deep in cold weather and a little deeper when the soil is warmer, spacing seeds 5–7 cm apart. For the dwarf growing early varieties up to 90 cm is needed between rows. All varieties will be more productive if supported by some form of trellis.

Sugar snap peas and snow peas also are worth growing in Canberra. In both types the pod and peas are eaten, as the pod lacks the stiff parchment-like walls of pod peas. Snow peas have flat pods, whereas the peas of sugar snap peas have grown a little and the pods are plumper and have more snap. Both types need to be picked regularly, as they will grow larger peas like pod peas if left on the vine.

Powdery mildew, a fungal disease, can occur at the end of the season.

Potatoes

Potatoes are easily grown and it is fun to try the gourmet ones and new varieties. Certified seed potatoes are available from garden centres, rural suppliers and the like. You should always use certified seed as an insurance against the spread of virus diseases.

Soil preparation should be deep and thorough. Potatoes may be planted in late August or September so that by the time the plants come up the frosts are over. Further plantings may be made later but maximum yield can be expected from a planting in early December. This is the crop to grow for storage and use in late autumn and winter.

For best results get the seed well in advance of planting time and spread it out in a spot that gets plenty of light but is not in full sunlight. This process, called greening, will result in the seed potatoes becoming quite green and in the development of short sturdy shoots. Greening promotes a good yield. Seed that hasn't been greened will still grow, but doesn't come on as well, or if the seed is left in a bag in the absence of light the shoots will be weak and spindly. Small whole seed, the size of chats is best but large seed potatoes can be cut into chat-sized pieces. Cut the seed potatoes at planting time, ensuring that each piece has at least one good 'eye' on it.

Plant in trenches about 60–75 cm apart placing the seed about 15 cm apart. Early planted potatoes should not be placed deeper than 10 cm from the surface but in hotter weather they can be placed down to 15 cm. Water regularly to maintain steady growth but avoid keeping the soil excessively wet. Mulching the whole potato patch is an excellent way to ensure that tubers are all covered. If exposed to the light the tubers will become green and poisonous and are also exposed to attack by potato moth larvae. Hilling is not essential as it has little if any effect on the yield.

Early sown crops can be used as soon as the tubers are large enough. These tubers are 'new' potatoes, which come from plants that are still green and the skin of the tubers is soft and easily rubbed off. Let the main crop mature completely before digging and generally it is better to leave them in the ground until the frosts have killed the tops.

Potatoes for storage should not be dug when the soil is wet. It is better to let it dry out for a time so that the potatoes will come out as free from soil as possible. Sort out any damaged tubers for use first and store only sound tubers. Potatoes damaged during digging will not keep well. Tubers for storage should always be kept in the cool and dark. Potatoes can also be reliably 'stored' in the ground as long as they are covered well with soil, through the autumn and winter; they will not start to grow again until September.

Pumpkins

For growing requirements see information under the heading Cucurbit family.

Pumpkins and Winter Squash are mostly long trailing plants, and they need to be spaced about 2 m each way in hills of 2 or 3 plants. If meant for storage these fruits should be allowed to fully mature on the plants but must be put under cover before any frosts occur. Pumpkins are ripe when the stalk dries out a little. Harvest with the stalk attached and store in a cool, dry and well-ventilated place. If the skin is damaged at all use these first. Butternut is a most useful variety as it is not as rampant as others but is a very prolific cropper and keeps quite well. Some pumpkins are bush varieties, which grow as a bush without a trailing habit, similar to a zucchini plant. Golden Nugget is a bush variety that produces smallish fruits of good flavour. It is well suited to small gardens and needs a spot of about 1 metre in diameter.

There are sometimes problems in getting the flowers to pollinate because ants get to the pollen first or because temperatures are too high. You can help the plant by hand-pollinating. Pick male flowers, remove the petals and then brush the pollen onto the sigma of the female flowers. Female flowers have a baby fruit at the base of the flower.

Radish

There are small round types, red or red and white in colour and long tapering varieties in white or red. Radish should be grown quickly for the best quality, so they need good rich soil with plenty of organic matter. The varieties of radish generally grown mature very quickly — in about a month from sowing. Quality deteriorates rapidly soon after the roots reach usable size, so a succession of small sowings at short intervals is desirable to maintain supplies. Sow the seed in rows 25–30 cm apart, thinning the seedlings to 5 cm apart. The roots should be eaten as soon as large enough and before they become pithy.

Rhubarb

Rhubarb is extremely hardy and will grow under almost any conditions including partial shade, but for the best results it needs plenty of attention and full sunshine. It is a particularly heavy feeder and should be given an abundance of organic matter and fertiliser. Mulch rich in nutrients would be best for rhubarb.

Rhubarb is a perennial but it is better to establish fresh beds each two or three years as younger, more vigorous plants produce the best stalks. Seedlings are variable; the best and easiest approach is to grow rhubarb from a piece of the crown of a good plant. It doesn't matter whether the stems are red or green, the taste will be the same. Green rhubarb cannot be changed to red.

Crowns should be planted out in late winter or early spring, selecting pieces with good buds from the outer portions of the old crowns. Plant the pieces about 60 cm apart and about 7–8 cm deep. Remove completely all flower stalks as they appear. Mature leaf stalks should be completely removed from the crown by pulling, not cutting, to avoid damage to the crowns and only the leaf stalks should be eaten, as the leaves are poisonous.

Silver Beet

Silver beet, or Swiss chard, is one of the most popular green vegetables. Rainbow chard, with red, yellow or pink ribs is an attractive plant even in places other than the vegetable garden. It is easier to grow than spinach.

Silver beet is not only attractive, it is also delicious and very useful as a plant you can pick continuously. Mature leaves should be removed from the plants regularly even if not required for use. Growth should be promoted at all times by regular watering and an occasional spray on the leaves of liquid manure would be beneficial. Silver beet is very attractive to slugs and snails.

Spinach

The true spinach is a difficult crop to grow except under ideal conditions and is less satisfactory as a home garden vegetable than silver beet. Spinach needs rich soil and will not tolerate acidity. It must be grown quickly but even given every attention the plants are liable to bolt to seed prematurely, particularly from spring sowings. It should be sown where the plants are to grow in rows 40–45 cm apart. You can take care to place seed 20 cm apart when sowing, or scatter it and later thin the plants to 20 cm or so apart. Individual leaves may be picked or you can cut the whole plant below ground level as soon as large enough.

Rainbow Chard, another vegetable that earns a place in an ornamental garden.

Sweet Corn

Sweet corn is characterised by high sugar content while the kernels are still young. The sugar rapidly changes to starch as the cobs mature, so it must be eaten while young, and soon after picking. The new super sweet hybrids are specially worth growing. The best indication of maturing for eating is the browning of the 'silks' at the tip of the cobs. It should be eaten while the kernels are still in the creamy stage. It needs fairly rich soil and can be planted to advantage following a crop such as cabbage, which has been heavily manured and fertilised.

Seedlings can be planted, or, if using seeds sowing may commence as soon as the soil has warmed up in the spring, usually by mid to late October. A succession of small plantings at intervals of 2 or 3 weeks can be made until early January. Sow only a small number at each time so that the cobs can always be used while young. Sow the seed 5–7 cm deep and 25 cm apart, spacing the rows 75 cm apart. Sweet corn is wind pollinated and should be grown in blocks, not in rows. Hill soil around the plants to prevent wind from blowing them over. If you use manure to form these hills the plants will make roots from the stems and grow stronger from the extra nutrients they take in. Aphids and corn earworms (Heliothis caterpillars) may feed in the tips of the cobs.

Tomatoes

Tomatoes like deeply worked and well-prepared soil so start preparing for the crop well in advance of planting. Oversupply of fertilisers, particularly if they contain a high proportion of nitrogen, during the early stages of growth will promote heavy plant development but delay fruiting. It is therefore better to be sparing with fertiliser until the plants have set fruit on the first two clusters.

A heritage tomato.

You may raise your own plants or purchase them from garden stores. If you want an early crop, sow seed of an early maturing variety (Apollo is a reliable one) early in September in a seed box or in a seedbed. Some protection will be necessary against the low night temperatures at that time. Wait until the end of October before planting out the seedlings. The common varieties are very susceptible to cold weather, and the most frequent cause of disappointment is planting too early. In cold weather the plants make very slow growth even if given protection at night; and unless the season is unusually warm, planting out into the open is not worthwhile much before early November.

Varieties with compact growth are very good in pots, or in the garden bed without stakes. The taller varieties do require staking otherwise the fruit lies on the ground and becomes hidden by the leaves and is prone to slug attack and rotting. Also, on stakes the plant will produce more fruit per area and better quality fruit. If more than one row is to be planted allow 90cm between the rows. The plants can be put in the ground 5–7 cm deeper than they were in the seedbeds as new roots will develop from the stem and give a stronger plant. Give the plants a good watering when they are put out but water subsequently only as frequently as is necessary to keep growth proceeding at a steady pace. Don't be too generous with water and fertiliser in the early stages, as this will only delay flowering and the setting of the fruit.

Once the plants commence to crop and particularly in hot weather, it is essential to maintain adequate and even moisture in the soil for growth and to avoid blossom end rot. As the plants grow they will develop lateral shoots where each leaf joins the stem. Some gardeners like to remove these lateral shoots leaving only the main terminal shoot to grow, but this reduces the yield. The plants should be tied to the stakes every 30 cm or so as they grow, or use the cylindrical wire cages that can be constructed of heavy gauge 10 x 10 cm wire mesh (also called tomato wire). As the weather becomes hotter tomatoes grow very rapidly and it will be necessary to attend to pruning out the laterals (if you choose to) and the tying up at least weekly. It may, however, be advisable to remove some of the lateral shoots to keep the plants manageable. A second crop of tomatoes can be planted in December–January to give a crop of tomatoes in autumn as the yield from spring plantings diminishes.

Do not allow fruit to overripen on the bush attracting fruit fly and other insects. Allowing the fruit to finish ripening indoors will increase the keeping quality without affecting the flavour. At the end of the season, as the first frosts approach, you can gradually ripen the remaining crop by pulling up the entire plant and hanging it upside down in the garage.

Diseases that affect tomatoes are blossom end rot, spotted wilt and big bud. To help avoid blossom end rot water regularly,

avoid waterlogging and protect plants from hot dry winds. Pests of tomatoes are the tomato caterpillar and green vegetable bugs. Tomatoes can also be affected by fruit cracking, which occurs during periods of fast growth when temperatures are high and there is plenty of soil moisture. If you think it is necessary, a tomato dust or spray will control most tomato pests and diseases.

Turnips

White turnips grow much more rapidly than swedes, but lose quality quickly after maturity and should be eaten while young. White turnips are sown in rows 30 cm apart; they germinate well and should be thinned to 10 cm in the row. They are best grown in late February to late March to mature in winter. They can be grown as small crops throughout the spring, summer and autumn.

Sow swedes in summer in rows 30 cm apart and about 1–2 cm deep. When the plants are established thin to 10–15 cm. While they are subject to the same pests as the others in the Brassica family, the pests are not of the same concern for a root crop.

Zucchini

For growing requirements see information under the heading Cucurbit family.

Zucchini is a versatile vegetable with a delicate, unassuming flavour. It is basically an immature marrow, and if left on the bush it will grow into a marrow. Several different types of zucchinis are available as seedlings (green, yellow, Lebanese), or you can grow them from seed. Zucchinis should be grown on 'hills' and spaced about 1 m apart each way. If using seed, sow a few seeds in each 'hill' to ensure that one good plant will result. Zucchinis require an open sunny spot, as air circulation is important in maintaining a healthy bush. Zucchinis produce prolifically and the fruit matures quickly; the more fruit you cut the more the plant produces. Late in the summer spring-planted zucchinis invariably succumb to powdery mildew. To maintain a supply of zucchini well into autumn grow a second plant or two in January.

Planting and harvesting calendar for vegetables

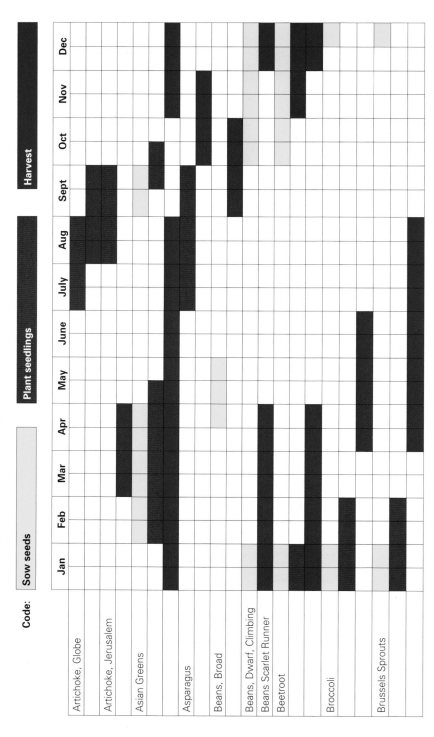

Planting and harvesting calendar for vegetables

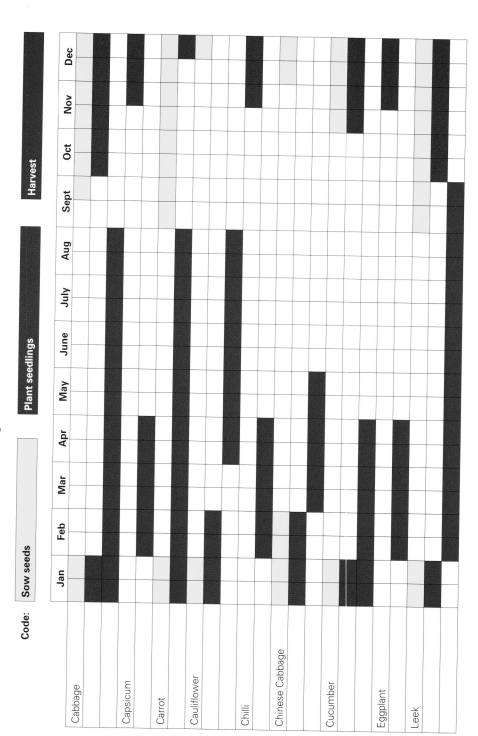

Planting and harvesting calendar for vegetables

Code: | Sow seeds | Plant seedlings | Harvest

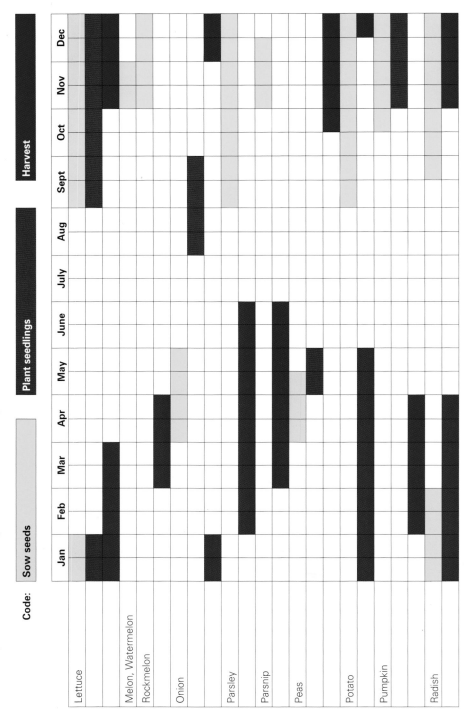

	Jan	Feb	Mar	Apr	May	June	July	Aug	Sept	Oct	Nov	Dec
Lettuce												
Melon, Watermelon												
Rockmelon												
Onion												
Parsley												
Parsnip												
Peas												
Potato												
Pumpkin												
Radish												

Planting and harvesting calendar for vegetables

Code: Sow seeds   Plant seedlings   Harvest

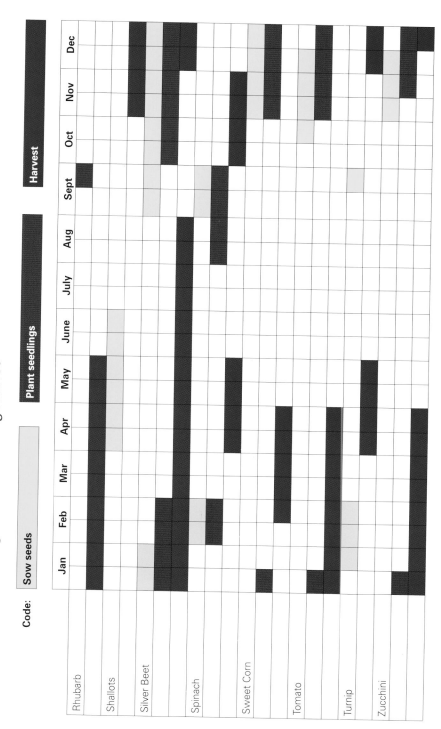

A corner in a highly productive North Canberra vegetable garden.

CHAPTER 23: Herbs

Jane Lindsay, revised by Chris Ryan

Herbs have a long and fascinating history of use in medicinal, cosmetic and household applications, and are a source of a number of modern drugs. Some are added to modern cosmetics and shampoos. Herbs are usually grown in the home garden for culinary use, as companion plants or for their decorative value. This chapter deals only with culinary herbs.

Many plants can be described as dual purpose, for example the onion could be described as a herb and as a vegetable. Some of these plants are covered elsewhere in this book.

Herbs are easy plants to grow; most require little in the way of maintenance, feeding and water. Even the smallest garden or balcony can be home to a good range of herbs, provided the position is sunny and the soil or potting mix is very well-drained.

Traditional formal herb gardens, plantings in rockeries, between pavers and even in the flower garden, as well as in containers, are excellent ways to add herbs to the garden. A container planted with a range of herbs for the cook can be situated on a deck or near an entrance close to the kitchen.

Herbs can be dried for later use. For this purpose they should be picked before the plants flower, preferably early in the morning in the hotter weather, and in a period of low humidity. They can be dried in a low temperature oven, a microwave oven on its lowest setting, a dehydrator or just hung upside-down in a well-ventilated

Like many of the herbs, thyme makes a really attractive feature plant.

place under cover. Spread the herbs thinly on trays to allow air to circulate freely. Keep temperatures below 30^c if possible. When dry, the leaves are removed and stored in containers with tightly fitting lids. Parsley and basil are probably best chopped and stored frozen in ice cubes for later use.

Some useful herbs

For ease of reference the following herbs are listed alphabetically by common name, with the botanical name in brackets.

Angelica (*Angelica archangelica*). Biennial or perennial. 1.5–2 m. Young stems can be stewed with rhubarb or candied for cake decoration. Sow seed in spring.

Anise (*Pimpinella anisum*). Annual. 45 cm. Fresh leaves are used in salads, liquorice-flavoured seeds used in soups, vegetable curries, cakes. Also used in medicines and liqueurs. Sow seed in spring, thin to 30 cm apart.

This formal herb garden was planted by members of the Horticultural Society in the grounds attached to the School of Horticulture's former campus at Weston Creek.

Basil (*Ocimum basilicum*). Annual, needs ample moisture to grow well. Not frost hardy. 15–50 cm, depending on the plant. There are many cultivars, all having aromatic leaves which can be used fresh or dried to flavour fish, meat, soups, eggs and salads, pesto and vinegar. Bush basil is a dwarf variety suitable for pots (*O. b. minimum*). There is also a perennial variety, sacred basil (*O. b. sanctum*) growing to 70 cm, used in salads and cold dishes. All prefer a sunny position. Sow seeds in spring, thin to 15 cm apart. Tip prune regularly to keep plant bushy and to delay flowering. Grows well in pots.

Bay, Sweet or Bay Laurel (*Laurus nobilis*). An evergreen tree which needs protection when young. Grow in a container to control size or clip to shape in a formal garden. Bay leaves may be used fresh or dried to flavour fish, game, soups and sauces. An excellent foliage plant for use in floral art and for inclusion in posies.

Bergamot (*Monarda didyma*). Perennial, Needs ample moisture and good soil to grow well. To 60 cm. It is an essential ingredient of Earl Grey tea and has attractive scarlet flowers. Prefers partial shade.

Bergamot, lemon (*Monarda citriodora*) Annual. 50–70 cm. Young leaves are used for tea or gourmet dishes, especially fish. Also useful garden plant with attractive, scented white, pink or purplish flowers. Will thrive in partial shade.

Borage (*Borago officinalis*) Annual. 30 cm. the blue flowers are used to garnish soft drinks or as a decoration. The leaves have a light cucumber flavour. Sunny dry position. Very attractive to bees. Sow seeds in spring and thin to 15 cm apart.

Herbs growing happily together with flowers and vegetables in a Canberra garden.

Caraway (*Carum carvi*) Biennial. 30–70 cm. Grown mainly for its seeds, which are used in cakes, breads and many vegetable dishes. Young leaves may be used for salads and cheese recipes. Roots are edible. If seed is left to fall it can create a weed problem. Sow seeds in spring or autumn.

Chamomile, Roman (*Chamaemelum nobile* syn. *Anthemis nobilis)*). Perennial. 30 cm. An aromatic spreading plant that can be used for herb tea or a hair rinse. There is also a more erect form, German chamomile.

Chervil (*Anthriscus cerefolium*). Annual. 45 cm. Aniseed-flavoured leaves are used in French cuisine, especially salads. Prefers a shady position and does not transplant well, so sow in permanent position. Seeds germinate quickly. Thin to about 30 cm apart. Ready to harvest in 6–8 weeks. The French blend of Fines Herbes, includes parsley, chervil, chives and tarragon.

Chives (*Allium schoenoprasum*). Perennial. 15 cm. Onion-flavoured leaves used to flavour soups, salads, eggs, potatoes, meat etc. Cut young leaves as required. Sow seed in early spring or divide existing clumps. Grow 15 cm apart.

Chives, Garlic (*Allium tuberosum*). Perennial. 20cm. Flat garlic flavoured foliage. Adds subtle garlic flavour to oriental dishes, soups, stir-frys and egg dishes. Propagate by division. Can become a dreadful weed.

Coriander (*Coriandrum sativum*). Annual. 60 cm. Mainly grown for seeds, which are used in sauces, soups, curries, cakes and breads. Leaves also are used in continental and Indian dishes. Sunny position. Seeds are sown in spring 6 cm deep in rows 30 cm apart. Runs to seed quickly in warm weather.

Dill (*Anethum graveolens*). Annual. 60–80 cm. Sow seeds in spring. Leaves are used in continental dishes and as a garnish. Known as the fish herb, it is lovely with salmon. Seeds are used in pickles, sauces and vinegar. Seedlings can become a nuisance. Will cross-pollinate with fennel and angelica.

Fennel, Sweet (*Foeniculum vulgare*). Perennial. 100 cm. Strong resemblance to dill, but with aniseed flavoured leaves which are used in salads, sauces and meat dishes. Will cross pollinate with dill and angelica. Florence fennel (*F. v. var. azoricum*), also called finocchio, is grown mainly for its swollen leaf base which can be steamed or used in salads. Red fennel is a good ornamental dark red foliage plant in the herb garden.

Garlic (*Allium sativum*) Perennial. Widely used in soups, curries and meat dishes. Harvest when leaves die down and hang up to dry. Cloves are planted in autumn or early winter 8 cm apart in rows 30 cm apart.

Lavender. Perennial grown for its culinary and cosmetic flavourings. A range of cultivars is discussed in the Annuals and Perennials Chapter.

Lemon Balm (*Melissa officinalis*). Perennial. 60 cm. Lemon scented leaves used in soups, fish and meat dishes, cold drinks, herb tea. Sunny position. Very attractive to bees. Also known as Bee Balm. Sow seed in spring, thin to 30 cm apart. Will self-seed.

Lemon Grass (*Cymbopogon citratus*). Perennial. 100–150 cm. A tropical grass which, though initially frost-tender, will grow in Canberra near a sunny wall. Fresh leaves are used in curries, or to make a tea. Fleshy base of leaves can be used in stir fries. Cut to ground level in late winter. Propagate by division.

Many of the culinary herbs are very well suited to growing in pots and so they can be kept in even the smallest garden.

Lemon Verbena (*Aloysia triphylla* syn. *A. citriodora*). A hardy deciduous lemon-scented shrub growing to between 1.5 and 2 m with pale mauve flower spikes in late summer. Its leaves have the fragrance of lemon sherbert and make a refreshing tea. It can also be used for sachets and pot pourri as its dried leaves retain their scent for several years.

Lovage (*Levisticum officinale*). Perennial. 100–150 cm. Fresh leaves are used in salads, meat and fish dishes. Dried leaves are used in soups, sauces, casseroles etc. Can also be used to make a savoury tea. Dies down each year and shoots again in spring. Also known as Maggi herb.

Marjoram, Sweet (*Origanum majorana*). Perennial. 40–60 cm. A very versatile herb, its leaves can be used fresh or dried for many dishes. For drying, cut before flowers appear. Seed is sown in spring. The golden form is a good ground cover for the rose bed.

Mint, Common (*Mentha cordifolia* syn. *M. officinalis*). Perennial. 30 cm. Fresh leaves are used to flavour drinks, potatoes, peas and for mint sauce. There are many other mints of the species used for flavouring,

You can grow quite a range of attractive peppers. It is best to buy them with the first fruit showing as Canberra's summer is too short otherwise to do them justice.

such as spearmint, peppermint, ginger mint, apple mint etc. Korean mint (*Agastache rugosa*), used to make an aromatic tea, and Vietnamese mint (*Persicaria odoratum*), used sparingly in salads, rice and meat dishes, are not the same species as the common mint, though all are vigorous creeping plants and have the potential to be invasive. They are best grown in a tub or large pot.

Nasturtium. (*Tropaelum majus*) Annual. Leaves and flowers add peppery flavour to salads, sandwiches and garnishes. Used to flavour butters, cream cheese and vinegar. Sow seed in early spring. Good summer ground cover or in pots.

Oregano (*Origanum vulgare*). Perennial. 30–50 cm. Another widely used versatile herb. Leaves are used fresh or dried in many Mediterranean dishes. Also known as wild marjoram. Propagated in spring or autumn from seed or division.

Parsley (*Petroselinum crispum*) Biennial. 20 cm. Best treated as an annual, as leaves become coarse in the second year; can be left to self-seed. Seed can take up to 6 weeks to germinate. Pick regularly to encourage a good supply of fresh young leaves. Very popular herb with fine tightly curled leaves, frequently used as garnish, also in salads, egg dishes, casseroles etc. Other varieties include Italian parsley (*P. c.* 'Neapolitanum'), with flat leaves and a stronger flavour, and Hamburg parsley (*P. c. var. tuberosum*), which has an edible tuberous root. Sow seed or plant out seedlings in early spring.

Rosemary (*Rosmarinus officinalis*). Perennial. 100 cm. Hardy evergreen bush with aromatic leaves and small lilac to purple flowers. Leaves are used fresh or dried to flavour soups, vegetables, meat and fish. There is also a prostrate form. Normally propagated from cuttings in autumn, but can be grown from seed.

Sage (*Salvia officinalis*). Perennial. 45–60 cm. Pinch out tips to encourage bushy growth. Leaves are used fresh or dried in seasonings, meat and poultry dishes. Propagated from spring-sown seed or from cuttings or divisions.

Salad Burnet (*Sanguisorba minor*). Perennial. 25 cm. Slight hint of cucumber flavour. Use only young leaves in salads, dressings and herb vinegar.

Savory, Summer (*Satureja hortensis*). Annual. 30 cm. Sweet flavour, used in meat dishes, poultry seasoning, eggs, salads and vegetables, particularly beans. Easily grown from seed; plant 25 cm apart in a sunny position.

Savory, Winter (*Satureja montana*) Perennial. 45 cm. An attractive cushion of fine green leaves with small white flowers; evergreen in sheltered locations. Uses are as for summer savory. Grow from seed, cutting or division.

Tarragon, French (*Artemisia dracunculus*). Perennial. 50 cm. Leaves are used in salads, fish, chicken and egg dishes, and to flavour vinegar. Withstands dry conditions. Spreading plant with underground runners, propagated from seed, cutting or root division.

Thyme (*Thymus vulgaris*). Perennial. 15 cm. Leaves can be used fresh or dried in a multitude of dishes. There are a large number of variants on common thyme with flavours such as lemon or caraway; some have variegated leaves, and all can be used for culinary purposes. Grown from seed or division.

CHAPTER 24: Fruit, nuts and berries

Phillip Unger

A wide range of fruit can be grown successfully in this district. While we cannot grow everything we find in our fruit markets, our cold climate is ideal for a good range of apples, pears, stone and other fruit varieties. Citrus fruits thrive in a warmer climate but, with a little care, you can still enjoy a bountiful crop from a number of citrus trees.

Experiencing the sheer pleasure of growing fresh, flavoursome and crisp fruit can be a great pleasure and can outweigh any effort you need to make in protecting your crop from pests and disease.

For some gardeners, growing varieties that are not readily available in the markets will be an attraction (for example, a Victorian apple tree specialist nursery lists 143 different eating and cooking apples) and the satisfaction gleaned from being able to point to the results of your own efforts is a reward in itself.

In our climate, though it's not possible to be totally self-sufficient, much of a family's fruit (and vegetable) requirements can be produced on a small suburban block. A significant quantity of fruit can be produced from a small area, and often the same plants will double as ornamentals. With good storage and/or preservation you can enjoy home-grown fruit or fruit products most of the year. It is also possible to enjoy a chemical-free garden by using an integrated organic approach to growing fruit. There are many physical and cultural controls which will assist in the production of good crops so

Feijoa flowers can be cut and used indoors. They make a great Christmas decoration in a float bowl.

look around and see what others do. Using chemicals can be a quick option, but another very satisfying option is to be able to produce good clean fruit without pesticides and it can, most certainly, be done.

Before choosing your trees there are a few things to think about. To produce healthy good quality fruit, you will need time, effort and the right cultivars.

For small gardens, it's important to select carefully, choosing smaller cultivars, or those grown on dwarfing stock, as they will fit better and in many cases, are far easier to prune and maintain. If you want quality peaches, nectarines and apricots it's going to take a little more time and effort, so as you can see, there are some choices to be made before you begin planting.

Some fruits will only produce well if the pollen of another compatible variety or cultivar, flowering at the same time, pollinates their flowers. If you are lucky, a neighbour will have a similar tree flowering at the same time, reasonably close to yours. To save space, some gardeners grow multi-graft trees, having two or more compatible cultivars grafted on to the one rootstock; and some plant complementary cultivars in the same hole.

The list later in the chapter indicates where cross-pollination is necessary.

Fruit tree rootstocks

Most fruit trees are grafted and comprise two distinct parts, rootstock and scion. The rootstock is the underground part of the tree while the scion or variety is the above ground portion.

When buying fruit trees it is most important to check the rootstock of the chosen variety as it is infinitely easier to control the growth and maintenance of a tree on a dwarf or semi-dwarfing rootstock in the home garden.

The reasons for using a rootstock are varied but primarily it is to control the tree's size, and as well to provide resistance against pests and diseases, drought and cold, and to assist the tree to cope with different soil types and

A specially designed 'fruit sock' has been fitted over this apple at an early stage and the fruit is now ripening perfectly, the sock expanding with the fruit.

the effects of waterlogging. For example, Northern Spy, an American rootstock is used extensively here and in New Zealand for its woolly aphid resistance and reliability on poor soils.

Using differing varieties on the same rootstock can result in quite different tree growth. For example 'Jonathan' apple grows with increased vigour on the rootstock Malling 7 as opposed to 'Granny Smith' and this phenomenon is not unusual in a rootstock-scion combination even with identical soil and cultural practices.

Pear trees are usually budded or grafted onto *Pyrus calleryana* but this is a very vigorous rootstock and it is difficult to control tree size. One way of dealing with size is to train the pear tree as an espalier against a wall or on a framework of wires supported by timber posts set in concrete. Even then the tree requires summer pruning as well as the usual winter pruning to keep it manageable. A better alternative is to choose a pear on quince rootstock such as Quince A or Quince C. Pear trees on these rootstocks may have to be purchased from a specialist grower and are usually advertised in trade magazines. It may be possible to order them from a local nursery a few months before their winter stock is delivered.

Citrus trees are also budded on rootstocks which will influence the size of the tree, disease resistance, and suitability for changes in soil and locations within Australia.

Trifoliata is a cold hardy rootstock suitable for most Citrus varieties except Eureka lemon. Citronelle (Rough Lemon) can be used for Eureka and will give a vigorous tree in most soils.

Citrange (Sweet orange x trifoliata) is the preferred rootstock for oranges and mandarins. It can also be used for Grapefruit and other lemons with the exception of Eureka.

There is a growing choice of small or dwarf fruit trees, especially suited to pot culture and for patio gardens. Local garden centres carry a few of these but you could also look at the selections offered by

» Daley's Fruit Tree Nursery, PO Box 154, Kyogle, NSW 2474 (02) 6632 1441 www.daleysfruit.com.au

» Diggers (03) 5984 7900 www.diggers.com.au

» Flemings Nurseries www.flemings.com.au

» Kendall Farms (07) 4779 1189 www.kendallfarms.com.au

» Woodbridge Fruit Trees (02) 6267 4430, www.woodbridgefruittrees.com.au

Daley's and Kendall Farms are in warmer climes than Canberra but both carry fruits which will do well here.

Pest and Disease Control

Hygiene is particularly important to counteract pests and disease. Decaying fruit and fallen leaves should be collected and placed in the bin, rather than composted. A winter cleanup beneath the trees is essential and the bare soil should be thoroughly sprayed when the trees themselves are sprayed.

If you keep poultry, it's a good idea to let them forage amongst your fruit trees for they will very effectively rid you of fruit fly and codling moth larvae. Next, a proprietary spray of a copper fungicide or lime sulphur during winter will help deal with fungal diseases during the growing season.

www.Greenharvest.com.au is a source of yellow sticky adhesive wrap which can be applied to tree stems as an effective method of trapping moths. This can be done from December to May, but remove the wrap periodically and burn it. Alternatively, corrugated cardboard can be wrapped around the trunk and main branches. Older trees with rough bark provide a refuge for pupating grubs so remove any loose bark. Orchardists use pheromone lures.

Spraying of fruit trees during the growing season is obviously a personal choice. Neglected trees in nearby gardens can be a constant source of infection of codling moth on apples and the increasing population of fruit fly on fruit and vegetables is a worrying trend. Both of these pests are appearing earlier in the season with more generations as a result. The loquat (Eriobotrya) is the prime suspect for the latter's increase as it flowers in mid winter and is the first fruit of the season. The main diseases of fruit trees continue to be brown rot and leaf curl on stone fruit while black spot and mildew can devastate susceptible varieties of fruit trees.

Suggestions for the control of pests and diseases are included with the discussion of specific crops. The possible problems and their control are discussed more fully in Chapter 28.

Nets and cages

Perhaps the most useful all round protection for your fruit will be provided by nets or cages which will keep out birds, possums and insects. There are quite a few ways of doing

It is not hard to net a fruit tree. This tree is netted each year by one small woman, without assistance.

this, ranging from protection of individual fruit to the erection of cages to enclose whole groups of trees. All of these approaches will be much easier if you have chosen to grow smaller trees and have pruned them to keep the fruiting branches manageable.

Individual fruit can be protected from insects and perhaps other pests by enclosing them in a bag. There are products designed especially for this such as shown in the earlier photo of an apple. You can also net selected branches of a tree, or enclose ripening grapes in paper bags.

Another common approach is to net a whole tree. This can be hard work if the tree is large. Nets will usually keep out smaller birds and possums. There are recent reports of fruit bats being caught in the nets; and cockatoos seem to be able to break through. Summer

pruning of excessive shoot growth should be done when the fruit begins to ripen as netting can be more easily erected over the tree to deter marauding birds.

At the more elaborate end of the scale you can erect a permanent cage, using bird wire for the sides and top, and including a door.

Choices for Canberra

In the following pages, the fruits, nuts and berries commonly grown in Canberra are listed, with their maintenance needs and any special care. Pruning is a major part of maintenance, so later in the chapter, general advice is provided on the principles of pruning. At the end of the chapter is a table telling you when you might expect to pick your crops. With a few exceptions the popular fruits are deciduous.

Fruits

With fruit trees we include three vine crops — grapes, Kiwifruit and passionfruit.

Apples (*Malus domestica*)

Apples are one of the most popular fruits and grow well in this district as most varieties have a high winter chilling requirement. They are long-lived trees and like pears, they flower late (late September–mid October), so are less prone to late frost damage in spring than stone fruit. They will grow on a wide variety of soils including heavier clay soils, but like most fruit will not take prolonged waterlogging.

If you want, you can have apples for a variety of uses (fresh, bottled, dried, frozen, juice, cider, jelly, jam, vinegar etc). Apples can be harvested and stored for long periods. Late maturing varieties such as 'Granny Smith' will keep for up to six months in a cool place.

They make attractive spring-flowering trees and are good for espalier and cordon training. There is a range of dwarfing rootstocks which will limit the ultimate size of the plant while not affecting fruit size and quality. Popular varieties grafted onto these are available through nurseries so that even in a very small garden it is possible to have one or more apple trees.

There are countless named cultivars and new cultivars each year. The home gardener can choose from catalogues for most needs and the more unusual cultivars can be located through specialist nurseries.

The Ballerina range of dwarf apples, growing from 1–3 m tall, are useful plants for smaller gardens, as feature plants in pots, and along borders or fences. Fruit is produced on spurs close to the main stem and they normally don't require much pruning.

Golden Delicious apples.

By using a mix of cultivars you can vary ripening times through summer and autumn see list on next page.

Some points to keep in mind:

1. Probably the single most important problem is codling moth. You cannot grow unblemished apples without controlling this pest. There are a number of organic controls, including horticultural oils to smother the moth eggs. Dipel, containing *Bacillus thuringiensis* (Bt), is an organic bacterial control for caterpillars. Timing of application is important for, once the caterpillars are inside the fruit, control is difficult. Combining 1% pest oil with Bt is helpful.

2. Two other possible pests are Woolly aphid (you can spot spray small infestations) and Queensland Fruit Fly. When you find the fly it is too late to control it but be sure to collect all fallen fruit and destroy the pest by securing the fruit in a plastic bag in the sun for three days.

3. Apples may get black spot and powdery mildew. They are not a great problem and there is not much you can do.

Examples	Approx ripening	
'Gravenstein'	February	Very old variety, big tree.
'Cox's Orange Pippin'	March	A famous English variety
'Fuji' 'Gala' 'Lady William' 'Pink Lady' 'Jonathan'	March	Aromatic, popular but can get powdery mildew
'Snow Apple' ('Pomme de Neige')	March	Small red, ideal children's apple. White flesh.
'Spartan'	March	Red similar to 'Jonathan' but more resistant to powdery mildew
'Bonza'	March	Similar to 'Jonathan' in appearance, good keeping qualities
'Delicious', various strains 'Early', 'Starkcrimson'	Early April	Attractive eating apples. Some varieties do not keep well and go 'floury' very quickly.
'Golden Delicious'	Early April	Popular yellow crisp apple when fresh
'Rome Beauty'	April	Red striped, excellent keeper, heavy cropper
'Granny Smith'	April/May	Green, vigorous tree. Heavy cropper. Wide range of uses.

4. For good fruit set cross-pollination is required. Crab apples may serve as pollinators.

5. Apples are alternate bearing trees. One year will see a heavy crop, the next year less. Pruning lightly after a heavy crop and slightly harder after a light crop and early thinning of excess fruit (just remove some of the small fruit) in the spring when there is a heavy fruit set can help reduce this.

6. Apples grow to be large long-lived trees. Espalier training or purchasing trees on dwarf root stocks is worth considering where space is limited.

To prune your apple tree, begin by thinning out excess new wood (ie, completely remove some shoots if there are too many packed into an area) rather than removing older wood with spurs. Spurs are where most of the fruit forms on apple trees. Shorten branches going too far where you do not want them, such as into adjacent trees, over a path or driveway. Leave uncut if not in the way, any horizontal or arching branches approaching the horizontal, especially if these have spurs on them.

Spurs may last twenty or so years. If too crowded, then carefully remove some. Some trees such as 'Jonathon' and 'Golden Delicious' also produce fruit at the end of the growing shoot so do not shorten or tip the ends of branches for cosmetic reasons.

Apricots (*Prunus armeniaca*)

Apricots are one of the most popular stone fruit. The trees grow well, ultimately to a large size and are long-lived compared to peaches and nectarines. They are self-pollinating. The special pleasure of eating an apricot fresh off the tree can easily make up for the extra care you must give to get a good crop of apricots.

Apricots prefer a warm dry growing period and mature from December to January. Fruit on any one tree can ripen over a period of about two weeks. They prefer sandy to clay loams (lighter than for apples and pears), with good drainage.

Some varieties, all of which ripen in January, are 'Tilton' and 'Trevatt' about the same time, 'Moorpark' a week or so later.

'Tilton': Large good quality fruit with a good flavour

'Trevatt': Excellent quality fruit. A heavy bearer in a good season, strong growing tree. Prone to biennial bearing.

'Moorpark' (& 'Early Moorpark'); Orange with red blush, rich and juicy, excellent fresh and for drying. Fruit ripens unevenly. Fruit will often show some green colour even when ripe.

These are old varieties and for the home gardener are better than most produced by commercial growers.

Points to keep in mind:

1. Apricots are prone to bacterial canker or gummosis. Infected young trees and severely infected older trees should be removed. Where the disease is only slight on older trees. Don't prune in winter. Dip secateurs between each cut and between trees in 70% methylated spirits. Copper sprays in winter will provide some control.

2. Ripening fruit may be affected by brown rot. Remove and destroy all mummified fruit and infected shoots during winter pruning. Thin heavy crops and collect all fallen and infected fruit on the tree every 3–7 days during summer and autumn. Destroy fruit by securing in a plastic bag

and exposing to the sun for 3–4 days. Control of dried fruit beetles and oriental fruit moth is important for brown rot control.

3. Oriental fruit moth can cause the tips of shoots to wilt and later to die back. Fruit are also attacked, often where the fruit touches a leaf or small stem. Brown excreta and gum is seen if the fruit is green. Infested maturing fruits are very susceptible to brown rot. As a start to control, avoid lush growth due to hard pruning, over-fertilisation and overwatering. Cut off infested shoot tips where practical. Remove loose or rough bark which provides shelter for cocoons. Collect infested fruit every few days and destroy by securing in a plastic bag and exposing to the sun for 3-4 days.

4. Apricots flower in September and late frosts seem to do more damage and reduce yield in many years than is the case for most other stone fruits.

5. Like most stone fruit apricots will split if wet weather occurs at harvest time.

Apricot spurs remain fruitful for three or four years. Prune to conserve new wood (ie previous season's) where possible and eliminate wood with spent spurs or few buds on it. Try to reduce the volume of barren wood toward the centre of the tree. Where possible keep the straight shoots that have buds and shoots.

Cherries

There are two common types: sweet cherries (*Prunus avium*) and sour cherries (*Prunus cerasus*). Both grow well in this district. Because they mature in November to December sweet cherries are popular, providing fresh fruit when there is little else. Sour cherries mature December into early January.

The sweet cherry is most commonly grown and is luxurious. They can be preserved as well. The tree will grow quite large when mature and is long lived. There are a dozen or so varieties available to Canberra gardeners.

Sweet cherries require cross-pollination. A suitable variety not only needs to have an overlapping flowering period but needs to be compatible with the variety for which it is to be the pollenizer. The variety 'Stella' is self-pollinating. Otherwise, two plants will be required or a multi-grafted tree. Double and triple grafted trees are available. Some Sweet Cherry varieties: 'Bedford', 'Black Boy', 'Burgsdorf', 'Moss Early', 'Napoleon', 'Ron's Seedling' and 'St Margaret'.

Sour cherries can be used for dessert purposes if fully ripe but are particularly useful for jam-making, pie fillings, preserves and cherry wines. They are too tart for most palates to eat as fresh fruit. Two common varieties are 'Montmorency' and 'Morello'.

Sour cherries have the advantage of cropping at an earlier age, are small trees and so better suited to most home gardens and do not require a pollinator. The fruit are less prone to wet weather cracking and the trees seem less affected by bacterial canker. They have a slightly longer chilling requirement and will tolerate a colder climate.

Tolerance to adverse soil conditions depends on the rootstock used but like most stone fruit cherries do not tolerate waterlogged soil. Sour cherries seem to survive better in poorer soils.

Sour cherries are pruned similarly to peaches. With sweet cherries little pruning is required in established trees. Most fruit is produced on spurs that last some years. Summer pruning of shoots heading the wrong way is often sufficient for a number of years.

Some other points to keep in mind:

1. Netting part or whole of the tree is vital to save fruit from the birds.

2. Sweet cherries are prone to bacterial canker or 'gummosis' disease. Other than initial pruning for training or shaping, try to avoid pruning. When pruning is required do not do it in winter. Keep secateurs clean and if in doubt, dip in 70 percent methylated spirits between cuts. Summer pruning of unwanted growth will mean much less dormant-season pruning of hard wood.

3. Aphids are sometimes a problem. Ladybird beetles, which are active predators of cherry aphids, may provide some control. On a small tree spot spraying may help (not too close to harvest). Borers are an occasional problem. Scrape away the webbing and probe into the tunnels with wire to destroy the caterpillars.

4. The other main problem is Pear and Cherry Slug. Small, slimy dark larvae up to 12mm long skeletonise leaves. Severely affected leaves turn brown, shrivel and fall. Trees may look scorched. On small trees larvae may be squashed by hand. Garden dusts and sprays are available for controlling this pest on trees less than 3 m high.

5. Take care in harvesting. Rough picking easily damages the spurs, which should produce fruit for a number of years.

Citrus — Calamondin, Lemon, Lime, Grapefruit and Kumquat

The most commonly planted citrus are lemons, especially 'Meyer', which is cold hardy but less acid than 'Eureka' or 'Lisbon', both of which are excellent but more frost-tender. Most citrus show some signs of cold damage by the end of winter. Leave yellowed foliage intact until the tree is actively growing in spring, and prune off affected foliage.

'Meyer' lemons are smaller trees and make good tub specimens. They mature in late autumn and if picked and stored, will supply lemons for many months. 'Eureka' and 'Lisbon' lemons will grow and produce good crops if they are planted in a protected spot and if necessary given some cover during the winter months.

Kumquat and calamondin are small, attractive trees grown mainly for their ornamental value (excellent tubbed specimens) and their attractive bitter fruit which make excellent marmalade and preserves.

In grapefruit the variety 'Wheeny' appears to be more cold-tolerant than the popular 'Marshes Seedless'.

Oranges and mandarins can be grown in Canberra. They produce attractive but mostly inferior-flavoured fruit.

Dwarf citrus trees, ideal for either small gardens or pots, are now available. These are exactly the same as the larger trees, but are controlled by a dwarfing rootstock called 'Flying Dragons' and will grow to about half the size of the big trees. Those which will grow locally are Meyer 'Lots a' Lemons', dwarf mandarin 'Emperor', dwarf lime 'Sublime', and Tahitian lime.

Most citrus plants are from warm-temperate

Meyer lemons bear well in Canberra and will have fruit on the tree all year round.

to sub-tropical climates with high rainfall so think carefully about where you grow these plants. Generally they should be planted in a warm protected location, eg a north-facing wall or in a tub that can be placed under the eaves of the house or on a protected deck. It is likely that some of the leaves will be burnt by winter frosts but don't worry. Leave the affected leaves to protect others beneath and then trim them off in spring.

All citrus prefer a free draining sandy to loamy soil and do not like waterlogged soil. A good mulch of decayed organic matter is essential, particularly for winter. Regular watering especially in summer is another essential as they are shallow rooted. Because they are evergreen, occasional watering in winter will be necessary if they are grown under the eaves of buildings.

Planting is best done when the danger of frost has passed and the soil is warming (late October to early November is ideal). Planting in autumn may result in losses as trees will have little time to acclimatise before winter.

Some points to bear in mind:

1. Apart from frost damage, the most likely pest problems are aphids and caterpillars.

These figs are ripening well, protected from birds by their netting.

Hand picking is the best control for the caterpillars. Natural predators may get the aphids but if you have to spray do not do this close to harvest.

2. Scale insects sometimes attack. Small numbers can be rubbed off. Regular sprays with soapy water or pest oil will control them.

3. Snails and slugs like the leaves. The usual baits won't work as they feed up in the canopy. Hand pick and use types of mulch they dislike.

4. Nitrogen, magnesium and iron deficiencies cause leaf distortion. Correct by applying a complete citrus food in spring and again in autumn.

As an alternative to a lemon, consider the Finger Lime (*Microcitrus australasica*). This is an Australian plant occurring as an understorey tree in SE Queensland and northern NSW and growing up to 10 m. They have prominent thorns and contain some seeds. Don't be deterred by the origin and ultimate size, for it is comparable with Meyer lemons for frost tolerance and will make an excellent pot specimen. The fruit, normally green and cylindrical in shape, is up to around 10 cm long and only about 2–3 cm wide with acidic juice not unlike a lime. Juice vesicles are compressed and when the skin of the fruit is cut, they will burst out, enabling them to be used in creative ways for cooking. They are a surprising addition to salad dressings and whole fruit can be frozen without destroying flavour or texture on thawing. 'Rick's Red' is a cultivar with purplish red skin and red flesh.

Feijoas or Pineapple Guava (*Feijoa sellowiana*)

With its leathery green leaves and bright red and white eucalyptus-like flowers the feijoa can be, and is often grown as an ornamental shrub. The flowers are good for flower arrangements. It flowers October to December and fruit ripens April–May. It is hardy, being both frost and drought-resistant.

Fruits are green and aromatic with an edible pulp. Let them fall from the shrub and then they may be eaten fresh, used in jams and jellies or juiced.

Figs (*Ficus carica*)

Figs need a warm dry climate for best fruiting. There are both 'black' and 'white' varieties available, the 'black' being more popular. Although figs will produce two crops per season the late summer–autumn crop is the main one in this district.

Some points to keep in mind:

1. Birds love the fruit. Netting at least part of the tree is the best answer.

2. Frosts easily damage young trees, so select a protected spot.

3. Provide a well-drained soil, adding lime if needed. Trees do not do so well in acid soils.

4. The trees are relatively shallow-rooted so water accordingly in summer to prevent a check in growth and fruit quality.

5. Figs can successfully be grown in a large tub or barrel.

Trees are inclined to sucker and grow with tangled branches. Prune to correct these problems as needed.

Grapes (*Vitis vinifera*)

Grapes will grow well in Canberra and produce good crops if suitable cultivars are selected. Most table grapes come from the European grape (*V. vinifera*) and prefer a warm, dry summer. Hybrids of one of the American grapes (*V. labrusca*) are also popular as they are more mildew and fungal rot resistant. They have a distinctive strong flavour and do not suit all tastes but make excellent jellies and produce a juice with good flavour.

Grapes grow on a wide range of soils but need to be planted so roots can run deeply. They also need a regular water supply in summer months for best yields. Drip irrigation is best as it waters the roots rather than the foliage and so reduces bunch rotting and mildew development.

They need a support, whether a pergola or wire along a wall or fence. Trellises should be strong if the vine is to be allowed an extensive run although vines may be pruned hard to keep the main framework within a couple of metres. One of the main aims of pruning is to expose the vines to the maximum amount of sunlight and warmth. Therefore if possible, do not plant on the south side of a wall or fence, especially varieties that are late maturing and may only just ripen in a shorter summer (e.g. Waltham Cross).

These grapes are looking really good. Most of the year the area beneath the vine is a chook run but they are kept out as the grapes ripen.

Some varieties for the home garden follow; local nurseries may well offer more.

White:

'Sultana' (syn. 'Thompson Seedless'). Best in a warm dry location. Canes should be pruned longer than other types, about 10 buds. Vigorous.

'Italia'. Golden colour, large grape.

'Golden Muscat'. Large juicy berries, distinctive flavour — one of the American varieties. Disease resistant.

'Golden Chasselas'. Golden fruit when ripe, a good table grape for cool areas although usually regarded as a wine variety.

Red:

'Flame Seedless'. Good quality and flavour and will hold on the vine for a long period.

'Black Muscat'. Good home garden variety, reasonable vigour and good flavour. Has been a popular home garden variety for many years.

'Purple Cornichon'. Suitable in a warm location, later maturing, large elongate fruit but with only a neutral flavour.

'Isabella'. Distinctive black, strong and unusual flavoured grape, vigorous and bears well. One of the American hybrids.

There are many wine grapes growing in this district but they usually don't double as dual purpose grapes.

Grapes are vigorous and forgiving when it comes to pruning. They shouldn't be allowed to run wild or be neglected. Initial pruning should take the cane up the support and in the direction you want it to grow. Frequent tying is needed with this initial pruning. They are normally pruned hard in early winter. Pruning grapes essentially consists of cutting each cane back to two or three buds leaving these spurs with the two or three buds to shoot the following spring. On these shoots the bunches develop. Some varieties such as sultana are better pruned to six to eight buds (called rods) rather than to spurs. Unwanted vigorous growth. especially beyond the developing fruit, can be pinched back at any time in the growing season. Sometimes removal of leaves around bunches will improve ripening. Local experience is the best guide.

Most people don't have any problems apart from birds. Netting is the answer. Some other points to keep in mind:

1. Downy mildew appears initially as yellowish green oil patches on leaves, affected areas die. Downy white growth appears on undersides of leaves in humid weather. Flowers and bunches may be lost. This disease is favoured by wet spring weather. More resistant varieties include 'Improved Isabella', 'Golden Muscat'; susceptible varieties include 'Waltham Cross'. During winter prune out all affected shoots, dead fruit bunches. Copper sprays were originally developed to control this disease and are still used today.

2. Black spot causes 'bird's eye' spots on leaves and black pitting on canes. Dead brown areas with white centres develop on the berries. This is favoured by damp cool weather in spring. It is not as common as downy mildew. Control of downy mildew and powdery mildew will probably reduce the problem.

3. Grapeleaf blister mites cause blisters up to 10mm across to develop on upper surfaces of young leaves, and felty patches of plant hairs occur on undersurface of the blisters amongst which the mites feed. Patches are white initially but later turn brown. Fruit is not attacked. More resistant varieties include 'Isabella', 'Golden Muscat', 'Sultana', susceptible varieties include 'Black Muscat' . Lightly infested shoots may be pruned out. This mite does not infest the fruit and does not much damage the plant.

4. Caterpillars of grapevine moth may feed on the leaves. The best response is to pick off the offenders.

Kiwifruit (Chinese Gooseberry) *Actinidia chinensis* (yellow flesh), *A. deliciosa* (green flesh)

Male and female flowers are borne on different plants so you will need at least one of each to obtain fruit. Kiwifruit are rampant growers and need regular training and pruning in summer as well as winter, otherwise they will twine and tangle and become less productive. A vigorous vine may grow 10 metres or more in a season. Commercial

Kiwifruit grow very well in Canberra.

growers often prune the vine 5–6 times during the growing season. The male plant should be carefully tagged, and pruned after flowering to stop it taking over.

Heavy crops on mature plants need a strong, sturdy trellis, far more substantial than any grape or climbing rose would need. A good cropping mature plant could carry many kilograms of fruit.

Plants are shallow-rooted and so require regular summer water. An organic mulch of composted straw or even a thin layer of lawn clippings or similar will help.

Young plants especially are easily damaged by wind burn and spring frosts. The fruit mature late in the season, around April–May. Some people don't like the smell of the vines.

Loquats (*Eriobotrya japonica*)

There are good specimens of this large (5–8 m) evergreen glossy-leaved tree in Canberra. They are self-pollinating and flower through late autumn to mid winter with fruit developing from winter into spring. Small trees are subject to frost injury and fruit crops can be irregular compared with trees grown in milder coastal or inland climates. The fruit are yellow, apricot sized with large seeds

and juicy sweet to acid flesh. This tree has the first fruit of the season and appears to be responsible for an increase in local fruit fly numbers. See the Apple section.

Medlars (*Mespilus germanica*)

An attractive deciduous small to medium sized tree. Fruit are late maturing, brown and plum-sized and require a frost to change the texture from white woody to brownish creamy flesh. The flesh is acid-tasting and the seeds prominent.

Two varieties are most commonly available, 'Nottingham' with compact small leaf and fruit and 'Dutch', which has a spreading open habit and larger fruit.

The trees will double as an ornamental with attractive green foliage and single white flowers in spring as well as fine yellow-orange foliage in autumn.

Mulberries (Morus sp)

These are large spreading trees at maturity so allow plenty of room. They grow well in cool climates and are relatively trouble-free.

Some points to keep in mind:

1. The black or English mulberry (*M. nigra*) is the popular fruit, rather than the red (*M. rubra*) or white (*M. alba*) mulberry.

2. Birds are the major problem and will damage ripening fruit.

3. Fruits are juicy and staining may be a problem if trees are planted near concrete paths or from where they may be tramped inside.

4. Silkworms prefer the leaves of the white mulberry.

5. There are a couple of diseases. Bacterial Blight causes small, black, angular spots on the leaves, cankers may develop on infected shoots, twigs may die back. The best response is to prune back infected twigs in autumn. Another possibility is Fungal Leaf Spot so rake up and destroy the infected leaves in autumn.

Olives (*Olea europea*)

Olives are now widely grown across the country and grow well in this district. They require cold winters for good flower production and long hot summers to produce and mature good quality fruit. Climatic variation and late spring frost damage to flowers can affect cropping between seasons.

The fruit will need pickling, as they cannot be eaten raw.

'Manzanillo' and 'Verdale' are varieties suitable for green and ripe pickling. 'Sevillano' is recommended for green pickling. There are many other new varieities.

The African olive (*Olea africana*), whilst somewhat similar in appearance, does not produce edible fruit.

Passionfruit (*Passiflora edulis*)

The purple or black passionfruit can be grown here, but only in a warm sheltered spot. Plants are at their best for 3–5 years and should then be replaced as they have usually developed the 'woodiness' disease by then. 'Woodiness' results in the fruits being hard and woody. The only response is to replace an affected vine with a new virus-tested plant.

Seedling plants are satisfactory or named cultivars such as 'Nelly Kelly' are also popular because of the attractive size of and appearance of the fruit. You need to take care with grafted varieties that the rootstock does not overtake the scion (top). Advanced plants of non-grafted 'Nelly Kelly' are now available.

Provide a deep well-drained friable soil and warm sheltered aspect with good trellis support for several metres. Summer watering is needed to prevent shrinkage of the fruit. Plant in spring and prune lightly after the first season just to remove older laterals and to open up the thicker vines.

The plants may suffer a bit from the effects of frost. Plant in the warmest protected spot you can, cover if practical during winter and prune out damaged shoots in spring.

Peaches (*Prunus persica*) and Nectarines (*P. persica nectarina*)

Peaches and nectarines will require a bit more care than most other fruits, but grow and produce readily in this climate.

Late frost damage can make them marginal in very cold areas. They require a well-drained soil (more so than plums and pome fruit). All common varieties other than 'J.H. Hale' (Million Dollar Peach) are self-pollinating.

Peaches are commonly grouped according to flesh colour, white or yellow, and whether freestone or clingstone. White-fleshed peaches are considered by many to be more flavoursome and aromatic but they have soft flesh and bruise readily. There are a number of good varieties such as 'Fragar', 'Wiggins', 'Anzac' and 'Briggs Red May'.

White-fleshed nectarines such as 'Goldmine', 'Newboy' and 'Early Rivers' are good for the home garden, and like white-fleshed peaches, they are often considered more aromatic

Many fruit trees make a striking addition to the spring garden. Note how the soil around the trunk is kept clear. Pollinating insects will have no trouble getting access through this netting.

and flavoursome than the yellow-fleshed nectarines.

The yellow-fleshed varieties of fruit are attractive for preserving too, will stand more handling and include some quite late maturing varieties such as 'Golden Queen'. This is a useful feature to spread fruit ripening and harvest. Other yellow varieties include 'Elberta' and 'J.H. Hale'. Yellow fleshed nectarines include 'Flavortop' and 'Nectareds Number 2' (earlier maturing) to 'Number 10' (later maturing).

To control excess growth in any stone fruit, it's a good idea to grow trees in a fan shape against a wall or on posts and wires. Peaches and nectarines produce volumes of new growth. This new growth (now previous season's wood) produces flowers and fruit once only in the spring and summer. Remove

spent growth in autumn (some of the fruiting wood may go in this process). If you do not, fruit will be produced further out on the branches each year and there will be less of it as the years go by.

There is a growing range of smaller peaches and nectarine cultivars with names like 'Pixzee' bred especially for small gardens or for growing in pots. They require very little pruning but you may need to thin the crop and, if you are growing them in pots, will have to be careful to ensure the potting mix is kept in good condition. They have a fine spring blossom display and will grow to less than 2 m.

Some points to keep in mind:

1. These trees have a shorter life than plums, apples or pears but with care will last 15 or more years.

2. Feed the trees in August/September and again in December, providing a regular supply of nitrogen along with other elements.

Some pest and disease controls are needed:

1. Peach leaf curl and brown rot must be controlled for successful cropping. With peach leaf curl, new leaves in spring may be thickened, blistered, "curly", reddish–yellowish in colour. Affected leaves shrivel and fall off. Later growth is healthy. Affected fruit may appear scalded. Copper or lime sulphur sprays before mid-August are the only effective control. A wet spring may mean that complete control is impossible. Trees which have suffered severe defoliation may be fertilised in spring to promote new vigour.

2. Brown Rot can be a problem. See the discussion in the apricots section.

3. Shothole results in holes in leaves, and cankers on up to 3-year old wood may cause dieback. Fruit are rarely affected. Controlling peach leaf curl will generally solve this problem.

4. If attacked by aphids prune out dead tips in winter. Treat Queensland fruit fly as for apples. Control oriental fruit moth as for apricots.

Pears and Nashi pears (Pyrus)

The European pear (*Pyrus communis*) is most commonly grown and known to all. The growing requirements are similar to apples — two trees or at least a double graft will be needed for good pollination and fruit set. The trees are long-lived and can grow too large for home gardens. Avoid this problem by selecting a tree grown on a dwarfing rootstock, such as one of the Quince selections.

Trees will naturally produce vigorous upright growth in great quantity unless pruned carefully in winter and summer, but like apples they lend themselves to espaliering along a fence or wall.

Nashi pears (*Pyrus pyrifolia*) are round (commonly apple-shaped), crisp and juicy. They are slightly earlier-ripening and usually best left to ripen on the trees. They can be very sweet to taste.

Local soils are usually adequate for either type, provided the trees are fertilised seasonally. They prefer deep and well-drained soil with good moisture-holding capacity. As with apples, pears will tolerate wetter soils for lengthy periods, but water-logging is fatal. codling moth and pear and cherry slug need to be controlled if trees are to thrive and fruit well. See the apple and cherry sections respectively for advice.

Some varieties recommended for Canberra include:

'Beurre Bosc': Elongate, cinnamon-brown fruit. A good cropping sweet, juicy and aromatic variety. Matures February-March.

'Bartlett' (Syn. 'Williams Bon Chretien'): Vigorous, smooth skin medium to large sized fruit. Fruit firm, very juicy and good for preserving as it is the common canning variety. Matures earlier than most varieties, February.

'Red Sensation' ('Red Williams Bon Chretien') is similar but produces an unusual, very attractive bright crimson fruit when ripe.

'Packham's Triumph': An Australian variety

A nearly ripe persimmon.

with juicy smooth-textured flesh. Large, sometimes bumpy green-yellow fruit maturing in March.

'Josephine de Malines': Small to medium sized fruit roundish pale green skin. High quality and distinctive flavour but inclined to biennial bearing. Matures in March, but later than 'Packham's Triumph'.

'Winter Cole': Small to medium sized fruit green turning to yellow with russet (rough skin). High quality fruit matures March-April.

'Winter Nelis': Small to medium sized fruit similar to 'Winter Cole'. Good late home garden variety but not always readily available. Matures April (slightly later than 'Winter Cole').

'Glou Morceau': Heavy cropping large quince-shaped fruit, maturing late (April) and will hang on tree for long period. Flesh is sweet, white and smooth textured. Not always readily available.

'Nijiseiki' ('20th Century') is the most commonly available Nashi. Heavy cropping with round, yellow mottled fruit. Crisp and very sweet and juicy.

Prune pears similarly to apples.

Persimmons (*Diospyros kaki*)

As well as being fruiting trees these make attractive ornamentals. They have deep green glossy foliage, produce beautiful orange to red autumn leaves and strikingly attractive fruit in late autumn. They prefer a moist soil. Most varieties do not need cross-pollination although some will produce better quality, larger fruit if available.

There are non-astringent and astringent types. 'Hachiya' ('Nightingale seedless'), 'Flat seedless' and 'Tanenashi' are recommended.

Fruit are usually harvested when the fruits turn orange in colour. With the astringent varieties clip fruit with a small section of stalk attached and store until the flesh is soft and sweet, the texture of jam. Ripening may be hastened by placing persimmons in a bag with one or two ripe bananas. Non-astringent cultivars may be eaten crunchy.

Birds enjoy the fruit so netting is very worthwhile.

Plumcots

These are a cross between an apricot and a Japanese plum. The fruits are characteristically large and often resemble an apricot externally. The fruit is slightly fuzzy, like apricots, but the colour may range from bright yellow to mottled red, the flesh texture and seed about the same as a plum. The flavour is probably closer to that of an apricot than to a plum. They mature from late January through most of February. Cultural requirements are similar to apricot. Prune plumcots in the same way as Japanese plums.

Plums (European, *Prunus domestica*) (Japanese, *Prunus salicina*)

The most common types of plums are the European and the Japanese. Plums are one of the most popular fruit for home gardens as they are easily grown and can be used fresh, for dessert purposes, jams and other spreads. Certain European varieties can be dried (prunes) as well as eaten fresh.

European plums are well suited to cool districts. They have firm flesh and usually have either green-yellow or purple skin with yellow flesh. They prefer deep rich soils and adequate summer water. Some varieties flower a week or so later than Japanese plums and so are less likely to be frost-damaged in spring.

Japanese plums are usually larger, more vigorous trees, yellow to red or purple in skin colour and with yellow or red flesh (blood plums). The blood plums also make excellent jam and preserves.

Both types of plums produce an abundance of flowers and the Japanese varieties require a cross pollinator. Japanese and European plums normally do not cross pollinate each other.

The other less common plums are Damsons (*Prunus insititia*) and Cherry plums (*P. cerasifera*). Both of these are inferior for eating fresh as they are quite tart around the seed but are quite useful for jam making especially the Damsons.

Some varieties include:

European plums:

'Coe's Golden Drop' and 'Greengage': Both light coloured fruit with good flavour. 'Coe's Golden Drop' is later maturing; mid to end of March.

'Angelina Burdett': Dark purple fruit, heavy bearing, good quality flesh matures toward end of January.

'Damson-Crittenden': Purple rounded fruit with golden flesh. Excellent jam. Matures toward end of March.

'Grand Duke': 'Large purple fruit with yellow flesh and a heavy bearing tree. Matures late February into March.

'President': Large fruit matures in March, good flavour.

'D'Agen' (Prune): Red, firm sweet flesh, popular fresh and the main drying plum. Matures early-mid March.

'Robe de Sargent' (Prune): Dark purple, prolific bearer matures about the same time as 'D'Agen'.

Japanese Plums:

'Mariposa': Superb large fruited blood plum. Excellent flavour both fresh and processed. Matures February.

'Narrabeen': Very large round fruit, yellow flesh; skin yellow-red. Skin tough, prolific bearer in March. Spreading tree.

'Santa Rosa': Large good quality dessert plum similar in skin colour and size to Satsuma but with yellow flesh. Matures January into February.

'Satsuma': Blood plum with very dark firm flesh. Juicy with good flavour. Excellent for fresh fruit and processing. Matures February.

'Wickson': Very large yellow heart-shaped fruit with a red blush on the tip. Firm texture and excellent flavour. Upright trees that yield well. Matures February.

Point to keep in mind: Plums are inclined to

overcrop and therefore should be pruned back at any time other than winter. Thinning the fruit will lighten the load and thus reduce the chance of limb breakage. It will also reduce the risk of brown rot transfer from fruit to fruit along a limb.

Japanese plums are also vigorous and will easily over crop. Long branches may develop and intertwine. Prune reasonably heavily in autumn and some summer pruning can reduce much of the autumn work. European plums are usually not quite so vigorous and can be treated more lightly.

Quinces (*Cydonia oblonga*)

These grow to about 4 m and produce well in cool climates. They are compact, sometimes rather crooked-growing with soft foliage and attractive white–pink tinged solitary flowers followed in autumn by large golden yellow fruit, many of them on the tips of long annual growth. Quinces make a fine ornamental fruiting tree and can look especially well if espaliered.

If the fruit is left on the tree until it is ready to drop, it develops a strong pleasant aromatic fragrance. This fruit is excellent stewed or preserved or made into jams or jellies as it has high pectin content. The cooked fruit develops a pink to red colour which makes it especially attractive on its own or mixed with other fruit such as apples and pears. Do not store fresh fruit in a refrigerator as its distinctive aroma can taint other food such as dairy produce and meat.

Quince trees grow best in deeper heavier soils with good moisture retention but in pockets of alkaline soil will readily show yellowing associated with iron deficiency. Water regularly during the growing season.

Fruit production is better with a cross pollinator but one tree can still set fruit adequately.

Varieties available include:

'Champion'. Large size pear-shaped golden fruit from a compact tree. Tender fruit of mild flavour matures early to mid April. Furry skin.

'Smyrna'. Very large, pale yellow fruit with smooth skin. A strong and productive tree at an early age. Matures early to mid April.

Some points for consideration:

1. Comparatively little pruning is needed but new growth must be developed each season to ensure fruitfulness. Enough cutting to stimulate a number of new side branches and twigs is required each year.

2. Remove suckers as they appear at the base of the tree.

3. Quince Fleck is a fungal leaf spot that can defoliate and crack fruit in wet seasons. Control it by pruning regularly to remove old wood. Birds may cause damage late in the season. Trees may need to be covered to prevent this.

4. Codling moth and Pear and Cherry slug are relatively minor pests. Treat as for apples and cherries respectively.

Quinces develop a lovely aroma as they ripen. The tree is most ornamental.

Nuts

A range of nuts will grow readily in Canberra and the surrounding area. The main problems are in making space available and protecting the mature nuts from birds. The need for cross-pollination increases the space needed for satisfactory growth.

Almonds (*Prunus dulcis, syn Prunus amygdalus*)

Almonds prefer a shorter winter than the tablelands provide. They are early-flowering (end of August) and in some years frosts and spring rains may damage flowers and developing fruit. In a good year the blossoms are a wonderful curtain-raiser for spring.

Cross-pollination is needed so choose a double or triple-grafted tree. Netting is an effective barrier to birds but, if left unprotected, parrots will happily feed on the developing fruit leaving little of the crop for you.

Varieties are usually grouped as paper-shelled, soft-shelled or hard-shelled. Varieties for the home garden include:

'Brandes Jordan' (soft shell), 'Chellaston' (soft shell), 'Hatch's Nonpareil' (paper shell), 'Johnston's Prolific' (paper shell), 'Ne Plus Ultra' (paper shell). 'All in one' is a self-pollinating one and 'Nonpareil' is said to be good.

Apart from birds, the only other problem could be the fungal Shot Hole — see the discussion under apricots above.

Chestnuts (*Castanea sativa*) Spanish or European Chestnut

These grow well if provided with a deep well-drained friable soil free of lime. They grow to be a large spherical tree (up to 20 m) and are unsuitable for smaller gardens. Chestnuts do make an attractive ornamental tree. Male and female flowers are borne on the same tree but trees are often self sterile so cross-pollination from another tree is often required.

Mature fruit will break open and fall to the ground. Wear gloves when collecting these, as the spines on the husks are very sharp. Chestnuts are floury in texture and, as they contain about 50 per cent moisture and lower oil content, do not keep as readily as other nuts. Storing in paper bags in a refrigerator will improve keeping quality.

Varieties: Seedling varieties have been grown successfully. Try some of the Fleming's series. There is little information on named variety yields in tableland climates.

These should not be confused with Horse Chestnuts (*Aesculus hippocastanum*) which have inedible fruit.

Hazelnuts (*Corylus avellana*), Pecans (*Carya illinoinensis*) and Pistachios (*Pistacia vera*)

These grow well if given adequate summer water. Hazelnuts and Pistachios are small trees 4–5 m high by 2–3 m wide at maturity, and Pecans approximately twice this size. Hazelnuts naturally grow as a multi-stemmed tree by suckering from the base but if basal shoots and suckers are removed they can be grown to a single trunk. The Turkish Hazel (*Corylus colurna*) is non-suckering and has greater drought tolerance, but can reach 15 m.

The trees bear separate male and female flowers on the same tree and are wind pollinated. However as they are usually self-sterile, two or more trees of a different variety from an acceptable pollination group are required.

Named cultivars are available and guidance for selecting should be obtained from your nursery. Some growers have achieved success by planting a range of seedling plants or a range of varieties to ensure at least one adequate pollen-providing plant. For a home gardener close planting along a fence could be a practical space saving solution.

Hazelnuts mature February–March by turning brown and dropping with or without the husk attached. They may then be raked up and stored dry. They are popular with parrots.

Some named varieties of Hazelnut include: 'Atlas', 'Wanliss Pride', 'Barcelona', 'Kentish Cob'. These varieties have been selected overseas. Other varieities that have potential are 'Tokolyi/Brownfield Cosford' (TBC), 'Tonda di Giffoni' and 'Tonda Romana'.

Pecans and Pistachios will grow well as trees in the tablelands but require a long hot summer to mature the fruit. They are not generally recommended, unless grown primarily as an ornamental tree.

Walnuts (*Juglans regia*) English or Persian Walnut

These are large deciduous trees growing to 15 metres high and wide at maturity and are unsuitable for most home gardens. Additionally, walnuts produce a root exudate that will suppress the growth of many plants grown in the vicinity.

They grow well in the tablelands particularly if provided with deep soil that allows a good root run. If the tap root is intact at purchase, deep soil is essential. Trees require irrigation in most summers to prevent fruit (kernel) shrinkage and defoliation. Cross-pollination will usually provide better yields.

The fruit on this old walnut are developing well, the tree itself about 10 m all round.

Walnuts, like chestnuts, are prone to soil-borne root diseases, particularly in poorly drained soils. The other main problems are bird (parrot) damage to fruit and bacterial canker. Bacterial blight causes fruit to blacken and wither as well as damaging foliage and newer shoots. Control this while the tree is young as later it will get too big for control measures to be carried out. Prune out blackened shoots and nuts. Collect all nuts on the ground. Irrigate tree during summer.

Some varieties include: 'Wilson's Wonder', 'Franquette' (somewhat blight resistant) and some recent French, German and American varieties.

Berries

Blueberries (*Vaccinium corymbosom*) and other Vaccinium species

The type most commonly grown in Australia is the high bush blueberries. They will grow well in the cool tablelands areas as well as coastal and northern areas of NSW so long as the appropriate varieties are selected.

The blueberry is a bushy shrub 1 to 2 m high with attractive glossy green leaves which turn yellow to red in autumn before falling.

Numerous shoots or canes develop from the crown; they may survive indefinitely and you can expect at least 20 years from a bush.

Blueberries require an acid soil (from pH 4.8 to 5.2), well-drained and high in organic matter. They need plenty of soil moisture between blossoming and fruit development (from late November to early February) and, though they do best in a sunny location, they will tolerate partial shade. Good air circulation is important, so don't plant blueberries in a sheltered corner of the garden or in a position surrounded by shrubbery.

Plant the young shrubs in early spring. Several weeks before planting, dig plenty of organic material into the bed. The soil pH should be reduced to about 5; if necessary, rake in sulphur powder to achieve this. Plant the blueberries singly or in rows about 1.2 m apart, taking care to keep the roots moist throughout the operation.

Birds enjoy blueberries as much as, if not more, than we do, so netting is vital.

Strawberries (*Fragaria species*)

Strawberries have long been a popular fruit to grow especially for those with limited space. A range of varieties is available that will produce fruit from spring until autumn with just a short break over the summer period. Healthy plants may yield up to half a kilogram of berries per season and they start maturing in mid spring when few other fruit are yet mature.

A warm sunny location is ideal. Trickle irrigation is the best form of watering for these shallow-rooted plants.

Thorough soil preparation is essential for consistently high yields. Beds should have

The traditional method of protecting strawberries from dirt and fungal diseases is to mulch them with straw.

compost and a slow release complete fertiliser and/or old manure thoroughly incorporated through the soil. If necessary, lime may be added to bring soil close to neutral pH. Beds should be raised to provide good drainage.

Strawberries for home garden use are most commonly planted in autumn and will yield the first crop the following spring. Cool stored plants are available at other times of the year. Late autumn planting of runners may require plants to be covered as a protection against frost damage to the crowns at least for the first few weeks until they establish. Plant 30 cm apart in the row and about one metre between rows.

Mulching is critical to good production, particularly to aid in weed control and in keeping berries clean. Clean straw or pine needles make excellent mulch and allows water to penetrate to the soil readily. Mulches such as weed mat or black plastic are popular as they also make baiting for snails and slugs easier. With these mulches the sheets should be set down on well prepared beds and planting done through slits cut in the sheet.

Strawberries can be grown in barrels or

specially designed pots and will then double as an attractive ornamental on deck or patio. Thorough soil preparation and regular moisture in summer is essential.

It is better to buy named, certified virus-tested varieties from your local nursery than accept runners or plants from friends or to propagate from your own plants (at least after the first season.) The few dollars spent replacing plants every few years will be more than rewarded in increased yield and fruit quality. Treat them as a short-life plant, replacing all plants every three or four years when the yield will be declining markedly.

'Red Gauntlet' is the main variety grown in cooler climates. It is high yielding and has an attractive appearance but the plant deteriorates quickly.

Other good varieties include: 'Temptation', 'Cambridge Rival', 'Chandler, 'Toyonoka', 'Kunawase', 'Alinta' and 'Hokawase'. New varieties become available each year and may be worth trying.

A couple of other points to keep in mind:

1. If fungal leaf spots appear make sure the plants have good ventilation. Affected leaves may be handpicked. If the plants are ageing it is best to replace.

2. Grey mould (Botrytis) can attack. This appears as grey powdery growth on flowers and ripe or near ripe fruits during wet weather. It is also a problem on picked fruit. Avoid overhead irrigation. Ensure plants get plenty of air, keep weeds down, and prune excessive growth. Pick only sound fruit, handle crop carefully.

3. Earwigs, snails and slugs can damage the fruit.

Trailing berries and bush fruit

These are ideal for Canberra and surrounds provided they have adequate water.

The raspberry grows from suckers of the spreading root system. The black currant is usually grown as a multi-stemmed bush, but the red currant tends to have a stout main stem and can be grown as a standard. Gooseberries can be grown in a variety of forms, ranging from trailing plants to upright bushes, but are usually grown as miniature, vase-shaped trees.

Loganberries, Boysenberries, Youngberries and Blackberries	Rubus hybrids
Raspberries	Rubus idaeus
Gooseberries	Ribes grossularia
Black Currants	Ribes nigrum

Blackberries, loganberries, boysenberries, youngberries, raspberries and black currants bear fruit on the previous year's growth only. Gooseberries and red currants produce fruit on spurs of old wood and on the previous year's growth. Training and pruning are different for the two types.

Raspberries are normally grown along a trellis or wires. During the first season allow only one main shoot to develop and cut this back to 15 cm the following winter. In the second winter, cut back to ground level all except two or three of the strongest canes; this will encourage the plant to develop a strong root system.

These plants produce their fruit on one-year-old wood. In the third and subsequent seasons tie the year-old fruiting wood onto the trellis and allow new growths to develop along the ground. When the plant has finished cropping, cut off the old wood and any weak or superfluous new growths at ground level, and tie the new wood up on the trellis.

Gooseberries and red currants are usually trained in the shape of a miniature vase-shaped tree with a short main stem of 10 cm. The plants are often bought with three or four strong shoots, and should be planted with the lowest shoot about 10 cm above the ground, and the shoots shortened to about 15 cm. If most of the shoots are weak and only one is vigorous, remove the weak shoots and encourage the strong shoot to form the main stem by planting more deeply, with the base of the strong shoot just above the ground.

Red currants bear on two-year-old wood so a proportion of older canes should be cut out each year.

For all of these berry plants prepare the ground thoroughly before planting and add a liberal dressing of manure or incorporate a green manure crop. Apply general purpose fertiliser regularly. Plants that are bearing do not respond to large amounts of fertiliser: too much nitrogen will stimulate growth of the canes without increasing the fruit crop.

The berries of all trailing berry and bush fruits are ready for harvesting when fully grown and darkening in colour. They can be picked when slightly under-ripe if required for cooking, but need to be fully coloured and soft if required as fresh fruit.

Warning: If you live near open land or a reserve, then first consider whether you are able to mesh your berries to protect them from birds. Remember, seed spread by birds may result in unwanted seedlings in the wild.

A few extra points:

1. Caterpillars may appear in or on ripening fruit. Float them out by placing the berries in water after picking.

2. Fungal leaf spots and Botrytis should be handled as with strawberries.

3. Sometimes rose scale appears on the older canes. Cut the canes out.

Pruning

Correct pruning is a major key to successful fruit growing. One of the ways to learn is to try pruning. Note and record what you have done and observe how the tree responds over the seasons. Watch out also for practical demonstrations, advertised from time to time in the media. The Horticultural Society regularly holds public pruning demonstrations. Pruning is not as hard as written descriptions tend to suggest.

Some general tips:

The aim is to remove parts of the plant to encourage it to grow, flower and fruit in the way you want. The degree of pruning could range from the removal of a large limb to the pinching out of soft shoots with thumb and forefinger in summer. Some fruit trees will thrive with only very limited pruning. Most fruit trees will produce without pruning but the quality of the fruit produced and the yield over time will not be up to the potential of the plant. Pruning in itself will not guarantee a good crop. It is futile to prune if the plant is not cared for in other ways. Soil preparation, drainage, irrigation, fertilising, pest and disease control are equally important.

Basic aims and principles

For fruit production, appearance is not so important. A simple examination of most shoots shows they end in a terminal bud. The terminal bud is the dominant bud, and it produces a chemical which inhibits the growth of side buds. You can manipulate and direct growth by removing selected buds. Removal of the terminal bud on any shoot will encourage side buds to shoot.

The more upright the branch or shoot, the more dominant the terminal bud becomes. Horizontal branches often are more fruitful. They grow less each year and usually require less cutting.

Early training and pruning

The roots of bare rooted stock will have been damaged in lifting before they reach the retail nursery. Because of this damage, the top of the young tree should be cut back by a third to one half to compensate until the new tree has become established. (Recent research also suggests that the intrinsic vigour or healthiness of the young trees is what will see it grow successfully the first growing season.)

The first pruning of a young tree usually involves heading back the best three to five scaffold branches to about half their length, and removing the rest (thinning out). The nursery may already have done this for you. If the tree has no branches, ie is a straight stem, then make one cut above the point at which you want branches to develop, possibly about hip high. In the first season a number of shoots will develop and these can be treated as mentioned above. At the risk of oversimplifying things the procedure will be similar for the first three or four seasons on

In Canberra the display by our fruit trees has been a traditional part of spring.

the framework branches as they develop.

Young trees and vines are usually pruned then to establish a shape or trained along a support to make management activities such as spraying and harvesting easier.

The most common training systems (shown in the diagram) are:

Central leader: These trees are strong and with more of the fruit closer to ground level.

Vase or open centered: This allows more light into the tree centre. These trees are not as strong as the central leader. They are more likely to split limbs under a heavy fruit load.

Modified central leader: Combines the best features of the central leader and vase shaped trees.

As the tree forms the shape you are aiming for, pruning needs to be maintained or reduced according to bearing habit and the nature of the plant.

There are two basic cuts that can be made.

1.   Thinning out — the removal of an entire branch back to the main branch or trunk. For example, where there are two branches of similar size too

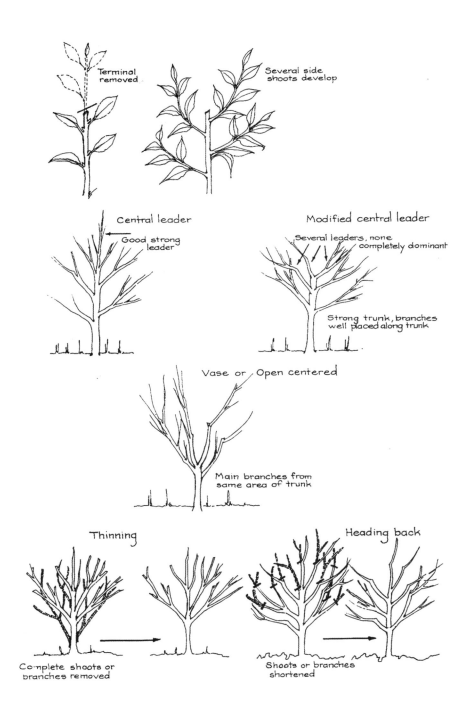

Terminal removed

Several side shoots develop

Central leader

Good strong leader

Modified central leader

Several leaders, none completely dominant

Strong trunk, branches well placed along trunk

Vase or Open centered

Main branches from same area of trunk

Thinning

Heading back

Complete shoots or branches removed

Shoots or branches shortened

close together, remove one entirely. This is usually the first cut made when approaching a tree or a vine to be pruned.

2. Heading back — instead of removing an entire shoot or branch it can be shortened to a suitable side branch or bud. In place of one shoot or branch you may in time have several. Remember, once you have removed the terminal bud, side buds will normally break into growth.

Pinching back and rubbing out unwanted shoots heading in the wrong direction during the growth season is a good way of saving a lot of heavy pruning in the winter dormant season. Late spring to early summer is a good time to apply this technique to many plants, eg grape vine and kiwifruit shoots heading in unwanted directions.

Once they are well-established some fruits will require very little pruning, while others will need attention each year. However, remove all dead, diseased and crossing wood at any time of the year.

Equipment for Fruit Growing

The basic minimum would be:

» A good quality pair of secateurs will be expensive but, if cared for, will last many years. Good quality secateurs are much easier on the pruner and the plant. The more expensive brands also offer replacement blades.

» A good quality pair of long-handled loppers (or 'parrot beaks'). Most branches that cannot be cut comfortably with secateurs should be cut with loppers (or if very big, a pruning saw). Attempting to cut an oversized branch with secateurs can damage both the tree and the secateurs.

» For mature trees, a pruning saw. There are two types — the two-edge straight saw with coarse and fine tooth set; and the curved saw with pointed nose. This second type of saw normally cuts on the back stroke and is easier to use in narrow confined spaces between branches. Pruning saws are designed to cut green wood and are better than bow saws or carpentry saws. At present European and Japanese brands seem to be the best quality, though substantially more expensive.

» Equipment for dealing with pests and diseases will depend on what you choose to grow. In the early years at least these can probably be dealt with by using formulations such as dusts, aerosols or hose-on products. Later, a reliable small spray unit is useful if tree fruit are grown. These can also be used to apply foliar fertilisers. If pesticides are used, then directions for application and protective clothing as indicated by the product label should always be followed.

» A sharp knife such as a budding knife is useful for smooth paring branches that have been cut by a saw.

» A good step ladder is necessary if tree fruit are to be grown, for pruning and harvesting. Ideal are aluminium 'orchard ladders'. They have a wider base and spiked legs and so are much more stable. Such ladders usually have to be ordered, but can often be practical for other uses as well.

The equipment suggested will not all be needed in the first year or two but is worth the investment if you aim to grow tree fruit. Saving in time and effort will soon repay the cost of purchase.

Fruit trees requiring minimal pruning after initial establishment of tree shape (ie two to four years):

Cherry - sweet	Medlar
Citrus - Kumquat	Mulberry
- Calamondin	Nuts - Hazel (Filbert)
- Lemon	- Walnut
- Orange	- Almond
- Grapefruit	Olive
Crabapple	Persimmon
Feijoa	Pomegranate
Figs	Quince
Loquat	Strawberries — No pruning necessary but shearing foliage at end of winter season will help fruiting in the new season.

Fruits that do better with regular pruning each year.

Bearing Habit	
Current season's growth	Grape Kiwifruit Passionfruit Brambleberries
Previous season's growth	Peach Nectarine Blueberry Raspberry Sour Cherry
Combination of previous season's growth and older wood	Apricot Plum Plumcot
Mainly two seasons' old and older wood (such as spurs that are long lived).	Apple Pear

Approximate maturing periods for fruit, nuts and berries in Canberra

The maturing dates will vary a little from season to season and from variety to variety for a given type of fruit.

	Aug	Sept	Oct	Nov	Dec	Jan	Feb	Mar	Apr	May	June	July
Almond								X	X	X		
Apple							X	X	X			
Apricot					X	X						
Blueberry						X	X					
Cherry				X	X							
Chestnut									X			
Currants						X						
Feijoa								X	X			
Fig								X	X			
Gooseberry						X	X					
Grape							X	X	X			
Hazelnut								X	X			
Kiwifruit										X		
Lemon (Meyer)									X	X		
Loquat			X	X								
Medlar										X		
Mulberry						X						
Olive									X			
Passionfruit									X	X		
Peach/Nectarine					X	X	X					
Persimmon										X		
Plum					X	X	X	X				
Quince								X	X	X		
Raspberry					X	X	X					
Rubus sp (other)						X	X					
Strawberry				X	X	X	X	X	X			
Walnut								X	X	X		

Planting on the grand scale. Canberra's new Arboretum is being planted with thousands of trees. They will be there a very long time so thorough preparation of the site and careful planting is essential. The photo shows some of the swales which will slow the passage of rain water, allowing it to sink into the ground. Some of this will reach a dam at the bottom and then be used to irrigate higher levels.

PART E: Caring for your garden

Your garden requires some simple procedures and some ongoing work.

In this section we begin with planting trees and shrubs, ways of growing your own plants, and the use of supplemental fertilisers.

Chapter 28 discusses the sorts of pests and diseases you might encounter. Often you can ignore these but sometimes you have to intervene. It's best that you do this in ways which will not damage you, your family or the environment.

The final chapter of the book provides some month-by-month guidance as to the jobs you might be doing, and some suggestions for new ideas and plants.

CHAPTER 25: Planting trees and shrubs

Revised by Adam Burgess

Preparation is the secret to successful planting. Because trees and shrubs are long-lived be sure that they are planted properly and given the best possible start in your garden. They will repay your efforts.

If you are like most people, you will have seen a plant, liked it and bought it.

You may have been attracted to the sheer look of it growing in a pot, but a better plan is to hold off buying until you have seen that plant growing in a garden. Ask the attending horticulturist at your garden centre about it, or go to Horticultural Society Shows and ask there. Whatever you do, it's best to find out a whole lot more before you buy, and especially so before you plant.

For example, does the plant need sun or shade, protection from winds and frost, lots of water, and will it need an acid soil? How big will it grow, so how much space must you allow for it? Far better to give the plant what is needed right at the start than be disappointed with the result for the next 20 years.

Some general points

In siting trees, next time it rains take notice of the water flow and try to plant in areas where water may be soaking in. A swale could help slow down water flow and make that water useful for the plants you grow. Don't plant directly under powerlines, close to the house or immediately above sewerage, gas and water pipes. Think also about the shade that the tree will cast when fully grown and the

effect it might have on other structures and plants in your garden. If the plant will require pruning or spraying, try to place it in an area where you can get at it.

Next, prepare the soil well before planting. It will be worth the extra effort. In Canberra's heavy soils, try to avoid digging a pot-sized hole because the hole will invariably fill with water and your plant could well become waterlogged and die, or at the very least, not thrive. Better to dig a bigger area than you need for the plant so that the roots will grow out into the good soil. Mix in some well-rotted compost with the existing soil and, if you can, leave for several weeks before you plant your shrub. Add plenty of water to the hole, allowing it to soak in before planting, as this will reduce the stress on the tree.

Most plants will tolerate a wide range of soil types, so long as the soil is well drained and reasonably fertile. If you have imported soil to the garden to improve soil texture ensure that it is well incorporated into the topsoil before planting so as to avoid drainage problems and a shallow root system. The soil should feel moist rather than wet. Put your finger in and feel the soil.

If you are planting a whole bed of shrubs, then begin by placing the pots in position to get spacing correct. Walk around the bed looking from many angles and imagine the trees and shrubs as mature specimens asking yourself is this the best position? Once you are happy, plant the centre of the bed first so you do not have to walk over or through those already planted. Dig a hole for each plant deep and wide enough to take the root system well spread out. If the plant is a grafted type, plant so the bud union will finish at or just above ground level — this will give a much better supported plant on our windy days than those planted higher as recommended in some publications.

All plants should be watered well after planting to settle the soil around the roots and to eliminate any air pockets. Do not allow the soil to dry out during the first twelve months after planting as moisture will help newly planted shrubs to extend their roots into the new soil. This is especially important.

Where trees are planted in turf it is best not to allow the grass to grow against the trunk. Remove the turf to a distance of approximately 30 cm from the trunk.

Regardless of position, dig a catchment around the tree to slow down any run off and allow water to soak in. Even if there has been rain you may still need to apply further water — feel the soil. In the first eight weeks it is critical not to let the tree dry out. In some cases a wetting agent may help. Take note of how much rain we have had, maybe a rain gauge will help, and adjust your watering accordingly.

Planting bare rooted trees and shrubs

It is common to plant deciduous trees and shrubs in winter while they are without their leaves. For many of these plants it is common also to buy them without soil round their roots. Roses and smaller shrubs are now readily available as potted plants at anytime of the year, but deciduous trees are usually planted bare rooted.

Always keep the root system moist when travelling from the nursery until planted. Wet newspaper wrapped around the roots is a good method.

Planting time for bare rooted trees, roses and other shrubs in our climate is anywhere from early June through to early September with August the ideal time. Bare rooted plants from local garden centres are not packed for long storage and must be planted immediately. Figure 1 shows the details of how to plant a bare rooted shrub or tree.

Plants from some outlets will be bagged in plastic to prevent them from drying out. If you are not ready, or the weather is too bad for planting, they will normally be quite happy left in their packaging for up to a week, but discuss this with your supplier. Leave the unopened package in a cool dry area such as the garage or shade house.

You will find plastic-wrapped roses on the shelves as early as April, but this is just too early to plant in Canberra. Extreme frosts may kill early growth in our climate and plants often do not recover. Reject any plants with stems shrunken or shrivelled, as this is a sign it has dried out at some stage.

Reject any plants with broken stems, showing signs of die back or having dried out excessively, showing signs of too much early growth or if the bud graft is not firmly attached to the understock. A seaweed solution, a soil conditioner rather than a fertiliser, will help reduce stress and will encourage the growth of new feeder roots.

Trim any damaged stems to just above a firm undamaged bud, and shorten any damaged roots. Be particular with the bud union to check it is not fractured from the under stock

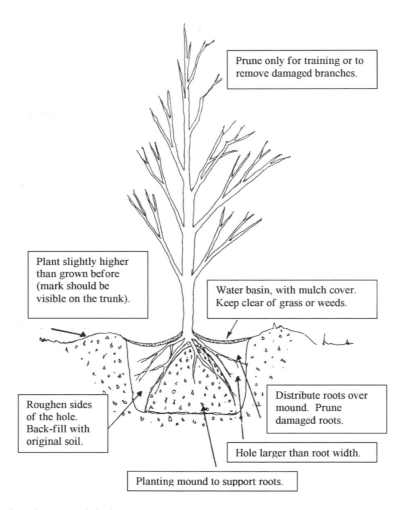

Prune only for training or to remove damaged branches.

Plant slightly higher than grown before (mark should be visible on the trunk).

Water basin, with mulch cover. Keep clear of grass or weeds.

Roughen sides of the hole. Back-fill with original soil.

Distribute roots over mound. Prune damaged roots.

Hole larger than root width.

Planting mound to support roots.

Figure 1: Planting a bare rooted shrub or tree.

as it is not very strong in young plants. Handle all plants by the under stock for the same reason.

When you bring your plants home, after unpacking soak the plants in a bucket of water for at least two hours. You could add up to 20 ml of seaweed or fish emulsion for good effect. Carry plants in the container of water to the planting site so the roots do not dry out.

A quarter-cup of nine-month slow release fertiliser may be spread into the soil at the bottom of the planting hole. Form a firm mound of soil in the centre of the hole, spread the roots of the new plant over and down on the mound, making sure the ends of the roots are facing down. Backfill the hole with soil, firming by hand only, to about two thirds of the depth of the hole and gently fill the hole with water. This water will help settle the soil around the roots and remove any air pockets. If drainage is correct this water will drain away in less than thirty minutes and then the hole should be backfilled to ground level. Because you will be planting bare-rooted plants in winter, keep the soil moist rather than wet. Use your fingers to feel the soil.

Stem (standard) roses should be planted in a similar way to bush roses but a little shallower as they are supported in the main by the stake. The top of the mound in the planting hole should be about 15 cm below ground level.

Staking

Staking is generally not necessary, except where plants are naturally weak-stemmed, but always check with the nursery if staking is required. Your site conditions will be important in deciding whether or not to stake. The need for a stake depends largely on whether or not the plant will be exposed to lots of wind. Once established, most plants will be better off without a stake. Stakes should always be used with grafted or standard plants.

Never tie the plant tightly. It should be able to move freely in the wind with the tie firm enough to support the tree and to allow the root system to develop. Inspect ties regularly to ensure that, as the tree grows, the tie has not become too tight as this may ringbark the tree. Hessian or an old pair of stockings makes good ties. You can use strips of Velcro to make an easily adjustable girdle. The top tie is the most important and the only one really required.

Do give standards a strong stake, particularly stem or tree roses, including weeping types, as all need permanent staking from the time of planting. It is important too for

other grafted or weeping specimens such as Japanese maples, special conifers, weeping cherries etc.

Planting container-grown trees and shrubs

Figure 2 shows how to plant a container-grown tree or shrub. Trees planted from containers generally benefit from a light teasing of the roots and loosening of the soil at the root base immediately prior to planting. Often the soil mix in the pot will be quite different to that in your garden and the new roots may be loathe to venture into the surrounding soil. Teasing out the roots will help this process. Some plants are particularly prone to keeping their roots in the tight ball they formed in the pot. Removing as much of the old soil as possible, though it appears drastic, will help a lot, but remember to keep the new plant well-watered.

Water the container well the day before planting and then plant it using the details of Figure 2 as a guide.

Planting into pots

Growing trees or shrubs in pots can bring a number of advantages. Pot-grown plants can be used as features to be brought forward into view when at their best. They can provide a real lift to a section of your garden in their special season. You can place a potted shrub into a position where, if it were directly in the ground, it would have to compete with a much stronger grower. Trees and shrubs that are frost-sensitive can be given shelter during the colder months and then brought into the open. They are very useful too if you are likely to move — you can take your ready-made garden with you.

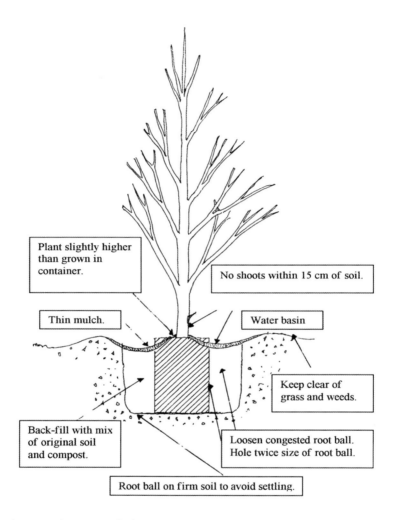

Plant slightly higher than grown in container.

No shoots within 15 cm of soil.

Thin mulch.

Water basin

Keep clear of grass and weeds.

Back-fill with mix of original soil and compost.

Loosen congested root ball. Hole twice size of root ball.

Root ball on firm soil to avoid settling.

Figure 2: Planting a container grown shrub or tree.

The main disadvantage of growing long-living plants in pots is that they exhaust the nutrient value and the structure of the soil with time. This means they have to be repotted regularly, so it is important to be sure you have the strength and willingness to handle a large pot.

The method of planting is no different to that in the open ground. It is very important that you use a good quality potting mix and not garden soil. Even so, the nutrients in the mix are finite and must be replenished on a regular basis. The old idea of using broken crocks in the bottom of the pot to ensure drainage is unnecessary with modern potting mixes. In hot weather keep an eye on the ability of the potting mix to absorb moisture and, if necessary, use a soil wetter. Regular

New plantings at the National Arboretum are protected from wind and moisture loss by plastic tree supports and well mulched with coarse woodchips.

use of seaweed solutions is a great help to plant health.

Do not put a young plant immediately into a large pot. Instead, gradually move the plant into a larger pot as it grows.

When repotting an established plant, remove it completely from its container. A strong wooden bench will be an aid here so you can invert the pot and then by tapping it against the edge of the bench remove the plant safely. Do not try to pull the plant out by its stem but rather let the weight of the plant and soil do the job upside-down. Trim a few centimetres off the roots all round, tease out the roots a bit and then return the plant to its container with fresh mix.

Watch in case the holes in the bottom become blocked as this will in time lead to death of the plant. Placing your pot on pot

feet or some old pavers, or in some other way raising it off the ground, will help prevent this and will also ensure that the plant roots do not find their way into the soil below. Some plants do this very speedily. Wheeled bases can prevent this and make the plant easier to move.

Because repotting is necessary every now and then, make sure that your pots are widest at the top. Many pots have a slightly convex shape and it can be impossible to remove a plant without damage to the plant or its container.

Any ceramic pot is better than plastic for a long-living plant, but terracotta pots will dry out more quickly that glazed pots. Plastic much more readily absorbs heat from the sun and this is harsh treatment for both plant and potting mix.

CHAPTER 26: Hints on propagation

There are many ways of growing your own plants, some of them very easy, and others more complicated. For *The Canberra Gardener* we have concentrated on three of the easiest methods — dividing existing clumps of perennials or bulbs, growing from seeds, and growing from cuttings and layers. Gardeners who wish to try grafting or budding, tissue culture and twin scaling of bulbs should refer to books devoted to plant propagation.

One thing to remember — growing from your own plants is only worthwhile if the selected plant is free of pests and diseases. From a diseased parent, the new plant will be diseased too.

Growing from divisions

This is the easiest method of all and ideal for increasing your supply of bulbs or herbaceous perennials. There is some discussion of this method in the chapter on bulbs and that on annuals and perennials. In particular, there are suggestions about timing and any special requirements in the notes on individual plants, so this chapter will simply give some general guidance in propagating your plants.

Regardless of whether or not you wish to increase the number of your plants, division of bulbs and herbaceous perennials is an essential part of prolonging their life. Every three or four years you should dig up existing clumps, rejuvenate the soil and replant the healthiest and most vigorous part of the plants.

Bulbs and the like

Bulbs and bulbous plants may be propagated

» by natural increase when new bulbs develop around existing bulbs;

» from bulbils, cormlets and the like which form on various parts of the parent;

» by division of rhizomes, tubers and tuberous roots;

» from seed which has been pollinated by bees or other insects (or hand pollinated with a view to breeding a plant superior to the parents);

» from scales of a parent bulb (the common method for most lilies);

» and by some more complicated methods such as twin scaling.

In the first three methods, carefully lift the bulbs and divide them. For best results, tulips, hyacinths and Gladiolus should be lifted and stored each year but many bulbs are best left in the garden from year to year and only need lifting when they become overcrowded and cease to flower.

When you dig bulbs and corms after flowering, they should be dried, cleaned, sorted and any damaged or diseased ones discarded as most pests and diseases of these plants can be carried over in the bulbs, etc. Before storing bulbs and corms make sure they are dry, and then dust them with an insecticide/fungicide powder and place them on raised trays with screen or slat bottoms to allow air circulation (seedling trays are ideal).

The easiest way of increasing stocks of narcissus is through natural increase of the bulbs. For a special bulb you could consider twin-scaling which allows a greater expansion in numbers.

Most rhizomes and tubers are best replanted at the time of division. If necessary, they can be stored in some slightly damp medium such as sphagnum moss. Very commonly you are advised to divide bulbs only during their dormant periods. The difficulty with this approach is that, if you can find them at all, you risk putting a fork through them, and it is difficult to avoid disturbing other plants. If you are careful you can move them at any time, with little damage to the bulbs or to surrounding plants.

Herbaceous perennials

Herbaceous and soft-wooded perennials are commonly divided to produce new plants and to rejuvenate the plant itself. Division can be done in either late autumn as plant growth slows, or in early spring just before the new growth begins. To divide a plant, firstly give it a light prune. Using a garden fork, loosen the soil around the plant and lift it from the ground, being careful not to damage the root system too much. Wash the clump to remove any soil. In some cases the clump may be pulled apart by hand, in others such as agapanthus, you may need a spade or even an axe. Cut the clump into pieces, discard the older centre, and replant the younger, more vigorous, outer growth. Do not allow the roots to dry out.

Raising from seed

Seedlings raised by the gardener are cheap to produce in quantity and can be raised in seedbeds, trays, or punnets. There are some very useful propagating boxes with clear plastic lids on the market.

Sow your seeds in a commercial seed raising mix. Level the sowing surface and lightly firm it so that the top 1–2 cm is capable of holding the tiny roots in place. Sow the seeds on the surface and water the containers lightly. (Don't apply fertiliser to the seed raising mix at seed sowing time as it is unnecessary and excess salts can build up in the mix and impair germination.) Next the seed should be lightly covered with washed sand or finely sieved seed raising mix.

Cover the seed tray with glass or clear plastic until the seeds germinate to help keep them evenly moist and for extra warmth as well. Bottom heat is beneficial if available but it is important not to let the seeds dry out.

Another approach is to sow your seeds in small containers which will rot easily in the ground — peat pots, milk cartons or rolls of paper can be used. Cucumbers and the like, tomatoes, silver beet, etc, can be raised in this way and planted into the garden once they have developed; this way there will be very little disturbance to the roots.

Germination time of annuals can vary considerably, but on average it will be between two and four weeks, provided the right temperature is maintained and sufficient water is available. Some seed requires pre-treatment to overcome dormancy. Those with hard seed coats may need abrasion (acacias), some need soaking (peas and beans), and others require exposure to high (some native plants) or low temperatures (maples). The seed packet will usually provide adequate instructions for when and how to plant your seeds, and on any special needs to ensure success.

When the seedlings are at the true leaf stage, gently prise them free of soil, holding them by a leaf so as not to damage the baby plant. You can then replant into a nutrient-rich potting mix or directly into the garden. Feed them frequently with a weak strength liquid fertiliser.

Most seeds germinate more successfully in a warm soil (15–20°C is ideal). If you are germinating seeds in winter, then seed trays should be placed in a warm spot until the seedlings are established. Until the seeds germinate, light is not usually necessary. To achieve the optimum result in our climate, timing is vital and seedlings should be planted out in mid-December for summer–autumn flowering and late March for spring flowering.

The more hardy seeds can be sown where they are to grow and thinned out. Plants like peas and beans, which have very large seeds, are best handled this way. Some seedlings hate being transplanted so they too are best sown direct where they are to grow and then thinned at an early stage. The seed packet should tell you if this is the case. Very fine seeds can easily be lost in the garden or carried away by ants so they are best sown in containers where you can look after them properly.

Transplanting seedlings into the garden should be done, if possible, in the cool of the day with a good ball of soil retained around each seedling.

To limit moisture loss, cover the seedlings with some kind of shading on sunny days until they are established. Frequent misting or watering helps. After transplanting and the seedlings are upright, a liquid fertiliser high in phosphorus will help to get the roots established.

Many gardeners prefer to omit the seed-raising process and purchase seedlings ready to be transplanted into the garden. Seedlings are usually offered in punnets. Avoid punnets where seedlings are overcrowded, and select those containing no more than about twelve sturdy, well-spaced seedlings, which are not overgrown or flowering prematurely. Transplanted seedlings should be gradually hardened off to acclimatise them to survive hot or cold temperatures, fluctuating water conditions and the effects of wind. Young plants will need fertilising, watering and protection from pests during hardening off. Water regularly but not in the evening as fungal diseases are more likely to enter in the moist night conditions. Remember to keep snails, slugs and insects in check — their main food source is the tender young leaves of seedlings.

Collecting your own seed

This can be rewarding, and is certainly cheaper than purchasing seeds each year. However, remember that many of the choicest plants nowadays are hybrids. If you are saving seeds from a hybrid plant, then the chance of reproducing plants identical to the parent is low. Even so, the seedlings may be better than an old variety, but they are most unlikely to be as good as the parent.

The main reasons for collecting your own seeds now are because you have something difficult to find, or because you are growing a heritage plant. For most of us, who only want a few plants of any particular type, collecting and then storing correctly is generally not worthwhile.

Timing is important as the seed must be ripe, yet must be harvested before the natural bursting of the seed pod. Store in a cool, dry, well-aired space away from pests that could destroy the seed. Some seed will need cleaning if it has outer coverings of pulp, hard chaff, papery wings or shell.

It is no good selecting for seed a big attractive tomato from a bush on which most of the other tomatoes are of poor quality. The seeds will reproduce the general quality shown by the bush. So, in selecting for seed, save seeds from the plants showing the best overall crop of uniform high quality flowers, pods, fruits or whatever is produced.

Seed collection from crops like sweet peas, garden peas, beans, lettuce and tomatoes is simple. No special precautions are needed, the seed being collected before it is shed. When the seedpods containing the seed are obtained, thresh out the seed, dry it thoroughly, and then store in dry airtight containers. If seed is still moist or is stored under damp conditions, it will become mouldy and will not germinate. Seed often stores better in airtight jars in the bottom of the refrigerator.

With tomatoes, pick well-ripened fruit, cut open and scrape the seeds with adhering pulp out into a fine mesh kitchen sieve and then wash by rubbing under a good flow from the tap. Then they must be dried, labelled and stored.

Damping off is a fungal disease which rots seeds before they emerge or rots young seedlings. Commercially, susceptible seeds are usually treated with a fungicide prior to sale to protect them against damping off. Damping off diseases are easily avoided by only planting seeds and seedlings when temperatures favour optimum germination and growth, by providing good drainage and by not overwatering. It helps also to water the seed at sowing time with a solution of a fungicide, following instructions on the label. Only one application should be necessary, but if damping off does occur, remove and destroy any infected seedlings and water the remaining seedlings with fungicide.

Cuttings

Many plants can easily be raised from pieces cut from a stem. Softwood cuttings are made from the stems of herbaceous plants, such as chrysanthemum, carnation, geranium and fuchsia. Hardwood cuttings of deciduous trees and shrubs are taken during the winter from dormant plants. Vines and most roses strike readily from such cuttings. It is most important to select cutting material from strong healthy plants that are pest and disease-free. Hardwood cuttings are usually around 15–30 cm long.

With softwood cuttings, usually taken in the spring, use a terminal cutting consisting of a growing point and one or more nodes below, or a leaf cutting comprising a piece of stem with one node and the leaf attached.

Hydrangeas are readily increased by cuttings, either in winter or in summer using new growth. In summer you will have to maintain humidity around the cuttings.

Many of the cuttings can be rooted in a warm, well-drained portion of the garden, especially if a little sand is worked into the soil. Softwood cuttings are planted about 2.5 cm deep, while hardwood cuttings are placed with least three-quarters of their length below the surface. The bed must be kept moist and sometimes a hessian shelter would be advantageous. In special cases, particularly with softwood cuttings and where cuttings are difficult to strike, a simple propagation box filled with sand or vermiculite is helpful. A polystyrene box with adequate drainage can be very useful for cuttings, as the polystyrene is a good insulator and keeps the soil temperature fairly constant.

The usual approach with softwood cuttings is to remove healthy and actively growing tips from the plant, 7–10 cm long. Cuttings can be taken at any time during the plant's active growing season. Use clean sharp secateurs to cut the shoot beneath a node, remove the leaves at the bottom end of the cutting and if the remaining top leaves are large, trim them off by half.

Make sure the cuttings do not wilt before planting. (They can be preserved in a sealed plastic bag with a little water for at least a few hours). Dip the newly re-cut end of the stem (just below a node) into a rooting hormone, being careful to follow the manufacturer's directions. Fill a pot with a mixture of clean sharp sand and peat moss which has been well-watered. Make a hole for each cutting, using a small stick or a pencil. Press the cutting down a little so as to be sure the base is in contact with the cutting mix. A number of cuttings can be placed into the same pot until it resembles a small forest (this is called community planting). Water well, allow to drain, and then place a plastic bag over the pot and seal to simulate humid conditions. Most softwood cuttings treated this way will strike in two to five weeks. (Hardwood cuttings can take two to six months.) There are always exceptions however, and daphne cuttings may take many months to develop roots even though they appear to be growing and developing new leaves. Be patient and wait for signs of root growth.

There are other methods of growing from cuttings. African violets can be grown by leaf, by simply inserting a cut leaf into a propagating mix, but you can grow them and many other soft plants by inserting a leaf with stem in a glass of water. Plant them into a pot when you can clearly see the new roots. Succulents are increased in a different way and this is covered in that chapter.

Layering

This is a useful form of propagation for some plants, and can occur naturally. In the simplest method a branch is bent to the ground in the spring and covered with 8 to 15 cm of soil, leaving the tip exposed to develop new growth. If one or two notches are cut on the underside of the layer and kept open with matches the formation of roots will be stimulated. Usually sufficient roots develop in the first season so that the new plant can be detached in the autumn or next spring. Rhododendrons, azaleas, daphne and roses can be propagated in this way. Many plants will layer themselves naturally in the surrounding mulch and the new bits can be detached and planted elsewhere.

Aerial layering is carried out the same way as normal layering, but the treated stem is enclosed in damp sphagnum moss or peat (sterilised for preference). The sphagnum moss is kept in place by a sheet of transparent plastic material wrapped round the moss and tied around the stem at each end. Developing roots can be seen through the clear plastic and when they almost completely fill the sphagnum envelope, the branch is cut off below the roots and planted. This is a useful way of propagating magnolias and rhododendrons.

CHAPTER 27: Supplemental fertilisers

Revised by Susan Orgill

Plants that are grown in soil which contains a reasonable percentage of humus should grow and flower well. However, the general health of the plants and the size of the blooms may be improved by the application of fertilisers. In new gardens it is unlikely that your soil will contain the humus and organic matter it needs and so you may well be dependent on supplemental feeding for a while.

Australian soils are ancient which means that many elements such as phosphorus, present long ago, are available now only in small quantities. Others such as nitrogen are readily leached away so that nutrient application in some form is essential for healthy plants. Various elements have various effects on growth.

» Nitrogen (N) promotes leaf growth. If leached by rainfall or watering below the root zone, the subsequent deficiency of nitrogen causes an initial yellowing of older leaves and then plant stunting.

» Phosphorus (phosphate, P) promotes root formation and stimulates flower production. Deficiencies show up as reduced growth, yellowing and sometimes a purple colour in older leaves.

» Potassium (potash, K) gives increased plant vigour and disease resistance. Deficiencies result in poor growth, with scorched margins and spots on older leaves.

The above (N, P and K) are the main elements for healthy plants but others such as calcium,

Do not use phosphorous rich fertilisers around some of the natives, such as this Grevillea. Because our soils are phosphorous poor some of our plants have adapted to grab every bit they can and can quickly get too much with fatal consequences for the plant.

magnesium, sulphur, iron and molybdenum are also necessary for good growth. If one essential element is in short supply, then the others will not make up for it, and growth will be poor. The converse is true also. An over-supply of a particular element (possibly through over-enthusiastic fertilising) can cause distress and perhaps death in a plant and can 'tie up' other nutrients through imbalances.

Suitable fertilisers can be either organic, such as cow or sheep manure, or inorganic, such as ready mixed plant-specific foods or complete general-purpose fertilisers. It is important, when using fertilisers, to heed some general principles. These are:

» Fertilise only when the soil is moist, and avoid fertilising if the soil is too saturated or waterlogged.

» Avoid fertilising in cold conditions.

» The fertiliser should be spread evenly in the area of the dripline and not against the main stem.

» Too much fertiliser could damage the plant and even cause it to die.

» Fertilisers should be applied strictly in accordance with directions.

» When comparing product quality and price, compare the nutrient content (i.e. P% per 100 g product) of the input.

» It is especially important to consider the nutrient content in relation to other nutrients. For example, you may over-apply phosphorous because you apply a lot of poultry litter to achieve a certain amount of nitrogen while phosphorus is required in lesser amounts (poultry litter on average contains N (% of dry matter) 2.6 versus P (% of dry matter)1.8).

The best time to fertilise is when a plant is beginning its active growth, with a consistent follow-up in mid-summer.

The degree of acidity or alkalinity in the soil is important for many plants and is measured by the pH of the soil — see the glossary. Generally, Canberra soils are in the pH range of 5.5–7.0 (in water). Most plants like a pH slightly acidic as this is when the majority of plant nutrients are available. If your pH is less than 5.5 (in water) you may need to consider liming. Excessively alkaline soils are uncommon in this area.

Plants such as daphnes, azaleas, rhododendrons and camellias prefer a somewhat acid soil, so be careful of liming near them.

It is possible to change the pH of your soil, but it can be a difficult and slow process. It is

A vegetable garden as healthy as this depends on lots of feeding, but mostly we do that with composts, mulches and animal manures.

probably much easier to stick with plants that like neutral or slightly acid soils.

When planting, either inorganic or organic fertilisers can be placed in the bottom of the planting hole provided they are well worked into the soil. Where clay is near the surface, wide shallow holes are preferable to deep ones.

Organic fertilisers

These are materials which contain carbon and are derived from plants or animals. Organic materials can be regarded as slow-release fertilisers as the nutrients are dissolved slowly and are released into the soil over several months. This has the advantage of minimising both the risk of over-fertilising and nutrient loss after rain or watering. Generally, organic fertilisers are required in larger amounts than inorganic fertilisers as they contain lesser amounts of nutrients. Organic materials are very important for encouraging soil microbial processes including nutrient mineralisation.

As discussed in an earlier chapter, compost can be used to improve the physical structure of the soil but since it contains decomposed plant material, nutrients are also present.

These tuberous begonias are perhaps most easily fed using a pelletised slow release product or, alternatively, regular weak solutions of a liquid fertiliser.

Composting is thus recommended wherever it is practical.

Other organic fertilisers include blood and bone (5-7% N, 5% P) and animal manures (1–8% N). Some of these such as fresh poultry manure or litter may burn plants. Fresh manure is best put through the compost heap.

Inorganic fertilisers

These are chemicals derived from non-living sources and usually sold in packaged form as granules or powders. Some, such as lime or gypsum, occur naturally while others such as superphosphate and sulphate of ammonia are manufactured. Most of the latter type are soluble in water and so can be applied as sprays on the soil or on plants (as well as being incorporated dry into the soil).

Simple fertilisers such as sulphur may contain only one basic element; more complex fertilisers will contain many, including trace elements. They have the following advantages over organic fertilisers:

» There is a fixed composition which is stated on the bag. Some 'complete'

fertilisers contain the stated amounts of N, P and K but not necessarily the other elements needed for plant growth;

» The concentrations of elements supplied are usually relatively high so that bulkiness is reduced;

» Nutrients are more readily available to plants (when in solution), whereas organic fertilisers may break down only slowly.

There are however some disadvantages in their use:

» It is easy to over-fertilise with inorganic fertilisers, so follow directions and water before and after application;

» Nutrients, particularly some of the nitrogen and sulphur, can be leached out of the rootzone;

» Most importantly, they do not add organic matter to the soil.

Rates of application will vary with soil type — in general the higher the clay level, the more buffered the soil so therefore more fertiliser is required to achieve change. The feeding roots of established shrubs and trees are likely to be some distance away from the centre of the plant so fertiliser can be applied in a band under the outer foliage. This will help to overcome the problem of fixation especially with phosphorus and make more available to the plant.

Don't apply a lot of fertiliser at the one time — stay within the recommended limits. Water in well if feeding plants via the soil and ensure the outer roots are sufficiently supplied.

Slow release fertilisers

One of the great advances in recent years has been the development of pelletised, slow release fertilisers. You can buy many different formulas which provide a choice of nutrients and also of release speed so you can use them for any sort of plant — you simply have to work out what the fertiliser needs of your plant are going to be and then buy an appropriate type. In this regard, many of the fast-growing ornamentals such as annuals, as well as vegetables and grass have much higher nutrient requirements than established shrubs and trees.

Use them in planting holes, in pots and sprinkle them around established plants. There is no danger to plants in using them as nutrients are only released when there is sufficient moisture. The gardens and lawns of Parliament House are fed almost exclusively with pelletised products which give a timed and gradual release of food. The plants receive their food as they need it, rather than in sudden burst, which is more usually the case with traditional fertilisers.

At the time of writing the main problem is in finding bulk supplies of this sort of plant food. As well, you should be aware that the pellets may not work well if the soil temperature is low. Conversely, if the pellets are left on the soil surface and subjected to fluctuations of moisture and temperature, they may burst and release all their nutrients well away from the roots where it is needed. Bury them rather than sprinkling them on the soil surface.

Liquid fertilisers

These are another relatively new product although of course homemade liquid fertilisers and manures have been around for years. Seaweed based products are good for just about any sort of plant. They have to be applied regularly as they contain only low concentrations of nutrient, but can also be used to give plants a boost. Some Canberra gardeners have had very good results by spraying their roses with mixes derived largely from seaweed or fish products.

There are also concentrated inorganic powders which are good for flowering annuals and perennials in particular. A more extensive range of this type of product is gradually coming onto the market, designed for specific plants.

HOME GARDEN FUNGICIDE

ACTIVE CONSTITUENT: 940 g/kg POTASSIUM BICARBONATE

CHAPTER 28:
Leaning towards organic gardening

Ruth Kerruish

BFA ALLOWED INPUT
CERTIFIED
PRODUCT FOR
ORGANIC GARDE

This chapter covers a number of areas. To help you find your way, the main topics are listed below, together with the starting pages for their discussion. The many pests and diseases discussed are all listed in the index at the end of the book.

Growing healthy plants

Home gardeners are in a good position to maximize the use of organic methods by using integrated pest management, that is, combining good cultural practice and encouraging beneficial insects. In doing this there will be less need for pesticides to keep the garden healthy. Many of the insects seen on plants are not pests. Some are beneficial in that they feed on pest species; others do so little damage that control is not necessary. Learning more about your garden and what constitutes a pest is vital to success with this approach.

Effective control does not mean 100 per cent control of pests and diseases and as home gardeners we can accept a few damaged leaves, flowers or fruit.

Many gardeners (especially fruit and vegetable gardeners) use organic techniques. They rely on cultural methods such as compost, careful sanitation and pruning out diseased plant parts, preserving predatory insects, selecting hardy problem-free plants or resistant varieties, hand weeding and digging, to control pests, diseases and weeds. In organic systems products are grown and processed without the use of synthetic chemicals, fertilisers, or genetically modified organisms. For those home gardeners who may wish to pursue this more seriously there is now a domestic standard (AS 6000-2009 Organic and Biodynamic Products) which outlines minimum requirements to be met by growers wishing to label their products 'organic' or 'biodynamic'. Some organic pesticides are listed in the Table beginning on page 375; the logo for organic certified products is shown on a label on page 341.

Annual flowers, fruit crops, vegetables, roses and lawns all require maintenance to obtain a crop or look attractive so careful selection of species and varieties to suit your garden is important. Trees and shrubs can be regarded as low-maintenance plants providing attention is given to selection for size, water requirements and resistance to pests and diseases.

The type of problem often determines the method of control used, eg virus diseases in roses and strawberries are avoided by using only virus-tested nursery stock and runners respectively. For some plant problems several methods of control may be involved, eg for fruit fly in Canberra, sanitation and the application of fruit fly baits are usually necessary.

By and large, most garden problems can be addressed without need for pesticides; on the other hand pesticide applications may be needed to prevent some key problems, eg peach leaf curl on very susceptible varieties of stone fruit.

Canberra gardeners are very fortunate in having a wonderful source of advice through regular plant clinics at the School of Horticulture, Canberra Institute of Technology, Bruce campus. For more information call on 6207 4610.

Cultural methods

Plants should be provided with their correct growing conditions. For example, avoid planting azaleas in areas with poor drainage as they are sensitive to waterlogging. Conifers in Canberra frequently suffer from moisture stress during the summer months although their needles will not brown until several months after.

Environmental conditions can also affect the development of pests and diseases. For example, twospotted mite infestation is favoured by hot weather. Some of these conditions can be avoided, others not. Damping off is common in seedlings and cuttings when low soil temperatures favour development of these fungi and bacteria rather than plant growth. Tomato spotted wilt is more serious when tomatoes are planted early.

The main reason for crop rotation in a vegetable garden or flower garden is to make the best use of soil nutrients and to reduce the likelihood of some soil borne diseases.

Nutrient deficiencies and excesses should be avoided. For example, lush growth on stone fruit trees is susceptible to attack by the oriental fruit moth.

Companion plants are usually plants which have been grown in combination and found by observation to be mutually beneficial. There are many books available on the art of companion planting. Some plants are reputed to actively discourage neighbouring plants. For example the roots of black walnut secrete a toxin which inhibits the growth of tomatoes, potatoes and birch trees. Chemicals washed by rain or irrigation from bark of eucalypts trees, shed bark and leaf litter, may inhibit the growth of surrounding plants. Fibrous-barked eucalypts are more inhibitory than smooth-barked species and the effects are likely to be more significant if irrigation or rainfall is inadequate.

Remember, many trees and shrubs have an optimum life span beyond which they tend to deteriorate.

Sanitation

Sanitation prevents or delays the spread of pests, diseases or weeds and is often combined with other methods. Crop residues from vegetable and annual flower crops should be removed promptly and be properly composted to prevent diseases multiplying on them. Only a few diseases overwinter in autumn leaves falling from trees and shrubs, and most fallen leaves may be composted or placed on garden beds.

Destruction of an affected plant may be sensible if problems arise which are extremely difficult to control, eg young stone fruit trees infected with bacterial canker or indoor plants severely infected with powdery mildew or infested with mealybugs.

Tree surgery involves the removal of wood from trees which are infested with wood rot fungi, borers or damaged in some other way. Advice should be sought on procedures or the services of a tree surgeon obtained.

Stationary insects such as scale can be wiped or brushed off a plant. Chewing insects, eg beetles and many caterpillars are easily picked from plants. Wear gloves when handling some insects, eg hairy caterpillars. A strong jet of water will dislodge and drown some insects such as aphids.

Biological control

Biological control is part of the overall phenomenon of natural control and put simply, is the deliberate use of natural enemies to control a particular pest, disease or weed. Biological control does not aim to eliminate the pest but tends towards stability at a low level of infestation, ideally, below the level of economic injury. The attacked plant

may, however, be seriously damaged before natural controls become fully effective.

Some gardeners keep a range of plants which are thought to attract beneficial insects. You can buy a range of seeds for these.

Home gardeners can assist natural and biological controls by learning to recognize beneficial insects such as ladybirds, parasitic wasps and lacewings. Many local insects, mites and pests are controlled or partly-controlled by biological control agents which have been released on a large scale or occur naturally, eg woolly aphid, greenhouse whitefly and twospotted mite. Some of these problems though may occasionally require additional control measures.

Home gardeners can buy a range of insects which attack and control specific pests, for example a predatory mite which feeds on twospotted mite, a pest of roses, beans, tomatoes and many other plants. The internet is a good source for these but you might begin with www.ecoorganicgarden.com.au

Many agricultural weeds are now biologically controlled to some extent by insects and fungal diseases, the most famous being

Ladybird beetles (6–7 mm long) feed on scales, aphids and other insects.

A tiny **parasitic wasp** lays an egg in a scale insect.

Praying mantis (often 20–120 mm long) feed on other insects.

Lacewings are delicate insects with lacy wings (commonly up to 20 mm long). They may feed on other insects.

READ SAFETY DIRECTIONS

eco-fungicide®

HOME GARDEN FUNGICIDE

ACTIVE CONSTITUENT: 940 g/kg POTASSIUM BICARBONATE

FOR THE MANAGEMENT OF FUNGUS DISEASES IN ROSES, GRAPEVINES, VEGETABLES & STRAWBERRIES IN THE HOME GARDEN AS PER DIRECTIONS FOR USE.

BFA ALLOWED INPUT 222AI
CERTIFIED PRODUCT FOR ORGANIC GARDENS

NET CONTENTS
500g

ORGANIC CROP PROTECTANTS PTY LTD
42 Halloran St Lilyfield 2040 NSW Australia
Telephone (02) 9810 4566　Fax (02) 9610 4674
A.C.N 003 149 719

AUSTRALIAN MADE & OWNED

Note the symbol in the bottom right hand corner that tells you this product has been certified by the BFA as suitable for organic gardens.

prickly pear which is controlled by the cactoblastis caterpillar.

Few diseases can be biologically controlled. Compost encourages the multiplication of beneficial bacteria and fungi in the soil which suppress disease-causing organisms.

Resistant varieties

Plants can suppress or retard the activities of a pest or disease. This, and the use of problem-free plants, are preventative methods of control. Some plants have multiple resistance but even slightly resistant varieties or species are useful in that they reduce the number of pesticide applications or may allow natural or biological controls to be effective.

For many plant problems such as rusts and soil fungal diseases, sensitivity to frost, waterlogging or drought, the use of resistant

varieties may be the only practical control. Perennial plantings such as trees, hedges, specimen plants and those beside swimming pools, in addition to being selected for their general features, should be selected for their resistance to pests and diseases.

Quarantine

Australia has many introduced pests, diseases and weeds, eg poplar rust, rabbits and Paterson's curse. However, the number of problems recorded overseas which still do not occur in Australia total many thousands. Coffee rust and Dutch elm disease are only two examples. Information on how to import plant material may be obtained from the Australian Department of Agriculture, Forestry & Fisheries (DAFF).

Regional and Interstate quarantine measures are designed to prevent the spread of diseases, pests and weeds already in Australia to 'clean' areas. They are not intended to interfere with the movement of produce or plant material when this can be done without danger of spreading diseases and pests. Codling moth and starlings do not occur in Western Australia. Information on importing plant material from other regions of Australia to Canberra may be obtained from Canberra Connect Tel 6207 9777 (ACT Government).

In a home garden, all plants should be inspected carefully for pests and diseases after purchase, prior to planting. Check that you are not giving your friends insect pests or weeds, when parting with cuttings or potted plants.

Disease and pest-free planting material

Diseases, especially virus diseases and occasionally insect pests and weed seeds, are often carried in, on, or in association with seeds, bulbs, cuttings and other propagation material. Select cuttings, bulbs and seeds only from healthy plants. Some plant species, eg strawberry, bulbs, potatoes, carnations and chrysanthemums, available through garden centres, are guaranteed free from certain diseases.

Physical methods

Devices such as scarecrows, bird-scaring kites and humming lines are probably the best known approaches to frightening off pests. Bird netting and other barriers keeps birds from fruit. There is a range of exclusion bags, fruit socks, insect traps and tree wraps available — see, for example, www.greenharvest.com.au

Upturned flower pots stuffed with paper provide shelter for earwigs which can later be collected and destroyed. Yellow sticky traps attract whiteflies, aphids, leafhoppers and moths. Beneficial insects may also be attracted. Lures will trap and monitor fruit flies and codling moths, indicating when they are around. Rough mulches prevent snails and slugs from reaching your seedlings.

Fallen, infested fruit can be collected and placed in a plastic bag in the sun for 3 days to kill codling moth caterpillars and fruit fly maggots.

Soil solarisation prior to planting involves trapping the energy from the sun under clear plastic sheeting laid on soil beds for at least 4–6 weeks during summer. The soil may be heated to a depth of 30–25cm and summer soil temperatures can rise to 60°C which may assist control of some soil fungal diseases. Water the beds before solarisation to improve control. Home gardeners can put soils and mixes in plastic bags and leave in sun for 2–3 weeks.

Composting temperatures (60°C for at least 30 minutes), are high enough to destroy soil disease organisms but not some beneficial bacteria and fungi. These temperatures are not high enough to kill weed seeds and rhizomes.

Pesticides

A wide range of pesticides (fungicides, insecticides, herbicides or weedkillers, snail baits, repellents) are available for home gardeners. Some are specific for particular pests or diseases, others are broad spectrum and will control more than one pest or disease. Multi-purpose garden sprays and dust mixtures, controlling both insects and diseases, are available for roses, vegetables, etc. They avoid the need for buying several different products. Home gardeners should be aware that some pesticides are 'biological' products and have been approved for organic systems and carry the BFA organic logo. The more toxic pesticides are not available from retail garden centres and are restricted to commercial horticulture or agriculture where users must undergo regular chemical user training courses. Some pesticides available to home gardeners are not approved for use on food producing plants. The safe use of pesticides is described on page 370.

Diagnosing plant problems

By correctly identifying the problem (if it is a problem) the appropriate control (if considered necessary) can be chosen. The majority of insects, mites, fungi and other organisms are 'beneficial'. Probably less than 1 per cent are really harmful to plants and even then, comparatively few cause serious problems.

The tableland's relatively dry climate does not generally favour the extensive development of diseases and the cold winters reduce

insect populations. Many plant problems in Canberra are caused by unsatisfactory growing conditions.

Identify the plant

Identification of the affected plant narrows the list of possible problems. Problems affecting some hosts, eg roses, lemons, azaleas, Australian plants, vegetables, fruit crops are listed in earlier chapters. For other plants you may need to refer to specialist sources of information.

Symptoms

If you can actually see the insect causing trouble, identification of the problem is often relatively easy. Diseases are not so easy to recognize as you cannot see the actual organisms causing the problem, but only its effect on the plant. It is useful to know what the plant looks like normally at different times of the year.

History of plant

Ask yourself what has happened to the plant, eg fertiliser and mulch applications, frequency and type of irrigation, drainage, pesticide

Identify plant, eg banksias, rose.

Look for symptoms, eg leaf spots.

History of plant, eg sun, frost, rain, fertiliser, irrigation, herbicide injury. Soil pH, nutrient deficiencies or excesses. Too dry, too wet, too windy.

applications, when purchased, if it is a tree or shrub, how tall it is, when was it planted, how old is it, etc. Answers to these questions often solve the problem.

Getting help

Garden advisors not only identify plant problems but also may do soil pH tests and provide advice on control. Take fresh specimens from both healthy and damaged parts of the plant. Collect soil for testing from 4–5 spots around the plant to a depth of 10–12 centimetres. Try to include part of the fine root system, for small plants bring the entire plant including top, roots and soil. Photographs of affected plants can be emailed to garden advisors.

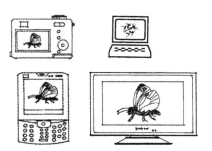

Get help. Telephone, email or better still, take or send insect or affected plant to a garden advice service.

Pests

Some pests may affect a wide range of plants while others may only attack one family, genus, species or one variety. Remember many of the insects seen on plants are not pests. Insect pests damage plants mainly by their feeding habits. They chew, suck or rasp plant tissue. Insects which damage plants change from egg to adult by one of two ways.

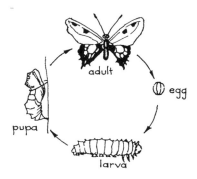

Young (larvae) hatch from the egg in a form totally different from the adult, egg ants, bees, butterflies and moths, beetles, spitfires, wasps.

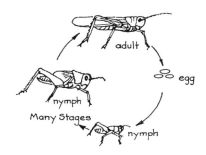

Young (nymphs) hatch from the egg in a form resembling the adult but initially they have no functional wings, eg aphids, mealybugs, thrips, whiteflies.

Chewing insects such as beetles, caterpillars and sawfly larvae, eat and swallow pieces of the plant. Sucking insects such as aphids, bugs, leafhoppers, lerp, mealybugs, scales, whitefly and mites, pierce the plant surface and suck plant juices from within the plant. Thrips rasp the plant surface and then suck up the plant juices. Some sap-sucking insects, like aphids, leafhoppers and thrips may also transmit virus diseases. Honeydew, insect excreta and webbing produced by some insects, may disfigure plants.

Ants

Ants are easily recognized, as they have a distinctive 'waist', adults have two pairs of gauzy wings. Ants are attracted to the honeydew produced by aphids, some scales, and other sap-sucking insects. Sticky material around the base of trees and shrubs will stop ants climbing up the trunk. Ants also nest in lawns and may eat newly-planted seed. They may sting humans and pets. Various ant baits are available from garden centres.

Aphids

Aphids are small, globular, soft, winged or wingless insects from 1–4 mm long, which often cluster and suck sap from young shoots, flower buds and under young leaves which curl under and often die. Aphids vary in colour, eg cabbage aphids are yellowish-green when young and mature forms are dull greyish green, green peach aphids are shiny green to pale yellow or pink, citrus aphids are black and woolly aphids secrete white woolly waxy threads. Aphids have long legs and antennae and two cornicles on their rear. Some species secrete honeydew which attracts ants and on which black sooty mould grows. The ants protect honeydew-producing aphids and scales from their natural enemies. Some aphids also transmit virus diseases.

Wingless aphid (commonly 1-2 mm long). Note two cornicles at rear end.

Ants vary in size from tiny to quite large.

Parasitised aphid in which a wasp has laid one egg which hatched into a larva. When fully fed, the larva pupate inside the by now swollen body of the aphid and emerge through a hole on its back.

Typical ant trail

Aphid sucking sap and excreting honeydew.

Pest cycle. Aphids may lay eggs or live young and large populations build up quickly especially in spring and autumn. Young aphids (nymphs) resemble the adult but are wingless; adults may be winged or wingless.

What to do: Aphids do not like very hot or very cold weather. Heavy rain decreases aphid populations. A strong jet of water will dislodge aphids from sturdy plants such as roses, but they tend to return within a day or so. Parasitic wasps and fungal diseases reduce aphid numbers but do not generally provide adequate control. Some gardeners, with varying degrees of success, use companion planting. On edible and ornamental plants, pyrethrum and soap sprays give some control but several applications are usually required. On ornamental outdoor plants more effective insecticides provide control over a longer period.

Bees

Bees, like ants, have a waist and two pairs of gauzy wings; they also have hairs on their body. Their main value to the gardener is as pollinators. Adult leaf-cutting bees cut pieces from soft leaves of roses, lilac, etc to build their nests. Some species sting.

Bee, honeybees are 10–20 mm long.

Leaf-cutting bee injury to rose leaves.

Pest cycle. Eggs hatch into legless larvae which pupate when fully fed. Adults emerge from the pupae.

What to do: Damage caused by leaf-cutting bees is seldom serious enough to warrant any action as damage is only noticed after bees have long since gone.

Beetles

Beetles have a hard and compact body; the front pair of wings is hardened into hard wing covers. The hind wings are gauzy and used in flight, when not in use they are neatly tucked under the wing covers. Both adult beetles and their larvae have chewing mouthparts and both may damage plants.

Christmas beetle and larvae (scarab grub). The grubs vary in size but are commonly about 20 mm long.

Beneficial beetles (about 5–7 mm long) feed on aphids, scales and other insects.

Pest cycle: Beetles lays eggs which hatch into legged or legless larvae depending on the species. When fully fed the larvae pupate, later the adult beetle emerges.

Christmas beetles feed on the leaves and young shoots of eucalypts and other plants during the daytime from December to February. Trees may be completely defoliated. Larvae are commonly called scarab grubs, and like the larvae of other scarab beetles, feed on the roots of grasses in lawns. Some other beetles feed on aphids, scale and other insects.

What to do: Depends on the species. Natural enemies of beetles and their larvae include birds and fungal diseases. Controls vary and are discussed under specific plants.

Birds

Parrots of various types, silvereyes, currawongs and other birds may damage flowers, fruit and vegetables.

What to do: Frightening devices such as scarecrows, rags and aluminium foil are commonly used with varying degrees of success to deter birds. If used only for short periods they may be successful but birds tend to become used to them. Humming lines and hawk kites are recent innovations. Netting for fruit trees and vegetable seedlings may be necessary. Shadecloth can be temporarily thrown over small trees during the ripening period and removed afterwards. Grape bunches may be protected by stockings, paper bags or open-ended plastic bags. Indian mynas compete with native birds and arboreal mammals for nesting sites, preying on eggs, chicks and young mammals. They nest in trees, especially pencil pines, soiling the ground underneath. Food scraps around outdoor eating areas attract them. Traps and more information are available from The Canberra Indian Myna Action Group. See http://www.indianmynaaction.org.au/.

Borers

Borers are mostly the larvae of beetles and moths which attack a wide range of trees and shrubs such as eucalypts, wattles, silk trees and tamarisks.

Pest cycle: Eggs are usually laid on the trunk and on hatching, larvae tunnel within the branch or trunk upwards or downwards and sometimes into the roots as well. When fully grown (may take years) the larvae pupate just below the surface of the bark. Adults emerge through exit holes on the trunk.

Fruit-tree borer. Caterpillars of this moth feed on bark and bore into the trunk of wattles, stone fruit and other trees and shrubs. Tunnels increase in size as the caterpillar grows to 7–10 cm long by the time larvae are fully grown. The tunnels are usually made in the forks of trees and damaged bark is always covered with a webbed mass of gnawed wood and excreta. During the day the caterpillar hides in the tunnel and at night comes out to feed on the bark surrounding the tunnel entrance.

Longicorn beetles. Larvae chew tunnels in trunks, limbs and roots of trees and shrubs. They are legless, whitish and measure up to 40 mm long. Adult longicorns are handsome beetles with antennae about three times the length of the body. Adult beetles usually emerge during spring leaving a circular exit hole in the trunk.

What to do: Control is difficult because damage may be extensive before the problem is noticed. Trees under stress appear to be more susceptible to infestation so maintain adequate watering and fertilising regimes; judicious pruning may help. Because tunnels made by the fruit-tree borer are short it is possible to kill the caterpillar by clearing the sawdust away and either poking a thin wire down the tunnel or squirting household insecticide into the entrance. There are no useful chemical controls for the home gardener. Advice may be sought on tree surgery.

Bugs

Bugs are usually large insects and are often called shield bugs because of their shape and tough exterior.

Green vegetable bugs are dark green, about 12 mm long and 8 mm wide, shield-shaped with a small head. They have well-developed legs and run and fly when disturbed, but usually drop to the ground when the plant is touched. They have an objectionable odour. Young black bugs emerge from eggs laid on the leaves. During successive moults they may be spotted with red, green, black and yellow. All stages cause serious damage to tomatoes, beans and other plants. Some bugs, such as the assassin bug, feed on other insects.

Pest cycle: The young resemble the adult in shape but may differ in colour. Young and adults feed by sucking plant sap and some exude offensive odours hence the common name 'stink bugs'.

What to do: A wasp which parasitises the eggs of the green vegetable bug has been released and provides some control. In a home garden the bugs can be collected when they are feeding on the tomato or beans etc during sunny periods of the day. Very occasionally during seasons particularly favourable to the pest, a garden dust or spray may be necessary.

Adult bug with 2 pairs of wings, front pair with a thickened front part. Often called shield bugs.

Green vegetable bug (12 mm long) suck sap from tomatoes, beans and many other plants.

Azalea lace bugs suck sap from the back of azalea and rhododendron leaves.

Left: Adult with lacey wings.
Right: Spiny nymph. Both 3–4 mm long.

Assassin bug (20 mm long) feeds on other insects by sucking out their contents.

Butterflies and moths (caterpillars)

Butterflies and moths feed mostly on plant nectar; it is the larvae or caterpillars which damage plants. As a rule of thumb, butterflies are day-flying with clubbed antennae, brightly-coloured, wings vertical when at rest. Moths are night-flying, antennae are other than clubbed, often drab-coloured, wings are held flat when at rest.

Pest cycle: Butterflies and moths lay eggs on plant tissue, which hatch into tiny caterpillars and feed on plant tissue. When fully fed they find a place to pupate and later the adult emerges. Usually there are several generations each season.

Cabbage white butterflies have white fore wings about 50 mm across. Hind wings are distinctly yellow. Caterpillars hatch from eggs laid on the undersides of leaves, are up to 25–30 mm long, velvety-green with a faint yellow stripe down the back and along each side. Initially they feed on leaf undersurfaces, and then eat holes through the leaves, only the veins may remain. Excreta (frass) is a sign of activity. Caterpillars pupate on leaf undersurfaces or in sheltered places such as fences.

Citrus butterflies are large and colourful and about 13 cm across the outspread wings which have brown, black, white, grey, orange, red and blue markings. Caterpillars feed on citrus, Mexican orange blossom and similar plants and when full grown are about 65 mm long and light brown to olive-green in colour. When disturbed, caterpillars extend a red, fleshy, forked scent organ from behind their heads which emits a pungent odour.

Codling moth is the No.1 pest of apples, pears and quince in the ACT, but only of trees in fruit. Holes are seen on the outside of fruit, sometimes also 'sawdust' or 'gum'. When fruit is cut open a tunnel leads to the core where a single creamy coloured caterpillar about 12 mm long is usually found feeding. Control is difficult and complex.

Quarantine regulations prohibit the movement of fruit to areas of Australia where codling moth does not occur. However, it is not compulsory for home gardeners in the ACT to carry out sanitation and spraying to control codling moth. Attempts should still be made to minimize the pest, which includes collecting all fruit on the ground and all infested fruit on the tree every 7 days, then destroying it by securing in a plastic bag and exposing to the sun for 3–4 days to kill the caterpillars.

As codling caterpillars also pupate on trunks and surrounding litter, brush trunks to remove any pupae. Trunks may also be banded with cardboard under which caterpillars like to pupate; it can be removed every three weeks and destroyed. There are lures which attract male moths and so indicate when moths are around and time to spray. As a rule of thumb for fruiting apple and pear trees this is about the end of October but varies. 'Desire' codling moth traps which attract both male and female moths can be purchased.

Corn earworm (also called tomato caterpillar) is a pest of many plants including vegetables, ornamentals, field crops and weeds. They are difficult to control because they often infest vegetable fruits as they are ripening. Caterpillars grow up to 4 cm in length and feed on young foliage and buds during moist warm weather. Large caterpillars may move from one tomato fruit to another and entry holes may be as large as 3 mm across.

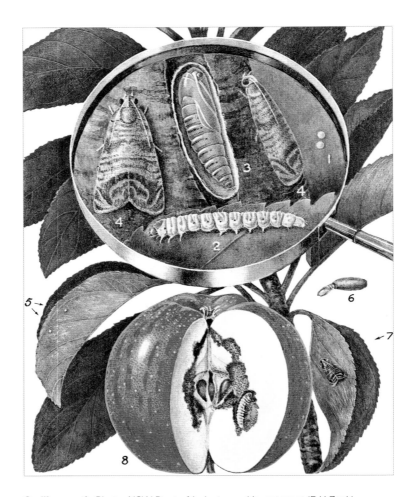

Codling moth *Photo: NSW Dept of Industry and Investment (E.H.Zeck).*

1. Eggs (about x4).

2. Caterpillar (about x3).

3. Cocoon spun in crack in bark cut open to show pupa.

4. Adult moths in resting position (about x4).

Actual size

5. Eggs on leaf.

6. Cocoon showing empty pupal skin from which a moth has emerged.

7. Moths resting on leaf.

8. Apple showing damage caused by the caterpillar feeding inside

Caterpillars of the **corn earworm** boring into tomatoes.

Infested tomatoes should be removed and destroyed. The tops of infested corncobs may be cut off after harvest.

Lightbrown apple moth is a common pest of a wide range of plants. Caterpillars are very active; 25 mm long and light green. They tie leaves and growing tips together and when disturbed drop and wriggle while dangling from a silken thread.

Citrus butterfly is Canberra's most beautiful butterfly, the. Larvae feed on citrus and Mexican orange blossom.

Cabbage white butterfly has club shaped antennae. Larvae feed on brassicas, stock and related weeds.

A **moth**, note feathery antennae.

Grapevine moth caterpillar (up to 50 mm long) has lots of legs.

What to do: Marix cloth may be spread over brassica plants to prevent cabbage white butterflies laying eggs on the foliage. Leaf-eating caterpillars may be hand-picked, but may be difficult to see or, if hairy, may cause skin irritation. Wear gloves as a precaution. Dipel®, is a biological bacterial insecticide specifically developed for certain leaf-eating caterpillars. To be effective it must be applied when caterpillars are small. In severe infestations a chemical insecticide may be necessary to provide faster control.

Earwigs

The European earwig, in addition to infesting houses, may also damage plants by chewing on leaves, flowers (petals) and fruit. Leaves and flowers develop a ragged appearance. They also spoil plants by their presence and their excreta.

Pest cycle: Young earwigs resemble adults, both stages are nocturnal and omnivorous feeders.

What to do: Earwigs may be trapped in rolled newspapers or other shelter traps and destroyed. Outdoors infested areas and plants can be treated with an insecticide.

Male and female **earwigs** (12–20 mm long).

Flies

Flies have only one pair of wings. It is the larvae or legless maggots of some species which cause plant damage. Maggots of leafmining flies may damage some chrysanthemum species.

Fermentation flies are commonly found associated with over-ripe fruit and vegetables. Unlike Queensland fruit flies which are slightly larger, they do not attack unripe fruit.

Queensland fruit fly. This pest occurs occasionally in Canberra in late summer and autumn in pome fruits, stone fruits, tomatoes and capsicums a few weeks before harvesting. Adult flies are a little larger than the house fly, wasp-like in appearance and reddish-brown in colour. The mid-portion of the body has distinct lemon-yellow patches. The wings have a narrow dark band along their front margins.

Pest cycle: Eggs are laid under the skin of developing fruit and many white to creamy maggots, about 8 mm long, burrow through fruit. Their presence is detected by the 'give' when fruit is pressed; fruit often decays. When fully grown, maggots spring from the fruit and pupate at a depth of 5–7 cm in the soil.

What to do: Control can be difficult in a home garden but attempts can be made to minimise the pest. Collect all fruit on the ground and all infested fruit on the tree every 3 days, then by securing in a plastic bag and exposing to the sun for 3–4 days you will kill the maggots. Select early maturing varieties which ripen before the appearance of fruit fly and keep trees pruned to a sprayable height. Ripening fruit can be protected from adult fruit flies (also possums and birds) by throwing bird netting over the fruit, or individual fruit clusters can be protected with paper bags, etc. Fruit fly lures, baits and sprays, based on spinosad derived from a soil bacterium, are available; the time of application will vary with the species of fruit.

An organc fruit fly trap (Richard Drew, CSIRO) can be made from a plastic bottle and placing the bait in the bottle: use 2 litres water, 1 teaspoon vanilla essence, 2 tablespoons cloudy ammonia and half a cup of sugar. Put several 6 mm diameter holes in the neck of a 1L bottle, place the bait in the bottle, and hang in a shady part of the tree just above the lower leaves. Female fruit flies are attracted to the smell of the bait in the bottle, enter the bottle and feed and die. Replace bait in trap twice a week to keep it fresh and attractive to fruit fly. The trap should be hung in the fruit tree about 6 weeks prior to the anticipated picking of the fruit until all the fruit has been picked as this is when the fruit is most attractive to fruit fly. This type of treatment may not provide adequate control when fruit fly numbers are high.

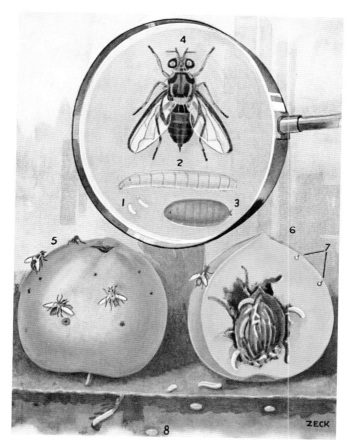

Queensland fruit fly *Photo: NSW Dept of Industry and Investment (E.H.Zeck).*

Enlarged x5

1. Eggs

2. Larva or maggot

3. Pupa

4. Adult fruit fly

Actual size

5. Apple showing punctures or 'stings' where eggs have been deposited

6. Showing decay and tunnels of the maggots

7. Egg clusters beneath the skin

8. Pupa in the ground

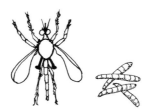

Typical fly with 1 pair of wings, larvae are called maggots and are legless.

Fungus gnat (2–3 mm long) and larvae (5–8 mm long) are found in over-wet soil and pots.

Garden soldier fly (12 mm long). Maggots (about 15 mm long) are commonly found in over-wet compost.

Quarantine regulations prohibit the movement of fruit to areas of Australia where fruit fly does not occur. However, it is not compulsory for home gardeners in the ACT to carry out sanitation and spraying to control fruit fly.

Leafhoppers

Leafhoppers have a quick hopping movement and adult wings meet tent wise. They are often brightly coloured and may feed on a range of plants. Both young and adults feed by sucking plant sap. Honeydew may be secreted which attracts ants and on which sooty mould may grow. Plant damage varies

and includes dotted feeding patterns on leaves of marigold, dahlia and other garden plants. Distorted growth, wilting and dieback may occur in Australian plants.

Leaf hoppers, many are no more than 1–2 mm long).

Passionvine hoppers (8 mm long) and nymphs.

Pest cycle: Young leafhoppers resemble the adults but do not have wings. The young gather in colonies. Nymphs of some species have prominent white waxy projections on their hindquarters which look like tails.

What to do: Control is not practical because damage is not usually noticed until the leafhoppers have gone. Common brown leafhoppers transmit tomato big bud disease (see page 366).

Leafminers

Leafmining insects are commonly the larvae of flies, moths and sawflies.

Pest cycle: The tiny maggots, caterpillars or larvae of sawflies tunnel between the upper and lower surface of leaves initially making scribble-like markings. As larvae grow in size, blotches may develop which eventually turn

Azalea leafminer damage.

Cineraria leaf miner damage to chrysanthemum.

brown. Most leafminers are host-specific and damage is common on some species and varieties of azaleas, chrysanthemums, eucalypts, oaks, wattles and other plants.

What to do: Controls vary and are discussed under specific plants.

Mealybugs

Mealybugs are up to 8 mm long and covered with a white mealy coating. White hairs radiate from their bodies. They are closely related to scale insects.

Mealybugs (up to 8 mm long).

Pest cycle: The young resemble the adults and both stages feed by sucking plant sap from both above ground plant parts and roots.

What to do: Adequate soil moisture will help infested plants cope with sap loss due to the sucking of the mealybugs. On lightly infested indoor plants, individual mealybugs may be brushed off with a small paint brush dipped in methylated spirits (very time-consuming) or sprayed with a soap or indoor plant spray. Severely-infested plants may have to be destroyed. Inspect all new purchases for the presence of mealybugs.

Mites

Mites can usually only be seen with a x10 hand lens. They have no wings and feed by sucking sap. The main one to cause problems is the twospotted mite (red spider). Adult twospotted mites are pale green with darker side spots. They have four pairs of legs and females lay eggs on webbing produced by the mites on the lower surface of leaves. They suck mainly from leaf undersurfaces causing leaves to look 'sandy' initially, later they may wither and fall. They may be a pest from early summer onwards, particularly in dry seasons.

Mites lay eggs which hatch into young (nymphs) which generally resemble the adults. They can multiply rapidly.

What to do: Twospotted mites react adversely to moisture so that spray irrigation directed towards the undersurfaces of leaves reduces populations. Adequate soil moisture must also be provided to make up for the amount of sap lost through the mites sucking. Natural enemies include predatory beetles and mites which may be killed by pesticides resulting in population increases. A list of suppliers of predatory mites is available from

Australian Biological Control (website is www.goodbugs.org.au/).

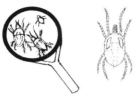

Twospotted mite (red spider) about 0.5 mm long. Easier to see with a x10 hand lens.

A **predatory mite** (rather pear-shaped), which feeds on twospotted mites.

Pear and cherry slug

This 'slug' is actually the larvae of an introduced sawfly. Larvae cover themselves with dark glossy slime concealing their true outline and making them slug-like. They feed on the surface tissues of leaves of pears, plums, cherries, hawthorns, rowan trees and other plants, skeletonising them.

Pest cycle. Female sawflies insert eggs into leaf tissue, eggs hatch and the larvae feed on leaves. When fully grown they usually fall to the ground and pupate in soil beneath the tree. There are usually several generations each year.

What to do: If the first generation is controlled, then the later generations may not cause so much damage. Insecticides such as pyrethrum and garlic sprays may be applied when the 'slugs' are seen, however, this pear

and cherry slug is a recurring pest so spraying only provides control for that season. Trees higher than 3 metres should not be sprayed. On small new plants, slugs may be squashed by hand. During dry weather they tend to shrivel up on the leaf surfaces and die. Avoid planting susceptible species as specimen trees, but site them in group plantings where damage is not so obvious.

Possums

Possums are protected native animals and are part of our urban environment. However, they are fond of ripening fruit and some flowers. Very occasionally they can become a pest, especially when they shelter in rooves etc. Block potential entry points or seek advice.

Sawflies (spitfires)

Sawflies are so-called because the adult females have a saw-like egg-laying apparatus which they use to insert their eggs into leaf tissue. The larvae which hatch from these eggs chew on the leaves of bottlebrush, eucalypts ("spitfires") and callitris, often causing much damage.

Spitfires (sawfly larvae) (up to 70 mm long) feed on eucalypt leaves. When disturbed they 'spit' a thick yellowish fluid with a eucalypt odour.

Sawfly larvae (up to 50 cm long) on bottlebush.

Black scale

Tick scale on wattle

Pear and cherry slug (up to 12 mm long) on stone fruit leaf.

Scales and lerp insects

Scale insects are flattened, disc-like, sap-sucking insects that remain stationary on the stems, leaves and fruit of plants. They may be difficult to see. Soft scales produce honeydew on which sooty mould grows. Hard scales do not produce honeydew but may be much more damaging to the plant and may eventually kill it.

Black scale is possibly the most common garden scale attacking a wide range of trees and shrubs including citrus. It is a large soft rounded scale. Its presence is often indicated by the occurrence of black sooty mould and ants.

Pest cycle: Eggs are laid and hatch into mobile nymphs which quickly settle permanently on leaves, twigs and other plant parts, developing a waxy scale covering.

Lerp insects mainly infest eucalypt leaves. The tiny flattened sap sucking insects produce a protective covering (lerps) in a shape and colour characteristic of the species. Some eucalypts are very susceptible. Lerp insects may occur in plagues.

What to do: The populations of most scales and lerp insects are to some extent controlled by natural enemies. Small branches where scales and other insects are clustered together may be cut off. Scales are readily- controlled with soap or oil sprays. On deciduous plants they are best kept in check during winter when the tree is bare of leaves by the application of one spray of oil. On evergreen plants two sprays, about 7–10 days apart, in spring and if necessary, again in

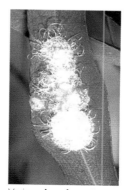

Various **lerp insects** on eucalypts leaves.

autumn, is usually effective. On indoor or pot plants, scales may be gently washed or brushed off using a tooth or paint brush; indoor plant sprays may assist control.

Scarab grubs

The larvae of several species of beetles are commonly called scarab grubs (see beetles above). These grubs feed on the roots of grasses in lawns and may cause significant damage in late summer and autumn. Control can be difficult and is best achieved by reducing the impact by maintaining turf in good condition. Healthy vigorous turf can support large populations of scarabs without apparent damage. Some grasses are less affected than others, clover is less severely damaged. Nematodes are available but require moist conditions for effectiveness.

Slaters, millipedes, centipedes

Slater (up to 10 mm long), more than 5 pairs of legs. Mainly feeds on organic matter but may feed on seedlings, ferns, staghorns.

Millipede (up to 30 mm long), round body, 2 pairs of legs on each body segment. Mainly feeds on organic matter.

Centipede (up to 100 mm long), flat body, 1 pair of legs on each body segment, poison fangs. Mainly feeds on other insects.

These pests feed mainly on decaying organic matter and do more good than harm. They are common in damp and sheltered places, such as rockeries, under stones, pieces of wood and pots. Slaters are grey, up to 10 mm long with more than five pairs of legs. Young slaters resemble the adults. They may nibble tender plants and in old shaded gardens, staghorns are particularly susceptible to attack. Places where slaters are likely to shelter can be cleaned up, or they may be trapped in scooped out oranges and then destroyed. Millipedes may invade houses, but remember they breed outdoors, not in the house, so they can just be swept up and disposed of. Centipedes do not harm plants, are mainly predators; they can inflict a painful bite.

Snails and slugs

Snails and slugs breed in any sheltered, damp place in the garden. Snails remain dormant during dry periods and in winter. They feed at night, after rain or on dull days. Some species are native to Australia and some are predatory.

Pest cycle: Snails lay masses of 30–50 small, white spherical eggs in the summer and autumn about 2–3 cm below the soil surface.

Snail damage to cabbage.

Young snails skeletonise fleshy leaves of gazania and other plants.

Young snails resemble adults but may be paler in colour. They take about 6 months to reach maturity and live for up to 2 years.

What to do: After rain or irrigation during overcast weather or at night, satisfaction can be obtained from stomping on them. Because snails and slugs require a smooth surface over which to move, sand or coarse mulches such as chip bark, eggshells, coffee grounds or kitty litter act as effective barriers. Eliminate potential breeding sites, although this may be impossible where there is a lot of groundcover. Female khaki Campbell or Indian runner ducks may be kept but are messy. Beer in shallow dishes attracts snails which then die from alcoholic poisoning or drowning. There are sprays which repel snails and slugs and are useful where there are children and pets.

Several of the snail and slug baits now available are are less hazardous to birds and other wildlife. Label directions must be carefully followed regarding the distribution of material as areas are easily overtreated. Do not heap. Baits are attractive to children and dogs. Consider growing plants less attractive to snails and slugs.

Thrips

Thrips are tiny elongated insects up to 1 mm long and can just be seen with the naked eye. They have two pairs of delicately fringed wings which can only be seen with a hand lens. They feed by rasping the plant surface and sucking the plant juice. There are many different species and some have definite plant preferences.

Plague thrips (1 mm long). *Right* — natural size

Pest cycle: Young resemble the adults but are usually paler in colour and wingless.

Greenhouse thrips commonly attack viburnum, indoor and many other plants causing silvering of leaves. Black dots of excreta may be seen on the undersurface of leaves. In heavy infestations thrips may also feed on the upper leaf surfaces. They occur often in the centres of bushes or in shady areas.

Plague thrips feed within flowers and when in plague numbers cause browning of petals and can reduce fruit set.

Western flower thrips feed in flowers and on young leaves, on strawberry fruit etc. They also cause major damage by transmitting the tomato spotted wilt and other virus diseases of vegetables, ornamentals and other herbaceous plants.

Thrips in flowers.

What to do: Control is difficult and may not be warranted. Rain or irrigation destroys large numbers. Because thrips feed in unopened flower buds they are difficult to reach with sprays and dusts. Regular spraying will at the most only provide limited control on outdoor plants; the type of insecticide used will depend on the plant. Leaves of affected indoor plants can be carefully wiped, affected plants can be moved to less favourable sites. Infestations of greenhouse thrips on viburnum and similar plants can be controlled by regular judicious pruning.

Wasps

Wasps are mostly beneficial insects. They usually feed on nectar and are often seen on flowers. They have 2 pairs of lacelike wings and a 'waist'.

Some wasps have an egg laying apparatus to parasitise aphids, scales, other insects.

Galls on wattles and other plants may be caused by fly or wasp larvae.

European wasp (worker) about 15 mm long - the commonest caste seen.
Photo: NSW Dept of Industry and Investment.

Paper wasps (14–25 mm long) also feed on other insects and may sting.

Pest cycle: Parasitic wasps lay eggs in other insects. The predatory European wasp feeds on bees, other insects and sweet foods. It stings aggressively. Only a few wasps lay eggs in plants, the larvae feed inside the plant often resulting in galls. Larvae are quite different from the adult.

What to do: Avoid using insecticides which kill beneficial wasps. Shoots and leaves of eucalypts and other plants which are infested with gall wasps may be pruned off and destroyed. If European wasps are suspected call XCS Consulting, a European wasp and insect identification service on 6162 1914.

Whiteflies

Whiteflies are not flies but are small white-winged sap-sucking insects, related to aphids, leafhoppers and similar insects. They are about 1 mm long, do not fly readily and usually remain on the undersides of leaves. However, if infested plants are disturbed, numbers rise in the air and flutter around. Nymphs and adults secrete honeydew with resulting sooty mould development.

Adult whiteflies (1 mm long).

Whiteflies on the undersurfaces of a tomato leaf.

Pest cycle: Eggs are laid on leaves which hatch into young. Some young stages are stationary on the undersurface of leaves and look rather like tiny scales.

Greenhouse whitefly may infest broad-leafed vegetables, ornamental plants and weeds. Ash whitefly infests ash and other ornamental trees.

What to do: Control is often not warranted. A wasp has been released, which parasitises the fourth nymphal stage of greenhouse whiteflies causing them to turn black (these are commonly seen amongst whiteflies on the undersides of infested vegetable leaves),

and provides some control. Yellow boards coated with clear grease are attractive to whiteflies — the boards have to be cleaned at regular intervals and recoated.

Diseases

Bacterial diseases

Only a few bacterial diseases cause problems for the home gardener in Canberra.

Disease cycle: In moist conditions, infected areas may produce drops of 'slime' consisting of myriads of microscopic bacteria which may be spread by water splash, insects, handling and pruning activities. Bacterial diseases of herbaceous plants may also be spread by infected seed, movement of infested soil and vegetative propagation from infected plants. They may overwinter in infected seed and plant debris, in soil or in lightly infected plant tissue in perennial plants.

Bacterial canker of stone fruit may infect other trees as well. Infection of young trees is particularly severe and often kills them. Dormant buds may die, blossom blight may develop in favourable weather and this may

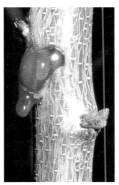

Gumming on stem   Bark removed, brown
                         dead tissue beneath

Bacterial canker of stone fruits.

Crown gall (*Agrobacterium* sp.) at the base of rose canes.

progress into twig blight. Watersoaked spots develop on leaves which rapidly become brown and drop out giving a shot-hole effect, defoliation may occur in spring. The most destructive damage is caused by the development of cankers — dead sunken areas on the branches, stems and twigs. These cankers may extend longitudinally more than 100 cm along the trunk and may produce water-soluble gum. Underlying tissue becomes brown. Some cankers are also sour-smelling but with little or no gumming. Where cankers girdle a branch, whole limbs may die. Stem infection of young trees is usually fatal. Fruit are not commonly attacked.

Bacterial soft rot is common on lettuce heads but attacks many other plants with soft, succulent tissues and fleshy storage organs. It is favoured by wet and humid weather and can be reduced by not planting seedlings too close together, and by avoiding overwatering.

What to do: The use of pesticides to control bacterial diseases has not been very successful, copper-based compounds being the only ones commonly used. Seek advice if you suspect bacterial canker. When pruning susceptible trees, pruning equipment must be sterilized between each cut and between each plant by dipping equipment in 70 per cent methylated spirits or a general disinfectant. On herbaceous plants control is usually obtained by the use of resistant varieties and bacteria-free seed or other planting material. Infected plant debris should be destroyed.

Fungal diseases

Everyone is familiar with the edible mushroom or the mould that grows on stale bread. Remember, though, that most fungi are beneficial and help breakdown organic matter.

Disease cycle: Most fungi reproduce by means of large numbers of spores which are mostly spread by wind. Water, soil, seed and movement of infected plants may also spread them. Some have stages resistant to unfavourable conditions such as dry weather. Generally fungal diseases are favoured by humid weather when diseases like brown rot in stone fruits, downy mildew of grapes and black spot of apples and roses may become epidemic.

Downy mildews are host-specific and commonly occur on grapes, stock and occasionally on brassicas and lettuce in the Canberra region. They are favoured by cool, rainy weather. Spores are produced on the undersurface of leaves with corresponding brown areas developing on the upper surface. Flowers and bunches of some varieties of grapes may also be attacked.

Powdery mildews are host-specific and the first signs of disease are usually the appearance of small white circular patches on leaves (both sides), stems, buds, petals and fruit. These increase in size to cover large areas of both sides of leaves which become powdery due to the production of windborne spores. Select varieties with some resistance to powdery mildew. Fungicides,

Fungal diseases of rose. *Upper left*: Black spot. *Upper right*: Powdery mildew. *Lower left*: Anthracnose. *Lower right*: Rust. Photo: NSW Dept of Industry and Investment (M.S.Senior).

at best, often just slow down disease development. Bicarbonate sprays (1 teaspoon sodium bicarbonate per litre plus some soapy detergent) have some effect against powdery mildew of roses. Spray both sides of affected leaves. Some annuals such as zucchini, crucifers develop mildew as they near the end of their lives and this is not worth treating.

Rust diseases are host-specific and generally produce pustules with bright orange, brown or black powdery spores on the undersurface of infected leaves and on stems. Defoliation may be severe during humid weather. Rust diseases overwinter on plant debris, infected perennial host plants and seed. Spores are spread mainly by wind and infected seed.

Control is difficult and is usually achieved by selecting resistant varieties, avoiding humid conditions. Fungicides may be applied at the first sign of disease.

Fungal leaf spots other than black spot of roses generally do not cause much damage. In addition to leaf spots, premature yellowing or collapse of leaves and defoliation may occur. Occasionally other plant parts may be attacked. They are often seedborne and spread by wind and water splash, use of seed from infected plants and movement of infected plants and plant debris. Wet and shady conditions should be avoided.

Root and collar rots may attack a wide range of plants. Symptoms resemble those caused by nutrient deficiencies or water stress and the only way to confirm diagnosis is to have the fungus isolated by a pathologist. *Phytophthora* fungi produce thick walled spores which can survive in the soil for up to 10 years. Spores and mycelium are spread in soil and water and root infections takes place through root hairs. Advice should be obtained regarding diagnosis and treatment. Root and collar rots are best prevented by providing good drainage and avoiding overwatering. Keep stems and trunks clear of mulch and other organic matter.

Damping-off is caused by soil-inhabiting fungi and bacteria which attack a wide range of seeds, seedlings and cuttings. Symptoms vary, seeds may rot before they emerge, roots and stems may rot and leaves may be attacked. Damping-off is less likely to occur in soil-less mixes and hydroponic systems. Otherwise, prevent by planting when conditions favour rapid plant growth and avoid crowding and overwatering. Good ventilation is essential to prevent aerial damping off during winter in unheated greenhouses. Destroy any affected punnets.

Sooty mould is not parasitic on plants but grows on the honeydew secreted by aphids, some scales, whiteflies and some other insects. Look around to discover the real cause of your problem.

What to do: Control methods include using resistant varieties. Symptoms may develop days, weeks or even months after the fungus is already well-established within the plant, so that control may have to be implemented well in advance of when the disease is likely to occur. Methods based on knowledge of the life cycle of the fungus include reducing humidity, pruning out infected stems and destroying affected leaves, and the application of sodium bicarbonate, oils or fungicides.

Death cap mushrooms appear after rain in autumn, at about the same time as edible mushrooms. Do not pick and eat any mushrooms unless you are sure of their identity. You need to see the colour of the gills and other features to be sure they are an edible species. Seek advice if in doubt. The Plant Enquiry Service in the Australian National Botanic Garden's Centre for Plant Biodiversity Research provides such advice.

Various types of **'mushrooms'** grow in organic matter in mulched areas and lawns.

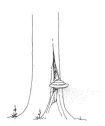

Fruiting body of a wood rot fungus growing out from the decay inside tree trunk.

Black spot of rose. Note spots are 'feathery'.

Nematode diseases

Nematodes (eelworms) are microscopic and wormlike in appearance. They are not related to true worms. Plant-parasitic species feed externally or internally in roots, leaves, bulbs and other plant parts. Nematode diseases which may occur in Canberra include root knot, foliar nematodes and stem and bulb nematode. Nematodes overwinter in the soil or in infected perennial host plants and are spread in soil on tools, footwear and in containers, by water and by the movement of infected plants.

Disease cycle: Female nematodes lay eggs which hatch into larvae which attack the host. They go through various stages until they are adults.

Root knot. Small galls up to 1 cm in diameter develop as a result of the nematodes feeding on the small roots and underground tubers of a wide range of plants. Root knot nematodes are favoured by light, sandy, well aerated, warm, coastal soils and are usually not a problem in Canberra. Control is usually aided by the use of resistant varieties, fallowing or trap plants such as marigold (*Tagetes patula*). Infested plant debris should not be placed on compost heaps. Some nematodes are 'beneficial' and are used to control scarab grubs in lawns.

What to do: Control can be difficult and may be aided by selecting resistant varieties, fallowing affected areas for a whole season, crop rotation and the removal of infected plants.

Virus and virus-like diseases

Virus diseases are common and the agents that cause them can only be seen with an electron microscope. They do not usually kill plants but many cause some stunting, reduction in yield and length of life of the host. Specific symptoms include mosaics, mottling and line patterns on leaves, malformations and greening of floral parts, ringspotting, russetting and malformation of fruit. For all practical purposes, even though symptoms are only observed on certain parts of a plant, all parts, including the roots, should be regarded as infected.

Disease cycle: Viruses can only multiply in living cells. Virus diseases may be spread by infected seed, cuttings, bulbs etc. Some are also spread by sucking insects such as aphids, leafhoppers and thrips and in sap adhering to hands, clothes and pruning tools.

Spotted wilt is caused by the tomato spotted wilt virus which infects a wide range of annual and herbaceous ornamental plants, vegetables, and weeds. It is spread by various species of thrips and by vegetative propagation. About 14–21 days after infection

Greening on chrysanthemum.
Left: Healthy flower *Right:* Green flower.

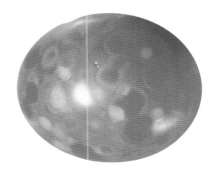

Circular blotches on tomato caused by tomato spotted wilt virus.

Mosaic on camellia.

of tomatoes, small areas of bronzing develop on the upper side of the leaf, while on older leaves; bronze spots or rings appear between the veins. Affected tissue later blackens and shrivels, brownish-black streaks may also appear on leaf stalks and stems. Fruit on infected tomato plants often show irregular or circular blotches as they ripen. On ornamental plants, yellow patterns may develop on leaves and brown and purplish streaking on stems.

Big bud or greening is caused by the tomato big bud phytoplasma which can infect a similar range of plants as tomato spotted wilt virus. It is spread by the common brown leafhopper and vegetative propagation. On tomatoes, stems become thick and upright, and stem splitting may develop high on the stems. Flower buds are enlarged, imperfectly developed and may be green. Abnormal flowers do not set fruit. Fruit which is immature at the time of infection, become distorted with a large woody core. On ornamental flowers, greening of the floral parts is a constant feature and there is no bud enlargement.

What to do: Once a plant is infected with a virus disease little can be done. The application of insecticides to control any insect vectors is not likely to be successful in the home garden and is not recommended. The most effective method of control is by the use of virus-tested planting material which is guaranteed free from specified virus diseases, eg strawberries, potatoes, gladioli, daffodils, carnations and chrysanthemums. Select plant propagation material only from healthy plants.

Environment, nutrition, genetic

Unfavourable environmental conditions, nutrient deficiencies and toxicities, mechanical injury, pesticide injury, pollution, lichens, dogs and vandals can cause you problems. Cultural and site-related problems are the commonest plant problems and most difficult to diagnose — they can be a real challenge.

Chimera (genetic abnormality) on tulip.

Left and centre: Either **too little moisture** (browned parts brittle) or **too much water** (browned parts soft).
Right: **Sunscorch injury**, often in centre of leaf.

Leaf scorch may be due to a general lack of soil water, insufficient moisture during hot, windy weather or excessive exposure to sun or other agents. Flowers, fruit and trunks of trees may also be burnt by the sun. Some plants may be damaged by frost in late autumn and early spring.

Fasciation mostly appears as a change in the appearance of a plant stem from its normal round shape to a flattened, ribbon-shaped structure. The exact cause is not known but is thought that it may be the result of a genetic abnormality, but other agents may be involved. It does not appear to spread from plant to plant, so that affected parts may be removed or left as desired.

Mechanical injury to trees and shrubs and other plants may result from cars, lawn mowers, tying wires and malicious damage. Damaged trees are more susceptible to borer and wood rot attack.

Fasciation (a genetic defect) on rose. Common on daphne and other plants.

Common nutrient deficiencies. *Left*: Iron deficiency occurs on the new leaves, when soil is alkaline on azalea, citrus. *Right*: Magnesium deficiency on older leaves, occurs in autumn on roses, citrus and many other trees and shrubs.

Echium candicans (Pride of Madeira) showing an extreme fasciation.

Nutrient deficiencies

Only a few nutrient deficiencies are common in home gardens.

Iron deficiency occurs under alkaline soils on azalea, rhododendron, citrus, banksia and some other plants. New leaves develop yellowing between the veins. Avoid planting susceptible plants beside cement walls or applying alkaline fertilisers. The deficiency may be corrected by altering the soil pH or applying iron chelates.

Magnesium deficiency is found on older leaves of citrus and other plants. The leaves begin to yellow near the midrib and this yellow blotch enlarges until the only green remaining is at the tip of the leaf and near the base in a V-shape. The entire leaf may yellow. An application of magnesium sulphate or Epsom salts will correct the problem.

Nitrogen deficiency is often found on citrus, camellia, daphne and other plants resulting in yellowing of both old and new leaves. Most general purpose fertilisers contain a sufficient source of nitrogen.

Boron deficiency causes brown heart of turnips and swedes, brown curd of cauliflower and corkiness in apples. Minute amounts of boron are incorporated in most general purpose fertilisers. Note excess boron is toxic to plants.

Excess fertiliser can result in browning of leaf edges and is common in container plants but may also occur on other plants including camellias and many vegetable plants such as lettuce. Excess nitrogen results in large leafy vegetables. More is not always beneficial.

Chemical injury

Herbicide injury to non-target plants, eg trees, may result from spray drift or the uptake of herbicide through green bark or roots. Roses and grapes are particularly susceptible. Insecticides and fungicides can also cause plant injury. Read all labels carefully. Leaking gas mains may damage plants. The gas itself is not toxic to plants but it kills roots by replacing oxygen in soil. After leaks are repaired wait at least six months before replanting the soil. Diesel fuel can remain in soil for some time, killing lawns, etc.

Weeds

Weeds are the home gardener's greatest 'pest'. They are often defined as 'pest plants growing where they are not wanted' and many plants including those considered to be beneficial, may be weeds at times in certain places. Apart from their untidy appearance in a garden, weeds compete with desired plants for space, light, moisture and nutrients. They may harbour pests and diseases.

On the other hand, some weeds may harbour the natural enemies of garden pests and diseases. Leguminous weeds such as clovers add nitrogen to the soil and many are a source of pollen and nectar for bees.

Reproduction and spread

Weeds reproduce mainly by seeds which are very efficiently dispersed by wind, explosive mechanisms, water, soil, birds and other animals and people. Many weeds also reproduce by means of root pieces, rhizomes, stolons and runners, tubers, bulbs, corms and suckers. Weed seeds and rhizomes may be introduced in soil deliveries.

Different types of weeds

Annual weeds flower, produce seeds and die within one year or less, eg chickweed. Control should aim to prevent further seeding. Roots are usually shallow and they are easily pulled out before they set seed.

Winter grass. Annual grass weed. Spreads by seed.

Couch grass. Perennial grass weed. Spreads mainly by stolons.

Cardamine, flick weed. Annual broad leafed weed. Spreads by seed.

Redflower mallow. Soft wooded perennial deep-rooted weed. Spreads by stolons.

Perennial weeds live for three or more years; most have deep roots, rhizomes, corms, etc. Cultivation should be avoided as this can lead to further spread.

Broad leafed weeds can be a problem in lawns. There are herbicides intended specifically to control broad leafed weeds.

Grass weeds include couch grass and paspalum, both of which are perennials. Summer grass and winter grass are common annual grass weeds.

In the ACT many garden weeds are merely nuisance plants. On the other hand, some plants are Declared Plant Pests covered by ACT Regulations and are listed in Appendix 2. Their declaration as 'pest plants' does not require the immediate removal of these plants from gardens in the ACT, but their propagation and spread should be controlled. Avoid growing or planting any of these plants.

What to do

Preventing weed infestation is important. Adequate preparation of ground prior to planting garden beds will kill germinating weed seedlings and reduce subsequent weed problems in the planting. The use of competing plants as ground cover and weed-free mulches are cheap and effective methods of controlling annual weeds in small areas. Annual weeds should be pulled or dug out before they set seed. Perennial weeds with a strong tap or other underground root system, must be carefully dug out to avoid leaving root pieces in the ground.

Mowing before seed has set is useful for annual weeds in lawns but not for perennial weeds. Systemic herbicides may be required for control of perennial weeds with deep roots, bulbs and other underground structures, eg dandelion which has a strong tap root. Take great care when applying herbicides to avoid drift to surrounding plants.

Some weed situations

Weeds in flower beds can be reduced to some extent if the ground is properly prepared prior to planting. If many perennial weeds are present the ground can be carefully dug over to remove weeds and roots or sprayed with glyphosate (Roundup, Zero) prior to planting. If necessary, weed seeds can then be encouraged to germinate; the area can then be raked or dug over to kill the germinating weeds while they are still small. The ground can then be planted. Any that develop amongst the flower seedlings can be hand-weeded or hoed, preferably when weeds are quite small. If mulch is used, it should be weed-free. Glyphosate may be applied using a weeding brush or gun to treat individual weeds of all types or as a spot spray with a shielded nozzle.

Weeds in gravel driveways and paths. Hand weeding may disturb the compacted gravel surface, bring underlying soil to the surface and so encourage more weeds. Isolated weeds may be spot sprayed.

Weeds around butts of trees. Cutting grass etc around trunks with a lawnmower or whipper-snipper can damage the tree. Play safe by keeping a weed-free area around the base either by hand-weeding, mulching or using a suitable herbicide, eg glyphosate.

Weeds amongst shrubs and trees. Start by removing all the perennial weeds either by pulling, digging or spot-spraying with glyphosate prior to laying a weed-free mulch. Any weeds that do develop in the mulch can be easily removed by hand or spot-sprayed with glyphosate. Glyphosate can be absorbed by the green bark of rose canes and by shrubs and trees less than two years of age, so take care to ensure that drift does not occur. If in doubt use a weeding wand or a spray nozzle with a shield over it.

Unwanted woody shrubs, small trees and suckers can be dug out or cut off diligently over a period. If herbicides are considered necessary, they must be applied according to label directions which usually indicate that they should be applied to the foliage or cut stem only, not to the soil, otherwise surrounding plants may be damaged. Herbicides should not be applied to suckers still attached to the parent plant. Some herbicides which are registered for use on woody plants may persist in the soil for varying periods of time.

Garden escapees are garden plants such as firethorns, privet, gorse, blackberry and some species of cotoneaster, which invade surrounding bush land causing serious economic and environmental problems in surrounding areas. Birds, wind, animals, vehicles and water spread seeds. Some weeds grow from stems, bulbs or corms after being dumped as garden waste in urban parkland or nature reserves. Most retail and wholesale nurseries have voluntarily stopped selling such plants and may display Bush Friendly Nursery signage. If you have any of the Declared Pest Plants for the ACT growing in your garden consider removing them and replacing them with plants which won't spread beyond your garden. Join your local Parkcare or Landcare group to take part in a united effort to control and eradicate environmental weeds in your local bushland areas. Weed swap schemes in Canberra are a useful means of replacing some of your garden environmental weeds with native species suited to your region.

Safe use of pesticides

Identify the problem and use the right pesticide

If you have doubts about what the problem is or what pesticide to use, seek advice. The staff at your local garden centre are usually trained in horticulture or you could attend a plant clinic at the CIT's School of Horticulture in Bruce. You may not need to use a pesticide. If you have to buy one, only buy sufficient to suit your needs for no more than the next two seasons.

Registered pesticides must have an intact original label attached to the container. Read directions carefully before opening the container and use only for the purpose stated on the label. This is not only commonsense, but a legal requirement.

Only apply to plants and pests listed on the label at the rate recommended. Check if any plants may be damaged by the pesticide. Only add wetting agents if the label says it is necessary, otherwise excessive run off may occur.

Ready-to-use-products

Ready-to-use aerosols, dusters, guns and granule dispensers are ideal for home gardeners. They avoid handling and diluting pesticide concentrate and the need for application equipment. Dusts are difficult to apply to large plants and are easily washed off by rain or overhead watering. Hold aerosols the prescribed distance away from the plant otherwise the plant may be damaged.

Preparing sprays.

Have different equipment for herbicides and insecticides/fungicides. When purchasing

Overalls, hat

Disposable overalls

Boots, gloves

Goggles, faceshield

Recommended respirators

equipment, look for the size of tank — how much spray am I going to need? Wide openings on the container make for easy spill-free filling and washing. Knapsacks carried over the shoulder or standup pumps are useful for spraying fruit trees. Small hand misters are useful for balcony gardens, pot plants and small shade houses.

Prepare spray in a well-ventilated area (eg outdoors) and where accidental spills cannot run into the storm water drain. Prepare only enough for immediate use.

Measuring equipment should be kept solely for this purpose. Many pesticide containers have measuring caps or inbuilt measuring wells. Rinse measuring equipment into the spray tank immediately after use

Prepare spray at the strength prescribed on the label. Measure quantities accurately, extra is wasteful, may cause plant injury or be dangerous to the person spraying or to the environment.

Rinse spray equipment, including nozzles, three times with water after each use in a remote area of the garden prior to cleaning your protective clothing and having a shower.

Storage and disposal

Store sprays and dusts in a cool dry place, out of reach of children or in a locked cupboard. Do not store in sunlight. Accidental swallowing of pesticides account for many poisonings of children under five. Do not store or transport with food, medicines, animal food or feed, seed or fertiliser.

Store all pesticides in their original container, in an upright position, with lid tightly closed and with label intact. Never store pesticides in food or drink containers.

Disposing of empty containers. Check label for instructions. Wrap empty containers, guns, dusters, aerosols and similar items in paper and place in garbage bin. Never re-use empty pesticide containers.

Disposing of old pesticides. Call Canberra Connect on 13 22 81 to obtain the latest procedures.

Do not pour excess diluted spray down storm water drains. Spray on bare gravel or cement or deposit in a deep hole in a remote area of the garden well away from water sources, roots of trees and shrubs, pets etc

Soak spills up with soil and bury in a little-used part of the garden. If the spill is on concrete, wash the area thoroughly with detergent and rinse with water.

READ THE LABEL

HAZARD WARNING

READ SAFETY DIRECTIONS
(Low to very low hazard)

More hazardous products have
CAUTION (Moderate hazard) or **POISON** (High hazard)

TRADE NAME
Name given to the product
by manufacturer

ACTIVE CONSTITUENT(S)
Material in the product
which controls the pest

CLAIMS FOR USE STATEMENT
Summary of the pests the
product will control and the
plants on which it can be used

HOW TO USE
Which plants?
Which pests?
Rate
How to apply

HOW TO PREPARE

NOT TO BE USED

DO NOT PICK

CAUTIONS

**STORAGE
& DISPOSAL**

FIRST AID

SAFETY DIRECTIONS

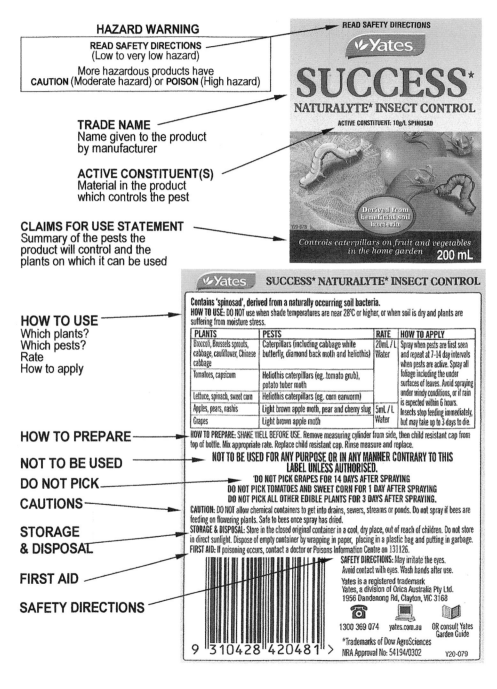

READ SAFETY DIRECTIONS

Yates

SUCCESS*
NATURALYTE* INSECT CONTROL

ACTIVE CONSTITUENT: 10g/L SPINOSAD

Derived from
beneficial soil
bacteria

Y20-078

*Controls caterpillars on fruit and vegetables
in the home garden*   **200 mL**

Yates   SUCCESS* NATURALYTE* INSECT CONTROL

Contains 'spinosad', derived from a naturally occurring soil bacteria.
HOW TO USE: DO NOT use when shade temperatures are near 28°C or higher, or when soil is dry and plants are suffering from moisture stress.

PLANTS	PESTS	RATE	HOW TO APPLY
Broccoli, Brussels sprouts, cabbage, cauliflower, Chinese cabbage	Caterpillars (including cabbage white butterfly, diamond back moth and heliothis)	20mL / L Water	Spray when pests are first seen and repeat at 7-14 day intervals when pests are active. Spray all foliage including the under surfaces of leaves. Avoid spraying under windy conditions, or if rain is expected within 6 hours. Insects stop feeding immediately, but may take up to 3 days to die.
Tomatoes, capsicum	Heliothis caterpillars (eg. tomato grub), potato tuber moth		
Lettuce, spinach, sweet corn	Heliothis caterpillars (eg. corn earworm)		
Apples, pears, nashis	Light brown apple moth, pear and cherry slug	5mL / L Water	
Grapes	Light brown apple moth		

HOW TO PREPARE: SHAKE WELL BEFORE USE. Remove measuring cylinder from side, then child resistant cap from top of bottle. Mix appropriate rate. Replace child resistant cap. Rinse measure and replace.

**NOT TO BE USED FOR ANY PURPOSE OR IN ANY MANNER CONTRARY TO THIS
LABEL UNLESS AUTHORISED.**
'DO NOT PICK GRAPES FOR 14 DAYS AFTER SPRAYING
DO NOT PICK TOMATOES AND SWEET CORN FOR 1 DAY AFTER SPRAYING
DO NOT PICK ALL OTHER EDIBLE PLANTS FOR 3 DAYS AFTER SPRAYING.

CAUTION: DO NOT allow chemical containers to get into drains, sewers, streams or ponds. Do not spray if bees are feeding on flowering plants. Safe to bees once spray has dried.
STORAGE & DISPOSAL: Store in the closed original container in a cool, dry place, out of reach of children. Do not store in direct sunlight. Dispose of empty container by wrapping in paper, placing in a plastic bag and putting in garbage.
FIRST AID: If poisoning occurs, contact a doctor or Poisons Information Centre on 131126.

SAFETY DIRECTIONS: May irritate the eyes.
Avoid contact with eyes. Wash hands after use.

Yates is a registered trademark
Yates, a division of Orica Australia Pty Ltd.
1956 Dandenong Rd, Clayton, VIC 3168

9 310428 420481

1300 369 074   yates.com.au   OR consult Yates
Garden Guide

*Trademarks of Dow AgroSciences
NRA Approval No: 54194/0302   Y20-079

Safe use and application

Do not apply pesticides in enclosed areas or in greenhouses unless the label indicates that product is for use indoors.

Avoid spraying or dusting if rain is expected, if temperatures are above 28°C or below freezing, or on windy days. A calm day is best. In Canberra it may be difficult or impossible to spray at the right time especially in spring. Have the correct pesticide, application equipment and safety equipment on hand so that you can spray whenever conditions and timing are correct. In most gardens, this will only take a short time. Early morning is usually the best time to spray as there is little or no wind and you are less likely to harm bees at this time of day.

Confine spraying/dusting to the plants or areas to be treated. Spot spraying is sufficient for some problems while for others, especially fruit trees, the whole tree may need to be thoroughly sprayed. For this reason, aim to keep trees at a manageable size; alternatively, plant dwarfing rootstock fruit trees. If herbicides are being applied to lawns using plastic containers attached to a hose, take care not to accidentally spray, or allow drift, onto surrounding plants.

Do not eat, drink or smoke during preparation or applying sprays and dusts.

Always wear the protective clothing recommended on the label attached to the container at time of use.

Skin absorption

Avoid contacting spray mist and dusts with skin or eyes at all times. Splashing may occur during preparation, mixing or application, handling sprayed plants or wearing contaminated protective clothing. Goggles (non-fogging) protect the eyes. Face shields protect the face and eyes against skin absorption, but not inhalation, during preparation or while spraying plants, especially trees. Cotton overalls, washable hat, rubber boots and gauntlet rubber gloves protect arms, legs, neck, feet and hands. Button overalls to the neck, wrist and have long trouser legs. Arms should extend over the gloves and legs pulled over boot tops.

Inhalation

Avoid breathing in dusts, spray mist or vapours at all times. Volatile pesticides, especially when used indoors or in an enclosed area, can cause poisoning. A recommended respirator (mask), if used correctly, provides protection. Beards interfere with the efficiency of respirators. In the open air, disposable half-face agricultural pesticide/herbicide respirators may be used with water-based chemicals which do not vaporise readily. Half-face-cartridge respirators remove both dusts and vapours (gases) in the air. Follow manufacturer's instructions for cartridge selection, use and cleaning.

Clean protective clothing

Hose down rubber boots outdoors, check that the insides are clean when they are taken off. Wash face shield and goggles in soap and water, rinse and dry. Wash outside of gloves in soap and water, rinse, discard any with holes or internal contamination. At the end of each use, clean and store respirator as recommended by the manufacturer. Launder overalls and hat on their own (not with the family wash).

Wash hands, face and arms thoroughly in warm soapy water immediately after spraying or dusting and always before eating, drinking or smoking. Better still, have a shower.

FIRST AID and Caution statements

FIRST AID. If poisoning occurs, follow First Aid instructions on the label. Contact a doctor or Poisons Information Centre 13 11 26.

Do not use sprays etc for any purpose or in any manner contrary to the label unless authorized.

Do not pick edible crops, eg fruit, vegetables or herbs, earlier than the withholding period on the label (time between last pesticide application and picking). It is a good idea to check withholding periods before spraying.

Do not allow chemical containers or spray to get into drains, sewers, streams or ponds.

Do not spray plants in flower as many insecticides are toxic to bees and birds. If unavoidable spray early in the morning before bees are active.

Birds, ducks, fish and other animals are very susceptible to many insecticides. Do not spray near swimming pools, fish ponds, tanks and animal bowls. Protect aviaries, ducks, fish tanks or ponds, pets' drinking or food dishes if spraying is to be carried out nearby.

Keep pets inside while spraying and until plant surfaces have dried. Dogs and other animals may be attracted to snail baits so do not heap powder or pellets.

Commercially available pesticides – including organic products (examples only)

Always read and follow label instructions attached to the pesticide container at time of use. Observe withholding periods on edible crops.

Some trade names	Active constituent	Crops and situations (not exhaustive)	Weeds, pests or diseases (not exhaustive)
Herbicides			
Beat-A-Weed Natural Weedkiller	acetic acid + sodium chloride	For the control of certain weeds in gardens, paths, driveways, around sheds and spot spraying in lawns and turf. Also controls moss and algae. Contact spray.	Re-application may be required if regrowth of annual weeds occurs. Perennial weeds may require repeated applications to obtain long term control.
Glypho, Glyphosate, Roundup, Zero	glyphosate	Garden beds and around shrubs. No residual effect on soil. Do not allow spray to drift onto surrounding plants. May be absorbed through green bark.	Broad leafed weeds and grasses. Absorbed by foliage and cut stems and moves downwards into the roots to kill plants. Apply when weeds are growing actively, do not disturb or cut weeds for two weeks.
Weed 'n' Feed, others	dicamba + MCPA	Certain type of lawns. Avoid drift onto surrounding plants.	Most broadleaf weeds and clover. Absorbed by foliage.
Once-A-Year Path Weeder, others	2,2-DPA + simazine + amitrole	Driveways, paths, tennis courts. Do not use on sloping areas. Do not use around plants or on lawns.	Most weeds. Soil herbicide, mainly absorbed through the roots. Residual activity lasts about 12 months.
Insecticides			
Natrasoap	potassium salts of fatty acids	Pot plants, vegetables, fruit trees, ornamentals. Do not apply to soft foliage or flowers.	Sedentary and semi-sedentary insects, eg aphids, thrips, mealybugs, mites, whitefly.
Natural Garlic Concentrate	garlic	Ornamentals, fruit, vegetables.	Aphids, thrips, cabbage white butterfly caterpillars, slugs.
Spray oils, eg Eco-Oil, EcoPest Oil and Pest Oil, White oil	botanical oils paraffinic oils petroleum oils	Ornamentals, some vegetable, flower and fruit crops, roses. Do not apply petroleum oil within 1 month of sulphur sprays or during hot weather or to soft-foliaged plants.	Aphids, mites, scales, mealybugs, whitefly, citrus leafminer, Check label for pests controlled. Petroleum oils may be applied to deciduous trees during winter
Caterpillar Killer Dipel Bio-insecticide	*Bacillus thuringiensis*	Vegetables, fruit, vines, herbs. Ornamental shrubs, flowers, trees.	Certain leafeating caterpillars only. Effective against young caterpillars. Slow-acting.
Success Naturalyte Insect Control	spinosad (soil bacteria)	Certain fruit and vegetables	Caterpillars, pear and cherry slug.

Some trade names	Active constituent	Crops and situations (not exhaustive)	Weeds, pests or diseases (not exhaustive)
Fruit fly lures, baits, sprays, eg Eco-naturalure, others	spinosad (soil bacteria)	Fruit trees in the home garden. Lures, baits and sprays. Band or spot spray to the trunk or lower parts of trees.	Fruit fly.
Fruit Fly & Insect Killer	fenthion	Fruit, ornamentals and vegetables. Very toxic to birds. **Anti-cholinesterase compound.***	Codling moth and oriental fruit moth, aphids, bugs, fruit fly, others.
Eco-neem	Azadirachtin (*Azadirachtin*)	Ornamentals, potting soil (for ornamental plants only). **Do not use on food-producing plants**.	Twospotted mites, aphids, whitefly, fungus gnats.
House & Garden Insect Sprays	pyrethrin	Indoor and outdoor plants.	Range of insects, aphids, whitefly.
Derris Dust	rotenone	Vegetables, grapevines, flowers, shrubs.	Aphids, caterpillars.
Confidor Garden Insecticide	imidacloprid	Flowers, shrubs, trees, fruit trees, roses, certain vegetables. Absorbed by plant.	Aphids, bugs, thrips, mealybugs, lace bugs, whitefly, scarab grubs.
Confidor Hose-on Lawn Insecticide	imidacloprid	Lawns.	Curl grubs (scarab grubs), billbug larvae.
Mavrik	fluvalinate	Ornamentals, roses, shrubs, brassica vegetables, tomatoes, certain fruit trees.	Plague thrips, green peach aphid, caterpillars, twospotted mite.
Baythroid Garden Spray	cyfluthrin	Ornamentals, outdoor areas, certain vegetables.	Aphids, lace bugs, caterpillars, sawfly larvae, thrips, whitefly, mealybugs.
Fungicides			
Kocide, others	copper hydroxide	Fruit trees, vegetables, ornamentals. May injure foliage of some plants. Preventative.	Downy mildews, rusts, leaf spots, peach leaf curl, shot-hole, bacterial diseases.
Copper oxychloride, Leaf Curl Spray	copper oxychloride	As above.	As above.
Mancozeb Plus Garden Fungicide	mancozeb + sulphur	Ornamentals, fruit, vegetables, lawns.	Powdery and downy mildews, rusts, leaf spot, brown rot, shothole, damping off.
Anti Rot	phosphorus acid	Citrus, ornamentals, avocado, grapes. Absorbed by plant. Moves up and down in the plant.	Phytophthora root and collar rots (ornamentals, citrus, avocado), downy mildew (grape).

Some trade names	Active constituent	Crops and situations (not exhaustive)	Weeds, pests or diseases (not exhaustive)
Fongarid	furalaxyl	Seedlings, bedding plants. Soil application, absorbed by roots.	Damping off and roots rots caused by *Pythium*, *Phytophthora*.
Eco-fungicide (Eco-rose is available for use on roses)	potassium bicarbonate	Roses, grapevines, strawberries, vegetables (tomato, capsicum, cucumber, zucchini). Contact fungicide.	Powdery mildews. Also black spot of rose. Mix with Eco-oil for increased effectiveness (see label on page 341)
Triforine Rose Fungicide	triforine	Roses (all types). Absorbed by plant.	Black spot, powdery mildew, rust. Suppresses mites.
Bayleton Garden Fungicide	triadimefon	Azaleas, apples, cucurbits, grapevines, lawns. Absorbed by plant.	Petal blight (azalea), powdery mildew (apple, cucurbits, grapevine), dollar spot (lawns).
Multi-purpose insecticides/fungicides			
Lime sulphur	sulphur polysulphides	Fruit trees and roses. Will scorch leaves of actively growing plants, smells, stains trellises.	Spray during dormancy for grapeleaf blister & pearleaf blister mite, aphids, scales, mites. Leaf curl, shothole, rust, powdery mildews
Dusting sulphur Fungicide/Miticide	sulphur	Pumpkin, marrow, grapevines.	Powdery mildew, also citrus mite on citrus.
Tomato Dust (Ready-to-use dust).	sulphur + copper + spinosad	Tomatoes.	Tomato caterpillar, tomato and other mites; early and late fungal blights, leaf spot.
Rose Black Spot and Insect Killer	triforine + pyrethrin	Roses (all types).	Black spot, powdery mildew, rust; aphids, thrips, caterpillars
Rose Shield Insect & Disease Spray, others	tau-fluvalinate + myclobutanil	Roses and ornamentals.	Aphids, caterpillars, thrips, mites, whitefly, black spot, powdery mildew, rust.
Yates Rose Gun Advanced	imidacloprid + tau-fluvalinate + myclobutanil	Roses and ornamentals in the home garden.	Insect pests (aphids, caterpillars, thrips, whitefly); mites; diseases of rose (black spot powdery mildew, rust).
Rose Pride	myclobutanol + bifenthrin	Roses, other ornamentals (shrubs, perennials, annuals).	Aphids, caterpillars, thrips, whitefly; mites; black spot, powdery mildew & rust on rose. Do not apply to food plants.
Rose & Ornamental Spray Garden Insecticide Fungicide	bitertanol + cyfluthrin (aerosol)	Roses and ornamentals.	Aphids, bugs, caterpillars, thrips, whitefly, black spot, powdery mildew and rust.

Some trade names	Active constituent	Crops and situations (not exhaustive)	Weeds, pests or diseases (not exhaustive)
Snail killers and repellents			
Dogs are attracted to baits. Do not heap, use other methods of control if children and dogs are present, or if snails are up in trees. All bran-based snail baits, typically pellets, contain Bitrex® which acts as a taste deterrent to discourage children and pets from eating them. Baits may contain a repellent smell (Petrepel®).			
Natural Garlic Concentrate Spray	garlic oil + garlic extract	Ornamentals, fruit and vegetables.	Slugs, also aphids, thrips, cabbage white butterfly caterpillars.
Escar-Go, Snail-Stop, Slugit	buffered copper complex	Surface barrier and repellent.	Snails and slugs. Useful where cats, dogs, birds are likely to be exposed.
Enviroguard Ferramol Snail & Slug Bait, others	iron phosphate (breaks down readily in soil)	Affected slugs and snails die within 3–6 days and crawl away to die in secluded places.	Snails and slugs. Kills snails and slugs more slowly than metaldehyde or methiocarb.
Multiguard Snail & Slug Killer (pellets)	iron-edta complex (breaks down readily in soil)	Iron is toxic to snails and slugs which crawl back to their shelter to die. Breaks down to add iron to the soil.	Snails and slugs. Kills snails and slugs more slowly than metaldehyde or methiocarb.
Snail & Slug Pellets	metaldehyde	Do not apply to edible parts of plants.	Snails and slugs.
Baysol Snail & Slug Bait	methiocarb pellets	Do not apply to edible parts of plants. **Anti-cholinesterase compound.** *	Snails and slugs, slaters, millipedes.
Dog, cat, possum and bird repellents			
Deter, Get Off, Keep Off	aluminium ammonium sulphate	Garden areas.	Dog, cat, possum, bird and wildlife repellent smell and taste. Effective for up to 8 weeks.
Keep off Dog & Cat Repellent	methyl nonyl ketone	Paths, non-crop, etc. Around ornamentals.	Dog and cat repellent (up to 4 days). May be used as a training aid.
Stay Off Dog & Cat Repellent Granules	citronella	Lawn, flower beds, shrubs.	Dog and cat repellent.
Skedaddle, Detour Dog & Cat Repellents	citronella oil, eucalyptus oil	Garden areas, lawns, paths, verandahs.	Dog and cat repellent. May be used as a training aid.
Poss Off Natural Possum Deterrent	plant oils, eg garlic, citronella, capsicum	Garden areas.	Possum repellent.

* **Anti-cholinesterase compounds.** A compound which interferes with the normal functioning of the nervous system.

CHAPTER 29:
A gardening calendar for Canberra

The calendar is intended as a collection of suggestions; refer to the relevant pages of the book for more information.

It is hard to remember the abundance of spring as gardens dry out in summer.

Hydrangea macrophylla 'Libelle' in February. This is a stunning white, especially when seen in a shady position.

This is one of the newer, double hellebores, flowering in late winter.

Pieris provides its flowers in late winter.

January

| The Ornamental Garden | The Kitchen Garden |

Bulbs: Lift spring flowering bulbs when leaves die off. If daffodils and jonquils are overcrowded or not flowering well, then it's time to lift them. Make first ties on dahlias and remove centre growth to promote strong lateral growth.

Roses: Summer prune mid-January for autumn display about fifty days later. Remove oldest canes from heritage roses to encourage new growth for next spring's flowers. Two spotted mite (red spider) may be a problem; humid stormy weather or watering foliage will increase the chance of black spot, rust and mildew on roses. Remedies may be needed.

Foliage loss on roses due to fungal or insect damage will expose the canes to sunburn, blackened stems and resulting lack of vigour. Use Confidor for thrip on roses or gladiolus.

Remove spent flowers from **annuals**. Seeds of many annuals can be sown now. Trim early-planted petunias to encourage new growth and a second flush of flowers. Nip out the centres of chrysanthemums to encourage stronger lateral growth. Half-strength fertilisers can be applied to fuchsias fortnightly.

Vegetables: Remove plants that are showing signs of disease. Clear broad beans and peas, and prepare bed for winter brassicas. Many seeds and seedlings can be sown now so check the vegetable calendar for a list. You can also plant seed potatoes. Apply liquid fertiliser fortnightly to vegetables. Mulch tomatoes and corn. Dig onions, shallots and garlic and store in a dry airy position indoors.

Bronze orange bugs appear in summer. Whether small and green, bright orange or adult, like large spiny cockroaches, they will suck sap. Tap them into a bucket of hot soapy water but take care. They squirt caustic liquid which can be very painful, especially to the eyes.

Fruit: Fruit-laden trees especially plums may need support to prevent limbs from breaking. Prune now to lighten the load on branches, sacrificing some fruit. Harvest stone fruit and remove damaged or fallen fruit. Keep in check. Protect apples and pears from codling moth.

Apply blood and bone to citrus trees. Water well once weekly. Remove any dead or twiggy growth and if you see scale, excessive ant activity or sooty mould, spray with pest oil. Confidor® should prevent future scale attack.

Prune berry bushes which have fruited by removing those canes which have produced fruit.

January

General Maintenance	Notes

Compost lawn clippings and other light prunings.

January is too hot for strenuous work in the garden but it is wise to continue weeding, watering and watching for pests and disease. Control as necessary. Try growing plants which attract insect predators as an extra control.

Remove any unwanted tree seedlings while small.

Check plants are well-mulched and if mulch has compacted, fork lightly to aerate the soil and allow moisture to penetrate deeply.

If applying fresh mulch ensure firstly that the soil is moist. Wetting agents will help.

Check watering system to see that all drippers are working properly. Remove blockages and replace faulty drippers.

Check individual plants, particularly those newly-planted as they may require more moisture, mulch and care to get them through summer, perhaps adding water storage crystals or a drench of seaweed planting gel or solution.

Don't forget to clean out and top up the bird baths.

Annuals are not a good option in drought, unless you opt for reduced plantings or grow a few in pots. Apply a liquid fertiliser fortnightly, but if water restrictions are in force, cut back on fertilisers.

In extreme heat, potted fruit trees can be moved to a cooler spot in the garden.

Water restrictions will determine when you can water your garden, but early in the morning or in the cool of the evening is best.

February

| The Ornamental Garden | The Kitchen Garden |

Bulbs: Obtain or order new spring flowering bulbs for planting in the next few months. Wait until cooler weather before planting, storing them in a cool dark place in the meantime. Established spring bulbs may still be lifted if they flowered poorly, or if they have been in the garden for 3 years or more. Replant in a sunny position in enriched soil.

Lift tulips and Dutch irises for storing in a dry cool place. Trim spent agapanthus heads.

Disbud tuberous begonias, leaving only the centre male flower on each flowering stem. Moisten but don't overwater.

Tie dahlias and tall chrysanthemums. Reducing the number of buds per stem will improve flower and stem quality.

Deadhead **rhododendrons**, camellias and azaleas, apply organic mulch, fertilise lightly and keep damp. Check for lace bug or two spotted mite infestation under leaves and apply remedy.

Deadhead flowering annuals as flowers pass their peak to help extend the flowering season. Liquid fertiliser will help. Sow most seed of annuals for spring this month ready for planting out in April.

Hydrangea heads may be trimmed or left to colour with age. If leaves show mildew, remove and bin rather than placing on the compost heap.

Vegetables: Sow seeds of Asian greens, Chinese cabbage, radish, spinach and turnip. A late sowing of beans may be made early in the month in warm protected areas. Plant seedlings of brassicas, lettuce and English spinach.

Vegetables should be producing good quality crops, but remember to keep the water up to tomatoes, capsicum and egg plants and apply liquid fertiliser fortnightly. Remove plants as they come to the end of their life cycle, so as to maintain good hygiene and to make room for winter crops.

Dig over the vegetable garden ready for more planting, or consider planting a green manure crop.

Remove excess growth from apples and pears. Feed citrus with a citrus fertiliser and keep well-watered as fruit begins to mature.

Gather mature **seed** if you wish to propagate your own seedlings. Seed will usually be ripe when it begins to turn brown. Store in paper bags and label with plant name and date. If you are using seed from hybrid plants, inferior seedlings may result.

Trim lavender and rosemary hedges. If lavender and rosemary are woody, prepare some cuttings for new plantings.

February

General Maintenance

Notes

This is normally the warmest month of the year, a month to enjoy the fruits of earlier planning.

Use **water** wisely, recycling from the household to keep plants alive. Remember to water trees and shrubs first, as smaller plants and lawn can be replaced at less cost.

Remove **weeds**. They compete for space and nutrients, as well as being host plants for some diseases and pests. Allowing weeds to produce seed will give you work for many years to come. Learn to identify your weeds and how to control them. Don't leave any weeds you've pulled to dry out where they lie, for they often mature and produce seed even after being pulled.

Watch for pests and disease, treat scale and aphids with horticultural oil, Mavrik® or MaxGuard®. Check in a week or two, and if necessary, repeat treatment. As ants will spread the scale, they should also be controlled. Caterpillars can be controlled with Dipel® or Success®.

Take semi-hardwood **cuttings**, using hormone gel, powder or unrefined honey to strike them. Don't allow cuttings to dry out, so this task is best done after good rains, late in the day or early morning.

Water roses well and apply a foliar fertiliser in late February to encourage autumn growth. Prune spring flowering heritage roses by thinning and shortening excess growth. With old plants, remove some of the older wood to ground level.

Protect maturing fruit from birds by netting or bagging individual fruits.

Check that new plantings, especially trees and shrubs, do not dry out. Other areas such as under eaves and tree canopies may also need watering.

Allowing weeds to produce seed will give you work for many years to come.

March

| The Ornamental Garden | The Kitchen Garden |

Bulbs: Prepare areas or pots for planting spring bulbs later in the month or during April. Divide and plant bearded iris if not done in late spring. Deadhead kangaroo paw flowers.

Continue tying and thinning buds of dahlias and chrysanthemums.

Plant new trees, shrubs, climbers, annuals and perennials.

Deadhead **annuals** and perennials as flowers fade. Annuals past their best should be removed and added to the compost heap if disease-free. Overgrown perennials may be divided, selecting vigorous fresh growth from the outside of the clump for replanting.

Sow sweet peas against wire frame or support.

Check local garden centres for evergreen **shrubs**. Your purchases should be planted now so that they can establish before the cooler weather.

Autumn is the best time to transplant evergreen shrubs if they need relocating.

Take note of outstanding roses for future planting.

Vegetables: Continue fortnightly foliar-feeding with seaweed extract or fish emulsion.

Complete planting of Asian greens, broccoli, cabbage and cauliflower seedlings and protect from caterpillars.

Remove vegetable crops as they mature and harvest the last of the cucurbits. Freeze excess produce or make pickles, preserves, jams or relishes.

Record vegetable plantings so that crops can be rotated next season. If you don't intend to plant for a while, spread some lime.

Mini vegetables are useful for small gardens where space is precious, as are 'cut and come again' leaf vegetables.

Fruit: Do not plant new citrus trees in the open garden now as the coming frosts may cause severe damage to young tender trees.

Some apples and pears will be maturing and should be harvested to avoid bird damage. If fully-developed, pears can be picked green and hard, and will still ripen indoors.

Astringent persimmon should not be harvested until you see bird activity on the tree, usually during April–May. Only then should the fruit be clipped from the tree and taken indoors to finish ripening. Non-astringent persimmon can be picked when fully-developed but still crunchy.

March

General Maintenance

A month of unpredictable weather, but spring flowering plants are beginning to show signs of growth.

Most shrubs and small trees can still be moved if required.

If your lawn is suffering and watering restrictions are in force, consider a smaller lawn or replacing it with drought-tolerant grass.

Water in the warmer part of the day and only where really required.

After rain, check that soil is moist around new plantings and give additional moisture if required. Plants growing under eaves and beneath the canopies of trees may also need water.

Clean out ponds and divide clumps of water irises, lilies etc.

Feed the soil. Trees and shrubs can have an application of manure to boost growth for spring.

Prune jasmines and late summer-flowering clematis.

Remove dead wood from deciduous shrubs and trees while it's easy to access.

Kiwifruit will not ripen till early winter, after the first frosts, so resist the urge to harvest them now.

Notes

Visit The Horticultural Society of Canberra Inc. Autumn Show featuring dahlias, orchids and floral art.

Mini vegetables are useful for small gardens where space is precious, as are 'cut and come again' leaf vegetables.

Before the warmer weather, check your mulch as you may need more. Dig in old mulch to aid moisture retention. Shredded prunings may be added to the compost heap or used as mulch.

April

The Ornamental Garden	The Kitchen Garden

Trim evergreen **shrubs** such as pittosporum, euonymus and conifers so they recover before winter. Do not trim shrubs which are in flower or about to flower. Remove dead growth from deciduous plants while it can easily be seen. This is not so obvious once the leaves appear.

Choose trees for **autumn colour** while still in leaf. You may be disappointed if you buy after the leaves have fallen, for not all have superior colour. A good time to plant or move camellias, rhododendrons, azaleas and pieris.

Check **conifers** for dead foliage. Running a gloved hand lightly over each branch will remove excess litter from the middle of the plant.

Look for lilium, hippeastrum and sprekelia **bulbs** at local outlets or order from specialist growers. Prepare a well-drained area for planting these in coming months or grow in pots.

Complete planting most of the spring bulbs. Tulips and Dutch iris may be planted later in the month when the soil cools.

Tidy the leaves of hellebores, winter iris and aquilegia. Tidy dahlias as they come to the end of their season, removing clumps not required for next year. Label remaining clumps with type and colour for later division.

Reduce watering tuberous begonias and move to a frost-protected area to die down for winter.

Harvest remaining summer **vegetables** and fruits.

Sow Asian greens, broad beans and peas. Onion seed may be sown in a protected area or in seed boxes for planting out later in winter.

Plant seedlings of Asian greens, peas and shallots.

Try growing brassicas in an improvised tunnel covered with fine netting to keep out the cabbage white butterfly.

Fruit: Hang fruit fly traps for lemons and pomegranates to help reduce next year's insect numbers.

Remove three-year-old strawberries and replace with new virus-free stock, preferably in a different bed. Remove any diseased leaves from remaining plants and bin, rather than compost.

All mummified stone fruit should be removed, bagged and binned. Do not compost.

It's a good time to repot potted **herbs** or other plants and replenish the potting mix, at the same time dividing them. Larger potplants may have the soil replenished by using a sharp tool to loosen the soil around the edges and on the surface of the pot. You can then replace the old soil with fresh potting mix and slow release fertiliser.

April

General Maintenance	Notes

Now is a great time to cultivate bare areas, incorporate extra humus if available or plant a green manure crop.

Complete sowing and repair of lawns.

Remove summer and autumn annuals including vines and crop residue from the vegetable and fruit areas. Dispose of any that might carry disease or pests and add all clean material to the compost heap.

Most herbaceous perennials and ground covers can be divided and tidied up.

If you've noticed an attractive shrub or tree in your suburb, try to get its name and research its potential size and characteristics. Bare-rooted and deciduous plants will become available later in winter.

Make use of autumn leaves. Compost, rake into a corner and cover with a little soil to prevent them from blowing around or put them in a black plastic garbage bag in the sun to break down. They can then be used as an excellent source of mulch and nutrients for those less drought tolerant plants which need a little TLC.

Cover ponds with wire to stop falling leaves fouling the water. Fish will be less active so food should be reduced.

Complete planting of alyssum, candytuft, cornflower, dianthus, linaria, pansy, primula, viola, aquilegia, delphinium, foxglove, nemesia, poppy, statice, sweet pea seeds, sweet William and wallflowers.

Growth slows as the weather cools, so reduce watering.

Band fruit trees with hessian, corrugated cardboard or Vaseline grease bands spread on pantyhose to trap codling moth. Remove and replace periodically, at the same time removing and destroying infested fruit.

May

| The Ornamental Garden | The Kitchen Garden |

Shrubs: Cut some hydrangea heads, autumn foliage and nerines for indoor decoration.

Evergreen shrubs can still be moved and new plants added. Note, Australian plants cannot successfully be moved, once established. A good time for planting new shrubs or for repotting.

Spring flowering camellias will benefit from disbudding, as this will improve the size of the flowers.

Bulbs: Tulips and Dutch iris can be planted now. Remove begonia tubers from pots when stems fall off. Overwinter in a tray of potting mix, covered with a plastic bag in a dry dark area.

The growing shoots of spring flowering annuals can be pinched back to strengthen growth and encourage root growth. Continue half strength foliage fertiliser.

Tidy hellebores now and apply a complete fertiliser together with dolomite lime. Hellebores can be moved if necessary.

Monitor **vegetable** crops for pests and weed infestations and adequate moisture.

After harvesting, it's time for a complete clean-up.

Final seed sowing of late maturing onions. Prepare area for planting onion seedlings in late winter. Sow seeds of peas until mid May. Seedlings of Asian greens may be sown until mid May. Plant strawberries now.

Think about planting new **fruit trees** and berries. Most fruit bearing plants require ongoing maintenance, but it will be worth it. Some fruit trees are worth a place in the general landscape for their shape, leaf and fruit colour e.g. olives and persimmons. Do some research before buying any. Some fruit trees will require cross-pollination with another cultivar so check with the horticulturist at your garden centre before purchasing. If you do plant fruit trees, they will benefit from good soil preparation to improve the texture and increase fertility with compost and well-rotted manure. Raised beds will improve the drainage in clay soils.

Birds and other animals can be a nuisance. Foil gift tape can be hung from poles and individual fruits can be bagged or covered with 'fruit socks'. Bird netting can also be used but must be pegged at ground level to ensure birds don't get trapped within.

General Maintenance

Notes

The end of autumn normally brings wonderful clear days with cold nights and cool mornings. Working in the garden is a delight on most days.

Water only as required. Remember overnight frosts will freeze any moisture left on plants and may cause damage, so water when its warmer. Keep newly-planted lawn areas moist.

Manual timers may need to be removed from taps at night in areas exposed to frost to avoid damage from freezing. Cover any exposed piping for the same reason.

It's time for a general tidy-up of the garden, but don't burn your leaves.

Think about any potted plants which might be affected by frost and relocate to a warmer site. or insulation, you can insert pots into larger pots, stuffing straw between them.

Hedge maintenance can be done.

If desired, remove lower branches of deciduous trees to allow access.

Deciduous plants will be available now. Don't be tempted to buy packaged roses if the new growth is pronounced, for winter's chills will hit them hard.

Collect the last of your fallen leaves and add to the compost heap or mix with lawn clippings and other material for mulch.

Weeding is not just pulling up dandelions, but also watching for the germination of woody weeds such as privet. These can be time consuming and costly to remove if allowed to grow on in awkward places.

June

| The Ornamental Garden | The Kitchen Garden |

Camellias are blooming so choose new plants now. Once established, they are very drought tolerant and are a valued plant for hedging or feature plant.

Older **hydrangeas** may be pruned in the next two months for good results. Remove old grey wood completely and reduce stems which have already flowered. Hardwood cuttings can be taken now.

Plant deciduous trees, shrubs, roses, fruit trees and vines. Some staking or supports may be necessary.

Dahlia tubers may be lifted, divided and placed in sawdust or a cheap potting mix and stored in a dark, dry area free from frost.

Check your trees for signs of stress eg dead limbs, weeping sap and excessive leaf drop. Borers may also be evident and limbs can drop. If concerned, call an arborist for advice rather than take the risk.

Houseplants should be moved away from heaters, perhaps nearer to a window for light -something you might not consider in summer, but still not so close to a window that they are affected by cold. Avoid draughts. Cut down on watering and nutrients and allow the soil to almost dry out between watering.

Do not allow **vegetables** to dry out. Keep weeds and pests under control.

Onion plants will be available, but best plantings are made in late winter. Sow seeds of shallots.

Prune pome **fruits**, grapes (both fruiting and ornamental) and .

Harvest before birds damage too many and store in a dark, draft-free position.

As citrus fruit begins to colour, harvest from outer canopy, leaving stalk attached for longer storage. Store indoors between sheets of newspaper. Fruit towards the centre of the tree can mature for longer, protected by the leaves.

Do not prune off frost-affected citrus foliage until spring, as it will protect the tree.

Plant new fruit trees and berries. When choosing fruit trees, check whether they are self-pollinating or need another variety for best pollination. Alternatively buy a multi graft tree.

A winter spray of horticultural oil for all fruit trees gets into the cracks and crevices of the bark where pests love to shelter or lay their eggs.

Replenish stocks of **manure** and if you want to dig it in immediately, make sure it is well-rotted. Otherwise, compost it.

Organic matter may be dug into the soil during winter in readiness for spring plantings.

Shred prunings either to use as mulch for the garden, or to add to compost .

June

General Maintenance

Notes

Have a general clean up of the whole garden while many plants are dormant.

Time to spray fruit trees and roses with oil or copper spray.

Remove any broken or crossing branches from trees and shrub. They may obstruct pathways or general access, so should be removed flush with the trunk. Do not leave a 'clothes peg' stump.

Mulching around tender new plants will reduce the damage caused by frost.

Carry out any construction or alterations needed to improve the site. Cover any cement work carried out late in the day to protect from frost.

Check lawns and shaded areas for unwanted moss growth, an indicator of poor drainage. Improved drainage and increased air flow will help.

Damp conditions can be perfect breeding grounds for fungal diseases so be observant Watering is best carried out in the warmer part of the day.

Consider installing a rainwater tank.

Australian plants are putting on quite a show and plants such as *Iris unguicularis* and *Jasminum nudiflorum* are in full stride. Many other plants are at their best in winter and some bulbs such as species cyclamen will be flowering. Look around, for there are many plants to brighten Canberra's winter.

When using horticultural sprays, be sure to follow directions carefully, wear gloves and protective clothing, and always spray on a still day to minimise drift.

Reduce watering as growth is minimal, but do not neglect areas in sheltered positions.

July

The Ornamental Garden	The Kitchen Garden

Remove flower buds from spring annuals to improve later display. Look out for outstanding winter-flowering shrubs and record their names for planting later in the year or in autumn.

Rhododendrons (including azaleas) and magnolias will appreciate extra moisture in the time leading up to blooming.

Attend a pruning demonstration by the Horticultural Society of Canberra Inc. Some local garden centres also advertise courses.

Prune wisteria and deciduous climbers.

Except for spring flowering shrubs, many shrubs can be pruned this month, removing dead wood and old canes as they are easier to see in winter.

Check catalogues and order summer flowering **bulbs**, such as liliums. Liliums should be planted or replanted as soon as possible to prevent drying out.

Fruit: Prune kiwifruit, remove weeds and mulch thickly.

Early flowering peaches and nectarines will soon be at bud-swell stage so spray with Bordeaux, copper or lime sulphur to help avoid leaf curl, a fungal disease which causes the new spring leaves to distort and thicken, and fall prematurely.

Newspaper or corrugated cardboard around the stem or between the pots of lemon trees may assist. Lemon trees in the garden require a cover while young. Older trees may yellow with frosts, but should be left untouched to protect the inner canopy. In spring the tree can be pruned to tidy it up.

Spray citrus trees with Pest Oil to smother the nymphs of bronze orange bug.

Vegetables: Sow globe artichokes and asparagus seeds.

July

General Maintenance	Notes

In winter time, clean and sharpen secateurs, loppers and saws

Wooden handles on all hand tools can be sanded and treated with linseed oil or other preservative.

It's a good time to check blades on mowers, edgers and trimmers and replace as necessary. Check or change oil in four-stroke machines.

Also timely to clean the glasshouse, shade house, garage or garden shed. Clean up and remove any rubbish.

Cultivate and improve any areas free of plants.

Remove any couch runners growing into gardens.

Water only when necessary in the warmest part of the day. It's a good time to install, alter or repair watering systems.

Watch for the Society's Rose and Fruit Tree pruning demonstrations

Potted lemon trees should be moved to a warmer position or covered at night. Pots can be insulated from the cold by placing inside a larger pot.

Remove weeds when you first see them, rather than leaving yourself a mammoth task later.

August

The Ornamental Garden	The Kitchen Garden

Prune and spray **roses** later this month or early September. Heritage roses which flower only in spring should be pruned after flowering. Plant new roses. Soak bare-rooted stock in seaweed solution and prune lightly before planting.

If you would like to add more **camellias** and azaleas to your garden, visit garden centres and make your purchases while they are in flower.

Magnolias will come into bloom this month. They require good drainage, acid soil and protection from hot or strong winds.

Early spring **bulbs** will also be appearing, hoop petticoat daffodils, crocus, galanthus, muscari amongst others.

Plant summer and autumn flowering bulbs.

Winter flowering **shrubs** will benefit from a trim as flowering finishes.

Prune and feed daphne after flowering. Picking for the house will help keep them in good condition and provide the necessary tip-pruning.

Prune Crepe Myrtle, which flowers on new wood.

Perennials may be divided as the weather starts to warm. Divide chrysanthemum or take soft tip cuttings.

If you prefer blue or darker blue **hydrangea** flowers, blueing tonic can be watered into soil around hydrangeas. Mark your calendar for follow-up applications a month apart in early and mid-spring.

Fruit: Spray peaches and nectarines again for leaf curl if the leaves have not yet appeared. If in leaf and leaf curl is evident, remove the leaves and bin them. Fertilise and water well. Fruit trees can still be planted.

Watch for signs of scale on citrus trees. Ant activity on stems is the first indicator. A couple of sprays with horticultural oil should smother these troublesome insects and kill eggs.

Seed **potatoes** will be available now but for better results, delay planting them until the weather warms. Plant onion seedlings, Jerusalem artichoke, asparagus crowns and spinach seedlings. Prepare beds for other crops. Little is gained by planting any other seedlings at this stage. Prepare beds by applying manure and blood and bone. Green manure crops may be dug in now. If necessary, lime vegetable plots.

Sow **tomato** seeds in a warm place. Seedlings may be grown on under glass or some other warm protected spot until the danger of frosts is over.

Check **herbs**. Some such as tarragon, marjoram, oregano or chives may need dividing and replanting. A few roots of mint are best grown in a large pot, which can then be placed near the house for easy access, or the pot put into the soil with the lip of the pot raised 5-10cm above soil level. From here it can be controlled as it tries to spread sideways into the soil.

August

General Maintenance

Spring plants are beginning to show signs of growth.

It's still not too late to move most shrubs and small trees.

Water gardens in the warmer part of the day and only where really required.

Do not forget to water new plantings if there has been no rain. If rain does fall, check your new plants to ensure rain has penetrated the soil around them. Also heck plants growing under eaves and beneath the canopies of large trees where rain may not reach.

Clean out ponds and divide clumps of water irises, lilies etc.

Feed the soil. Trees and shrubs should receive ample applications of manure to help them along.

Shredded prunings may be added to the compost heap or used as mulch.

Prune jasmines and late summer-flowering clematis.

Before the warmer weather, check your mulch and whether any more is needed. Dig in old mulch to aid moisture retention.

Notes

Camellias in bud will respond to a little extra water. This will increase the size and quality of blooms.

It's time to rejuvenate lawns or prepare for turf. Think about reducing lawn size, or using drought-tolerant grasses. South African Hybrid couches such as 'Grand Prix' and 'Santa Ana', though discolouring in winter, quickly revive in spring and have very low water needs. New grasses are continually being trialled but watch also for Australian native turf.

September

| The Ornamental Garden | The Kitchen Garden |

Container grown plants can be planted out at any time. Circling or balled roots should be unravelled and trimmed to encourage them to spread out.

Tie sweet peas to supports.

Dahlia clumps left in the ground can be divided before new growth commences.

Finish planting summer **bulbs**. You can also plant out new perennials and pot on any cuttings and divisions taken in autumn. Obtain seed of summer and autumn annuals for planting next month. Begonia tubers can be taken out of winter storage and placed in small pots to start growth in a frost-free area, such as glass or shade house.

Winter-flowering **sasanqua camellias** can be pruned after flowering. Feed camellias, azaleas, rhododendrons, daphne, pieris, erica and other shallow-rooted plants with a generous helping of old animal manure such as sheep or cow.

Tomato seedlings are available but best not planted in the open garden until mid November. They will not grow until the soil warms. It's the same for capsicum and egg plant.

Onion seedlings may still be transplanted.

Citrus trees should be planted in a warm position and kept well-watered and mulched as the weather warms. Prune any damaged stems from established trees at the end of the month and give them a feed.

Bronze orange bugs on citrus can be knocked into a bucket of soapy water. As a safeguard, wear long sleeves, gloves and glasses.

Use beer traps. heaped coffee grounds, copper strips or sprays to control slugs and snails.

September

General Maintenance

Notes

Weather can be variable, so do your gardening when you can. There is something new each day and the spring garden can be one of life's great delights.

Plant or repair lawn areas. If bindii is a problem, spray with a specific weedicide or remove by hand before the bindii flowers set seed. Once that seed is set, it is too late to do anything.

Water early in the morning where possible. Spring flowering bulbs require consistent watering, especially if grown in pots.

Keep paths and lawns clear of fallen flower petals as they can become very slippery in shaded areas.

Apply mulch to retain moisture in soil.

With new plantings of trees and shrubs, good preparation is vital. If the soil is dry, fill the hole with a bucket of Seasol solution to ensure the plant settles in. After planting, the soil should be kept moist, not soggy, for at least 12 months. Water crystals are useful to reduce the amount of water needed.

Visit the Horticultural Society Inc. Spring Bulb and Camellia Show in mid–September, featuring daffodils and camellias. Visit Floriade during September–October.

Make small sowings of cabbage, carrot, leek, melons, parsley, silver beet, spinach and turnip. Leave main planting for later.

As the weather warms, lush growth attracts insects. Squash caterpillars, aphids and other insects as you see them, before their numbers increase dramatically.

October

| The Ornamental Garden | The Kitchen Garden |

Prune flowering **shrubs** as they finish flowering. Thin out camellias and shorten drooping branches. Azaleas should be clipped back and any dead growth removed. Choose new azalea and rhododendron plants while they're in flower.

Roses will respond to fertiliser and added water from midmonth. Check for fungal problems and mulch well to retain soil moisture.

Remove last year's dead growth from bedding begonias and fuchsias now that frosts are less frequent. Divide or plant bedding begonias for a good border display in summer and autumn.

Nip out sweet pea shoots when they reach the top of their support to encourage lateral growth and flowers.

Plant dahlia tubers later in the month; insert stakes before planting tubers to avoid damaging them.

Gladiolus corms can be planted at two-weekly intervals, remembering that they flower in about 90–100 days.

Deadhead annual flowers and spring **bulbs**. All bulbs should be given a fertiliser high in potash and well watered before the foliage dies to improve next year's flowers. Resist the urge to remove the foliage until early December when they have completely died off.

Sow seed of summer and autumn annuals ready for planting out by mid December.

Vegetables: Sow seeds of tomatoes, zucchini, silver beet, beans and cabbage for successive cropping.

Make supports for peas and climbing beans.

Plant herbs in a well-prepared spot or in tubs.

Vegetables use more water than lawns, but can be a productive alternative. If you plant to turn your lawn over to vegetable production, cover the lawn with layers of newspaper and pile compost or good garden mix at least 10cm deep.

Even with a small space you can still enjoy growing some vegetables and herbs. Vegetables thrive in deep polystyrene boxes. Smaller cultivars of most vegetables are available, and it is possible to grow strawberries and some varieties of tomatoes in hanging baskets.

Fruit: Citrus can still be planted. Existing trees should be watered and mulched.

Compost tea or well-diluted fertiliser should be applied to strawberry plants, adding plenty of straw around the plants as berries mature.

October

| General Maintenance | Notes |

Warm days with plenty to do and see. Enjoy the spring garden and plan for autumn.

Now is the time to deep water your lawn if you are allowed to do so. A hose-on soil wetter will mean you will use less water overall, and if you let your grass grow longer than usual, with less evaporation, the soil will stay cooler.

Control weeds in your lawn. Newly-laid turf will need to be well-established before it will tolerate heavy foot traffic.

Increase watering as required and pay special attention to new plants as their root system becomes established in their new environment.

Mulch all shrubs and trees to retain soil moisture as the temperature warms.

If using stakes for rose bushes or young trees, remember that timber is better. Metal will transfer excessive heat or cold to the plant.

Wisteria should not be allowed to grow up into trees or onto roofs, where it can do damage. It may look lovely in flower, but it's best to train it early and save yourself some work in later years. Reducing rampant trailers each year will be work enough!

Visit The Horticultural Society of Canberra Inc. Iris, Rhododendron and Azalea Show

Main plantings of cabbage, carrot, leek and parsley can be done this month although frost-sensitive plants such as tomatoes, capsicum, eggplant and basil can wait until mid-November.

All fruit trees benefit from additional moisture as the fruit develops, so think about installing drip irrigation. Not only is it easier, it is a more efficient form of watering plants.

November

The Ornamental Garden	The Kitchen Garden

Spring is coming to an end and most roses are coming into flower.

Deadhead annuals and remove any that are past their best. At the end of the month remove spring annuals and prepare areas for summer and autumn plantings.

Continue to tie sweetpeas, picking flowers regularly to encourage more blooms. Keep deeply watered.

Tall bearded iris can be divided now if this has not been done for a few years.

Continue to plant dahlia tubers. Cuttings can be taken from growing plants. Strong stakes are required for taller-growing plants and should be put in prior to planting, to avoid damaging tubers.

Transfer tuberous begonias to larger pots. Leave plants in the shade house till next month and keep moist.

Trim evergreen shrubs and hedges.

Check roses for insect or fungal problems. If deadheading, trim back to a strong bud to produce the next flush of flowers. Continue to do this throughout season for best results.

Vegetables: Seedlings of beetroot, cabbage, cucumber, leek, melons, pumpkins, silver beet, sweet corn and zucchini may be planted.

Thin out and weed earlier plantings.

Tie and support peas and broad beans and harvest as they mature.

Remove old winter crops.

Remove weeds. They compete for nutrients and harbour pests and disease.

Continue small sowings of most vegetables to spread the best of crops over a longer period of time.

Frosts are still possible so if cold nights are predicted, have a roll of frost protection cloth (Marix®) on hand. Sections can be spread over plants such as citrus trees, tomatoes, capsicum, egg plants etc.

Pheromone traps are useful for monitoring the activity of codling moth so that controls can be effectively timed. Exclusion bags of waxed paper or cloth will help to keep your fruit unmarked.

November

| General Maintenance | Notes |

Regular trimming of buxus and most hedge plants encourages dense growth, but is best done before it gets too hot, for new growth may suffer sunburn.

Watering may have to increase in warmer weather with the possibility of drying winds.

Fill a pottery bowl with water for the birds. In dry times, the birds will greatly appreciate the water and will return regularly.

Water and feed container-grown plants regularly.

It is far better to water occasionally and deeply, than to water often and lightly.

All climbers must be tied regularly to frames, trellis or wire mesh to prevent them from smothering nearby plants.

Slow release fertilisers are particularly useful in the garden. For pot plants, you will find a Once-a-Year feeder, as well as specific formulations for trees, shrubs, citrus and roses.

Notes

Look for the Horticultural Society of Canberra Inc. Spring Exhibition and Rose Show

This is the main planting month for tomatoes, capsicum, basil and eggplant.

Keep your plants growing strongly, and they will be less susceptible to pests and disease.

Deep watering twice a week will keep most plants in good condition.

December

| The Ornamental Garden | The Kitchen Garden |

Plant summer and autumn annuals.

Remove weeds, top up mulch and water new plantings as necessary.

Continue to deadhead **roses**. Support new water shoots on roses with stakes and ties. Watch for sucker growth from below the graft. Tear away the suckering growth with a gloved hand or cut as close to the stem as possible.

Dahlias can still be planted, including cuttings.

Dianthus can be layered or cuttings taken at any time during the growing season, usually late summer to early autumn.

Look for autumn **bulbs** such as colchicum, sternbergia, lycoris and nerines for planting in the next two months.

Finish pruning spring flowering shrubs and evergreens.

Deadhead annuals and perennials to prolong flowering and tidy hellebores which may be showing signs of heat stress.

Take cuttings of daphne, grevillea and buxus.

Remove whippy growth from wisteria and continue to do so until main pruning in winter.

Twist off old rhododendron flower trusses. Spray azalea and rhododendrons for lace bug with MaxiGuard or Confidor.

Continue to make regular sowings of autumn maturing **vegetables**. Thin earlier sowings and keep weeded.

Just before Christmas, make a late planting of tomatoes and capsicums in a warm sheltered spot for a good late crop.

Begin to harvest crops as soon as they are of usable size.

Keep watering **fruit** trees. Net to prevent bird damage to stone fruit and spraying as required.

December

General Maintenance

Notes

This month will see the first touch of really hot weather.

Mow lawns regularly using a high setting. If you are going away, then arrange for someone to mow your lawn.

If watering the lawn, soil wetter will help to make best use of your water. Mulch all garden beds not already covered and keep soil lightly aerated under the mulch to help water penetration.

Water wisely, preferably when it's cooler.

A gift of a special plant can bring great enjoyment, while a pair of quality secateurs will give years of service. Don't forget to include a copy of the latest edition of *The Canberra Gardener* in your loved one's Christmas stocking.

Seeds of beans, beetroot, cabbage, carrot, cauliflower, Chinese cabbage, cucumber, leek, parsley, potato, pumpkin, radish, silver beet, sweet corn, zucchinis or parsnip can be sown until mid December.

Make first sowings of winter vegetables in seed boxes. Only sow enough for your needs and so save space and water.

Appendices

There are two appendices, one covering special terms you may find in gardening books, and the other reproducing the Weed Regulations for Canberra. Some of the weeds you will be unfamiliar with, but others are common garden escapees.

In the previous edition we provided contact information for the wealth of garden and similar clubs that operate in Canberra. Information on local clubs is now available on the links page of the Society's website, www.hsoc.org.au/ .

APPENDIX 1:
Glossary of terms used in this book

Acid soil. See pH.

Alkaline soil. See pH.

Annuals. Plants which grow from seed to full maturity within one growing season. They flower, set seed and die all within a single year.

Balled, Balling. Flowers failing to open due to petals clinging together, often due to damp or cold conditions.

Bare rooted. Plant removed from ground and sold without soil, usually in winter eg fruit trees, roses.

Bi-coloured. A flower with two distinct colours.

Biennial. Plants which complete their life cycle over two years, sometimes producing a few flowers in the first season, but most often just making foliage growth and establishing their root systems in the first year and then flowering in the second.

Biological control. The use of predatory insects or other natural methods to control pests or diseases.

Bloomers. Small annual plants in flower sold singly for instant colour.

Border. A garden planted as a strip with herbaceous perennials, shrubs or a mix of plants.

Bottom heat. Used to promote growth of seeds or cuttings, can be as simple as placing pots on your hot water system or electric horticultural heating pads may be used under the pots or trays.

Bract. Modified leaf below a flower or in place of flower e.g. on dogwoods it is the bracts we admire rather than the flowers.

Broad spectrum pesticides. Pesticides that will not restrict their actions to the problem insect but may also kill others, including beneficial insects.

Bud. Immature flower before petals unfold, or leaf shoot before expansion.

Budding. Inserting desired leaf bud in a cut in the bark of the rootstock for the purpose of growing a new plant.

Bud union. Position where leaf bud has been inserted in rootstock.

Bulb. Swollen base of stemless plants. Consists of layers of 'scales' made up of fleshy leaves as a means of storing nutrients during a period of dormancy. Eg daffodil, onion, lillium.

Bulbil. Small bulbs which develop in flowerheads (tree onion) or leaf axils (tiger lily). May be grown on to produce a mature bulb.

Bulblet. Small bulbs which form around the base of a mature bulb or on rooting stems below the ground (eg lily). May be grown on to produce a mature bulb.

Calyx. Outer set of perianth segments protecting the flower bud, may be green or decorative. Outer part of a flower enclosing the bud.

Catkin. A hanging stem of tiny bracts and flowers without petals, often looking scale-like eg garrya, silver birch.

Climber. Plant with stems too long to be self-supporting, which grow over, through, across other plants and may be trained to grow on supports.

Companion plants. Plants which, when grown close together, may be beneficial to each other.

Common name. Name by which some plants are known by non botanists, can vary in different localities. See Plant names.

Compost. Material made from waste organic material, used to fertilise and improve the soil.

Corm. Swollen base of a stem of a plant. Similar to a bulb but without layers of scales. Eg Gladiolus.

Cormel (or comlet). Small corms which form around the base of a mature corm. They may be grown to produce a mature corm.

Corolla. Flower formed by outer petals which may be separate or united into a tube.

Creeper. Plants which make long shoots normally along the ground.

Cultivar. A cultivated variety of plant, possibly a hybrid. See Plant names.

Cuttings. Pieces of stem or root used for the propagation of new plants.

Damping off. A fungal disease of seedlings and cuttings, very destructive.

Deciduous. A plant which loses its leaves each year at the end of its growth cycle.

Deadhead. Remove spent flowers to promote further growth or flowers, prevent seeding and improve appearance.

Dieback. Death of tips of plants or branches due to frost damage or disease.

Disbud. Removal of surplus buds to encourage better flowers and fruit.

Division. A method of propagation in which a plant clump is divided into separate clumps during dormacy.

Dormant. A plant in its non-growth period, usually winter.

Double flower. A bloom with multiple rows of petals completely covering the centre and male part of the flower (which contains the pollen), enclosing the stamens when in prime condition.

Dripline. The ground area where feeder roots are normally found. The dripline is generally below the outermost foliage of a plant.

Epiphyte. A plant which grows on another without being a parasite, obtaining nutrients and moisture without rooting in soil.

Espalier. Ongoing process of training a plant in horizontal directions on a flat area such as a wall, fence or wires.

Evergreen. A plant remaining in leaf throughout the year, though it will lose some older leaves regularly throughout the year.

Exotic. A plant introduced from another country or region.

Fertile soil. Contains an abundance of nutrients and organic materials for good plant growth and successful production of fruit and seed.

Fertiliser. A substance added to the soil to maintain or increase plant growth. May be organic or inorganic.

Foliar feeding. Fertilising by applying plant food in a liquid form to the leaves.

Formal. Bloom or plant with regular and consistent placement of petals or growth.

Friable. Soil which holds together well in the hand, but is easy to break up and crumbles readily.

Fungicide. A substance used to destroy fungi. Usually takes the form of spray or powder.

Genus. A group of closely-related species of plants.

Grafting. Propagation by which a piece of desirable plant is joined to a hardy plant or rootstock to give a stronger root system and plant.

Ground covers. Extensive planting of low-growing plants to cover the ground, normally aimed at suppressing weeds and holding the soil in place.

Habit. The way or shape in which a plant is expected to grow.

Harden off. Gradually expose plants to normal weather when they have previously been growing in a protected environment.

Hardy. A term used to describe plants which will survive easily in local conditions without protection.

Herbaceous. A plant with non-woody stems. An herbaceous perennial is one that dies down in winter and then recovers in spring.

Herbicide. A substance used to kill plants.

Hose-in-hose. Flower repeated within itself i.e. a corolla produced within another identical corolla.

Host specific. A pest or disease that prefers one particular type of plant and does not affect others.

Humus. The more-or-less stable part of soil organic matter remaining from the decomposition of plant and animal remains.

Hybrid. A plant resulting from the crossing of two different species. Plants produced this way are designated with a small 'x' within the botanical name, eg *Saxifraga x apiculata*.

Informal flower. A bloom with an irregular shape.

Inorganic. In terms of fertiliser, products derived from minerals rather than from once-living things. In terms of garden practices, methods which depend on the use of inorganic products to feed the plants and also to combat diseases and pests.

Insecticide. A substance used to kill insects.

Invasive. A plant which spreads rapidly into areas where it is unwanted.

Lateral. A side shoot arising from a main stem.

Layering. Propagation method, where part of a plant is fixed in contact with the ground to promote root growth for the production of a new plant. It occurs naturally with many plants.

Leader. The main growing stem of a plant.

Legume. A pod-bearing plant containing seeds which split along both sides, eg pea. Characteristically, legumes add nitrogen to the soil through their root systems.

Lime. A calcium compound which, when added to soil. increases alkalinity.

Loam. Soil of light texture with low clay content.

Mildew. Fungi of fine powdery webs on the surface of organic matter or living plants which appears in excessively moist conditions.

Miticide. A product used to kill mites or spiders.

Mulch. A surface layer of organic or mineral substance used to protect plant roots, help prevent evaporation, control weeds and improve the soil.

Neutral. See pH.

N:P:K. Indicates ratio of the three major chemicals in fertilisers which affect plant growth. (N) Nitrogen, (P) Phosphorous, (K) Potassium.

Native. A plant which is endemic to a country or region.

Node. Position on a stem where a leaf is attached or from where a leaf will emerge.

Offset. A small immature plant which remains attached to a parent plant until removed or the connecting tissue dies. Usually refers to cacti and some succulent plants. Plants reproducing in this manner may form clumps if undisturbed.

Organic. In terms of fertiliser, the remains of plants and animals such as compost, leaf mould, blood and bone, seaweed and animal manure. In terms of garden practices, methods which depend on the use of organic products to feed the plants and also to combat diseases and pests.

Ornamental. Plant grown for its appearance, rather than for food or other use.

Perianth. Outer part of the flower, consisting of the calyx and corolla.

Perennial. A soft stemmed plant lasting more or less permanently. Above ground parts may die down to ground over winter and reappear in spring.

pH. A scale which measures the degree of acidity or alkalinity of soil. You can think of it as a scale which indicates the amount of limestone in the soil. Acid soil, lacking in limestone, has a pH value below 7. Alkaline soil, rich in limestone, has a pH value above 7. Neutral soil, where the pH value is 7, is neither acid nor alkaline.

Phyllode. A flattened leaf stalk that functions as a leaf. Common in Acacias.

Plant names. Some plants share common names, but every plant has a unique botanical name. A botanic name, though often more difficult to pronounce, will tell you more about the plant and is less confusing than a common name: eg *Acer* (the Maple genus), *palmatum* (palm-shaped, describing the shape of the leaves), *atropurpureum* (describing the colour of the leaf, dark purple). *Acer palmatum* 'Atropurpureum' is a member of the Aceraceae, the Maple family.

Potting mix. A specially-prepared medium, used for growing plants in pots.

Recurrent. Repeat flowering. Also called remontant.

Resistant variety. Plant varieties that have been bred or selected to restrict certain diseases.

Rhizome. Stem of plants which grow under or along the surface of the soil. May be swollen (iris), thin and wiry (couch grass) or crowns (asparagus). May develop segments from which new plants develop.

Scion. Piece of desired plant used to graft onto rootstock or host plant.

Seed. Mature grain of a plant produced from a fertilised flower, which can be used to grow a new plant.

Seedling. A plant grown from seed, at an early stage of growth.

Self-seed. The shedding of seeds which then germinate readily.

Semi-deciduous. Describes a habit of losing some, but not all leaves.

Single flower. Bloom with central disc or centre exposed with very few rows of petals.

Soil profile. A cross section of soil in which the structure and depth of the various layers can be seen.

Species. A group of plants essentially alike when grown under similar conditions and which normally breed true among their own kind.

Stamen. Male part of the flower, which contains the pollen.

Stop, stopping. Removing the growing tip or tips to promote lateral growth.

Succulents. A general description of plants which have adapted to store water in swollen stems, leaves or roots to survive extreme dry conditions.

Sucker. A shoot which appears from an underground root. If it comes from below the graft union (for example, on a rose) it is undesirable.

Syn (an abbreviation of Synonym). A scientific or common name no longer accepted but still lingering in use. Another name by which a plant may be known in some places.

Tender. A plant subject to easy damage e.g. frost tender.

Tip pruning. Pinching out the end of new soft growth to promote branching.

Tuber and tuberous root. Swollen stem or root, with buds or 'eyes', which stores nutrients during a period of dormancy. New growth comes from the eyes. Eg potato and dahlia. A tuberous root is a swollen root which stores nutrients during a period of dormancy.

Variegated. A modification of the natural colour in plants which, by absence or variation of pigments, exhibit in various ways patches or streaks of unnatural colour. This may vary from a change in intensity of the normal green to white, yellow and even degrees of red.

Variety. Used to designate plants occurring in the wild which exhibit clearly defined but minor variations from the species plant and which are not usually lost when the plant is grown from seed. Synonymous with 'subspecies'.

Watershoot. A desirable new growth from the base of a plant (eg, roses) used to replace old stems once mature. See sucker.

Weed. Unwanted or nuisance plant.

Withholding period. A period, after spraying fruits and other edibles, before it is safe to eat them.

X. See Hybrid.

APPENDIX 2: Weeds in the Australian Capital Territory

The information which follows is extracted from the ACT's *Pest Plants and Animals (Pest Plants) Declaration 2008 (No 1).*

Pest Plants in the Australian Capital Territory

Botanical name	Common name	Plants which are notifiable pest plants	Plants which must be suppressed	Plants which must be contained	Plants whose Propagation and supply is prohibited
Achnatherum caudatum	Broad-kernel Espartillo	X			X
Alternanthera philoxeroides	Alligator Weed	X			X
Cabomba caroliniana	Cabomba	X			X
Centaurea maculosa	Spotted Knapweed	X			X
Equisetum species	Horsetail	X			X
Gymnocoronis spilanthoides	Senegal Tea Plant	X			X
Kochia scoparia	Kochia	X			X
Lagarosiphon major	Lagarosiphon	X			X
Myriophyllum aquaticum	Parrot's Feather	X			X
Nassella charruana	Lobed Needlegrass	X			X
Nasella tenuissima	Mexican Feather Grass	X			X
Parthenium hysterophorus	Parthenium Weed	X			X
Pistia stratiotes	Water Lettuce	X			X
Salvinia molesta	Salvinia	X			X
Senecio madagascariensis	Fireweed	X			X
Toxicodendron succedaneum	Rhus Tree	X			X
Carduus nutans	Nodding Thistle		X		
Cytisus (ALL species)	Broom species		X		X

Botanical name	Common name	Plants which are notifiable pest plants	Plants which must be suppressed	Plants which must be contained	Plants whose Propagation and supply is prohibited
Genista (ALL species)	Broom species		X		X
Lycium ferocissimum	African Boxthorn		X		X
Rosa rubiginosa	Sweet Briar, Briar Rose		X		X
Salix ALL species of willow, except for the permitted species: Salix babylonica Salix x calodendron Salix x reichardtii	All Willows except for the permitted species: Weeping Willow Pussy Willow Sterile Pussy Willow		X		X
Ulex europaeus	Gorse		X		X
Xanthium occidentale	Noogoora Burr		X		X
Xanthium spinosum	Bathurst Burr		X		
Carduus pycnocephalus	Slender Thistle			X	
Carduus tenuiflorus	Slender Thistle			X	
Carthamus lanatus	Saffron Thistle			X	
Crataegus monogyna	Hawthorn			X	X
Echium plantagineum	Paterson's Curse			X	
Echium vulgare	Viper's Bugloss			X	
Eragrostis curvula	African Love Grass			X	
Hypericum perforatum	St John's Wort			X	
Nassella neesiana	Chilean Needle Grass			X	X
Nassella trichotoma	Serrated Tussock			X	X
Onopordum acanthium	Scotch Thistle			X	
Onopordum illyricum	Illyrian Thistle			X	
Pinus radiata	Radiata Pine			X	
All Rubus fruticosus (aggregate) species except for the permitted cultivars: R. armeniacus and R. ulmifolius species hybrid	All Blackberry except for the permitted cultivars: Black satin Chester Thornless Dirksen Thornless Loch Ness Smoothstem Thornfree			X	X
R. armeniacus species Hybrid	Chehalem				

Botanical name	Common name	Plants which are notifiable pest plants	Plants which must be suppressed	Plants which must be contained	Plants whose Propagation and supply is prohibited
R. ursinus and R. armeniacus species hybrid	Murrindindi Silvan				
Acacia baileyana	Cootamundra Wattle				X
Acacia nilotica ssp. indica	Prickly Acacia				X
Acer negundo	Box Elder				X
Ailanthus altissima	Tree of Heaven				X
Alnus glutinosa	Black Alder				X
Annona glabra	Pond Apple				X
Asparagus asparagoides	Bridal Creeper				X
Celtis australis	Nettle Tree				X
Chrysanthemoides monilifera	Bitou Bush / Boneseed				X
Cortaderia jubata	Pampas Grass				X
Cortaderia selloana	Pampas Grass				X
Cotoneaster franchettii	Cotoneaster				X
Cotoneaster glaucophyllus	Cotoneaster				X
Cotoneaster pannosus	Cotoneaster				X
Cotoneaster salicifolius	Willow-leaf Cotoneaster				X
Cotoneaster simonsii	Cotoneaster				X
Cryptostegia grandiflora	Rubber Vine				X
Eichornia crassipes	Water Hyacinth				X
Hedera helix	English Ivy				X
Hymenachne amplexicaulis	Hymenachne				X
Lantana camara	Lantana				X
Lonicera japonica	Japanese Honeysuckle				X
Ligustrum lucidum	Broad-leaf privet				X
Ligustrum sinense	Narrow-leaf privet				X
Mimosa pigra	Mimosa				X
Parkinsonia aculeata	Parkinsonia				X

Botanical name	Common name	Plants which are notifiable pest plants	Plants which must be suppressed	Plants which must be contained	Plants whose Propagation and supply is prohibited
Phyllostachys aurea	Yellow Bamboo				X
Populus alba	White Poplar				X
Populus nigra 'Italica'	Lombardy Poplar				X
Prosopis spp.	Mesquite				X
Pyracantha angustifolia	Firethorn				X
Pyracantha coccinea	Scarlet Firethorn				X
Pyracantha fortuneana	Firethorn				X
Robinia pseudoacacia	False Acacia				X
Sorbus sp.	Service Tree, Rowan				X
Spartium junceum	Spanish Broom				X
Tamarix aphylla	Athel Pine				X
Vinca major	Periwinkle				X

Index